AF505632

André Kertész

André

POSTCARDS

Edited by Elizabeth Siegel

With essays by Sarah Kennel,
Sylvie Pénichon, and Elizabeth Siegel

The Art Institute of Chicago
Distributed by Yale University Press, New Haven and London

FROM PARIS

Kertész

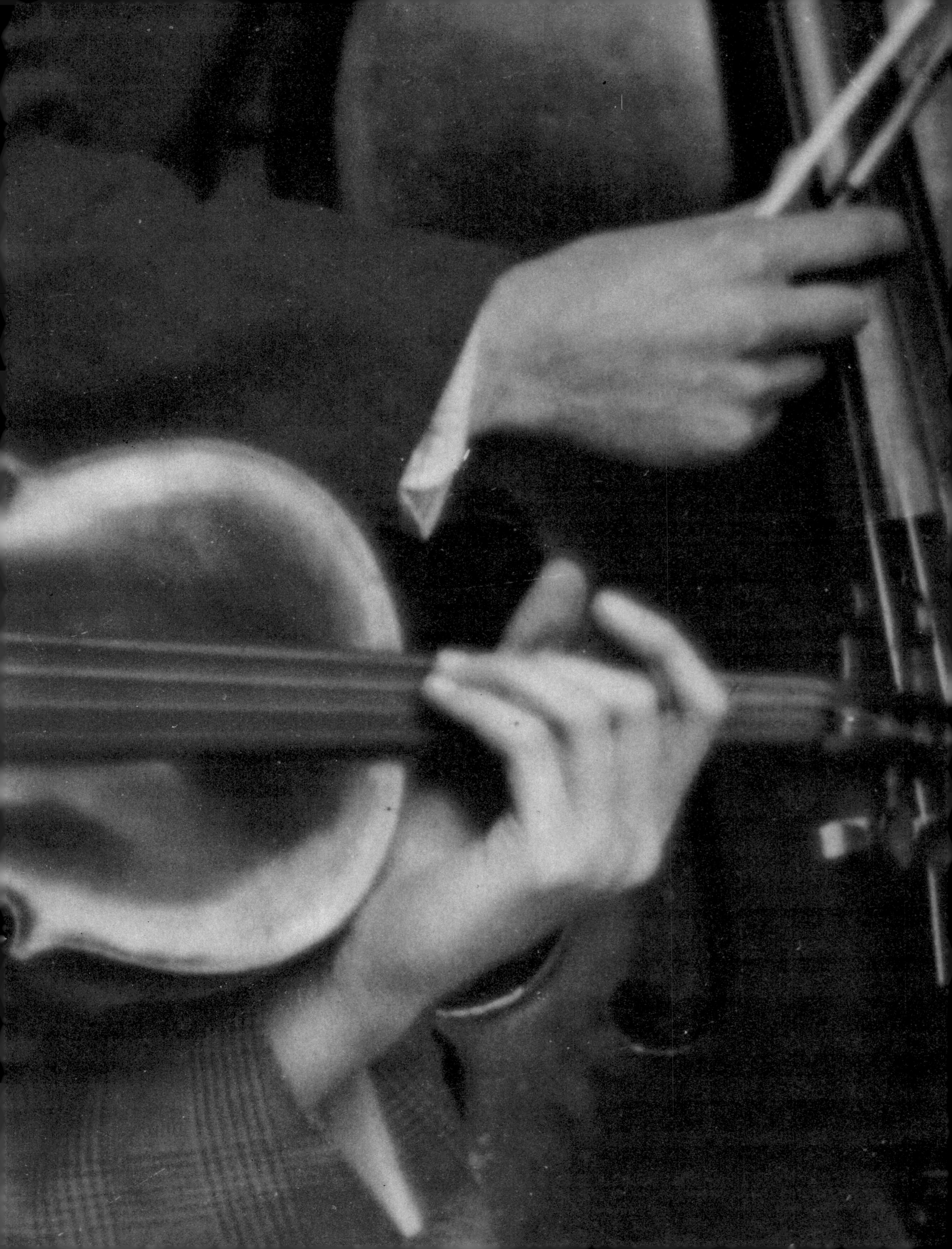

CONTENTS

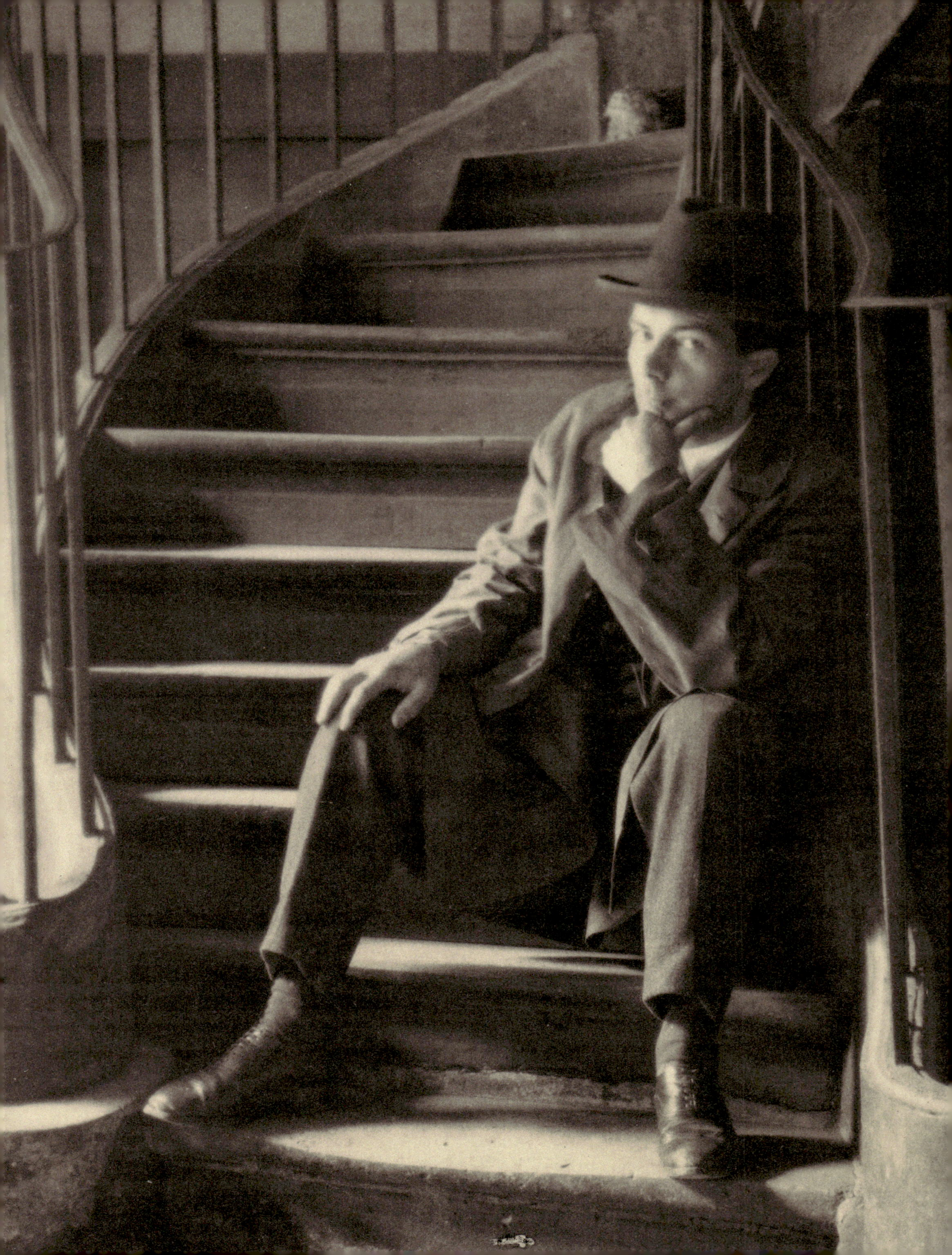

FOREWORD

A self-proclaimed amateur with the compositional rigor of a modernist, photographer André Kertész (American, born Hungary, 1894–1985) is well known for his timeless documents of everyday life in the countries he called home: Hungary, France, and the United States. *André Kertész: Postcards from Paris* is the first exhibition and catalogue to focus on the artist's earliest years in his first adopted city, when he produced most of his work as *cartes postales*, precise prints on inexpensive but lush postcard stock. During this time of freedom and experimentation in the 1920s, Kertész made many of his most enduring images and helped set the course of twentieth-century photography, taking inspiration from the bohemian community of international artists he befriended in the cafés of Montparnasse as well as from the aesthetics of the carte postale paper itself. This publication brings together, for the first time, all known carte postale prints from this period, highlighting more than one hundred of the finest examples and examining them not merely as images but as objects with physical attributes and tactile histories inextricable from their value and meaning.

The Art Institute of Chicago has presented and collected Kertész's work for decades. Seventy-five years ago, in the summer of 1946, it hosted the artist's first solo museum exhibition. Kertész had been disappointed by his reception in the United States in the decade after he left France to photograph for American magazines; his exhibition here marked a new beginning for his artistic reputation and initiated a relationship between photographer and museum that continues to the present. Prints by Kertész first entered the Art Institute's holdings in 1975, with the acquisition of the collection of New York gallerist Julien Levy, who exhibited his works in the 1930s. In 1985 the Art Institute mounted a major retrospective with a focus on vintage prints and new scholarship, solidifying Kertész's place in the history of photography; the artist proudly attended the exhibition's opening just months before his death. The Art Institute has continued to engage with Kertész's work and now boasts one of the broadest collections of his oeuvre anywhere, thanks to generous gifts from Nicholas and Susan Pritzker, Ellen and Richard Sandor, and the André and Elizabeth Kertész Foundation, among others.

Elizabeth Siegel, Curator of Photography and Media at the Art Institute, organized this comprehensive examination of a key period in Kertész's career and ensured its elegant and scholarly presentation; her commitment to recovering, studying, and preserving the material culture of photographs has suffused and strengthened the entire project. Sarah Kennel, Keough Family Curator of Photography at the High Museum of Art, Atlanta, and Sylvie Pénichon, Director of Photography and Media Conservation at the Art Institute, contributed original research to this publication that will no doubt spur new conversations regarding some of Kertész's most beloved works. It is immensely gratifying that the exhibition will travel to the High Museum, thanks to the collaboration of Randall Suffolk, Sarah Kennel, and Amy Simon. Special recognition is due to the many institutions and private collectors who entrusted us with the care and display of their artworks for the exhibition and the many more who contributed to the catalogue.

This exhibition and publication have been made possible by lead sponsors Nicholas and Susan Pritzker, whose stellar collection of Kertész's work and enthusiasm for this endeavor reflect their enduring dedication to both the artist and the museum, and by the André and Elizabeth Kertész Foundation. Members of the Luminary Trust provide annual leadership support for the museum's operations, including exhibition development, conservation and collection care, and educational programming. The Luminary Trust includes an anonymous donor; Neil Bluhm and the Bluhm Family Charitable Foundation; Jay Franke and David Herro; Karen Gray-Krehbiel and John Krehbiel, Jr.; Kenneth C. Griffin; Caryn and King Harris, The Harris Family Foundation; Josef and Margot Lakonishok; Robert M. and Diane v.S. Levy;

Ann and Samuel M. Mencoff; Sylvia Neil and Dan Fischel;
Anne and Chris Reyes; Cari and Michael J. Sacks;
and the Earl and Brenda Shapiro Foundation.

Although Kertész is now acknowledged as a major figure in the rise of fine-art photography in the twentieth century, his success was far from assured during his first years as an immigrant in an international city. This project celebrates the creativity born of the limitations and the possibilities of this brief moment in the young photographer's career while also reminding us that early work matters. The Art Institute is proud to champion and support artists as they hone their unique visions, just as we are proud to invite new reflections on Kertész's postcards from Paris.

James Rondeau
President and Eloise W. Martin Director
The Art Institute of Chicago

ACKNOWLEDGMENTS

André Kertész: Postcards from Paris is the culmination of several years of planning, research, and collaboration. From the beginning it was supported by individuals who shared the desire to explore this fertile yet under-examined part of André Kertész's career. Nicholas and Susan Pritzker, longtime benefactors of Photography and Media at the Art Institute of Chicago, have not only generously and passionately sponsored the project but have also made substantial gifts of Kertész's photographs to the museum. The André and Elizabeth Kertész Foundation, shepherded by curator Robert Gurbo, has been an invaluable partner at every turn, providing financial support for the exhibition as well as access to archives, objects, and memories.

In addition, members of the Luminary Trust provide annual leadership support for the museum's operations, including exhibition development, conservation and collection care, and educational programming. The Luminary Trust includes an anonymous donor; Neil Bluhm and the Bluhm Family Charitable Foundation; Jay Franke and David Herro; Karen Gray-Krehbiel and John Krehbiel, Jr.; Kenneth C. Griffin; Caryn and King Harris, The Harris Family Foundation; Josef and Margot Lakonishok; Robert M. and Diane v.S. Levy; Ann and Samuel M. Mencoff; Sylvia Neil and Dan Fischel; Anne and Chris Reyes; Cari and Michael J. Sacks; and the Earl and Brenda Shapiro Foundation. Funding for conservation travel and research was provided by the Karen and Jim Frank Photograph Conservation Research Fund.

I am thrilled that this exhibition will travel to the High Museum of Art, Atlanta. Randall Suffolk, Sarah Kennel, and Amy Simon were key partners in organizing and facilitating the tour, and I also thank Gregory Harris, Maria Kelly, Danielle Kiser, Tomasina Ray, and Kevin Tucker.

Museums throughout the United States and abroad lent photographs to the exhibition. I am grateful to Timothy Potts, Jim Ganz, Mazie Harris, and Miriam Katz, the J. Paul Getty Museum, Los Angeles; Max Hollein Meredith Reiss, and Jeff Rosenheim, the Metropolitan Museum of Art, New York; Matthew Teitelbaum and Anne Havinga, Museum of Fine Arts, Boston; Gary Tinterow and Malcolm Daniel, the Museum of Fine Arts, Houston; Glenn Lowry, Clément Chéroux, Tasha Lutek, and (formerly) Sarah Meister, The Museum of Modern Art, New York; Kaywin Feldman and Sarah Greenough, National Gallery of Art, Washington, DC; Alexandra Suda, Lori Pauli, and Ann Thomas, National Gallery of Canada, Ottawa; Susan M. Taylor and Russell Lord, New Orleans Museum of Art; James Steward and Kate Bussard, Princeton University Art Museum, Princeton, New Jersey; Neal Benezra and (formerly) Corey Keller, San Francisco Museum of Modern Art; and Philipp Demandt and Kristina Lemke, Städel Museum, Frankfurt. Several galleries also lent works, and I am indebted to Adam Boxer, Ubu Gallery, New York; Jane Corkin, Jane Corkin Gallery, Toronto; Stephen Daiter, Stephen Daiter Gallery, Chicago; Edwynn Houk, Edwynn Houk Gallery, New York; and Bruce Silverstein, Bruce Silverstein Gallery, New York. Many private collectors and foundations temporarily parted with their works for the exhibition: Stephen Brown, Gary Davis, Randi and Bob Fisher, Kevin Heneghan, Joy of Giving Something, Inc., the André and Elizabeth Kertész Foundation, the Estate of André Kertész, Michael Mattis and Judith Hochberg, Nicholas and Susan Pritzker, The Salgo Trust for Education, Richard and Ellen Sandor, Ealan and Melinda Wingate, and an anonymous lender.

Numerous other museums contributed to the research for this project by sharing their holdings of Kertész's photographs: the Amsab-Institute of Social History, Ghent; the Canadian Center for Architecture, Montreal; the George Eastman Museum, Rochester, New York; the Hungarian Museum of Photography, Kecskemét; the Hungarian Theatre Museum and Institute, Budapest; the Israel Museum, Jerusalem; the Los Angeles County Museum of Art; the Nelson-Atkins

Museum, Kansas City, Missouri; the Petőfi Literary Museum and the Kassák Museum, Budapest; and the Smart Museum of Art, University of Chicago. Many gallerists and private dealers provided access to other prints, including Christopher Cardozo, Keith de Lellis, Howard Greenberg, Wendy Halsted, Paul Hertzmann and Susan Herzig, James Hyman, Robert Koch, Alex Novak, Alain Paviot, Jill Quasha, Roger Szmulewicz, Davi Weston, and Ann and Jürgen Wilde. Additional private collectors emailed images or opened their homes for viewing prints: Jeanne Salgo Aboudrar and Bruno Nassim Aboudrar, Imad Ben Mariem and Vania Ferrat, Trish and Jan de Bont, Sondra Gilman and Celso Gonzalez-Falla, Sir Elton John, Betsy Karel, Christian Kietzmann, Boguslaw Maciuk, Nion McAvoy, Donald Mullen, Richard Pare, Dorothy and Alan Press, John Pritzker, Lisa Pritzker, Paul Sack, Gary Schneider, Steven Schwartz, Robert Yoskowitz, and several others who wish to remain anonymous.

This book reflects the work of many talented collaborators. The essayists shed welcome light on Kertész's work. Sarah Kennel deftly traced the many complexities surrounding the now-iconic *Satiric Dancer*. Sylvie Pénichon conducted an invaluable analysis of Kertész's preferred *carte postale* (postcard) paper. Jena Sher's sensitive design captures the spirit of Kertész's 1920s work while imparting a contemporary energy to the pages. The entire team in Publishing at the Art Institute, led by Greg Nosan, ensured that the book would be both intellectually rigorous and visually dynamic. Kit Shields enhanced each essay and tamed the voluminous back matter with great patience and skill. Joseph Mohan shepherded the book's production with his characteristic attention to quality. Kylie Escudero managed hundreds of images. Ben Bertin, Alissa Chanin-Kolaj, Lauren Makholm, Lisa Meyerowitz, and Amy R. Peltz all assisted with the project at various stages. In Imaging, directed by Bonnie Rosenberg, team members Elyse Allen, Owen Conway, Aidan Fitzpatrick, Jonathan Mathias, and Craig Stillwell collaborated on new photography of Art Institute works for the catalogue. Eriksen Translations transcribed and translated Hungarian text.

Many colleagues gave advice, shared research, made connections, and helped locate prints. I'm grateful to Stuart Alexander, Paul Berlanga, Denise Bethel, Emily Bierman, Stephen Bulger, Gabe Catone, Susan Cooke, Gabriella Cseh, Júlia Cserba, Caroline Deck, Carol Ehlers, Annie Flom, Victor V. Gurbo, Vanessa Hallet, Newell Harbin, Susan Harder, Darius Himes, Daile Kaplan, Lucie Kessler, Annette Kicken, Károly Kincses, Frank Kolodny, Michael Lee, Simon Lowinsky, Peter MacGill, Chris Mahoney, Peter Mustardo, Gyorgy Nemeth, Sandra Phillips, Attila Pőcze, Shlomi Rabi, Deborah Rogal, Ina Schmidt-Runke, Rose Shoshana, Agathe Sorel, David Travis, Thomas Walther, Amy Whiteside, and the late Daniel Wolf. Matthieu Rivallin at the André Kertész archive, Médiathèque de L'Architecture et du Patrimoine, Charenton-le-Pont, France, graciously hosted a research visit. Oliver Botar and Arpad Kovacs assisted with Hungarian translation on short notice. Research for the project benefited from an interview with the artist conducted in his home in the mid-1980s by Edwynn Houk, Nicholas Pritzker, and David Travis and filmed by Robert P. Gordan.

This endeavor has benefited from the guidance, support, and dedication of the Art Institute's leadership: James Rondeau, President and Eloise W. Martin Director of the Art Institute of Chicago; Sarah Guernsey, Deputy Director and Senior Vice President of Curatorial Affairs; Ann Goldstein, Deputy Director and Chair and Curator of Modern and Contemporary Art; Eve Jeffers, Senior Vice President of External Affairs; and Andrew Simnick, former Senior Vice President of Finance, Strategy, and Operations.

Colleagues throughout the museum enthusiastically contributed to the success of the exhibition and catalogue. In Photography and Media, Matthew Witkovsky, Richard and Ellen Sandor Chair and Curator and Vice President of Strategic Art Initiatives, championed the project from the start, securing support and offering sage advice along the way. Barbara Diener assisted with all Art Institute objects, and Sharrone Brumfield handled countless administrative tasks. Antawan I. Byrd and former colleague Michal Raz-Russo were congenial sounding boards. Curatorial fellow Joshi Radin intrepidly tracked down primary sources and auction records and organized a wealth of material. In Photography and Media Conservation, helmed by Sylvie Pénichon, Nayla Maaruf and Elsa Thyss facilitated the safe presentation of the works, while Jim Iska designed and oversaw a custom frame treatment that beautifully highlighted the objects' materiality. Ann Goldstein and Caitlin Haskell in Modern and Contemporary Art also facilitated loans of painting and sculpture for the Chicago presentation, and Christine Fabian, Emily Heye, and Katrina Rush a l contributed their conservation expertise to the non-photographic objects in the presentation. The team in Exhibitions, ably led by Megan Rader, organized the safe transportation of works from widespread collections and guided the exhibition's transfer to the High Museum, with Joyce Penn in Collections and Loans meticulously overseeing all aspects of crating and shipping. Becca Schlossberg was an indispensable partner in th s project from its beginning; her evident passion for the presentation of art is matched by her command of every detail.

A team of creative partners managed the content and design of the exhibition: Samantha Grassi des gned the space with great sensitivity and skill; Bronwyn Kuehler produced innovative digital interactives; K t Shields thoughtfully edited the didactics; Kirsten Southwell, assisted by Kristin Best, created bold yet elegant graphics; and Ginia Sweeney helped craft and guide the narrative. The exhibition would not have been possible without the skills of numerous collaborators in Experience Design, led by Michael Neault. The ever-resourceful Joseph Vatinno and his talented team ensured a smooth construction process. Art handlers Brandon Czaja and Christine Huck installed the works quickly and safely.

The Art Institute's External Affairs team, helmed by Eve Jeffers, helped secure the necessary support for this project. Colleagues in Marketing, directed by Katie Rahn, communicated Kertész's innovations to a wider public. Troy Klyber lent his expertise to all legal and intellectual-property questions. The dedicated teams in Engagement, led by Amy Katherine Allen, and Learning and Public Engagement, led by Veronica Stein, devised a roster of dynamic programs to accompany the exhibition. The Ryerson and Burnham Libraries— the starting point of every exhibition I have under-taken at the Art Institute—aided my research at every turn, especially through the assistance of Autumn Mather and Aaron Rutt.

Much of the work for this exhibition took place during a global pandemic. I am indebted to everyone named here for their generosity, flexibility, and resource-fulness in the face of unprecedented challenges. Special mention is due to my friends and colleagues in the support system of the Ongoing Moment: Sophie Hackett, Corey Keller, Sarah Kennel, Sarah Meister, and Casey Riley. And last but not least, thank you to my family: Greg, Audrey, and Nina.

Elizabeth Siegel
Curator of Photography and Media
The Art Institute of Chicago

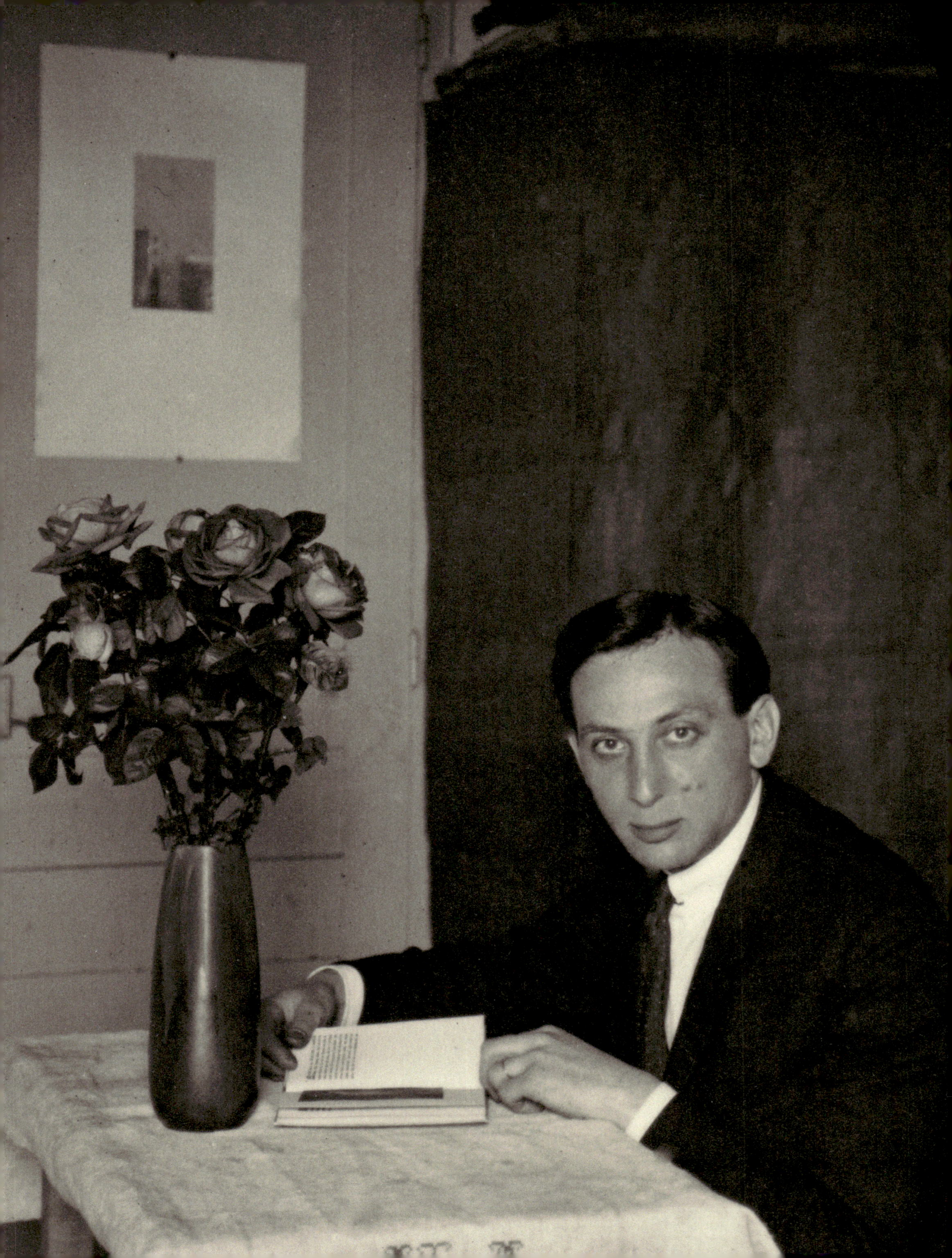

André Kertész's Carte Postale Period
Paris, 1925–28

ELIZABETH SIEGEL

Consider two portraits of André Kertész, each made
not long after he moved from Hungary to Paris, where
he intended to pursue a career in photography. In the
first (fig. 1), Kertész, vignetted in an oval, squints down
the barrel of a rifle held to his cheek, lights and
onlookers barely visible in the background. The artist
was taking advantage of a new fairground attraction
of the 1920s, the *tir photographique*, or photographic
shooting range: participants attempted to hit a target
with a toy gun to trigger a camera's mechanism and
create an image rewarding the marksman for his
aim.[1] Such amusements were popular among recent
veterans of World War I, like Kertész, as they afforded
them the opportunity to be photographed "in action."
Fairground workers printed the resulting shots on
common, inexpensive *carte postale* (postcard) paper
to produce a keepsake the subject could preserve
to commemorate an evening of fun or mail to share
the experience with friends or family.

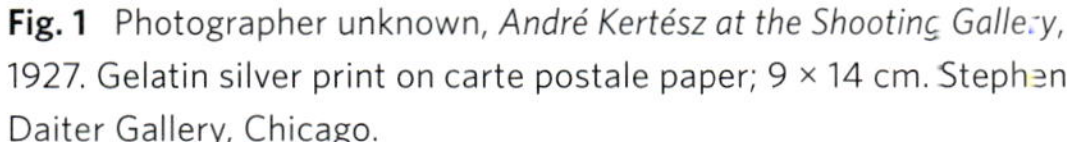

Fig. 1 Photographer unknown, *André Kertész at the Shooting Gallery*,
1927. Gelatin silver print on carte postale paper; 9 × 14 cm. Stephen
Daiter Gallery, Chicago.

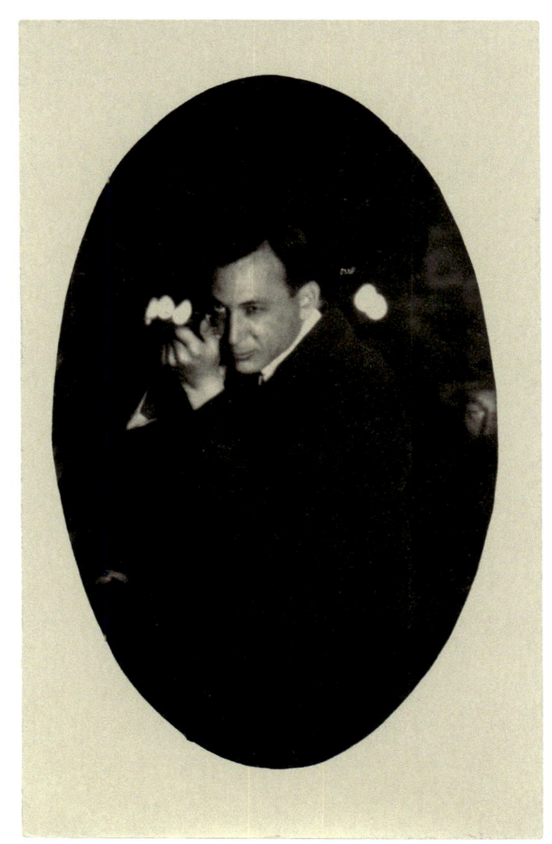

The second picture (cat. 1), which shows the artist in a setting he arranged himself, can more properly be considered a self-portrait. Seated on his bed at a table in his cramped apartment, Kertész gazes at the camera with determination, surrounded by talismanic objects from home as well as symbols of his new life: a tablecloth embroidered by his mother with his initials, Hungarian crafts on the shelf, a sculptural life mask of his face, and, prominently displayed over his head, one of the earliest photographs he made in Paris, of the Eiffel Tower shrouded in fog (cat. 6).[2] Unlike the playful shooting-range portrait, this portrait is contemplative and composed, a thoughtful, confident display of old and new, traditionalist and aesthete, Hungarian and Parisian; but like the shooting-range portrait, it was printed on carte postale stock. Kertész sent it back home to Hungary to his mother and his future wife, Elizabeth Salamon, as a declaration that he was fulfilling, in his adopted city, his promise to become a photographer.

The humble support for each portrait, the photographic postcard, would serve as the vehicle for Kertész's aesthetic aspirations during his first years in Paris, the moment in which he shaped his artistic identity.[3] Adapting a recently introduced innovation in modern material culture, he honed a personal style while generating new formal possibilities for photography generally. Although his decision to employ this format may have been born initially of economy and convenience, he soon embraced the paper's sensual properties: its velvety tones, pleasing surface texture, and restricted dimensions, the last of which opened up entirely new ways of editing and composing prints. The low cost enabled Kertész to distribute his pictures freely among friends or send them to loved ones, but as his renown grew he also occasionally included them, mounted, in exhibitions. Today these small, precise works are the premier objects in private and institutional collections of his art.[4]

This book assembles and analyzes—for the first time—Kertész's output of carte postale prints, which he made exclusively from 1925 to 1928.

It argues that the material form of these works cannot be separated from his innovative formal decisions; the carte postale format reflects the photographer's sense of freedom as well as the wide array of new artistic influences he found in 1920s Paris. In linking the image with the object, this catalogue also takes part in the current materialist turn in the history of photography, in which historians, curators, and conservators aim to understand the production and circulation of photographs through rigorous attention to their physical qualities.[5] This approach extends to the reproduction of the works in the plate section: unlike in most books on Kertész, which have suppressed this materiality by cropping reproductions to the edge of the image, here they are presented whole, in recognition that the expanse of the paper is part of the work and the image cannot be understood apart from its support. There exist carte postale prints of over 250 negatives; examined together, they show how, through his sustained exploration of the format, Kertész investigated a range of possibilities for the photographic object: from darkroom experiment to finished product, from pictures kept in pockets and shared intimately at café tables to those carefully mounted for display at groundbreaking exhibitions.

These works also show Kertész investigating different roles for the photographic artist in the interwar period. Looking closely at this focused moment and specific category of prints illuminates the artist's methods and concerns at a liminal point in his career. Many scholars have treated the full span of his time in Paris (1925–36) as a coherent chapter in his growth as a photographer, but in fact his first three years there—before his critical successes in exhibitions and magazines—stand apart as a chapter of particular independence and discovery. This gestational period would also prove extraordinarily productive, resulting in some of the most beloved and recognized works of Kertész's career. More importantly, it enabled him to combine a candid, amateur approach with lessons learned from an international circle of artists; to experiment with compositions, which he further refined in the darkroom; and to explore the relationship of image to ground that would continue to inform his later work. The carte postale prints also met the circulation and communication needs of an immigrant and budding professional, facilitating both connection with distant family and advertisement of his photographic skills.

"I am an amateur and I intend to remain so for the rest of my life," Kertész told a critic in 1930.[6] During those first years in Paris, before his output was dominated by magazine work with all its attendant constraints and demands, Kertész combined the best qualities of the amateur—freedom from assignment or convention, fascination with the small moments of everyday life, an open-eyed sense of wonder—with the sensibility of a modernist who had absorbed formal lessons from artists working in a wide range of media. During this brief but generative period, he discovered the city, expanded his social circle, and investigated picture making: he looked, he listened, he imagined, and he invented. In the process, he carved out an unprecedented path that allowed him to move between amateur and professional, photojournalist and avant-garde artist, diarist and documentarian. It was not until he retired from a career in magazine photography at the age of sixty-eight that he found that freedom again.[7]

HUNGARY

Although Kertész's first years in Paris were formative, by the time he arrived there in October 1925 he had already been practicing photography for over a decade in his native Hungary.[8] After a series of professional detours and frustrations (he had been a clerk in the stock exchange, a soldier, and a bee-keeper), he was finally, in the 1920s, beginning to find an identity as a photographer in Budapest.

As it later would in Paris, his approach synthesized a wide variety of influences, from mass media to avant-garde artist friends. The practices Kertész developed in his first years of experimentation— photographing diaristically, printing at a small scale, and even engaging the postcard form to distribute his images—found mature expression in his carte postale period in Paris.

The second of three brothers, Andor Kertész (he changed his name to André upon arrival in Paris and kept the French form after immigrating to the United States in 1936) was born to a middle-class Jewish family in Budapest in 1894. Family and photography went hand in hand for Kertész: in 1912 he and his younger brother, Jenő (see fig. 2), together began learning the technical and formal skills of photography using an Ica box camera, a gift from their mother. The two collaborated on images of the Budapest streets and portraits of relatives, a working relationship that would continue well

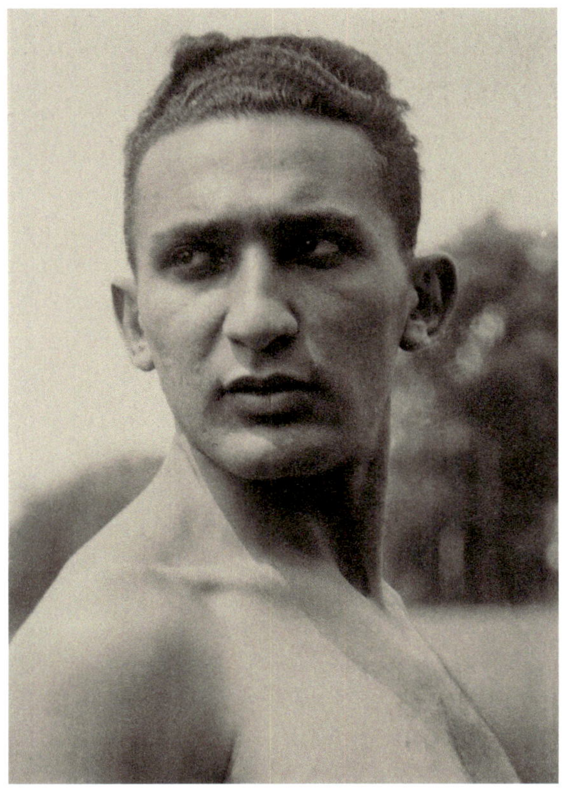

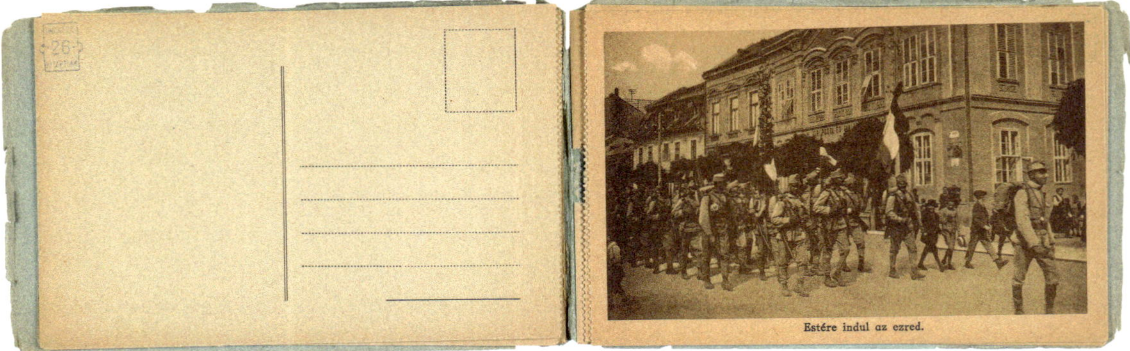

into André's professional career. When André joined the Austro-Hungarian Army during World War I, Jenő sent him a new Ica model with a faster lens, and the elder Kertész began to turn their shared pastime into something more serious, sending back negatives for Jenő to print and place in local newspapers and magazines. At the front and during convalescence after sustaining a wound, he photographed not the horrors of war but the quieter moments of soldier life; the free, youthful bodies of swimmers; and village scenes around the areas where he was stationed.

These early experiences likely informed the artist's work on carte postale paper during his first years in Paris. The Ica held only a limited number of plates, so Kertész learned the patience necessary to wait for the right moment and visual organization required to make a compelling photograph. He delighted in the precision of the 4.5-by-6-centimeter contact prints (made by placing the negative in direct contact with the photographic paper during exposure, without the use of an enlarger), describing one as "a tiny picture, but sharp. I can stare at it endlessly, and I am very happy."[9] During the war Kertész also became accustomed to seeing photographic postcards. Like many servicemen, he sent home postcards with scenes of army life and likely contributed to their production. Soldiers were encouraged to raise money for widows and orphans through the sale of photographs, often as postcards bearing the name and rank of the photographer. Kertész kept a booklet of ten detachable photographs

imprinted with his unit (fig. 3), some of which he probably took himself.[10]

After the war Kertész continued to investigate various outlets for and attitudes toward picture making. He became friends with many prominent Hungarian artists, some of whom he would encounter again in Paris; they imbued in the budding photographer an appreciation for Hungary's agrarian past while inspiring new compositional rigor in his pictures. He also gleaned lessons from the worlds of amateur and professional photography. His first published image appeared in the Budapest weekly *Az Érdekes Újság* in 1917, and he continued to submit to the Hungarian picture press with some success. Although Kertész was intrigued by the work he saw in illustrated magazines (and Jenő would exhort that "reportage is the only kind of modern photography"), he was not a news photographer, preferring subtler, more poetic moments to scenes of action or politics.[11] Nor did his work fit contemporary standards for fine-art photography: although he was a member of the National Association of Hungarian Amateur Photographers, he eschewed their preference for painterly printing, even denying himself the possibility of a medal in a 1924 contest by refusing to resubmit his gelatin silver photographs as fussy bromoil prints.

Fig. 3 Book of photographic postcards produced by Kertész's unit during World War I. André Kertész archive, Médiathèque de L'Architecture et du Patrimoine, Charenton-le-Pont, France.

The artistic practice Kertész developed in this early period was something of a middle way between reportage and fine art. In later years he would often assert that his photography functioned as a kind of "visual diary," a record of his daily life.[12] His early images of his family, friends, and environs, along with an extensive series of self-portraits for which he adopted different personas, show the young artist charting a path to personal expression between the poles of journalist and amateur. But even these photographs were not mere records; already he was grasping at a more modern approach— intuited more than learned, mingling nature and geometry, past and present, subjective expression and precise reportage—that would come to fruition in his first years in Paris.

PARIS, 1925–28

Kertész left Hungary for reasons both personal and professional. Although close with Jenő, he fought with his older brother, Imre, who wanted him to contribute to the family financially. At the same time, Salamon refused to marry him until he established himself and encouraged him to leave Budapest to do so. Unable to find secure footing as a photographer and plagued by self-doubt, Kertész saw the opportunities France afforded as an antidote to his stagnant career in Hungary. At the age of thirty-one, he left Salamon and his family behind to make his way as a photographer in Paris.[13] He arrived on October 8, 1925, with his cameras, a temporary visa, and enough money to sustain him for about a year or two.[14] If his ambitions were lofty, his expectations were modest.

In November he listed his profession as "photo reporter" in the police registry of foreign residents, and in January 1926 he obtained a press pass from the Budapest-based Continental Photo Agency; however, he would not receive regular commissions from magazines for a few years.[15] He worked for three months in early 1926 as a retoucher at a studio in the suburbs of Paris and received an auditor pass for courses in cinematography from the École d'Arts et Métiers. He carefully maintained a record of

his accounts, and his expense books from November 1926 on are primarily occupied with necessities of food, lodging, transportation, and photographic supplies. Letters from family express their concerns about Kertész's health, language skills, and ability to support himself. Although within a few years he would exhibit his work with other well-regarded artists and become a mainstay of the burgeoning picture press, his success at this early moment was by no means assured.

In Kertész's first days in Paris, the camera became an adjunct to his initial tours of the city. The first photograph he made upon arrival was the view from his room in a hotel on rue Vavin in Montparnasse, the area popular in the 1920s with expatriate artists and where Kertész spent nearly all of his eleven years in Paris, moving frequently within the neighborhood. He took his camera with him on walks through the city, photographing boats along the Seine at the Pont Louis-Philippe and the fountain sculptures at Place de la Concorde (cat. 9) with his smaller Hungarian camera.[16] He followed these with a view emblematic of his new home, the aforementioned image of the Eiffel Tower, as seen from a window in the apartment of a Hungarian architect he was visiting. Anything but a typical tourist snapshot, this moody photograph renders a specific vision of the famous landmark from the perspective of a local.[17] In these early months he also made his first night photograph in Paris, a view near the Hôtel de Ville (cat. 7), and began to document not only the monuments and streets but also the people of Paris. He photographed fishermen along the quay in a geometric composition, perhaps admiring their ease in their surroundings (cat. 10), and *clochards*, men camped out along the banks of the river (cat. 38), whose marginalized status drew the artist's sympathy; he was an outsider himself. Kertész's first photographs in Paris are more personal than those of a reporter, more composed than those of a tourist, and more experimental than those of an amateur. With little market or audience for the work, and thus few expectations to satisfy, Kertész was free to explore and record, refining his eye as he reviewed his images as contact prints on carte postale paper.

As he settled into his new home, the photographer also began to expand his circle of friends and acquaintances. With limited ability in French, he gravitated toward a group of Hungarian expatriate artists and writers. Through the painter Gyula Zilzer (see cats. 12, 82), whom he had known in Budapest, Kertész met two Hungarian artists who would become his closest friends and most important artistic influences in Paris. Lajos Tihanyi (see cat. 15), a painter who had been associated with the modern art movements Ma and the Group of Eight in Hungary, arranged small commissions for his countryman, exchanged work with the photographer, took him to places of interest around the city, and passed along ideas about pared-down form in painting.[18] Cubist sculptor Joseph (József) Csáky (see cats. 16, 80), one of the best-known Hungarian artists in Paris—on the back of a print he sent to Jenő (cat. 16), Kertész wrote, "Csáky, a sculptor of international renown by now"—gave his friend two sculptures he had admired.[19] Soon Kertész met and photographed, among many other artists and luminaries, musician and composer Paul Arma (Imre Weisshaus, see cat. 17), who had been a student of Béla Bártok in Budapest; puppeteer and folk-art restorer Géza Blattner (see cat. 108); abstract sculptor Etienne (István) Beöthy (see cats. 90–91); dancer Magda Förstner (see cats. 86–89, 91–92), who posed for the photograph that would come to be known as *Satiric Dancer*, one of Kertész's most famous works (cat. 92; see Sarah Kennel's essay in this book); journalist and writer Sándor Márai (see cat. 18); and designer and artist Eva Révai (see cats. 76–77), who shared with Kertész an affinity for traditional Hungarian textiles. In this circle—bound by a common language, limited resources, and an appreciation for the homeland from which they had broken—he found a like-minded group of fellow artists willing to help him along both practically and aesthetically. Photography historian and curator Sandra Phillips has described this group as preserving a playful "Budapest spirit" that referenced the folk art of Hungary's past as well as the Constructivism of its present.[20]

Through these new friends, Kertész began to expand his circle internationally, especially at the Café du Dôme, a gathering place for the expatriate set (see fig. 4). (The Hungarian "Dom" shows up regularly in his expense books, as do entries for coffee and pastry.) As the artist later recalled, "The Café du Dôme on the Montparnasse was the meeting place for all, and when I was not going around photographing I went there and it became my living quarters. I only went home to sleep."[21] Kertész was often the only photographer among a group of artists in other media, and his skill with a camera provided a kind of passport to this wider community. As he began to make portraits of new friends and acquaintances, he undoubtedly gleaned innovative approaches to composition, gained intimate access to artwork and studios, and exchanged ideas about modern art.

As he improved his French and accumulated acquaintances, the artist produced carte postale prints of French writer Pierre Mac Orlan (see cats. 22, 75), who would later publish sensitive criticism about Kertész's work and the photographic scene in Paris; Belgian poet Paul Dermée (see cat. 19), who penned verses in Kertész's honor for the opening of his first exhibition in 1927; French-Romanian writer, performance artist, film director, and

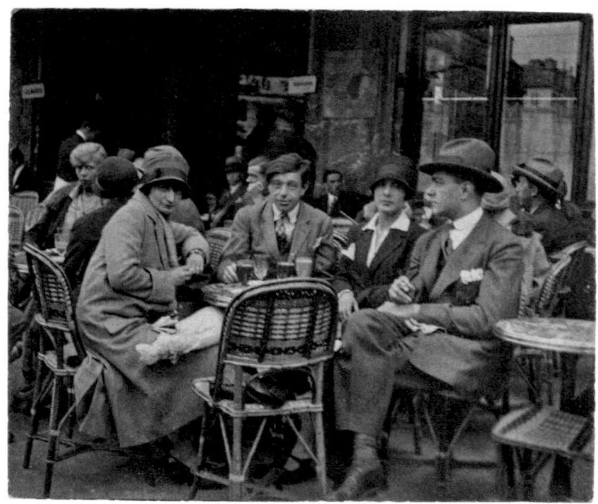

composer Tristan Tzara (see cat. 23), a co-founder of the Dada movement; and American writer, editor, and photographer Edwin Rosskam, often with his wife, Peggy, and their cats (see cats. 29–35). Perhaps intrigued by her references to folk art, he made portraits of Swedish painter Gundvor Berg (see cats. 71–72). He admired German artist Anne-Marie Merkel's "face of the Middle Ages" and photographed her in several different sittings (see cats. 25–28), one of which he used for the invitation to his 1927 exhibition.[22] Among the other artist friends in his portraits are Spanish ceramist Josep Llorens Artigas (see cats. 65, 78); Hilda Daus (see cats. 20-21), a German handcraft artist; Evsa Model (see cat. 73), a Russian-born painter and proprietor of a bookshop and gallery, L'Esthétique; and Dutch painter Piet Mondrian (see cats. 51, 82), whose meticulous studio would become the site of one of Kertész's most famous images. In these collaborative portraits, the photographer eschewed studio props and lighting in favor of isolating a striking close-up profile or situating his subject within the geometry of his or her everyday environment. Just as his early photographs of the city made visible his peregrinations, these portraits map his new community as well as his investigations of composition and form.

The Café du Dôme was a site not only for socializing but for distribution and display. There, photographs—first the small prints Kertész brought from Hungary and later the prints on carte postale paper he started making in Paris—became a kind of calling card and an advertisement of his skills.[23] "To my friends I gave photos for nothing, but some of my friends' friends began buying my prints for what must have been the equivalent of a dollar each," he recalled.[24] The artist's daybooks are peppered with tightly written lists of incoming funds, from portrait commissions and later from magazine

Fig. 4 *Lajos Tihanyi and Friends, Café du Dôme*, 1925–26 (cat. 187). Gelatin silver print on carte postale paper; image/card: 4.0 × 4.9 cm. André and Elizabeth Kertész Foundation.

assignments, that reveal not only an expanding network but also a blurring of the lines between work for hire and what we might now consider personal photographs. Some of his most successful portraits originated as commissions, but the fact that he kept personal copies, or sent prints to loved ones for their admiration and review, indicates that he valued them for more than the income they generated.[25] One undated entry in his daybooks (made sometime between October and December 1927) includes listings for commissions for an American woman, Mrs. Wheeler (cats. 45–46); American actress (later painter) Anita de Caro (cat. 43); and the wife of a doctor, Madame Perret (cat. 50).[26] Other apparent commissions from the period include a portrait of a German physician introduced to Kertész by Zilzer (cat. 39); the furniture designer Elizabeth Pfeiffer (cat. 44); and a young Yugoslav man who posed for the photographer as a bohemian artist (cat. 41) and a book collector (cat. 42). When printed at an intimate and easily portable scale (the standard postcard size was 9 by 14 centimeters, or about 3 ½ by 5 ½ inches), such portraits could readily be spread out on a table or passed around to fellow habitués of the café to demonstrate Kertész's increasing compositional prowess and attract new commissions. He continued to use them in this manner for decades: toward the end of his life, more than fifty years after he first came to Paris, Kertész was known to carry a set of twenty or thirty carte postale prints from the period in his pocket, always ready to show an interested viewer.[27]

Critically, the carte postale prints were small, lightweight, and sturdy enough that they could also be sent easily and affordably through the mail, and Kertész regularly sent prints back to his family and Salamon in Hungary and to Argentina, where Jenő had moved in 1926. Notably, however, he did not send them in the manner the manufacturers of the paper stock had intended—that is, by writing and stamping directly on the back of the card.[28] Instead, he mailed them in envelopes, accompanied by letters, as examples of his photographic progress or, as with the several self-portraits he made and sent (see cats. 5, 13), proof of his own well-being.[29] Like many immigrants, Kertész changed addresses frequently, struggled to find employment and make ends meet, and contended with the language barrier; communication with family back home was a necessary lifeline. He kept the many long, newsy missives his mother and brothers sent him during his years abroad, and they reveal great concern for his health and welfare. Although Kertész's own letters have not survived, the photographs he enclosed must have spoken for themselves, providing evidence of his new community and expanding competency. As Kertész later claimed, "My English is bad. My French is bad. Photography is my only language."[30]

Kertész did, however, append notes to the backs of his photographs; distinct from the chatty text on a typical postcard, they amplified the images with brief comments on his sitters or technique. Extant carte postale prints known to have been sent to Jenő bear pencil inscriptions informing his brother of his new acquaintances: "Magda Förstner, grotesque dancer from Pest"; "Miss Jaffe, American journalist, contributor to the world's largest Yiddish paper, *Der Tag*"; "Lajos Tihanyi, my most sincere advocate

and distributor. He is a well-known Hungarian painter who has gained a high reputation here, abroad, as well."[31] Sometimes the notes contained welcome news of professional success, as when he wrote on the back of *Chez Mondrian* (cat. 56) about the work's publication in a forthcoming avant-garde art journal.[32] At other times, the artist mused in inscriptions about his photographic thinking, as with an environmental portrait of one of Beöthy's cousins on a sinewy stairwell (cat. 70): "This is more like a movie than a photograph, but it is typical of the person depicted. The gorgeous stairwell is my discovery" (fig. 5). Jenő responded with thoughtful criticism and encouragement; about a year into the Paris venture, with André's prospects steadily improving, his brother wrote:

I know that the many words of recognition and the good reviews that you have earned by the sweat of your brow don't mean more for now than reassurance and encouragement for the future. I know that the fight is still ahead, but even if it will be grueling, it will be easy because you can already see the goal. But it isn't really this that I'm

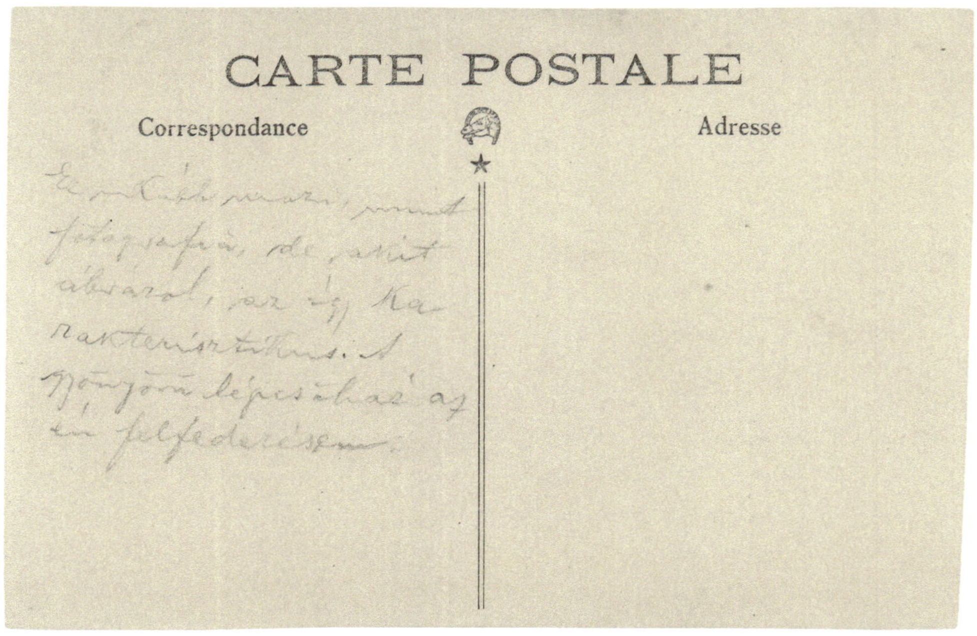

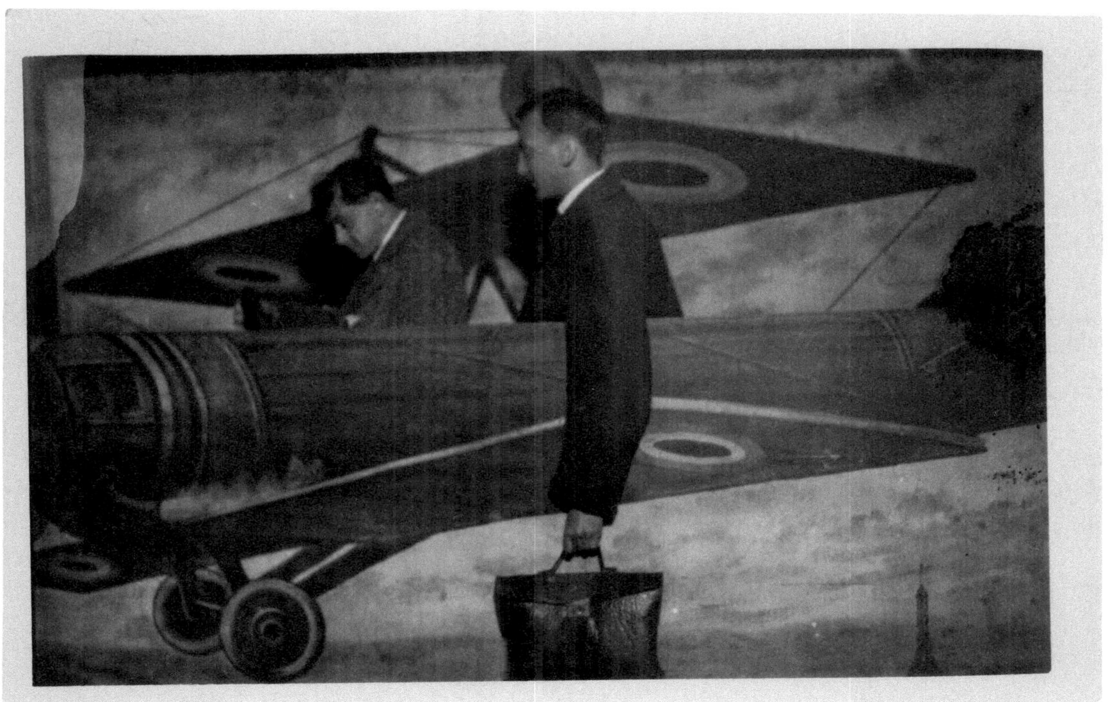

very happy about. What makes me happy is that you were able to become a photographer. If you had become a stockbroker, or if you were a beekeeper with an apiary so large that it would take two days for you to count your Papszt hives, you would only have become a rich man. This way, however, you'll be a contented man.[33]

Though Kertész did not treat these prints as a tourist would a postcard, their format (not only their size and durability but also the inclusion of designated areas for an address and a stamp) may nonetheless have inspired him to circulate them through the mail and use them to communicate with his family.

Kertész was not alone in using postcards as an artistic medium. By the 1920s photographic postcards had been in active use for some forty years. Enthusiasm for the novelty and convenience of these small, sendable images at times overwhelmed post offices.[34] Collectors assembled and traded their favorites. By the beginning of the twentieth century, a market had emerged for "fantasy cards"—images that were playful, suggestive, or simply bizarre—and opportunities abounded for people to insert themselves into these whimsical scenes. At fairgrounds across France in the 1920s, visitors could pose as aviators in a plane or passengers in a car or boat, sliding their heads or torsos into painted flats; Kertész took advantage of one such opportunity, posing with Tihanyi in a dangerously smoking propeller plane (fig. 6). Like the souvenirs from the popular tir photographique, fantasy cards were printed on postcard stock to be mailed to friends.

Unsurprisingly, the Surrealists were enamored of these images for the possibilities they provided for shape-shifting play. Artists and poets like André

Fig. 5 Verso of *Unidentified Sitter* (*Hungarian Woodcutter and Graphic Designer*), 1927 (cat. 70). Identifying marks of Kertész's preferred Guilleminot paper are visible (see Sylvie Pénichon's essay in this book).

Fig. 6 Photographer unknown. *Lajos Tihanyi and André Kertész*, September 29, 1927. Gelatin silver print; image: 6.2 × 10 cm; card: 6.9 × 10.9 cm. André and Elizabeth Kertész Foundation, courtesy of Stephen Daiter Gallery, Chicago.

Breton, Salvador Dalí, Paul Éluard, Max Ernst, Man Ray, Lee Miller, and many others frequented fairground photographers, posing in humorous sets or shooting photographic targets.[35] Several of these artists built impressive collections of fantasy postcards for inspiration, personal pleasure, or trading, and many other artists across Europe made their own work in the postcard format, producing new collages and photomontages on postcard backing or enhancing mass-produced cards with their own inventive additions. Perhaps due to the intimacy and economy of the format, some photographers simply used postcards as a different mode of distribution for unmanipulated images, like Man Ray, František Drtikol, and Germaine Krull in Europe in the 1920s and Walker Evans in the United States in the 1930s.

While Kertész joined numerous other artists of the twentieth century in using the materials of mass culture to make modern art, his sustained investment in the format of the carte postale marks a different kind of engagement. The photographer—who later insisted "I am not a Surrealist, I am absolutely a realist"—employed postcards not for visual games or fantastical amusements but rather because they enabled intimate scale, personal circulation, and precise compositions resulting from cropped and masked contact printing.[36] His initial motivations for using carte postale stock were likely economy and convenience: it was certainly easier and cheaper to make contact prints than enlargements.[37] But he also appreciated the semi-matte surface and rich tonal range of the Guilleminot paper and in later years maintained that the paper's beauty was its primary appeal for him.[38] The photographer may also have naturally gravitated to the format's small size. The standard postcard size, which he regularly trimmed even smaller, was not a significant departure in scale from the tiny contact prints he had made in Hungary and in his first months in Paris. Years later, while living in New York, he returned to this scale and precision when he began making Polaroid images of friends, scenes from his window, and domestic still lifes (see fig. 7).

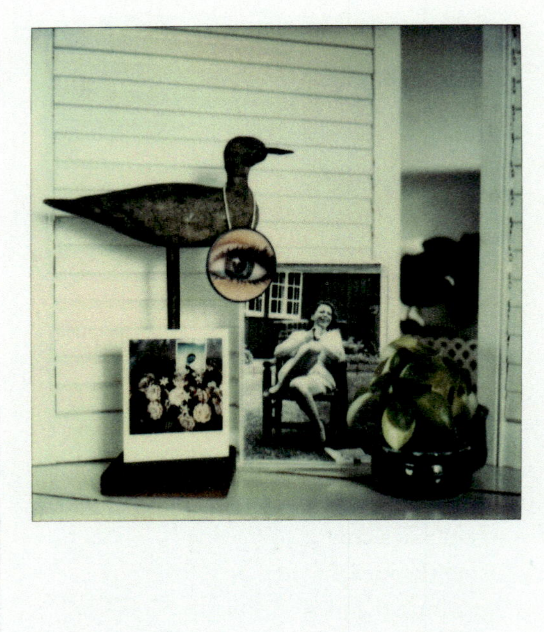

Though Kertész may have begun working with carte postale paper for largely practical reasons, the format was also part of a lifelong creative interest in pictures viewed up close in the hand.

If his printing choices were shaped in part by economy, they were conscious decisions nonetheless. For example, Kertész had the capacity, both financially and practically, to make enlargements. A self-portrait showing him at work (cat. 2) reveals trays large enough to handle bigger paper along with printed enlargements tacked up on the wall. Among the equipment promised by Jenő around Christmas 1925 were larger developing trays as well as a plate washer for negatives sized 6 by 9 to 13 by 18 centimeters. And his expense book shows, among purchases of 9-by-12-centimeter film plates and boxes of one hundred sheets of postcard paper, purchases of larger paper and the occasional

Fig. 7 *Untitled (Still Life with Bird, Eye, and Photographs)*, June 24, 1979. Internal dye diffusion transfer print; image: 7.9 × 7.8 cm; paper: 10.7 × 8.8 cm. The Art Institute of Chicago, Smart Family Foundation Fund, 2014.81.

outsourcing of enlargements.[39] Enlarging was technically possible as early as the mid-nineteenth century, but it became more common with advanced projection techniques and an emerging market for fine-art prints around the turn of the century. Associated with the pictorialist salons that Kertész disdained in Hungary, enlarged prints connoted handcraft, rarity, and exclusivity. After the mid-1920s they circulated much more widely and took on a different, less rarified valence with the arrival of the 35mm handheld camera, whose negatives were too small for contact printing.[40] In making contact prints on carte postale paper, Kertész prioritized a direct relationship between negative and print, maintaining that a work of art did not need to be large to be taken seriously, just as earlier he had protested the idea that a gelatin silver print could not constitute the final presentation of a work. He did not overtly espouse a philosophy, but his instinct was a kind of photographic purism, perhaps influenced by the genre of reportage and the format of postcards. His friend, frequent sitter, and incisive critic of photography Mac Orlan must have felt the same way, for in a 1928 letter requesting additional prints of a portrait Kertész had made of him, he added an underlined postscript: *"Do not make enlargements."*[41]

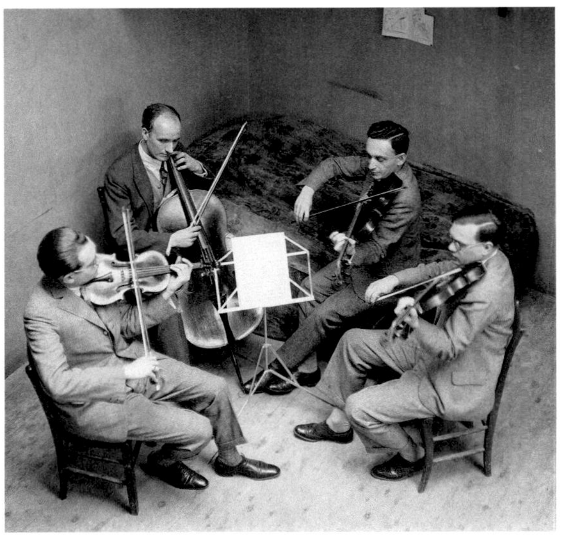

Although the artist eschewed painterly techniques and surrealist manipulations in his prints, he did take liberties with how much of the negative he printed. He seems to have intentionally left room at the moment of exposure for creative revision in the darkroom, where he could bring a more refined composition to the fore by cropping out select portions of the image.[42] A series of standard-format portraits (cats. 47–48), for example, became elongated verticals, amplifying the upright form of each sitter; he further emphasized the vertical by carefully trimming the card and leaving extra space at the bottom, using the altered proportions of the postcard to create a new kind of photographic object tailored to the individual image.[43] Kertész sometimes masked the negative, which allowed him to reprint his new vision more easily and consistently. For instance, he taped off the edges of an image of Château de Sainte-Mesme (page 55, fig. 6), shifting the focus from the building and trees to the decorative elements of the landscape and producing a panoramic effect (cat. 59).[44] A radical example of Kertész's approach can be seen in *Quartet* (cat. 95), a print made from a larger publicity image (fig. 8) commissioned by Feri Roth's string quartet. Not only did the artist drastically reduce the portion of the negative used in printing—eliminating the heads of the players and centering the white rectangle of the sheet music on the stand—but he placed the image at the top of the carte postale, leaving much of the expanse of the paper as negative space. This decision, which greatly heightened the impact of his darkroom cropping, reinforced the idea of the carte postale as a complete object and not merely the physical support for a picture. By so dramatically reconfiguring the negative, he also carved out a personal, experimental practice from his professional one: the whole image was for them, he later said in an interview; the cropped print was for him.[45]

Fig. 8 Positive scan from negative of *Quartet*, 1926 (cat. 95), showing uncropped image.

Often Kertész's carte postale prints seem to constitute a final presentation form, with the blank space around the image serving as a built-in mat or frame (see cats. 30–31, 73). In certain cases, like *Quartet*, the amount of blank space exceeds the area of the image. In one print made of a bookstore (cat. 96), the white of the page appears to squeeze the image into the uppermost reaches of the card, echoing the position of the photographer as he looked up at the man retrieving a book from a shelf near the ceiling. Through these precise printing and presentation choices, Kertész transformed his cartes postales into something very different from an ordinary postcard. Also atypical for the format, Kertész usually signed his prints on the front. This signature marks the carte postale prints as more than objects of mass culture or personal exchange, establishing them as finished works of art, signed by an artist and not a correspondent.

Kertész's carte postale years coincided with a remarkable period of growth in his photography, and this assured, purposeful style of presentation reflected a new maturity and self-confidence. In his photographs of the city, he moved away from the moody atmosphere of his early pictures and began to showcase the geometry of typography (see cats. 36–37). Along with images of fellow artists in their studios, he produced sophisticated "displaced portraits" absent of people, evoking their presence through their creative environments or personal objects, as with the sculptures, wineglasses, and kerosene lamp he photographed in the studio of Russian sculptor Ossip Zadkine (cat. 100).[46] In his portraits of Arma (cats. 93–94), he mimicked the process of cropping his cartes postales—selecting a new, more focused image out of a larger one—by making a second picture at closer range, zooming in on the gesture of Arma's hand holding his distinctive eyeglasses. During this time he also embarked on a series of still lifes, both found and arranged, whose print size echoes their intimate subject matter (see cats. 101–3). In his most overtly Surrealist work (an affinity he recognized even as he disavowed it), he photographed the overturned bottom half

of a mannequin in a sculptor's studio (cat. 99), its truncated legs erotically suggestive amid a chaotic mix of objects.[47] This period of cross-pollination with artists in other disciplines found its fullest expression in *Satiric Dancer* (cat. 92), which features Förstner in Beöthy's studio mimicking the sculptures that surround her. The informal and playful tone of the session echoes the circulation of carte postale prints at the Dôme: by photographing friends, working in their studios, and sharing his prints with them, Kertész achieved a consistent ethos of experimentation and exchange. Indeed, in these critical first three years in Paris, when he was free of professional photographic obligations and able to fully explore his chosen carte postale format, Kertész produced some of the most enduring images of his career, among them *Satiric Dancer*, *Fork* (cat. 111), and *Chez Mondrian*.[48]

His experience with Mondrian marked a turning point. The Belgian writer Michel Seuphor, who squired the photographer around Paris, introduced him to the Dutch abstract painter around August 1926; notes of subsequent meetings are scribbled in Kertész's daybooks. On several visits that fall, he made portraits of Mondrian, documented his studio (see cats. 53–55), and produced a still life evoking the presence of the painter through his pipe and glasses (cat. 52). Kertész scholars note a shift in his work toward more deliberate, geometric compositions after the encounters with Mondrian; some argue, for instance, that Mondrian's diamond-shaped lozenge paintings may have inspired Kertész to mount a carte postale portrait of Peggy Rosskam on an angle (cat. 32).[49] Even Mondrian's studio—by many accounts an extension of the controlled palette and rectangular forms of his paintings—exerted an influence on the photographs. The space was fastidiously clean, its possessions rigorously edited, with no instance of the color green allowed. "He simplified, simplified, simplified," Kertész later recalled. "The studio with its symmetry dictated the composition. He had a vase with a flower, but the flower was artificial. It was colored by him with the right color to match the studio."[50] Kertész photographed the environment from different angles, emphasizing its overlapping planes and rectilinear forms, which were softened only by the necessity of a bed for sleeping. When he made what would become his signature work, *Chez Mondrian*, he did so with great assurance, even moving a sofa in order to position his camera such that he could capture the contrast of the common hallway beyond the studio's entry. Split neatly down the middle, the composition is a marvel of balance and tension, with smooth against rough, rectangles against curves, and light against shadow.

Notably, Kertész produced more carte postale prints of *Chez Mondrian* than of any other image. The provenance of most other cartes postales—originating with friends, sitters, family, and Kertész's own estate—attests to their intimate circulation, and most exist in only a single known print or, occasionally, as many as five. In contrast, there are at least eight carte postale copies of *Chez Mondrian*, an indication of how much the artist appreciated it at the time of its making and also, potentially, of his belief that it would eventually be appreciated by a much wider audience. Most of these known prints feature Kertész's usual margin of blank space around the image, but a few he carefully trimmed to the edge and mounted on a larger, warm-toned, textured paper, which he often employed for exhibitions. When Kertész sold several works to New York gallerist Julien Levy around 1929, he included a mounted carte postale print of *Chez Mondrian*, ready for display in future exhibitions (fig. 9).[51]

This treatment of *Chez Mondrian*—mounting a carte postale print for display—was not typical for Kertész; more often, he made enlargements for exhibitions on single-weight paper and then mounted them, trimmed. This can be seen most vividly in installation shots (see fig. 10 and cat. 85) for the first exhibition to focus on his work, at Jan Sliwinsky's gallery, Au Sacre du Printemps, in Montparnasse, where for two short but important weeks in March 1927 Kertész exhibited some thirty mounted photographs alongside abstract paintings by Hungarian artist Ida Thal. Two of

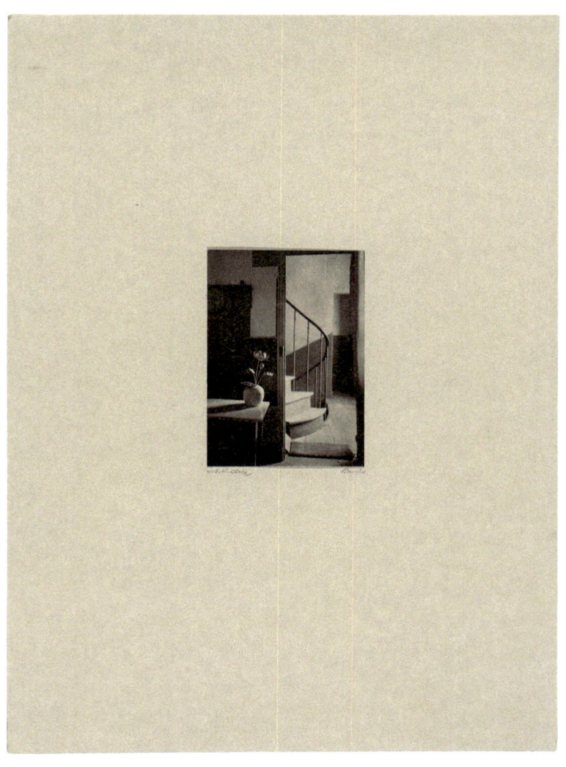

the works visible on the walls are postcard-sized, but most appear to be enlargements, including prints of works that otherwise exist in the carte postale format. In this respect, Kertész was following practices emerging from photography exhibitions of the late 1920s and early 1930s.[52] His choice to enlarge, trim, and mount his photographs for gallery display might seem to suggest that he did not consider the carte postale prints finished works in themselves or that he did not view the ground as an essential part of the photographic object. However, his presentation does seem to have been influenced by the scale and materiality of the carte postale format. For example, although he enlarged prints for the exhibition, their scale remained relatively intimate; that he pinned them right next to one another on the wall even recalls their informal display on the café table. Moreover, he employed the blank space

Fig. 9 Full mount of *Chez Mondrian*, 1926 (cat. 56).

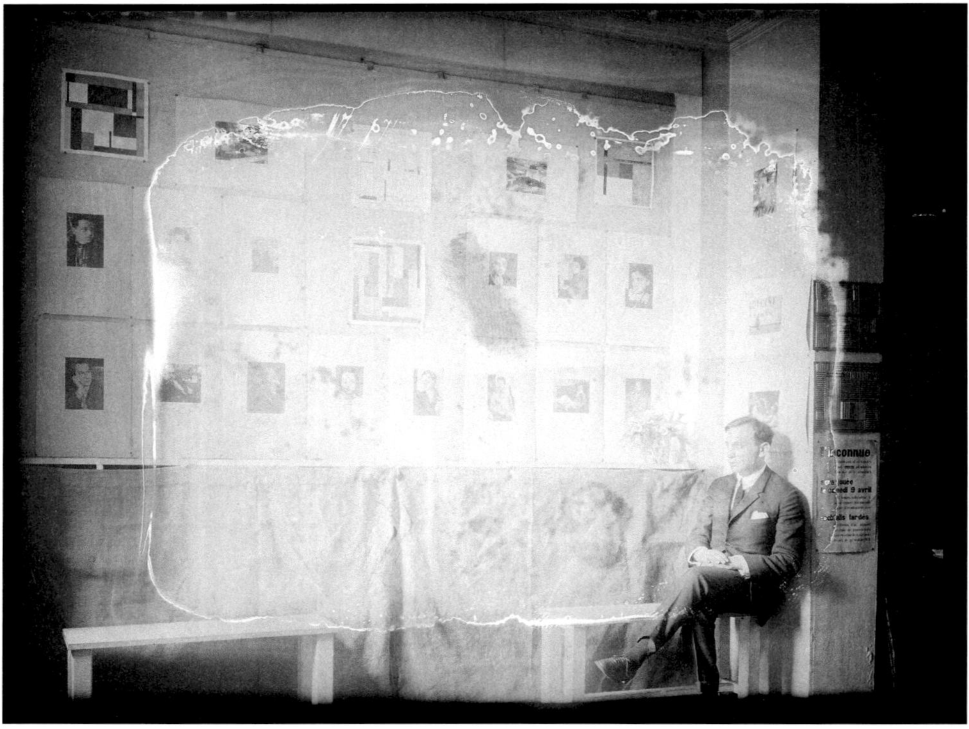

of the mats as margins for the images in a manner that harks back to the figure-ground relationship of his cartes postales, though the proportions differ.[53] In this translation of the postcard from the pocket to the wall, the artist remained indebted to his early experiments in Paris.

Kertész's first exhibition represented a break-through moment for his career and a striking demonstration of everything he had accomplished since leaving home. Nearly all of the photographs he presented had been made in the year and a half since he arrived in Paris, evidence of a remarkably fertile period. One wall featured scenes of Paris and studio still lifes, another portraits, primarily of fellow artists. Sliwinsky had earlier mounted shows for Tihanyi and Beöthy, as well as photographer Berenice Abbott, and his gallery was a gathering place for influential international figures. The exhibition opening was an extravagant soirée of music and poetry recited in multiple languages, a merging of art forms intended to celebrate the "esprit nouveau,"

according to one of Sliwinsky's three announce-ments advertising the show. On another, Dermée praised Kertész in a poem titled "Seeing Brother" that described *Chez Mondrian* and *Mondrian's Pipe and Glasses* (among other memorable images) and pronounced of their creator "your technique is as honest, as incorruptible, as your vision" (fig. 11).[54] For a small show of a relatively unknown photographer, it was well received by the press, with most remarking on Kertész's honesty, directness, and lack of trickery or guile. The Paris edition of the *Chicago Tribune* noted the intimacy of his portraits in

---

Fig. 10 Kertész in front of an installation of his works at Au Sacre du Printemps, 1927.

Fig. 11 Recto and verso of announcement for Kertész's 1927 exhibition at Au Sacre du Printemps. The recto is printed with one of the artist's portraits of Anne-Marie Merkel (cat. 26), the verso with a poem by Paul Dermée. The Art Institute of Chicago, Ryerson and Burnham Art and Architecture Archives, Artists' Papers, gift of Robert Gurbo and Louise Voccoli.

particular: "With two or three exceptions, the portraits are as unaffected as a snapshot. His sitters, seemingly unposed, are presented as casually and unemphatically as though they were sitting at a café table. Through this simplicity they show, like the still-lifes, land-scapes, and genres, the artistic possibilities of photography which depends purely on the most fundamental resources."[55] Important group exhibitions followed: Kertész showed alongside some of the best-known Parisian photographers at, among other exhibitions, *Le Premier Salon Indépendant de la Photographie*, also known as the *Salon de l'Escalier*, Paris, 1928; *Fotografie der Gegenwart*, Folkwang Museum, Essen, Germany, 1929; and, also in 1929, the legendary *Film und Foto* exhibition in Stuttgart, Germany. Soon he was

printing for the wall as much as for circulation among friends.

When the artist arrived in Paris in fall 1925, photographic practice was transitioning out of the studio and onto the pages of the new French picture press. Although photo-illustrated magazines had emerged earlier in Germany, the French journals that would come to publish his photographs regularly did not debut until the end of the decade: *Vu* was founded by Lucien Vogel in 1928 and was soon joined by other journals like *Art et Médecine* and *Voilà*.[56] Thus, although Kertész quickly became known through his published reportage, it is important to remember that the institutional support provided to him by the picture press was not available during his first few years in Paris. Nor was there

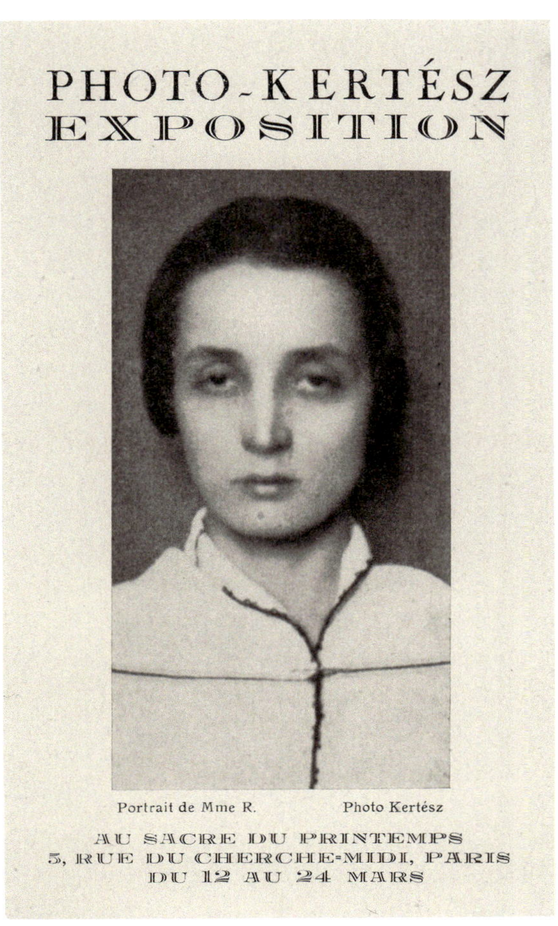

Portrait de Mme R.   Photo Kertész

Frère voyant

Ne fût-ce que pour la rime, Hamlet, tu devais ajouter : Il y a plus de choses dans la nature que dans les œuvres d'art et les littératures.

Seuls les découvreurs et les inventeurs créent, enrichissent le domaine public. Il n'existe que par eux, ce dont on leur sait mal gré.

Dans le monde visuel, pour faire de perpétuelles découvertes, il suffit d'y promener des yeux dont la rétine redevient vierge à chaque clin — film qui se dévide sans fin.

Mais tous, ne photographiez-vous pas la nature sur une plaque que vous n'avez pas changée depuis le jour de votre naissance !

Kertész,

des yeux d'enfant dont chaque regard est le premier ;

qui voient le grand roi nu, lorsqu'il est vêtu de mensonges ;

qui s'effraient des fantômes drapés de bâches hantant les quais de Seine ;

qui s'extasient devant les tableaux tout neufs que créent, sans malice, trois chaises au soleil du Luxembourg, la porte de Mondrian s'ouvrant sur l'escalier, des lunettes jetées sur une table à côté d'une pipe.

Pas d'arrangement, de rangement, de trucage, de contreplacage.

Votre technique est aussi loyale, aussi incorruptible que votre vision.

Dans notre hospice des Quinze-Vingts.

Kertész est un frère voyant.

Paul Dermée.

a photography community as such. Phillips has pointed out that other photographers do not figure among his early portraits of cultural figures; he did not associate closely with Man Ray, and he did not meet photographers Abbott and Krull until slightly later—Abbott through Sliwinsky in 1927 and Krull through work at *Vu*.[57] Kertész was often the only photographer in his circle, providing him a unique role as chronicler. If this limited his opportunities for professional advice, it also broadened his visual influences. As he had done in Hungary, in Paris he sought out connections with painters, sculptors, poets, and designers, and his distinctive approach to making photographs may well reflect his particular network and moment.

By 1928, the end of his carte postale period, the photography scene had changed, and Kertész was at the center of it. If his approach was intuited, as he often claimed in later interviews, it was certainly in keeping with—and likely helped to shape—the prevailing aesthetic.[58] Besides steady work as a magazine photographer, he was regularly mentioned in published articles (see fig. 12) in the same breath as Man Ray, and he soon began to be featured in group exhibitions that sought to define what modern photography should be.[59] The *Salon de l'Escalier*, for example, included works by Kertész, Abbott, Krull, and Man Ray, among others, with a separate section dedicated to Eugène Atget. Florent Fels, one of the organizers of the exhibition, wrote that in their selections they avoided "artistic photography" that imitated painting and drawing to focus instead on "exact, clear, precise" works. "A good photograph is, above all, a good document," he wrote.[60] Kertész agreed, finding inspiration in both reportage and snapshots: "Look at reporters and amateurs—both of whose sole aim is to make a souvenir or a document. That is pure photography."[61] For this brief, critical period in Paris, Kertész navigated through and between the available options of snapshooter, camera-club amateur, studio portraitist, and reporter to forge a new identity as a photographic artist and chart a path for other photographers to follow.

EPILOGUE

Kertész left Paris in 1936, relocating to New York for a job with the Keystone Press Agency and the promise of magazine work. His move marked a disappointing change in fortunes from the successes of Paris, and for many years he found little artistic opportunity or recognition in the United States. In his last decades, however, Kertész once again achieved the fame he desired and felt he deserved, with exhibitions, books, and a base of collectors hungry for his work. Interest in his prints paralleled wider developments in the burgeoning photography market: an affinity for ever-larger, new prints followed by an appreciation for the smaller, original prints that became known, in the parlance of fine-wine collectors, as *vintage*.[62] Correspondence in his archives, beginning around 1970, traces the demand for Kertész's work: clients write galleries requesting first 8-by-10-inch prints—the "natural" size for his photographs, Kertész told the Moderna Museet in 1971—then 11-by-14, and finally 16-by-20 (all three sizes, with commensurate pricing, were offered by Light Gallery by 1975).[63] By the mid-1970s, however, the word *vintage* increasingly crops up, with dealers and collectors jostling to obtain the earliest material and prices rising for rarer work. As the market shifted around him, it is possible that Kertész, too, changed his rationale for the carte postale prints, citing the quality of the paper over its cost and convenience as his primary motivation for employing it in the 1920s. Whatever his original impetus, today a combination of market forces, relative rarity, and aesthetic preferences have propelled these small, intimate prints to the forefront of his production in the view of museums and collectors.

Kertész made his last carte postale print in 1928. The various reasons he abandoned the format reflect his change in circumstances as well as changes in the field. The artist acquired a 35mm Leica camera that year, which gave him new mobility and spontaneity; but the camera's smaller negatives demanded enlargement. He began serious and sustained work for Parisian magazines, who cropped

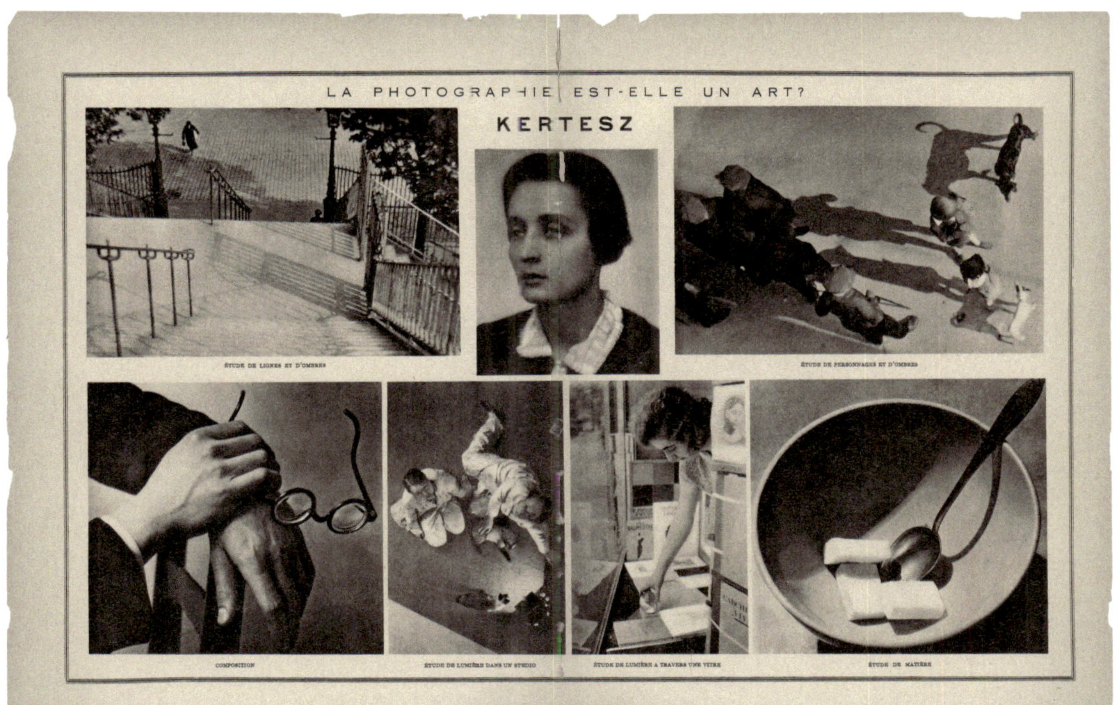

and sequenced his works according to their own preferences.[64] And he began to be included in more international exhibitions, for which enlargements were more desirable. Moreover, the photographer claimed in later years that the Guilleminot company discontinued his favorite carte postale paper stock.[65]

The last carte postale print Kertész may have made is one of his most famous: on the edge of a dinner plate, he posed an ordinary fork, its shadow tracing a faithful double along the tabletop and bending into slanted stripes along the plate's lip. Clean and modern, simple and unpretentious, it asserted that art could be made with the humblest objects so long as they were carefully observed. *Fork*, as it came to be known, was featured in international photography exhibitions in Arnhem, Amsterdam, Rotterdam, and Brussels in 1928 as well as *Fotografie der Gegenwart* and *Film und Foto* in 1929. It attracted widespread critical notice: "Among the still lives, one must above all admire a fork by André Kertész— yes, simply a fork—which is almost moving in its purity and tones," noted writer Pierre Bost. "It is perhaps the only image that gave me the impression of a true work of art."[66] Other reviewers argued that with *Fork*, Kertész "forces himself to validate the object" and "combines the pure plastic arts, the constructivist spirit."[67] This photograph marked Kertész's arrival as an equal among international photographers, heralding his acceptance and his future. Notably, he printed it at least once on carte postale stock. Whatever the reason he abandoned his beloved paper that year, its scale, at least, endured in other prints he made of *Fork* at the time, which, though on different paper, are also intimate contact prints around the same size as the negative.[68] There was no need to make it any bigger.

Fig. 12 Spread of Kertész's photographs from the March 1, 1929, issue of *L'Art Vivant*, including *Anne-Marie Merkel*, 1926 (cat. 27), *Edwin and Peggy Rosskam*, 1927 (cat. 29), *Paul Arma's Hands*, 1928 (cat. 94), and *Window, L'Esthétique*, 1927 (cat. 232).

NOTES

I am grateful to Robert Gurbo, Sarah Kennel, Sylvie Pénichon, and Matthew Witkovsky, who all read earlier versions of this essay and offered excellent suggestions for its improvement. All translations from Hungarian are by Eriksen Translations, New York, unless otherwise noted; all translations from French and German are my own unless otherwise noted.

1   See Clément Chéroux, "Portraits en pied . . . de nez: L'introduction du modèle récréatif dans la photographie foraine," *Études photographiques*, no. 16 (May 2005): 88–107, journals.openedition.org/etudesphotographiques/721. See also Clément Chéroux, "L'image inexpulsable," in *Si la vue vaut d'être vécue* (Paris: Textuel, 2019), 129–44. There is no evidence that Kertész sent this postcard to anyone.

2   On the iconography and circulation of this self-portrait, see Sandra S. Phillips, "André Kertész: The Years in Paris," in Sandra S. Phillips, David Travis, and Weston J. Naef, *André Kertész: Of Paris and New York*, exh. cat. (Chicago: Art Institute of Chicago, 1985), 30.

3   I am indebted to the art historians and curators who have produced thoughtful and thorough examinations of Kertész's life and career. The most essential sources, each building on the last, are Sandra S. Phillips, "The Photographic Work of André Kertész in France, 1925–1936: A Critical Essay and Catalogue" (PhD diss., City University of New York, 1985); Phillips, Travis, and Naef, *André Kertész: Of Paris and New York*; Sarah Greenough, Robert Gurbo, and Sarah Kennel, *André Kertész*, exh. cat. (Washington, DC: National Gallery of Art; Princeton, NJ: Princeton University Press, 2005); and Michel Frizot and Annie-Laure Wanaverbecq, *André Kertész,* exh. cat. (Paris: Jeu de Paume, 2010).

4   Though sale prices are only one measure of value, a 2020 ArtPrice search showed that half of the top ten Kertész auction records were for carte postale prints, with a carte postale print of *Chez Mondrian* (sold at Sotheby's, New York, October 10, 2005, lot 24) taking the top slot.

5   For just one of many examples, see Mitra Abbaspour, Lee Ann Daffner, and Maria Morris Hambourg, eds., *Object:Photo. Modern Photographs: The Thomas Walther Collection 1909–1949: An Online Project of The Museum of Modern Art* (New York: Museum of Modern Art, 2014), moma.org/interactives/objectphoto/#home.

6   Jean Vidal, "En photographiant les photographes," *L'Intransigeant*, April 1, 1930, 5.

7   As Phillips, Travis, and Naef put it, "he celebrated his fiftieth anniversary as a photographer by becoming an amateur again." Phillips, Travis, and Naef, *André Kertész: Of Paris and New York*, 11.

8   For background on the beginnings of Kertész's career in Hungary, see Sarah Greenough, "A Hungarian Diary, 1894–1925," in Greenough, Gurbo, and Kennel, *André Kertész*, 2–19; and Annie-Laure Wanaverbecq, "From Andor Kertész to André Kertész," in Frizot and Wanaverbecq, *André Kertész*, 21–29. For an overview of the general climate of Hungarian photography in the decade before Kertész left, see Péter Baki, "Hungary Between the Wars: A Photographic Portrait," in Abbaspour, Daffner, and Hambourg, eds., *Object:Photo* [online project], moma.org/interactives/objectphoto/assets/essays/Baki.pdf.

9   Cited in English translation in Greenough, "A Hungarian Diary," 5, from an entry dated June 24, 1912, about a photograph Jenő had made of a girl with whom André was obsessed.

10   See Wanaverbecq, "From Andor Kertész to André Kertész," 23. The album remains at the André Kertész archive, Médiathèque de L'Architecture et du Patrimoine, Charenton-le-Pont, France (hereafter cited as *MAP*), and Kertész included a postcard from the booklet in a collage now with the Kertész estate in New York.

11   Jenő Kertész to André Kertész, July 29, 1926, cited in English translation in Greenough, "A Hungarian Diary," 19.

12   By comparing archival documents against Kertész's stories of his career, Greenough has shown how he elided both historical fact and his own sophisticated intent, convincingly complicating the claim that his photographs served as a visual diary. See, especially, Sarah Greenough and Robert Gurbo, introduction to Greenough, Gurbo, and Kennel, *André Kertész*, xii–xiv.

13   Detailed accounts of Kertész's early years in Paris can be found in Phillips, "André Kertész: The Years in Paris"; Sarah Greenough, "To Become a Virgin Again, 1925–1936," in Greenough, Gurbo, and Kennel, *André Kertész*; and Annie-Laure Wanaverbecq, "Paris, the Garden of André Kertész," in Frizot and Wanaverbecq, *André Kertész*.

14   There are varying accounts of the different cameras Kertész used. We know that he brought a 4.5-by-6-centimeter camera with him to Paris; perhaps this was the Ica Bébé camera Jenő gave him during the war or a Goerz Tenax he favored (see Greenough, "A Hungarian Diary," 10; and David Travis, "Kertész and His Contemporaries in Germany and France," in Phillips, Travis, and Naef, *André Kertész: Of Paris and New York*, 58–59). Kertész recalled having the Tenax stolen from him as he napped in the Luxembourg Gardens, and Travis indicates that he replaced it with a 6-by-9-centimeter French reporter's camera. Jenő sent a Goerz Ango Anschütz folding camera with inserts for 9-by-12-centimeter plates, which Kertész likely received in late 1925 or early 1926 (see note 17). In 1928, all sources agree, Kertész acquired a 35mm Leica camera, which he often used for reportage. Sometime in spring 1930 his daybooks record the "camera purchase" of a 9-by-12-centimeter Silar, so he continued to employ that medium format even after the purchase of the Leica (MAP, undated page). Most of the negatives from the carte postale period at the MAP are 9-by-12-centimeter glass plates. A few rare extant prints of Hungarian 4.5-by-6-centimeter negatives on French carte postale paper (at the MAP and with the Kertész estate in New York) reveal that he brought his earlier negatives with him to Paris and continued to print from them.

15 The registry document and press pass are both in the MAP. Kertész published photographs in *Art et Industrie* and *Das Illustrierte Blatt* in 1926 and procured some commissions in French and German magazines in late 1927, but he was not a regular contributor to the picture press until 1928 or 1929. A complete list of the articles in which the artist published photographs can be found in Frizot and Wanaverbecq, *André Kertész*, 335–43, and supplemented by Sarah Kennel's chronology in Greenough, Gurbo, and Kennel, *André Kertész*, 246–67.

16 Kertész made two slightly different negatives of *Rue Vavin* his first photograph in Paris, but he did not produce this print in the carte postale format; *Pont Louis-Philippe* is a contact print made with a 4.5-by-6-centimeter negative (a print is at the J. Paul Getty Museum, Los Angeles) but not on carte postale paper.

17 The chronology of these earliest (fall 1925) photographs is a puzzle. I date them according to the primary research conducted by Sandra S. Phillips for her dissertation (see note 3) while Kertész was still alive, but the size of the negative confuses matters. In a letter to Kertész dated December 2, 1925, Jenő writes that he will be bringing him a large package of equipment including a "10-by-12.5 Goerz Ango Anschütz folding camera" and "dual cassettes with inserts for 9 by 12" (Jenő Kertész and others to André Kertész, December 2, 1925, MAP). He used the latter to make larger contact prints throughout the period. The negatives for prints dated 1925 discussed here (cats. 6–8, 10, and 38, all viewed at the MAP) were 9-by-12-centimeter plates; one wonders whether they were made after the new camera arrived.

18 Greenough discusses Tihanyi's philosophy and points in particular to the influence of his 1923 painting *Still Life with Pipe* on Kertész's photograph of Mondrian's pipe and glasses (cat. 52). Greenough, "To Become a Virgin Again," 65. The two works are also paired in Ernö Kallai, "Bildhafter Photographie," *Das Neue Frankfurt*, March 1928, 47.

19 Kertész owned the sculptures until his death according to Phillips, "André Kertész: The Years in Paris," 26.

20 Phillips, "André Kertész: The Years in Paris," 26.

21 André Kertész, *Kertész on Kertész: A Self-Portrait* (New York: Abbeville, 1985), 48.

22 Cited in the entry for cat. 13 in Phillips, Travis, and Naef, *André Kertész: Of Paris and New York*, 260.

23 Kertész later explained how the informal circulation of his prints slowly led to photojournalism commissions: "When I came to Paris in 1925, I brought these [Hungarian photos] with me and started to show them on the Montparnasse. First I showed them to the Hungarians because I had no contact with anybody else, Tihanyi, Brassaï, Csáky, Beöthy, [Béla] Czóbel,

these were the members of our little company. First they looked at them, then came a group of Germans—then, you know how it is, we mixed together, and they asked: is there anything new? Then I showed what I had. Then slowly journalists, reporters came asking if they can take them for their papers. Take them. And this is how the photojournalism started slowly." André Kertész, interview by Krisztina Passuth, Paris, October 25, 1982, transcript in English from Passuth's recording in Hungarian, André and Elizabeth Kertész Foundation, New York.

24 Kertész, *Kertész on Kertész*, 50. He also described this exchange for Peter Sager: "'André, can I have a photo,' they always said. First I gave them away, later I asked 25 francs"; Peter Sager, "Neugier als Kunst," *Die Zeitmagazin* 46 (November 11, 1983): 88. Christian Caujolle affirmed the artist's recollection of the price, specifying that Kertész sold artists their portraits on Guilleminot carte postale paper; Christian Caujolle, "André Kertész," *Camera International* (French ed.), no. 32 (Spring 1992): 62.

25 To the best of my knowledge (from conversations with Edwynn Houk and from Phillips, "The Photographic Work of André Kertész"), provenance for the commissioned works discussed here traces them to André or Jenő, not the sitter; they either remained with the Kertész estate or were mailed to Jenő.

26 MAP, undated page. Based on conversations with Kertész, Phillips identifies all of these works as commissions. Phillips, notes to cats. 1928.63, 1927.84, and 1927.83 in "The Photographic Work of André Kertész," II.244, II.405.

27 Nancy Reinhold relates a story from gallerist Peter MacGill, who, having traveled with Kertész by train in 1981, recalled that the artist had a set of twenty or thirty carte postale prints in his pocket. Reinhold speculates that they were perhaps too valuable or personal to leave at home. Nancy Reinhold, "Exhibition in a Pocket: The *Cartes Postales* of André Kertész," in Abbaspour, Daffner, and Hambourg, eds., *Object:Photo* [online project], 8–9, moma.org/interactives/objectphoto/assets/essays/Reinhold.pdf.

28 To my knowledge, the only exception is a print of *Le Soudier* (*Hands and Books*) in the Sir Elton John Photography Collection, which bears the address of György Bölöni, a postmarked stamp, and a note of greeting (see cat. 97).

29 Kertész also sent photographs to family for professional reasons as Jenő often served as his brother's agent, placing his work in Argentine newspapers.

30 Carol Schwalberg, "André Kertész: Unsung Pioneer," *U.S. Camera*, January 1963, 65, cited in Michel Frizot, "Kertész, Photography That Thinks," in Frizot and Wanaverbecq, *André Kertész*, 13.

31 Verso inscriptions from cats. 92, 14, and 170.

32 "*L'Esprit nouveau* is coming out in mid-January. A new artistic magazine, this picture will be published there." Cited in English translation in Phillips, "André Kertész: The Years in Paris," 35. Unfortunately, the photograph was not published and the revived journal lasted one issue. This print is now in the collection of the Museum of Fine Arts, Boston.

33 Jenő Kertész to André Kertész, November 13, 1926, MAP.

34 For the story of a post office meltdown owing to the "epic proportions" of picture postcards being sent during summer 1905, see Clément Chéroux, "The Small Change of Art," in Clément Chéroux and Ute Eskildsen, *The Stamp of Fantasy: The Visual Inventiveness of Photographic Postcards*, exh. cat. (Göttingen, Germany: Steidl, 2007), 197.

35 Many of these are reproduced in Chéroux and Eskildsen, *The Stamp of Fantasy*, along with works in the postcard format by Giacomo Balla, Herbert Bayer, Erwin Blumenfeld, Paul Citroen, Hannah Höch, Georges Hugnet, Gustav Klucis, and Sophie Tauber-Arp.

36 Thomas Cooper and Paul Hill, "Interview with André Kertész," *Camera* 58, no. 11 (November 1979): 40.

37 According to Reinhold's study, the most comprehensive to date regarding the material qualities of Kertész's carte postale prints, price lists and advertisements from the time show that postcard stock, made of heavier paper for durability in the mail, was actually more expensive than single-weight paper. The paper's smaller size, however, might still have made it more affordable. Reinhold, "Exhibition in a Pocket," 2. For more on carte postale paper, see Sylvie Pénichon's essay in this book.

38 "I liked the paper," Kertész later said. "It was unique. You see yourself, absolutely unique. I never seen something beautiful paper with this. Never after." André Kertész, interview by Edwynn Houk, Nicholas Pritzker, and David Travis, New York, c. 1984, video courtesy of Nicholas Pritzker.

39 On the promised equipment, see Jenő Kertész to André Kertész, December 9, 1925, MAP. Kertész's expense book includes several notations indicating funds paid to "Steuerman" for enlarging. In a letter asking for prints to place locally, Jenő indicates both that Kertész possesses an enlarger and that he doesn't wish to use it: "Can't you enlarge with the Leodon? Because you wrote that you want to have someone else do the enlarging"; Jenő Kertész to André Kertész, December 15, 1925, MAP.

40 See Olivier Lugon, "Photography and Scale: Projection, Exhibition, Collection," *Art History* 38, no. 2 (April 2015): 386–403. Lugon asks, "Is enlargement always a trigger for artistic dignity and, conversely, miniaturization necessarily a sign of the informational or documentary function of a photograph? And do such connotations remain stable through time?" (388).

41 Pierre Mac Orlan to André Kertész, July 16, 1928, MAP.

42 At times this cropping seems to have been done for practical reasons, as with *Eiffel Tower* (cat. 6), whose negative, viewed at the MAP, had processing defects in the areas Kertész cropped.

43 Kertész rarely left the postcard paper untrimmed, almost always carefully altering the original ratio to best suit his cropped print. For more on his trimming process, as well as other physical observations, see Reinhold, "Exhibition in a Pocket."

44 Very few prints at the MAP still bear evidence of masking. The negatives were cleaned as part of Kertész's 1974 John Simon Guggenheim Foundation grant to restore and reprint from his old negatives. I am grateful to Robert Gurbo, curator of the André and Elizabeth Kertész Foundation and Kertész's former assistant, for illuminating the artist's darkroom techniques.

45 Kertész, interview by Houk, Pritzker, and Travis.

46 Wanaverbecq, "Paris, the Garden of André Kertész," 68.

47 On the verso, Kertész wrote, "Interesting coincidence. They claim it as being surrealistic, if it suits people better." Cited in English translation in Phillips, Travis, and Naef, *André Kertész: Of Paris and New York*, 259.

48 For a thorough investigation of *Fork*, see Anne de Mondenard, *L'odyssée d'une îcone: Trois photographies d'André Kertész (The Odyssey of an Icon: Three Photographs by André Kertész)* (Paris: Actes Sud/Maison Européenne de la Photographie, 2006), 143–48. For contextualized accounts of *Chez Mondrian*, see ibid., 136–43; and David Travis, "André Kertész: The Gaiety of Genius," in *At the Edge of the Light: Thoughts on Photography and Photographers, on Talent & Genius* (Boston: David R. Godine, 2003), 34–50.

49 See Greenough, "To Become a Virgin Again," 66; and notes to cat. 50 in Phillips, Travis, and Naef, *André Kertész: Of Paris and New York*, 264.

50 Kertész, *Kertész on Kertész*, 53.

51 See Travis, "Kertész and His Contemporaries," 88. Levy showed Kertész's work in exhibitions in 1932 and 1937.

52 As photography historian Olivier Lugon has shown, the notion of an "exhibition print" in these years was not yet stable. Extant installation photographs of 1920s and 1930s exhibitions reveal a great heterogeneity of approach, but enlargement was typical. See Olivier Lugon, "Prints from the Thomas Walther Collection and German Exhibitions around 1930," in Abbaspour, Daffner, and Hambourg, eds., *Object:Photo* [online project], moma.org /interactives/objectphoto/assets/essays/Lugon.pdf; and his related essay in the print complement to the online project, "Photography and Exhibition in Germany Around 1930," in Mitra Abbaspour, Lee Ann Daffner, and Maria Morris Hambourg, eds., *Object:Photo. Modern Photographs: The Thomas Walther Collection 1909–1949* (New York: Museum of Modern Art, 2015), 366–75.

53 A folio of mounted carte postale prints with invitations from the exhibition tucked into its pages was discovered among the artist's possessions after his death. It may provide insight into his display methodology, since he may have experimented with mounting sizes or maintained a portable version of the exhibition for other purposes. The folio, along with related vintage work assembled by gallerist Jane Corkin, was dispersed at a Christie's sale, but several pages are reproduced in this book as plates. See *Stranger to Paris: André Kertész*, exh. cat. (Toronto: Jane Corkin Gallery, 1992); and *An Important Collection of André Kertész Vintage Photographs, Paris and Hungary, 1919–1927*, sale cat. (Christie's, New York, April 17, 1997).

54 I am grateful to Sylvie Pénichon for her assistance with translating this poem.

55 "Art and Artists," *Chicago Tribune* (Paris ed.), March 13, 1927, 5. Reviews also appeared in *Comoedia, Chantecler, Le Crapouillot*, and *Tageschronik der Kunst*. For a complete list of notices, see the bibliographies in Greenough, Gurbo, and Kennel, *André Kertész*, 295–98; and Frizot and Wanaverbecq, *André Kertész*, 334–43.

56 For more on Kertész and the picture press, see Travis, "Kertész and his Contemporaries," 57–91; and Michel Frizot, "Photo Essays and Illustration," in Frizot and Wanaverbecq, *André Kertész*, 183–97.

57 Phillips, "André Kertész: The Years in Paris," 26. Brassaï, his countryman, was at this point still a writer, not a photographer.

58 In many interviews and quotes from his later years, Kertész sought to position himself as having few external influences, citing his innate vision as his only guide. For example, he told Cooper and Hill: "There is no explanation, I was born with these instincts. . . . The moment always dictates in my work. What I feel, I do. This is the most important thing for me. Everybody can look, but they don't necessarily see. I never calculate or consider; I see a situation and I know that it's right"; Cooper and Hill, "Interview with André Kertész," 33, 40. He aimed to prove the originality of his work by noting how it differed from the prevailing ethos of mid-1920s photography in Paris: "At the time, photography was zero—only the ordinary commercial kind of shots with little or no artistic value. Nobody photographed the chairs in the parks, in the Luxembourg Gardens, and in the Tuileries. I did. Of course, at that time I did not know that this was modern or unique"; Kertész, *Kertész on Kertész*, 75.

59 For articles that mention both Kertész and Man Ray as key figures, see, for example, Pierre Mac Orlan, "L'Art littéraire d'imagination et la photographie," *Les Nouvelles littéraires*, September 22, 1928, 29; and Pierre Mac Orlan, "La Photographie et la fantastique sociale," *Les Annales politiques et littéraires*, no. 2321 (November 1, 1928): 414.

60 Florent Fels, "The First *Salon Indépendant de la Photographie*," trans. Robert Erich Wolf, in Christopher Phillips, ed., *Photography in the Modern Era: European Documents and Critical Writings, 1913–1940* (New York: Metropolitan Museum of Art/Aperture, 1989),

26; originally published as "Le Premier Salon Indépendant de la Photographie," *L'Art Vivant* 4, no. 90 (June 1, 1928): 445.

61 Vidal, "En photographiant les photographes," 5.

62 For a detailed overview of the shifting market for Kertész's photographs in the 1970s and early 1980s, see Mondenard, *Odyssey of an Icon*, 173–79.

63 André Kertész to Ake Sidwell, Moderna Museet, Stockholm, February 4, 1971, MAP.

64 Frizot notes that Kertész continued to use his 9-by-12-centimeter camera for reportage, while using his Leica for "his rambles." Frizot, "Photo Essays and Illustration," 188.

65 Pénichon, in her essay in this book, disputes this assertion, although it is possible that something about the formula changed to his dissatisfaction.

66 Pierre Bost, "Le Salon des Indépendants de la photographie," *La Revue hebdomadaire et son supplément illustré* 37, no. 24 (June 16, 1928): 358.

67 [Georges] Charensol, "Les Expositions," *L'Art Vivant* 4, no. 91 (June 15, 1928): 486; and A. L., "Compte rendu de l'exposition à la galerie L'Epoque," *Variétés* 1, no. 7 (November 15, 1928): 401; both cited in English translation in Mondenard, *Odyssey of an Icon*, 144–45.

68 For a discussion of the presentations of vintage *Fork* prints, see the catalogue entry for the work in Phillips, Travis, and Naef, *André Kertész: Of Paris and New York*, 266. The Art Institute of Chicago is fortunate to have two such vintage contact prints (not on carte postale paper). Other examples can be found at The Museum of Modern Art, New York; the Metropolitan Museum of Art, New York; and the Nelson-Atkins Museum of Art, Kansas City, MO.

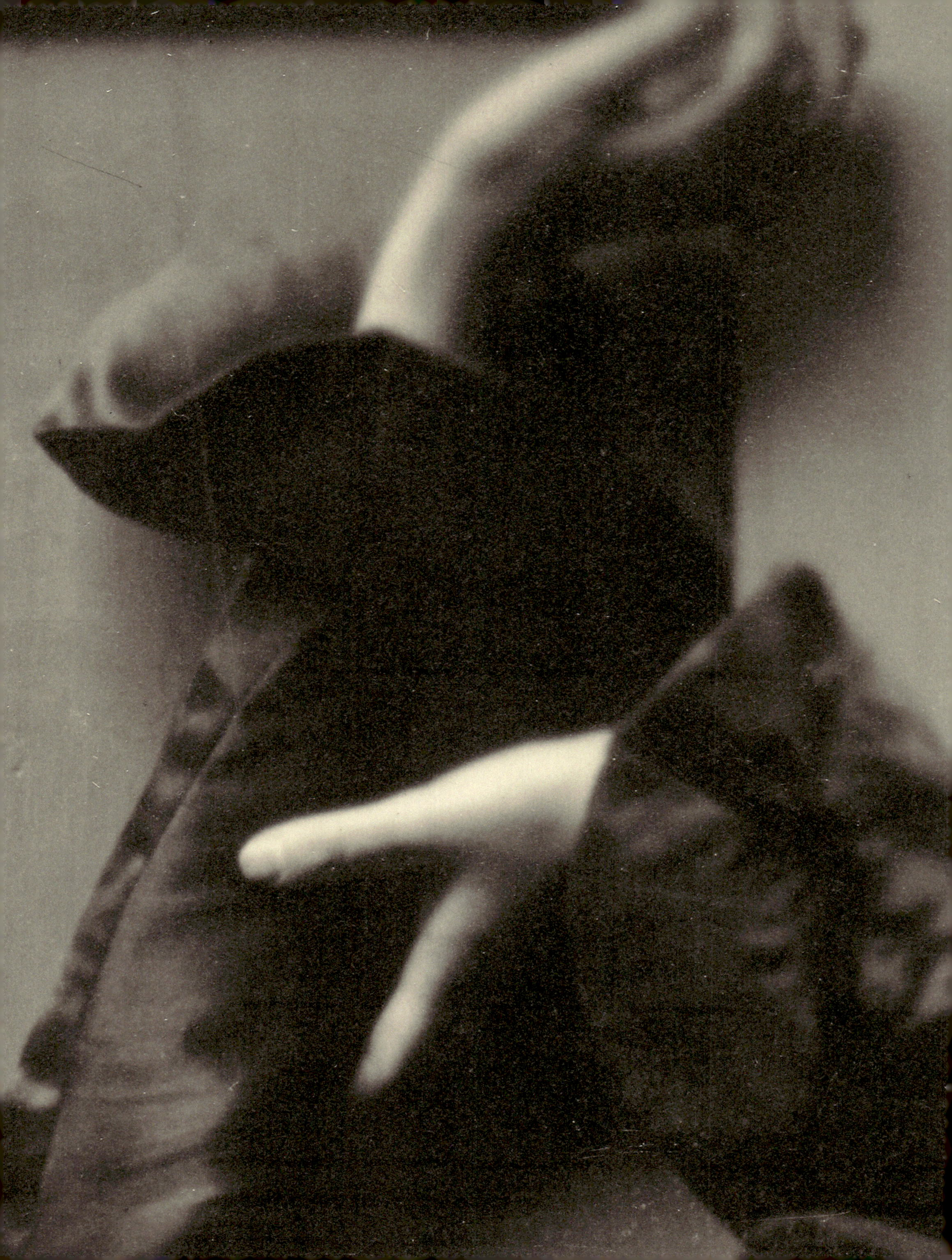

"The Grotesque Dancer from Pest" Magda Förstner and the Making of *Satiric Dancer*

SARAH KENNEL

O body swayed to music, O brightening glance,
How can we know the dancer from the dance?

—William Butler Yeats, "Among School Children," 1928[1]

Satiric Dancer (cat. 92) holds pride of place among André Kertész's most widely reproduced and sought-after works. It has been included in almost every major exhibition devoted to the artist, and its frequent appearance at auction over the past two decades—mostly in the form of modern prints made in the 1970s and 1980s—is rivaled only by *Chez Mondrian* (cat. 56). It is unclear, however, how much Kertész esteemed the image at the time he produced it. Although he made at least two, and possibly up to four, *carte postale* (postcard) prints of *Satiric Dancer*, as well as one slightly larger print, at or around the time he created the negative, he did not, as far as we know, submit this picture to any of the important photography exhibitions in which he participated from 1927 onward. Nor did he include it in either of the publications he devoted to his adopted city, *Paris vu par André Kertész* (1934) and

Day of Paris (1945). Aside from two appearances in magazines in 1927 and 1932, *Satiric Dancer* was not published until 1964, when John Szarkowski included it in a retrospective devoted to the artist at The Museum of Modern Art, New York, at which point it assumed its current title and began its second life as one of Kertész's most recognizable photographs.[2]

With the resurgence of interest in Kertész's photography in the mid-1960s, *Satiric Dancer* emerged as a centerpiece of his career, emblematic not only of his artistic achievements but also of the spirit of Jazz Age Paris. Over the next decade the picture appeared in nearly every major publication devoted to his work. By the mid-1970s it was one of Light Gallery's best-selling works, with modern prints offered in three sizes, the largest (at $450) commanding a fifty-dollar premium over most other works by the artist.[3] It was also included in Kertész's first portfolio, produced by Light in 1973, a collection of the photographer's "greatest hits" from the Hungarian and Parisian periods. This moment, which coincided with the beginning of a substantial market for fine-art photography, also contributed to the creation of a new category: the vintage print, that is, a print produced at or near the same time as the negative. Although initially slow to take off, vintage prints of Kertész's Parisian photographs—especially those printed on carte postale paper—eventually became the most desirable works by the artist. As one index of this meteoric shift, in 1976 a dealer offered Kertész's "French period vintage prints" for $1,500. By 2008 the only known vintage print of *Satiric Dancer* to come to auction sold for £228,000, or more than $440,000.[4]

Given the iconic status this picture now enjoys, it is all the more curious that so little is known about its production, including its original title and date of creation. Especially shrouded in mystery is its main subject, dancer Magda Förstner, who poses on a couch in sculptor Etienne Beöthy's studio.[5] Although scholars have politely noted the dancer's feminine charms, her artistic identity and the influence of her dance practice on Kertész's famous photograph remain largely unexplored. Yet Förstner's training as a dancer—especially her embodiment, through performance, of the modern "New Woman"—distinctly shaped the making and meaning of *Satiric Dancer*. Just as Kertész's *Chez Mondrian* is commonly understood as the photographer's canny response to the painter's rigorous pursuit of abstraction and pictorial harmony (see pp. 24–25 of Elizabeth Siegel's essay in this book), we must also recognize *Satiric Dancer* as an astute collaboration between the dancer, the sculptor, and the photographer. Tracking this photograph from origin to afterlife with its main subject, Förstner, at the center of the story reminds us that even "masterpieces" are rarely achieved alone.

Recovering Förstner's agency in the making of *Satiric Dancer* also illuminates Kertész's transition in the later 1920s from a young émigré in a city that embraced women like Förstner to a more sober and professionally driven artist whose changed circumstances (including the end of one marriage and the start of another) ultimately impelled him to leave Paris and the personal and professional freedoms it had provided.

ENTER LA GARÇONNE

When Kertész made *Satiric Dancer* in 1927, he was in the full flush of his first major success.[6] Just a year and a half after he arrived in Paris as an immigrant with poor French-language skills, limited funds, and few contacts, he mounted an exhibition at the Au Sacre du Printemps gallery that garnered significant critical praise and opened up new professional opportunities for publication and international exhibition. By this time he had also firmly established himself within a robust artistic community comprised mainly of other émigrés. Although he was initially closest with fellow Hungarian expats, his circle of acquaintances expanded rapidly in 1926 to encompass many of the leading international artists of the day, including many women working across a variety of genres who served as Kertész's subjects and provided him with inspiration and commissions. In numerous photographs from 1926 to 1928, Kertész documented his friendships with Viennese designer Vally Wieselthier (see cat. 79), Swedish painter Gundvor Berg (see cats. 71–72), German sculptor Anne-Marie Merkel (see cats. 25–28), and Hungarian designers Hilda Daus (see cats. 20–21) and Eva Révai (see cats. 76–77).[7] Kertész also made portraits of other professional women, including American actress (later painter) Anita de Caro (see cat. 43) and pioneering American journalist Jean Jaffe (see cat. 14), by then a globe-trotting field reporter for the prominent Yiddish newspaper *Der Tag*.

Judging from the numerous photographs Kertész made of convivial gatherings and parties, his social life flourished from 1926 onward and directly nurtured his creative output, particularly as this expanded social network provided opportunities for commissions and introduced him to the leading artists, writers, and publishers of the day. His personal life was equally eventful. Though he never mentioned it, Kertész probably had a brief affair with Révai, whom he photographed on several occasions, both alone (see cat. 76) and with her mother (see cat. 77), who was also a photographer.[8] During this time he was involved with at least one other woman, a Hungarian

art student named Rosza Klein. In October 1928
Kertész and Klein were married, and he began to
teach her the mechanics of photography. Soon after,
she assumed the professional name Rogi André,
a hybrid of the couple's first names, and launched a
successful career as a professional photographer
specializing in portraits.[9]

Etienne and Anna Beöthy, who were close to
Rogi, probably introduced Kertész to Förstner.
As Kertész later recalled, he first met the dancer at
a party at Etienne's studio following one of her
performances and asked her to pose for him.[10] Two
unpublished carte postale prints that originally
belonged to Förstner may document this after-party
One depicts the dancer and another woman, both
wearing men's suits, raising their wine glasses in
celebration (fig. 1). An inscription in Hungarian
on the verso reads "Paris 1927, the Monday after
Whitsun."[11] If, accordingly, this photograph was
made on June 6, 1927, then it followed Förstner's first
run of performances in Paris, which had begun
a few days earlier.[12] Although the identity of the other
woman is not known, a second inscription provides
a tantalizing clue: "I hope you all can recognize Lidi."
Another photograph that seems to have been made
at this party shows Förstner by herself, now wearing
the tuxedo "Lidi" wore in the first photograph
(fig. 2). These outfits were likely theatrical costumes,
as cross-dressing was a common feature of cabaret
performance in the 1920s and 1930s. However, pants
and menswear-inspired suits were also among the
most recognizable expressions of the New Woman,
the sexually liberated, self-determined, and inde-
pendent figure that captivated the public imagination
and dominated discussions of gender during the
interwar years.[13] Förstner, with her bobbed hair and

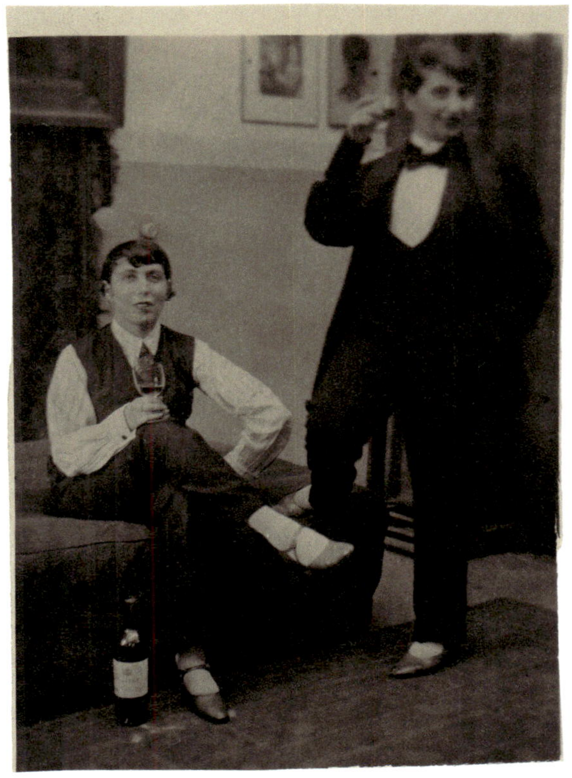

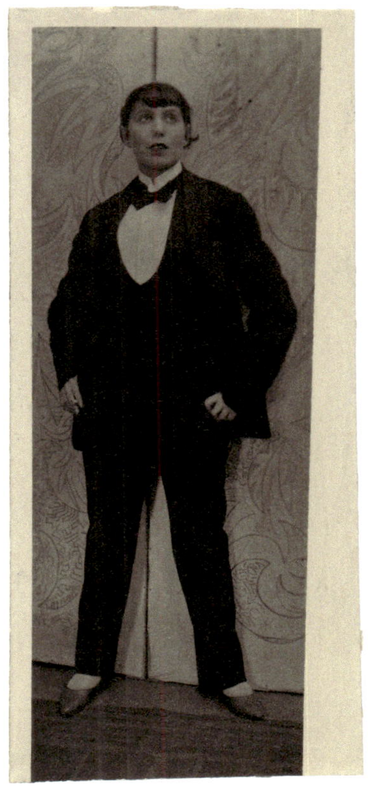

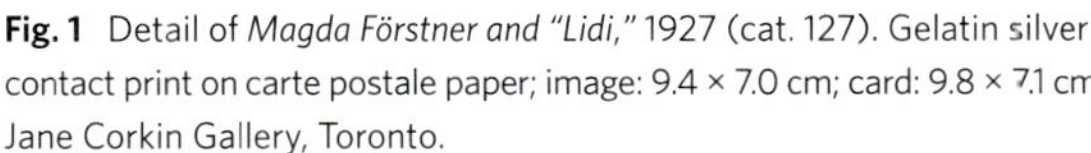

Fig. 1 Detail of *Magda Förstner and "Lidi,"* 1927 (cat. 127). Gelatin silver
contact print on carte postale paper; image: 9.4 × 7.0 cm; card: 9.8 × 7.1 cm.
Jane Corkin Gallery, Toronto.

Fig. 2 Detail of *Magda Förstner*, 1927 (cat. 126). Gelatin silver contact
print on carte postale paper; image: 9.7 × 3.7; card: 9.9 × 4.6 cm.
Jane Corkin Gallery, Toronto.

penchant for pants, as well as her career as a stage performer, certainly fit the image of *la garçonne* ("bachelor girl" or tomboy), the titular type of Victor Margueritte's bestseller of 1922.

Förstner's publicity photographs from around this time reveal that she adopted a range of personae on stage (see fig. 3), and Kertész's first images of the dancer capture the gender-bending aspect of her performance. In one carte postale by Kértesz she wears a short, shiny frock with puffed sleeves resembling dance dresses from the early 1920s (cat. 88).[14] The somewhat stilted pose and plain background in this work are typical of theatrical photographs from the time, and it may thus have been commissioned by the dancer to promote an upcoming show. (An entry in Kertész's diary notes that he received twenty-five francs from Förstner in July 1927, presumably for photography services.[15]) While this more typical view tells us little about Förstner as a performer, other photographs of the dancer—including a vertically trimmed carte postale print in which she reaches upward, mouth agape in laughter or ecstasy (cat. 87)—help us see the nature of her dance practice and, by extension, what Kertész meant when he identified her as "the grotesque dancer from Pest" (see fig. 4).[16]

MAGDA'S MODERN DANCE

In Hungary, as in Europe more broadly, women led the development of modern dance as they sought to redefine the expressive possibilities for the female body.[17] During the first three decades of the twentieth century in Hungary, women dancers, choreographers, and movement theorists created new pedagogies that drew from a wide range of dance-based practices, including expressive or "free" dancing, cabaret performance, avant-garde theater, rhythmic training, and gymnastics. While some of the Budapest schools of modern dance promoted a quasi-classicism inspired by the teachings of American dancer Isadora Duncan, Förstner's training may have been more similar to *Ausdruckstanz*, a term for an array of dance practices that arose in Central Europe between the wars.[18] Often considered a parallel to Expressionism in the visual arts, Ausdruckstanz was less a unified school than a philosophy of gesture. It disrupted the conventional relationships between movement and signification by rejecting the codified gestures of ballet and pantomime, instead exploring compression, dissonance, distortion, pose, speed, stillness, tension, and weight to convey emotions and ideas. With an emphasis on individual subjectivity, extreme bodily states, and the use of irony and masquerade,

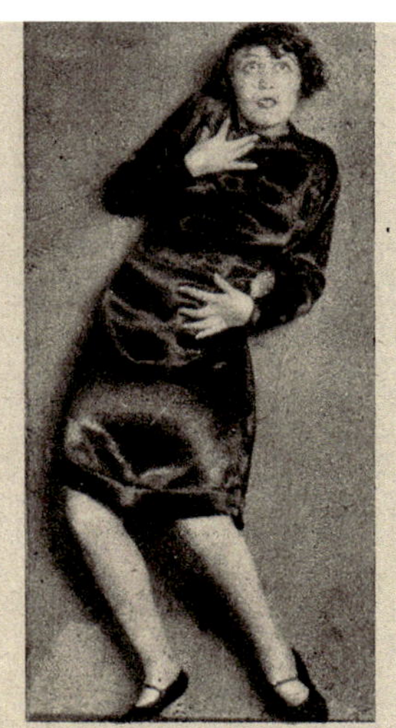

Uj magyar siker Párizsban

Egyre több és több fiatal magyar tehetség hódítja meg Berlin és Párizs közönségét a magyar művészetnek és a magyar kultúra megbecsülésének. Bizonyos, hogy nincs még egy nép a világon, amely kis lélekszámához képest a művészi tehetségeknek olyan garmadát dobná ki a világ minden küzdőterére, mint éppen a magyar.

Muzsikusaink és festőink számos sikert értek el már Párizsban, ezúttal a magyar táncművészet aratott odakinn babért. A párizsi Olimpia-színház a rendkívül tehetséges magyar *Förstner* Magdát ünnepli estéről-estére. Nemrég tartotta meg Förstner Magda első párizsi táncmatinéját is, amelynek keretén belül tizenegy táncot mutatott be modern zenére. A francia kritikusok mind nagy dicsérettel írtak Förstner Magda táncairól, kiemelve sokoldalú fantáziáját, vidám számainak nagyszerű karikirozását és a „Vak leány" című táncfantáziájának megrázó erejét. Megemlítik, hogy *Oteró, Argentina* és Raquel *Meller* szintén az Olympiában léptek fel először Párizsban s bár a magyar táncosnő modernebb idők gyermeke, hasonló sikereket jósolnak neki is.

Táncmatinéját január első napjaiban fogja követni egy újabb, melyet máris nagy érdeklődéssel várnak. Förstner Magdát különben londoni, berlini és stockholmi szerződéssel is megkinálták.

Förstner Magda

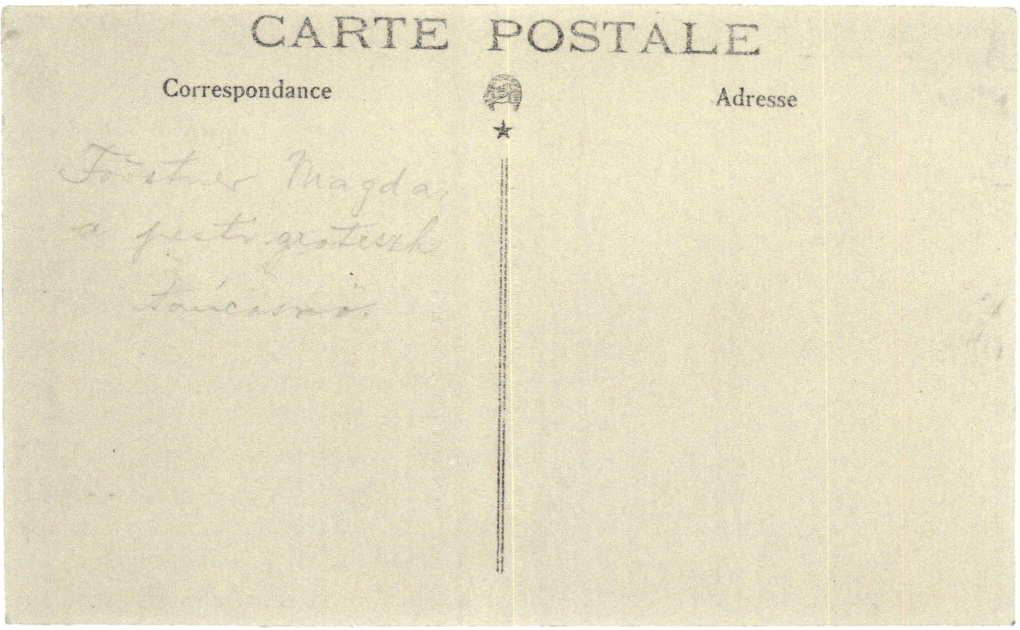

these transgressive performances were sometimes described by contemporaries as "grotesque" because of how they exaggerated or deviated from the norms of classical beauty.[19]

Although we do not know much about Förstner's early training, by 1922 she was performing solo dances in Budapest with an avant-garde troupe. In 1926 she starred in one of the *Új Föld estek* (New earth evenings), a series of avant-garde musical and theatrical performances associated with the journal of the same name. One review of the performance described Förstner's dances as "grotesque" and compared her to Valeska Gert, the famous German dancer, cabaret performer, and film star who appeared throughout Europe in the 1920s and claimed to have invented the "modern dance satire."[20] An innovator in the genre of grotesque dance that

combined caricature, expressive movement, and pantomime, she deployed broken and angular poses, exaggerated movements, and extreme facial expressions to parody all manner of subjects: contemporary social types, dance traditions from ballet to the Charleston, and even abstract concepts such as nervousness and fear.

Gert's most transgressive performances, however, involved a critique of gender. In these dances, she would often assume a recognizable female "type"—the streetwalker, the procuress, the wet nurse—only to violently defamiliarize and destroy this persona through exaggerated, vulgar movements. Flailing, thrusting, bending, and twisting, Gert, as one scholar put it, "used her solos to disrupt the representational economy of women's bodies and the history of women's representation in dance"; in so doing, she "exposed female sexuality as performance."[21]

The comparison of Förstner with the more famous Gert illuminates the former's aesthetics. Förstner would certainly have been familiar with Gert, who was not only well known in Hungary but had caused a mini-riot in Paris in 1926 among supporters and

Fig. 3 Profile of Förstner in the Hungarian newspaper *Tolnai Vilaglápja*, December 7, 1927. The headline hails her as a "New Hungarian success in Paris."

Fig. 4 Verso of *Satiric Dancer*, 1927 (cat. 92) with Kertész's inscription, "*Förstner Magda, / a pesti groteszk / táncosnő*" (Magda Förstner, grotesque dancer from Pest).

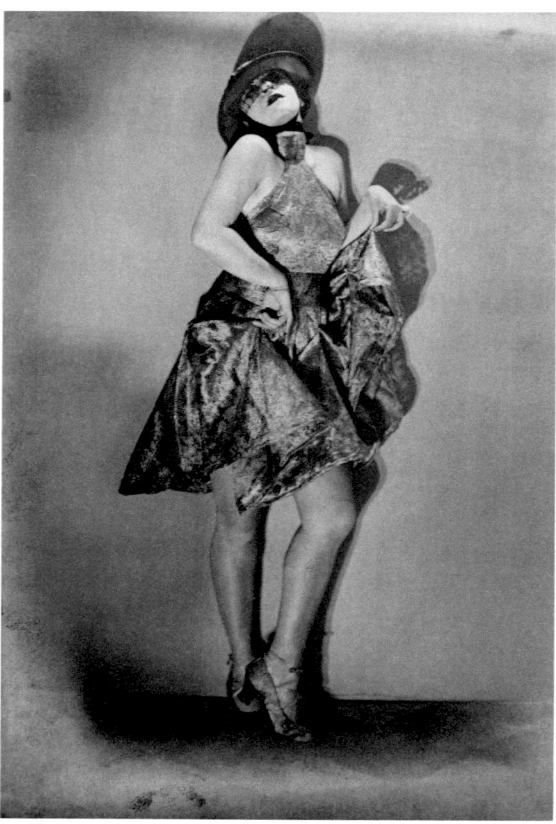

detractors of her controversial performance style, an event that attracted attention even in the Budapest newspapers.[22] A photograph by Man Ray (fig. 5), possibly made during that same Paris tour, shows the dancer wearing a dress strikingly similar to the body-skimming halter dress Förstner wears in *Satiric Dancer*.[23] Förstner's dance also resembled Gert's in its commingling of mimicry, caricature, and exaggerated movement to produce a series of ever-changing personae. Reviewing Förstner's performance at the Sorbonne in 1927, critic Jean Marèze lauded her ability to make her entire body expressive: "Magda Förstner has inaugurated caricatural dance. . . . Watch her eyes vibrate, her nostrils quiver, her body sways, bends, offers

Fig. 5 Man Ray (American, 1890–1976). *Valeska Gert*, c. 1926. Gelatin silver print; 26.7 × 20.3 cm. Courtesy of Joel Soroka.

itself . . . . Here she's one character, and now here a totally different one."[24]

Satiric Dancer is usually described as a light-hearted homage to Beöthy's work. By this time, of course, Kertész had already produced a number of startlingly original studies of artist's studios that broadcast his aesthetic sophistication by subtly aligning his views with those of the artists whose spaces he depicted. In his photographs of Mondrian's studio (see cats. 53–54), for example, Kertész responded to the Dutch painter's Neo-Plastic principles of purity and harmony with his own rigorous assemblage of geometric shapes. In his image of the painter Fernand Léger's studio (cat. 105), the perplexing spatial rendering and intersecting pictorial fragments that characterize the painting at center seem to have provided the visual language for the photograph: stacked and layered canvases, pasted pictures on the wall, and even objects carefully set askew create a dynamic tension between two and three dimensions. Likewise, in the seemingly casual arrangement of objects in the corner of Ossip Zadkine's studio, Kertész created a symbolic portrait of the Russian sculptor, alluding to his interest in puppetry and his penchant for drinking as well as his engagement with Cubist form (cat. 100).

In *Satiric Dancer*, however, Förstner is treated as the main artwork on display, a riposte to Beöthy's works, which are visible on the left corner and right wall in the picture. Her potent facility for imitation is, of course, the primary joke in *Satiric Dancer*. As many have noted, she deliberately mimics Beöthy's sculpture *Action directe* (fig. 6) on the pedestal at left. Förstner's pinwheeling form and gleaming alabaster skin echo the strong torque of the plaster work. The triangles formed by the dancer's raised arm, legs, and even the silky folds of the dress near her crotch repeat the triangular shape at the base of the sculpture. Perhaps Kertész and Beöthy highlighted this sculpture in particular because it represented a major stylistic shift toward a more dynamic mode of abstraction.[25] The evolution of Beöthy's sculptural language becomes clear when *Action directe* is compared to the work hanging on the opposite wall, a bas-relief depicting the ample breasts, belly, and hips of a female figure. Made only two years earlier, Beöthy's serene *Opus 17, Femme* counterbalances *Action directe*, the solid, inert feminine to the latter's propulsive, phallic energies. Spanning the distance between these two sculptures, Förstner, the garçonne with the bobbed hair, kicked-up legs, slinky dress, and toothy grimace, seems to mock both works and the polarities of gender they exemplify.

Förstner's playful caricature extended to the photograph's entire setup. Although Kertész was undoubtedly interested in her capacity for physical

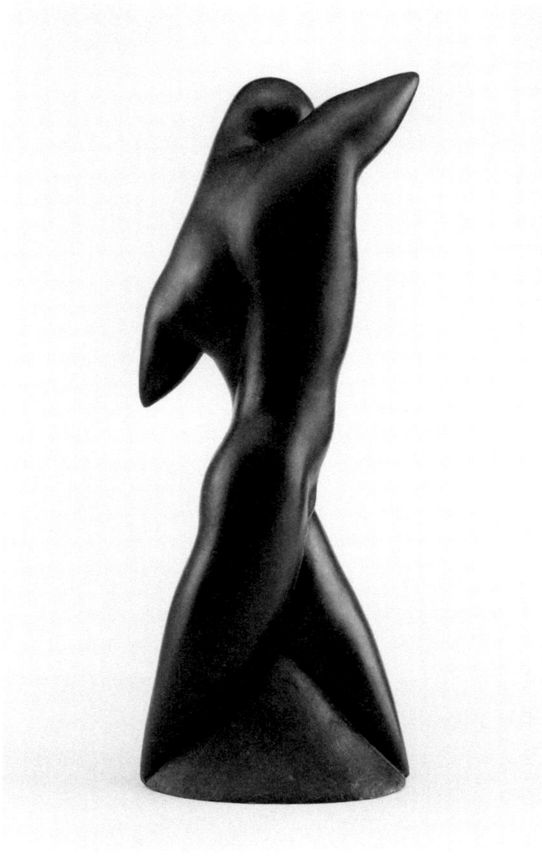

Fig. 6 Etienne Beöthy (Hungarian, active France, 1897–1961). *Action directe*, 1927. Bronze; 74.9 × 20.3 cm. Family Holdings of Nicholas and Susan Pritzker.

expression, he later claimed that he was the one to suggest she take "inspiration from these lovely sculptures."[26] Yet it seems just as likely that Förstner herself, invited to pose in relation to Beöthy's sculptures, assessed her context and assumed her chosen role: a satirical take on the erotic fantasy of the "artist's model." She played a well-known character, the scantily clad model lounging flirtatiously on the bohemian artist's shabby couch. An alternate version of *Satiric Dancer*, which exists as a unique carte postale print (cat. 86), also presents Förstner in the guise of the knowing modern woman. Now perched on the edge of the sofa, she angles and inverts her arms and knees in imitation of the Charleston, a dance sweeping European stages at the time thanks in no small part to Josephine Baker, who immortalized it in the 1927 film *La Sirène des tropiques*. The Charleston, which exposed and emphasized the bare legs of the performer, was closely associated with the New Woman. It was also a common feature of cabaret performance by figures like Gert, who deployed the dance to signify both libertinism and modernity. While Förstner's reclining pose on the sofa deliberately mirrors the angled lines of Beöthy's *Action directe*, here her inverted pose, derived from a highly recognizable popular dance, more directly mocks the sculpture's thrusting energies.

Another photograph of Förstner, presumably made the same day, depicts her sitting atop a table like a sculptor's model as those around her contemplate her charms (cat. 91). Of course, the history of photography is filled with photographs, some more overtly erotic than others, that sustain this same narrative fiction. But Förstner was not the model for any of the works on view in *Satiric Dancer*; instead she appears to poke fun at the genre itself, inverting the well-worn cliché of female bodies inspiring male genius such that the lithe sculpture serves as the model for her own artistry.

Both the erotic charge and ironic intent of *Satiric Dancer* were clear to the first publisher of the picture, the German fashion magazine *Die Dame*. Reproduced with the title *Das Modell des Bildhauers*

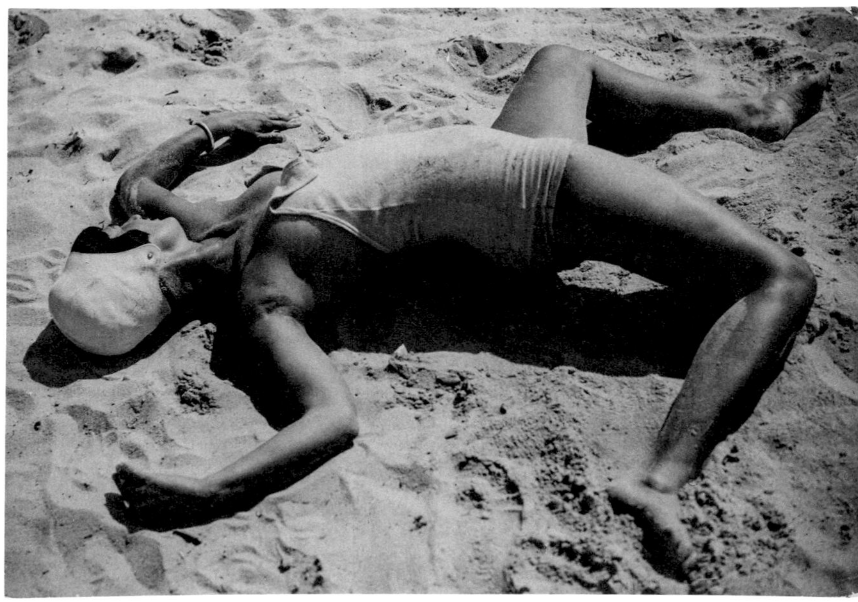

(The sculptor's model), it accompanied a humorous piece entitled "Kleine Lugen" (White lies), a fictional dialogue between a suspicious husband and his unfaithful wife, who expertly deceives him as she spins an increasingly complex tale to cover her tracks.[27] Five years later Kertész published *Satiric Dancer* in the September 1932 issue of *Paris Magazine*, where once again it accompanied a ribald article—this one by Paul Reboux and entitled "Ménage Moderne" (Modern couple)—that detailed (and lauded) the infidelities of the modern woman.[28] Even though he contributed to twenty-seven issues of *Paris Magazine*, or about one third of the seventy-seven issues published between 1931 and 1939, Kertész—who was an otherwise avid keeper of records, including clippings, diaries, letters, receipts, and other documents—retained no evidence of his participation in this publishing venture, nor did he mention it in any of the interviews he conducted in his later years. As a result of this omission, the second appearance of *Satiric Dancer* has only recently been noted.[29] Perhaps Kertész simply thought the publication unimportant. Carefully treading the line between suggestive photographs and pornography while covering such subjects as dance, film, nudism,

sports, and other transgressive or bohemian lifestyle trends, *Paris Magazine* was nowhere near as pictorially innovative as publications like *Vu* or as experimental as the Surrealist *Bifur*, each of which published numerous photographs by Kertész around this time. Additionally, the photographer may have been reluctant to reveal his association with the publisher Victor Vidal, who also ran an erotic bookstore and founded a fetish-wear company, Diana Slip, for which he commissioned leading photographers like Brassaï and Roger Schall to produce advertisements.

Although Kertész did not celebrate *Satiric Dancer* as a significant work until decades later, other artists may have taken note of its few early appearances. Brassaï, a frequent contributor to *Paris Magazine*, knew Kertész and his work well.[30] Kertész even claimed he was the one to teach photography to Brassaï, thus launching the latter's career. Brassaï likely saw *Satiric Dancer* before its 1932 publication in *Paris Magazine*, and we can gauge its possible impact by looking at his *Swimmer* (fig. 7). Executed around 1930, the photograph shows a woman lying on the sand with her limbs bent in a windmill-like formation that strongly recalls Förstner's pose in *Satiric Dancer*. Perhaps *Swimmer* was Brassaï's way of acknowledging his debt to Kertész or perhaps it was just a clever counterpoint, an attempt to one-up his friend and competitor. Whatever the case, by the early 1930s the differences between the two photographers were greater than their commonalities, and Brassaï's photographs of the sexual economy of bohemian Paris were certainly far more explicit than anything Kertész would ever produce.

There is another reason why Kertész may have distanced himself from the salacious *Paris Magazine* and its tales of marital infidelity. As Brassaï wrote to his parents in 1932, "Kertész has divorced his first wife and now lives in seclusion with his second."[31] Even before Kertész and Rogi were officially divorced in the fall of 1932, he had rekindled his romance with his former girlfriend of many years, Elizabeth Salamon, whose rejection of the photographer in 1924 was, in great part, the impetus for his move to Paris.[32] Salamon and Kertész were married in 1933, and while it is unclear whether she initially knew about his marriage to Rogi, we may deduce from Kertész's adamant silence about it—to the point of erasing his first marriage entirely from all later accounts of his life—that the subject of his romantic and sexual life in Paris before her arrival was a complicated one for the couple. Perhaps because he was hoping to avoid an encounter between Elizabeth and Rogi, who remained close with many of his friends (including the Beöthys), the photographer's once-active social life also dwindled around this time.[33] Instead, as his 1933 portrait *Elizabeth and I* (fig. 8) suggests, Kertész's marriage increasingly took center stage in his life. The tenor of his work also changed in the early 1930s. Although he continued to contribute sporadically to magazines, he focused increasingly on making books. He dedicated his

first publication, 1933's *Enfants* (Children), to his new wife and to the memory of his recently deceased mother. Sweet and sentimental, the book suggests Kertész's newfound investment in family and domesticity, a far cry from the freewheeling atmosphere that produced *Satiric Dancer*.

Yet that same year Kertész also undertook a radically different experiment by making nude photographs using funhouse mirrors. His first and only works for the mildly titillating magazine *Le Querelle,* they eventually came to be known as the Distortions and ranged from moderately distended figures to monstrous deformations, prompting one critic to compare them to "strips of ectoplasm" (see fig. 9).[34] When the artist later exhibited these works in New York in 1937, he titled them *Grotesques*, a term he had used to describe Förstner's performances a decade earlier.[35] But this time it was the photographer and not the model who enacted the bodily transformation, and the vision of the female body that emerges from these pictures

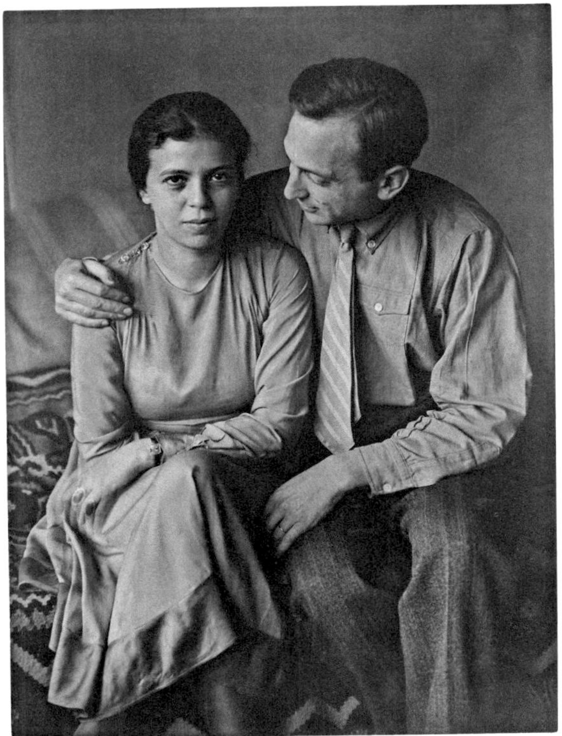

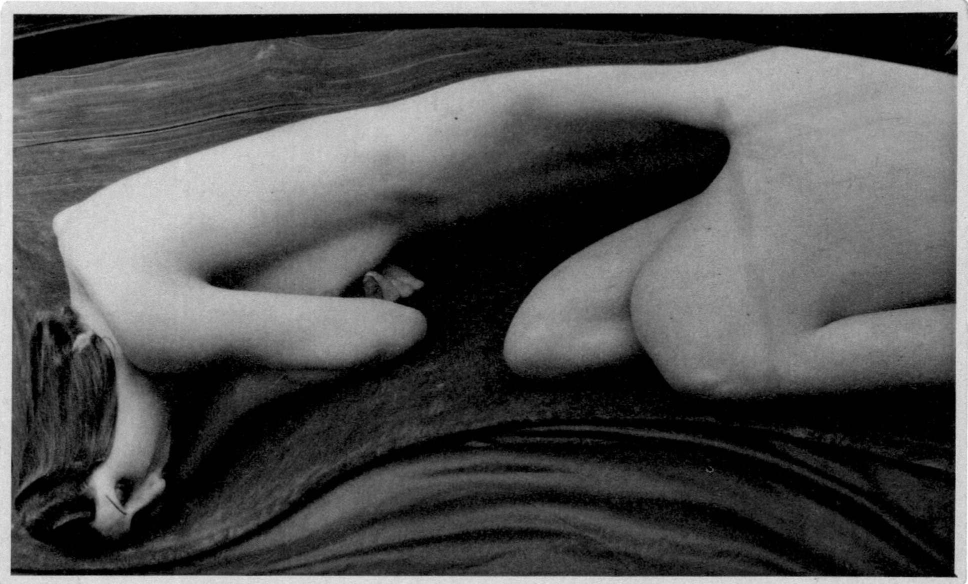

is far more foreboding, aggressive, and unsettling than the playful performance of *Satiric Dancer*. The latter had been produced in and nurtured by the social bonds of friendship and community and shaped by the dancer's embodiment of a modern, liberated sexuality; the environment from which the Distortions emerged was very different. New pressures, including rising anti-Semitism in Europe and the extended economic impact of the Great Depression, had forced Kertész and many of his émigré friends away from the bohemian world that had birthed *Satiric Dancer*. In 1936 Kertész's gradual separation from that world was made absolute when he and Elizabeth set sail for New York, leaving Paris behind in hope of greater success and stability in America.

RECLAIMING SATIRIC DANCER

In his 1983 book *Kertész on Kertész*, the photographer, intent on demonstrating to historians and critics the originality and consistency of his vision, noted

similarities between *Satiric Dancer* and his 1917 photograph *Underwater Swimmer* (fig. 10), in essence establishing a lineage for what he understood as his greatest hits: "This picture of Magda was taken in Beöthy's studio. I said to her, 'Do something with the spirit of the studio corner,' and she started to move on the sofa . . . . People in motion are wonderful to photograph. It means catching the right moment—the moment when something changes into something else. It shows a kind of distortion similar to that in the photograph of the swimmer."[36] Around this time, *Satiric Dancer* also took on greater weight as a symbol of his uneven career, from leading figure of the avant-garde to twenty-five years as a "dead man" in America, and, finally, critical rediscovery in the early 1960s.[37] When late in his life a journalist asked the photographer about the circumstances of the work, he replied that *Satiric Dancer* had made him an overnight sensation in Paris which, as we know, was hardly the case. In that interview, he also complained bitterly that although he exhibited the photograph soon after his arrival in the United States in 1936 (no record of this exists), it failed to elicit a single line from American critics.[38]

Fig. 9 *Untitled* (*Distortion #126*), 1933. Gelatin silver print; image: 7.9 × 13.3 cm; paper: 8.3 × 13.7 cm. The Art Institute of Chicago, gift of Charles Levin, 1991.1243.

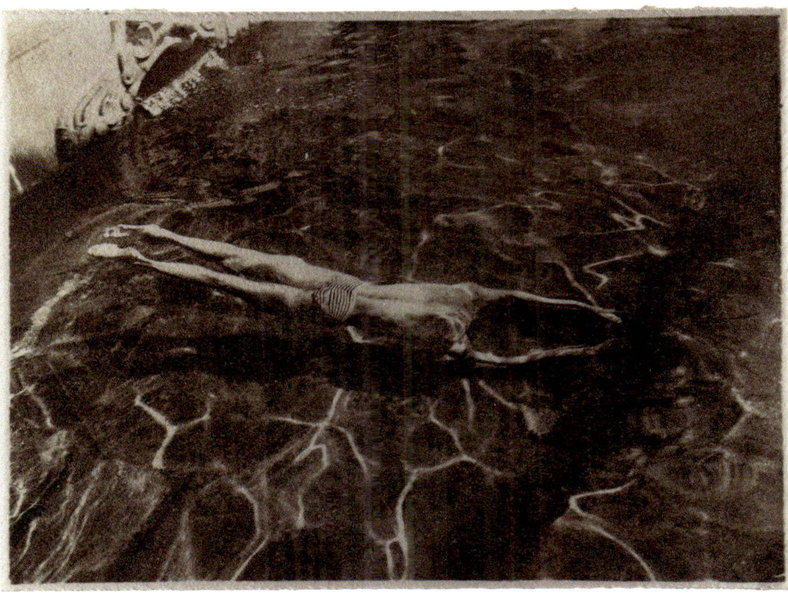

Kertész's tendency to embellish and elide aspects of his past has, of course, been well documented. The fact that *Satiric Dancer* was by then among his best-known and best-selling photographs only made his story of its origins more compelling. But as the lines from Yeats that began this essay remind us, creative acts are often so intimately connected to the lived experiences of the artists who made them that trying to fully untangle the truth—trying to tell the dancer from the dance—risks the perfection of the whole. We know the life that Kertész was living when he made *Satiric Dancer*, and we know that once he turned away from that bohemian existence to assume a more settled position he left no evidence that he considered this work as important and characteristic of his artistry as others have judged it to be. Among those others, eventually, was the older Kertész, who, after fleeing Paris and after many years of obscurity in America as a commercial photographer, was determined to recapture and define his time as a great artist in the City of Light.

Likewise, it may be impossible to untangle the artist from the art in appraising Förstner's role as Kertész's collaborator and inspiration for *Satiric Dancer*. Nevertheless, our richer understanding of who she was and of her role in the making of the photograph allow us to better appreciate the nuances of the work as well as its shifting meanings for the photographer over time, from document of his artistic and erotic liberation to reminder of the profound alienation he faced in the United States to symbol of his eventual triumph over obscurity. We should remember, too, the absences in these retellings: of Förstner herself, of course, but also of the many other women—colleagues, friends, lovers, models, wives—who shaped Kertész's life and yet have rarely been considered significant to his work, whose influence has been overlooked and at times deliberately suppressed, both by the photographer himself as well as by those who continue to study and celebrate his extraordinary accomplishments.

Fig. 10 *Underwater Swimmer*, 1917. Gelatin silver print; 3.8 × 5.1 cm. The Metropolitan Museum of Art, New York, promised gift of Ann Tenenbaum and Thomas H. Lee, in celebration of the museum's 150th anniversary.

NOTES

I wish to thank Elizabeth Siegel for sharing her extensive research, access to numerous archival documents, and especially for her incisive comments that strengthened this essay. I also wish to thank Robert Gurbo and Alex Novak for sharing their knowledge of Kertész. All translations from Hungarian are by Eriksen Translations, New York, unless otherwise noted; all translations from French are my own unless otherwise noted.

1   W. B. Yeats, "Among School Children," in *The Collected Poems of W. B. Yeats: A New Edition*, ed. Richard J. Finneran (New York: Palgrave Macmillan, 1991), 217.

2   According to Michel Frizot, the photograph (incorrectly titled *Magda Zahler*) appeared on a list that Kertész provided to Romeo Martinez in 1962 in preparation for his solo exhibition at Long Island University. In contrast, the print was not included in the 1963 exhibition at the Bibliothèque Nationale de France. See Michel Frizot, "A Lost Cloud," in Michel Frizot and Annie-Laure Wanaverbecq, *André Kertész*, exh. cat. (Paris: Jeu de Paume, 2010), 327n92.

3   Light Gallery to André Kertész, October 1, 1975, André Kertész archive, Médiathèque de L'Architecture et du Patrimoine, Charenton-le-Pont, France (hereafter cited as *MAP*). Prints of *Underwater Swimmer* and *Distortion #6* also commanded premiums.

4   Nicolas Ducrot to Marjorie Neikrug, March 4, 1976, MAP. The only known vintage enlargement of *Satiric Dancer* (measuring 16.8 by 11.8 centimeters) sold as lot 7 for £228,500 at Christie's, London, on May 15, 2008.

5   The exception is Gabriella Vincze, the first scholar to research Förstner in the context of Hungarian dance. See Gabriella Vincze, "Adalékok a magyar mozdulatművészek párizsi korszakához," *Enigma* 76, no. 4 (2013): 25–28; and Gabriella Vincze and Judit Faludy, eds., *Mouvement. Rythme. Danse: Les débuts de la danse modern en Hongrie, 1902–1950* (Paris: Institut Hongrois, 2013).

6   Although this photograph is almost always dated 1926, following Kertész's signature, I concur with Péter Baki, who dates *Satiric Dancer* to 1927 based on Förstner's appearances in Paris; Péter Baki, "Hungary Between the Wars: A Photographic Portrait," in Mitra Abbaspour, Lee Ann Daffner, and Maria Morris Hambourg, eds., *Object:Photo. Modern Photographs: The Thomas Walther Collection 1909–1949. An Online Project of The Museum of Modern Art* (New York: Museum of Modern Art, 2014), moma.org/interactives/objectphoto/assets/essays/Baki.pdf, 3. Additionally, Sandra S. Phillips notes that Anna Beöthy claimed this photograph was made in 1927; see Sandra S. Phillips, "The Photographic Work of André Kertész in France, 1925–1936: A Critical Essay and Catalogue" (PhD diss., City University of New York, 1985), II.59. My own survey of announcements and reviews of Förstner's performances in the Parisian press affirm that she first performed there in June 1927, with a return trip in October 1927.

7   Phillips notes the importance of Kertész's association with many professional women in Paris in "The Photographic Work of André Kertész," I.184.

8   Alex Novak learned this information from Csaba Morocz, a Paris-based Hungarian art dealer who knew Révai well. Alex Novak, conversation with the author, October 2020.

9   Sarah Greenough notes that Rosza Klein assumed the professional name Rogi André (a hybrid of *Rosza* and *André*) soon after she began publishing photographs in the 1930s. Sarah Greenough, "To Become a Virgin Again, 1925–1936," in Sarah Greenough, Robert Gurbo, and Sarah Kennel, *André Kertész*, exh. cat. (Washington, DC: National Gallery of Art; Princeton, NJ: Princeton University Press, 2005), 86.

10   Kertész tells of meeting Förstner at a party at Beöthy's studio in an interview with Bela Ugrin. Bela Ugrin, "Dialogues with Kertész, 1978–1985," 70, transcript of taped interviews and notes compiled by Manuela Caravageli Ugrin, Getty Research Institute, Los Angeles.

11   According to Jane Corkin, the writing is Förstner's hand. Jane Corkin, conversation with Elizabeth Siegel, August 2018.

12   See "Une célèbre danseuse hongroise dansera en Sorbonne," *Le Soir* (Paris), May 26, 1927, 5.

13   In her study of gender between the wars and the rise of the New Woman in France, Mary Louise Roberts notes that the garçonne's "lack of distinctly female form symbolized the unrestrained social and cultural space she seemed to inhabit. A 'being' without a waist, without hips, and without breasts, she symbolized a civilization without churches, without palaces, and without sexes." Mary Louise Roberts, *Civilization without Sexes: Reconstructing Gender in Postwar France, 1917–1927* (Chicago: University of Chicago Press, 1994), 20.

14   I am grateful to fashion historian Debra Mancoff for providing insight about Förstner's clothing selections. She dates this dress slightly earlier than Förstner's costume in *Satiric Dancer*, which features a neckline that was popular around 1926. Debra Mancoff, email to the author, August 31, 2020.

15   André Kertész, daybook, July 1927, MAP.

16   From the inscription on verso of cat. 92.

17   For an overview of the development of Hungarian modern dance, see János Fügedi and Livia Fuchs, "Doctrines and Laban Kinetography in a Hungarian Modern Dance School in the 1930s," *Journal of Movement Arts Literacy Archive* 3, no. 1 (2016), digitalcommons.lmu.edu/jmal/vol3/iss1/3.

18   See Karl Toepfer, *Empire of Ecstasy: Nudity and Movement in German Body Culture, 1910–1935* (Berkeley: University of California Press, 1997), 97–154.

19   The term *grotesque* was also used to describe an older form of comic theatrical dance (*danse grotesque* or *ballo grottesco*) that emerged in the courts of Renaissance Europe and peaked in the eighteenth century. For an overview of the long history of grotesque dance, see Anna Kisselgoff, "Dance View: Grotesque Imagery Has Come to Dance," *New York Times*, April 15, 1984.

20   László Fenyő, "Az Új Föld előadóestje," *Nyugat* 19, no. 21 (1926), accessed in English translation September 21, 2020, arcanum.hu/hu/online-kiadvanyok/Nyugatnyugat-1908-1941-FFFF0002/1926-51C88F/1926-21-szam-68E090. On Gert, see Alexandra Kolb, "'So watt war noch ni da!!' Valeska Gert's Performances in the Context of Weimar Culture," *European Legacy* 12, no. 3 (2007): 293–309.

21   Karen A. Mozingo, "Crossing the Borders of German and American Modernism: Exile and Transnationalism in the Dance Works of Valeska Gert, Lotte Goslar, and Pola Nirenska" (PhD diss., Ohio State University, 2008), 38–44.

22   See Jacques Heugel, "Échos et nouvelles: Valeska Gert," *Le Ménestral* 88, no. 46 (November 26, 1926): 484. See also "Viharos botrány után hosszasan ünnepelt a párizsi közönség egy német táncosnot: Valeska Gert Diadalmas harca a 'surrealistákkal,'" *Pesti Napló*, November 12, 1926, 14.

23   Mancoff notes that the exaggerated collar, as well as the short, body-skimming fit, mark this dress as a stage costume. Mancoff, email to the author.

24   Jean Marèze, "La Danse caricaturale Magda Förstner," *Le Soir*, June 9, 1927, 5. In his review, Marc Blanquet also lauded Förstner's gift for expressive caricature. See Marc Blanquet, "Un concert en Sorbonne," *Le Soir*, May 29, 1927, 5.

25   See Serge Lemoine, *Etienne Beöthy, 1897–1961*, sale cat. (Artcurial/Art Déco, Paris, May 27, 2014), lot 81, 81.

26   Ugrin, "Dialogues," 36.

27   Hermann Ungar, "Kleine Lügen: Dialog zwischen Eheleuten," *Die Dame*, October 1927, 2. I am grateful to Claudia Einecke for her assistance with translating this article.

28   Paul Reboux, "Ménage Moderne," *Paris Magazine*, September 1932, 473–75. Kertész's work for this magazine was brought to light by Michel Frizot, "Photo Essays and Illustrations," in Frizot and Wanaverbecq, *André Kertész*, 194.

29   As Frizot notes, Kertész's participation is even more curious because many of his photographs in the magazine were sober city views and reportage that stood apart from the publication's more salacious offerings. Notably, Kertész submitted older photographs rather than making new ones, which suggests that the magazine's publisher, Victor Vidal, may have tapped highly respected photographers to lend his enterprise greater legitimacy. See Frizot, "Photo Essays and Illustrations," 194.

30   Kim Sichel discusses Brassaï and Vidal in Kim Sichel, *Making Strange: The Modernist Photo Book in France* (New Haven, CT: Yale University Press, 2020), 77–78. For more on *Paris Magazine*, see Christian Bouqueret, *Des années Folles aux années Noires: La Nouvelle vision photographique en France, 1920–1940* (Paris: Marval, 1997), 169.

31   Brassaï, *Letters to My Parents*, trans. Peter Laki and Barna Kantor (Chicago: University of Chicago Press, 1997), 202, cited in Greenough, Gurbo, and Kennel, *André Kertész*, 275n138.

32   As Sarah Greenough notes, Salamon's disappointment that Kertész was not more professionally established was a major factor in his decision to move to Paris. Sarah Greenough, "A Hungarian Diary, 1894–1925," in Greenough, Gurbo, and Kennel, *André Kertész*, 29.

33   See Phillips, "The Photographic Work of André Kertész," l.487–88n4.

34   Bertrand Guégan, "Kertész et son miroir," *Arts et Métiers graphiques*, September 15, 1933, 24–25.

35   Greenough, Gurbo, and Kennel, *André Kertész*, 81. He may have started using this term after the publication of an article entitled "Mirror Photography Gives the Grotesque Touch, Finding Design in Distortion," *Photography* 4, no. 46 (June 1936): 1.

36   André Kertész, *Kertész on Kertész: A Self-Portrait* (New York: Abbeville Press, 1985), 55.

37   André Kertész to Brassaï, c. 1956, cited in Brassaï, "My Friend André Kertész," *Camera* 42 (April 1963): 32.

38   Magda Zalán, "André Kertész," *Új látóhatár* 27, no. 1 (1986): 107–10.

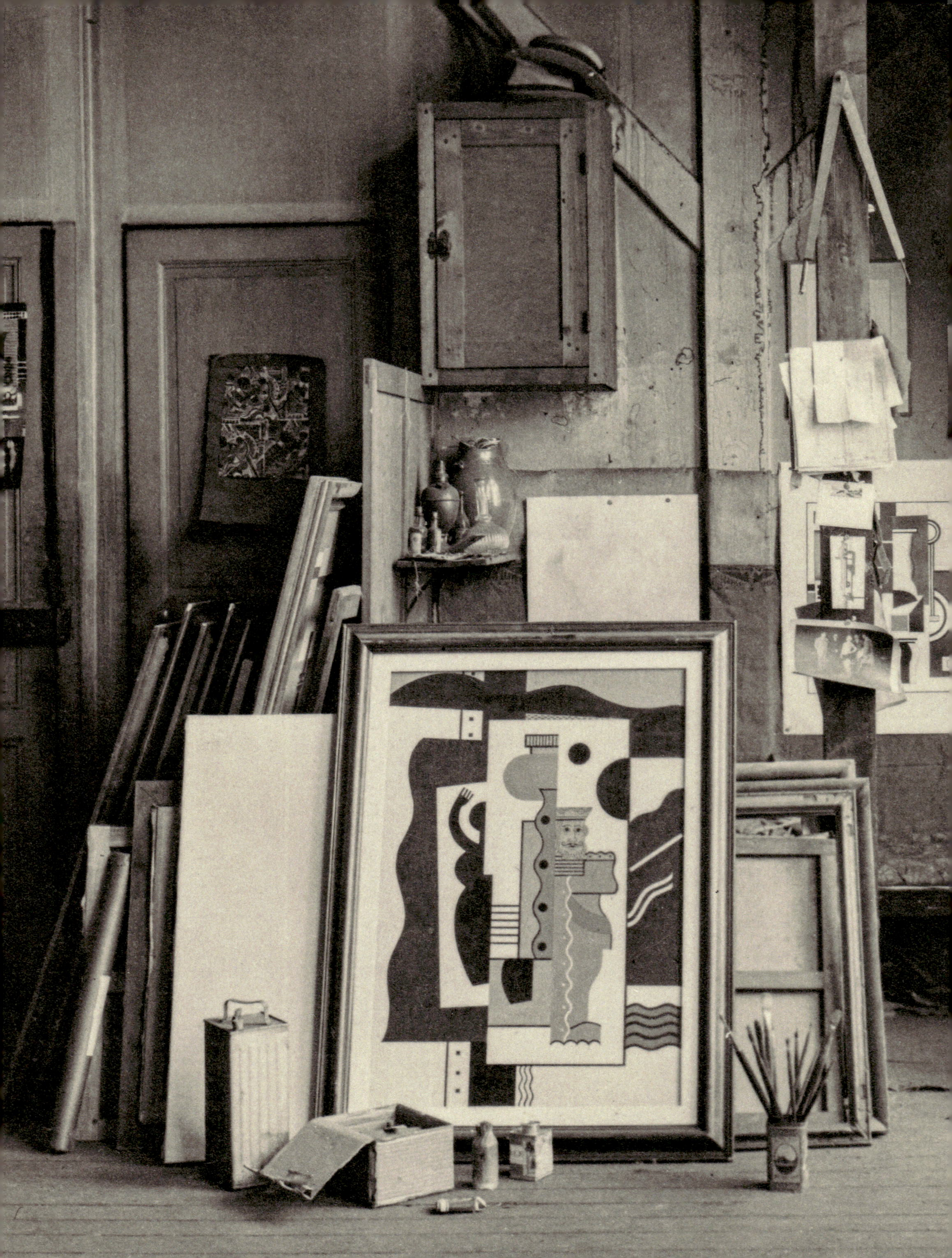

"It Was a Beautiful Paper"
Notes on Guilleminot Cartes Postales

SYLVIE PÉNICHON

André Kertész's photographic postcards, known as *cartes postales,* occupy a singular place in the photographer's oeuvre. Produced during his first years in Paris, between 1925 and 1928, they capture a burgeoning aesthetic of unaffected simplicity and "deliberate artlessness" that became his signature.[1] The mounting of the exhibition *André Kertész: Postcards from Paris* has provided an opportunity to take a closer look at the artist's materials and build upon previous technical research.[2] Close examination of the postcards, combined with research in the artist's archive and in photographic literature, sheds light on the aesthetic, practical, and economic motivations that led Kertész to print on this unassuming support during his early years in Paris. In addition, by disproving his late-in-life assertion that he stopped making prints on postcard stock because the paper had been discontinued, this research demonstrates that, as his work enjoyed renewed interest, Kertész reinvented his narrative of his early years to emphasize his aesthetic and artistic agency, originality, and independence.[3]

For the short period during which Kertész routinely printed his photographs on postcard paper, he seems to have consistently favored a card stock manufactured by the French company R. Guilleminot, Bœspflug et Cie. Among the hundreds of photographic postcards known to be produced by the artist, only a handful do not bear the company's logo consisting of a horse's head crowned by a horseshoe, with a five-pointed star underneath (see p. 20, fig. 5).[4]

R. Guilleminot, Bœspflug et Cie, better known simply as Guilleminot, was one of the early manufacturers of photographic materials in France, established in Paris in 1858 by Gustave Guilleminot. By 1925, when Kertész arrived in Paris, the company had relocated its operations north of the French capital to the city of Chantilly, on the site of an old woolen mill along the banks of the Oise, which provided the water necessary for the making of fine photographic plates and papers (see fig. 1). The family-run enterprise was one of a half dozen prominent French manufacturers specializing in the production of photographic goods that supplied most

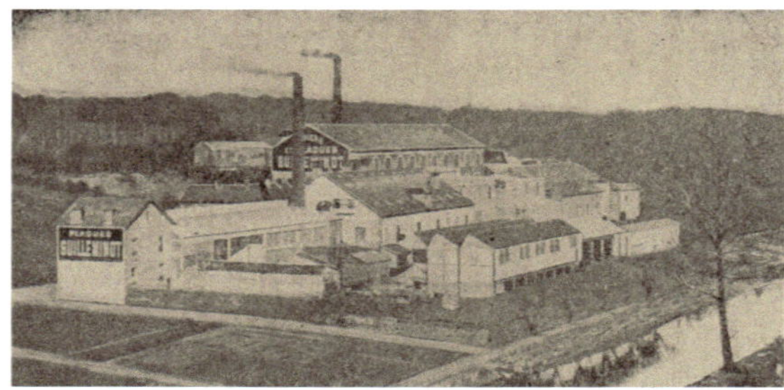

of the national market, the others being Bauchet, Crumière, Grieshaber & Cie (maker of the popular brand As de Trèfle), Lumière, and Pathé Frères.[5] Key to the success of the Guilleminot brand was the quality of its products, all manufactured in Chantilly. Instead of outsourcing the coating of its papers to foreign suppliers like most of the competition, the company treated its own high-quality baryta papers with a preparation perfected by chemist René Guilleminot, son of the founder. It also boasted that its emulsions featured the highest silver content on the market.[6]

This emphasis on quality may have prompted Kertész to select Guilleminot's product. An expense book in which the artist carefully noted his daily expenditures between November 1926 and January 1927 (see fig. 2) offers glimpses of a frugal but socially dynamic life paired with vigorous photographic activity. In the course of three months he purchased 877 francs worth of photographic materials, equipment, and printing services—a substantial sum considering that he paid a monthly rent of fifty francs. The purchases comprised glass-plate negatives, photographic paper, and at least five boxes of one hundred cartes postales each, three of them described by the photographer as "Sedar," a Guilleminot brand.[7]

Sédar paper was most likely introduced around 1909, as samples were presented to the members of the Société Française de Photographie at its July 16 session that year. The reporter at the meeting noted that images developed rapidly on the paper, in forty to sixty seconds.[8] A 1921 review in the *British Journal of Photography* admired the product's rich, warm, black-to-brown color and concluded that it was

"evidently of high-class manufacture."[9] Catalogues published by Guilleminot noted that the Sédar emulsion, available on single- and double-weight (*cartoline*) papers as well as postcard stock, was specially formulated for contact printing and that its deep, rich blacks were similar in range to those obtained with platinum papers. The words *tons platine*, or platinum tone, figure prominently on the package label, underlining the enduring appeal of the platinum printing aesthetic during the first decades of the twentieth century.[10] In addition, the manufacturer advertised in its product catalogues that the slightly grained finish of Sédar papers resulted in modeling of "incomparable artistic effect." These catalogues also show that in 1926 Sédar cartes postales were available in two base colors, standard or chamois (buff); the standard cards came with a semigloss surface finish, but the chamois were offered in both matte and semigloss, with a deckle-edge option for the matte.[11] By 1928 Guilleminot also offered standard Sédar cards with a glossy surface finish and chamois semigloss with deckle edges.[12]

To determine whether the group of Kertész's cartes postales at the Art Institute of Chicago were all printed on the same type of paper, we measured them to compare their thickness, surface sheen, and color.[13] The postcards are remarkably consistent in their physical attributes (see fig. 3).[14] Following the classification established by Paul Messier for the characterization of gelatin silver prints, they can be described as having a luster surface finish (between 10 and 20 gloss units), an off-white or warm-white base color (between 7 and 15 or above 15 b* color values, CIE L*a*b*, respectively), and a double-weight support (above 0.25 millimeters).[15] The slight variations recorded among the prints could derive

---

Fig. 1 Guilleminot plant in Chantilly, France, c. 1926.

Fig. 2 Pages from Kertész's expense book for November 6–14, 1926. The entry for November 12 records the purchase of one hundred Sédar postcards for 15.80 francs. André Kertész archive, Médiathèque de L'Architecture et du Patrimoine, Charenton-le-Pont, France.

from manufacturing differences between batches of paper as well as natural aging.

We then compared the physical characteristics of Kertész's postcards with samples of Guilleminot postcards (Sédar and other varieties) in an effort to pinpoint which line he used.[16] Inspection of the logos was particularly revealing, since the company typically identified its different product lines with a letter, number, or symbol below the horse's head.[17] Sédar was the only variety bearing the star observed on Kertész's carte postale prints, strong evidence that the artist consistently used this specific paper.

During the 1920s manufacturers of photographic papers competed against each other by producing an immense variety of brands, surfaces, and finishes.[18] In spite of the many choices available, Kertész seemingly remained faithful to one product. The decidedly warm color that characterizes the base and back of Kertész's cartes postales (b* values in fig. 3, in which the warmer tones are characterized by higher numbers) also points to the photographer's preference for chamois-based cards over the standard variety.[19] Guilleminot advertised its chamois papers as the most appropriate for artistic work and especially fitting for portraits, qualities that might have attracted Kertész.[20] Messier has argued that, historically, papers used to print utilitarian or commercial photographs were generally thin, cool-toned, and glossy, whereas thick, warm-toned, and matte papers were associated with fine art.[21] Kertész's predilection for a thick paper with a warm-toned base and reduced surface sheen may reflect the artistic trends of the time and, as such,

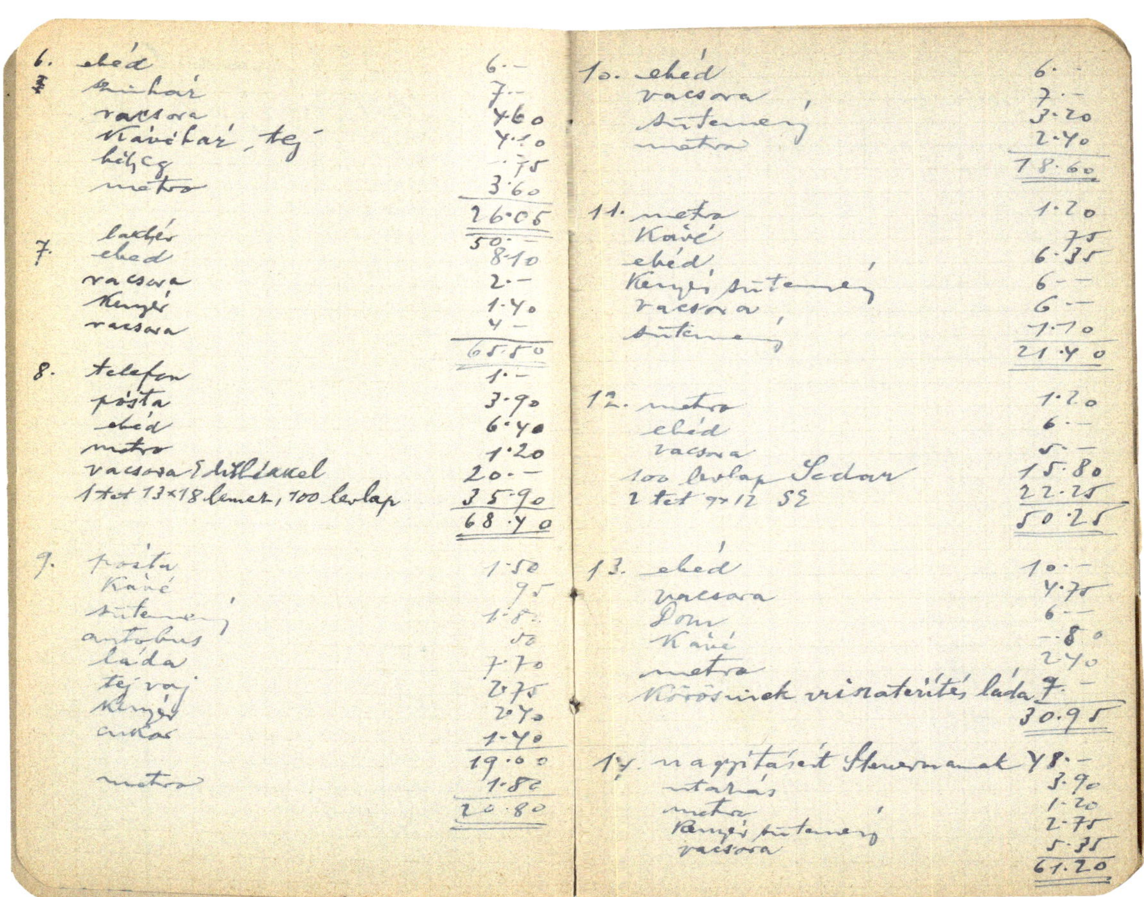

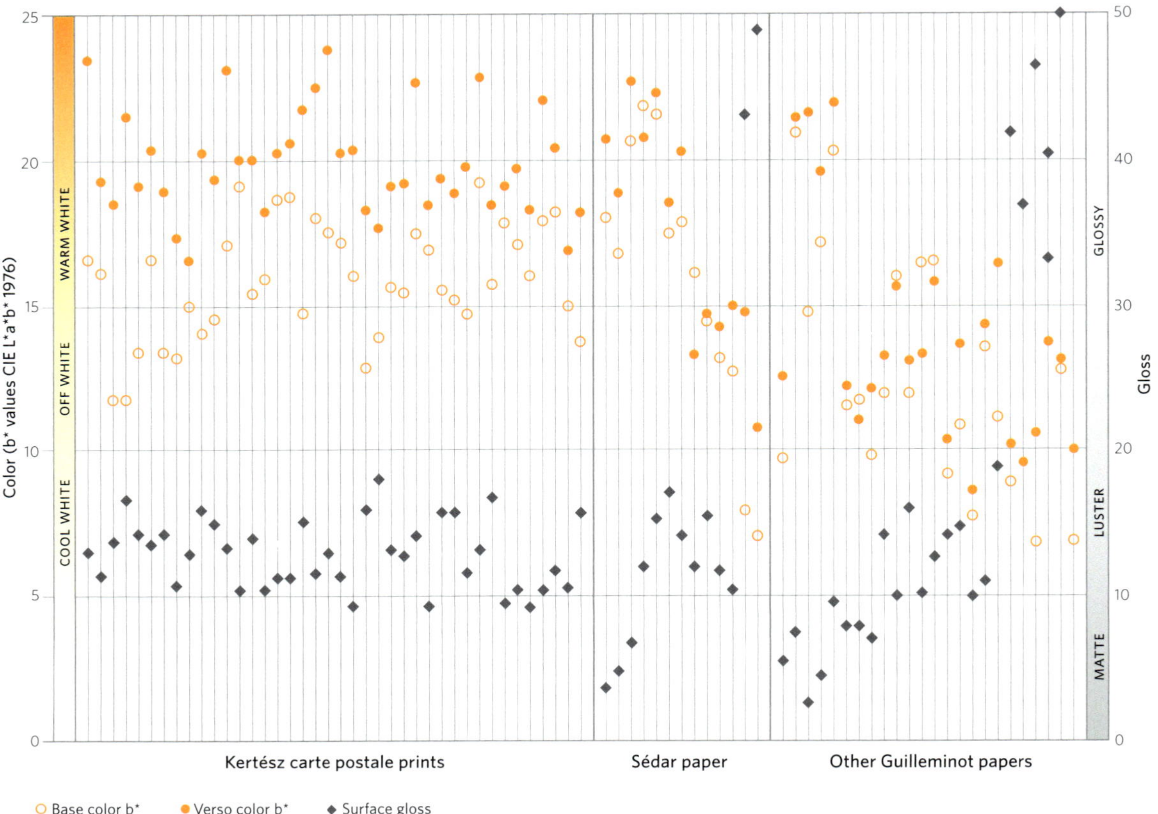

Comparison of Kértesz's Prints and Guilleminot Carte Postale Papers

may suggest a desire to infuse his photographs with greater aesthetic value. However, his use of the popular postcard medium—favored for commercially produced images and amateur snapshots—complicates any simplistic conclusions about the artist's intentions.

The standard size of postcards (9 by 14 centimeters) allowed Kertész to print his 9-by-12-centimeter glass-plate negatives by contact and perhaps dispense with the use of the cumbersome enlarger he kept in his cramped quarters. Furthermore, postcards bought in bulk were cheaper than regular photographic paper of the same size in smaller quantities, a factor that the cash-strapped artist would likely have considered. In the 1926 price list published by Guilleminot (fig. 4), boxes of one hundred Sédar cartes postales are listed at 16.10 francs (or sixteen centimes per card) while packets

of ten sheets of single- or double-weight Sédar paper of the same size are listed at 2.05 francs (or twenty centimes per sheet) and 2.25 francs (or twenty-two centimes per sheet), respectively. Even smaller sheets of the paper, meauring 9 by 12 centimeters and available in packets of twenty (at seventeen and nineteen centimes per sheet), still would have been slightly more expensive than the cards.[22] In addition to financial practicality, the thick postcards also would have fared better physically

---

Fig. 3 Graph showing base color, support color, and surface gloss of cartes postales by Kertész in the collection of the Art Institute of Chicago compared with Guilleminot samples. Higher b* values indicate a yellower or warmer tone; a higher number of gloss units indicates a glossier surface.

Fig. 4 Guilleminot catalogue from 1926 with prices for different product lines. The available varieties of carte postale stock are listed in the far-right column.

than thinner stock when passed around at the tables of the Café du Dôme or carried in the photographer's pocket (see Elizabeth Siegel's essay in this book). Close to a century later, the cards that have survived are in remarkably good condition.

Kertész's postcards were expertly printed and finished.[23] All but six of the cards studied were trimmed, and many bear the photographer's signature, *A Kertész / Paris*, in graphite in the lower margin below the image. Examination of original glass plates in the Kertész archive at the Médiathèque de L'Architecture et du Patrimoine, Charenton-le-Pont, France, revealed thorough retouching of the negatives, most likely by the photographer, who had been employed for a few months in 1926 as a photo retoucher at the Atelier Moderne, a photography studio in the Boulogne-Billancourt suburbs of Paris.[24] Under close inspection the borders along many of his photographs appear slightly irregular, a consequence of the fibrous quality of the black paper tape masks the artist used to precisely crop his images in the contact-printing frame (see fig. 5).

Some negatives in the Kertész archive even retain these masks (see fig. 6).

The artist did not print exclusively on postcard stock and, occasionally, he made or had someone else make enlargements. A few postcard prints in the collection of the Art Institute, notably *Chez Mondrian* (cat. 56), were mounted by Kertész onto larger secondary supports for exhibition purposes. A photograph taken in 1927 at the Au Sacre du Printemps gallery on the occasion of the photographer's first exhibition (cat. 85) shows a group of his friends at the event. An enlargement of *Chez Mondrian* can be spotted on the wall behind them, but several other prints are small enough to be contact prints, although it is impossible to say whether they are postcards. The Art Institute holds several vintage works printed by contact on single-weight paper, including two examples of the renowned *Fork*, of which at least one carte postale print also exists (cat. 111). These prints are similar in size and cropping to their postcard counterparts but with decidedly different paper attributes (thin, cool-toned,

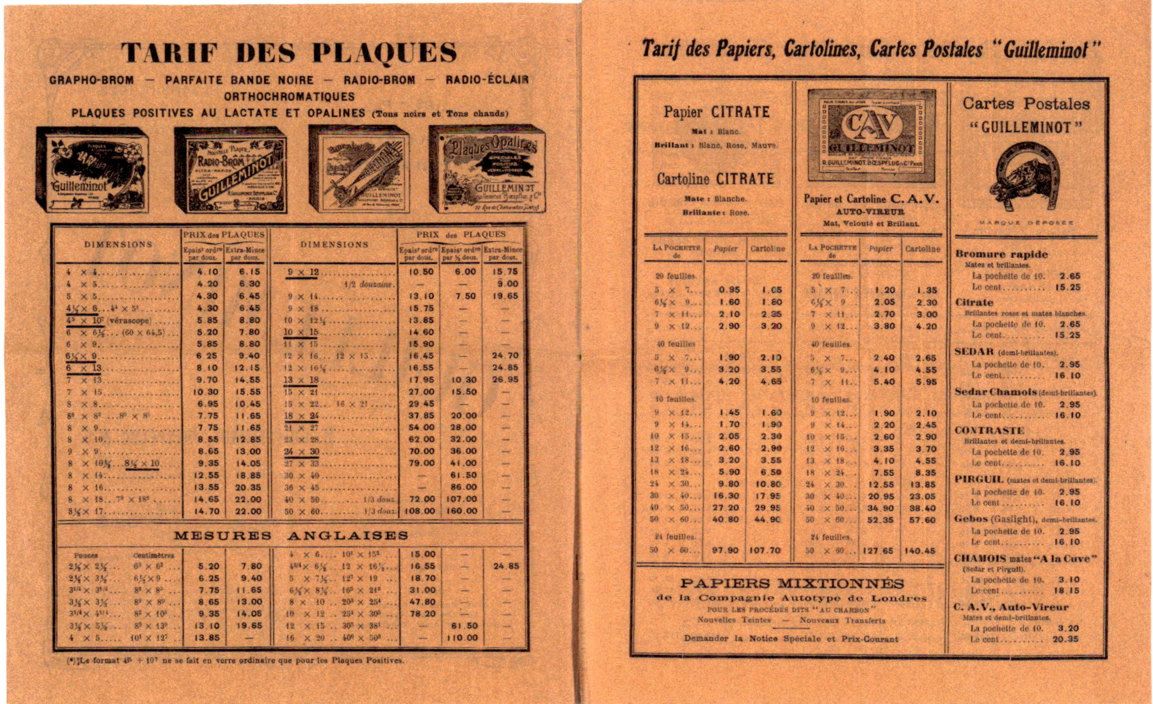

TARIF DES PLAQUES

GRAPHO-BROM — PARFAITE BANDE NOIRE — RADIO-BROM — RADIO-ÉCLAIR
ORTHOCHROMATIQUES
PLAQUES POSITIVES AU LACTATE ET OPALINES (Tons noirs et Tons chauds)

DIMENSIONS	PRIX des PLAQUES — Épaisr ordre par douz.	PRIX des PLAQUES — Extra-Mince par douz.
4 × 4	4.10	6.15
4 × 5	4.20	6.30
5 × 5	4.30	6.45
4½ × 6 … 4⁴ × 5⁵	4.30	6.45
4⁵ × 10⁷ (vérascope)	5.85	8.80
6 × 6½ … (60 × 64,5)	5.20	7.80
6 × 9	5.85	8.80
6½ × 9	6.25	9.40
6 × 13	8.10	12.15
7 × 13	9.70	14.55
7 × 15	10.30	15.55
8 × 8	6.95	10.45
8³ × 8³ … 8⁵ × 8⁵	7.75	11.65
8 × 9	7.75	11.65
8 × 10	8.55	12.85
9 × 9	8.65	13.00
8 × 10½ … 8½ × 10	9.35	14.05
8 × 14	12.55	18.85
8 × 16	13.55	20.35
8 × 18 … 7⁹ × 18⁷	14.65	22.00
8½ × 17	14.70	22.00

DIMENSIONS	PRIX des PLAQUES — Épaisr ordre par douz.	Épaisr ordre par ½ douz.	Extra-Mince par douz.
9 × 12	10.50	6.00	15.75
(½ douzaine)	—	—	9.00
9 × 14	13.10	7.50	19.65
9 × 18	15.75	—	—
10 × 12½	13.85	—	—
10 × 15	14.60	—	—
11 × 15	15.90	—	—
12 × 16 … 12 × 13	16.45	—	24.70
12 × 16½	16.55	—	24.85
13 × 18	17.95	10.30	26.95
15 × 21	27.00	15.50	—
15 × 22 … 16 × 21	29.45	—	—
18 × 24	37.85	20.00	—
21 × 27	54.00	28.00	—
23 × 28	62.00	32.00	—
24 × 30	70.00	36.00	—
27 × 33	79.00	41.00	—
30 × 40	—	61.50	—
36 × 45	—	86.00	—
40 × 50 … 1/3 douz.	72.00	107.00	—
50 × 60 … 1/3 douz.	108.00	160.00	—

MESURES ANGLAISES

Pouces	Centimètres	Épaisr ordre	Extra-Mince
2½ × 2½	6³ × 6³	5.20	7.80
2½ × 3½	6½ × 9	6.25	9.40
3¼ × 3¼	8³ × 8³	7.75	11.65
3½ × 3½	8⁹ × 8⁹	8.65	13.00
3¼ × 4¼	8² × 10⁸	9.35	14.05
3½ × 5½	8⁹ × 13⁹	13.10	19.65
4 × 5	10¹ × 12⁷	13.85	—

Pouces	Centimètres	Épaisr ordre par douz.	Épaisr ordre par ½ douz.	Extra-Mince par douz.
4 × 6	10¹ × 15³	15.00	—	—
4³/⁴ × 6½	12 × 16½	16.55	—	24.85
5 × 7½	12⁷ × 19	18.70	—	—
6½ × 8½	16⁵ × 21⁵	31.00	—	—
8 × 10	20³ × 25⁴	47.80	—	—
10 × 12	25⁴ × 30⁵	78.20	—	—
12 × 15	30⁵ × 38¹	—	61.50	—
16 × 20	40⁶ × 50⁸	—	110.00	—

(*) Le format 4⁵ + 10⁷ ne se fait en verre ordinaire que pour les Plaques Positives.

Tarif des Papiers, Cartolines, Cartes Postales "Guilleminot"

Papier CITRATE
Mat : Blanc.
Brillant : Blanc, Rose, Mauve.

Cartoline CITRATE
Mate : Blanche.
Brillante : Rose.

LA POCHETTE de	Papier	Cartoline
20 feuilles.		
5 × 7	0.95	1.05
6½ × 9	1.60	1.80
7 × 11	2.10	2.35
9 × 12	2.90	3.20
40 feuilles.		
5 × 7	1.90	2.10
6½ × 9	3.20	3.55
7 × 11	4.20	4.65
10 feuilles.		
9 × 12	1.45	1.60
9 × 14	1.70	1.90
10 × 15	2.05	2.30
12 × 16	2.60	2.90
13 × 18	3.20	3.55
18 × 24	5.90	6.50
24 × 30	9.80	10.80
30 × 40	16.30	17.95
40 × 50	27.20	29.95
50 × 60	40.80	44.90
24 feuilles.		
50 × 60	97.90	107.70

Papier et Cartoline C.A.V.
AUTO-VIREUR
Mat, Velouté et Brillant.

LA POCHETTE de	Papier	Cartoline
20 feuilles.		
5 × 7	1.20	1.35
6½ × 9	2.05	2.30
7 × 11	2.70	3.00
9 × 12	3.80	4.20
40 feuilles.		
5 × 7	2.40	2.65
6½ × 9	4.10	4.55
7 × 11	5.40	5.95
10 feuilles.		
9 × 12	1.90	2.10
9 × 14	2.20	2.45
10 × 15	2.60	2.90
12 × 16	3.35	3.70
13 × 18	4.10	4.55
18 × 24	7.55	8.35
24 × 30	12.55	13.85
30 × 40	20.95	23.05
40 × 50	34.90	38.40
50 × 60	52.35	57.60
24 feuilles.		
50 × 60	127.65	140.45

PAPIERS MIXTIONNÉS
de la Compagnie Autotype de Londres
POUR LES PROCÉDÉS DITS "AU CHARBON"
Nouvelles Teintes — Nouveaux Transferts
Demander la Notice Spéciale et Prix-Courant

Cartes Postales "GUILLEMINOT"
MARQUE DÉPOSÉE

Bromure rapide
Mates et brillantes.
La pochette de 10. 2.65
Le cent 15.25

Citrate
Brillantes roses et mates blanches.
La pochette de 10. 2.65
Le cent 15.25

SEDAR (demi-brillantes).
La pochette de 10. 2.95
Le cent 16.10

Sedar Chamois (demi-brillantes).
La pochette de 10. 2.95
Le cent 16.10

CONTRASTE
Brillantes et demi-brillantes.
La pochette de 10. 2.95
Le cent 16.10

PIRGUIL (mates et demi-brillantes).
La pochette de 10. 2.95
Le cent 16.10

Gebos (Gaslight), demi-brillantes.
La pochette de 10. 2.95
Le cent 16.10

CHAMOIS mates "A la Cuve"
(Sedar et Pirguil).
La pochette de 10. 3.10
Le cent 18.15

C. A. V., Auto-Vireur
Mates et demi-brillantes.
La pochette de 10. 3.20
Le cent 20.35

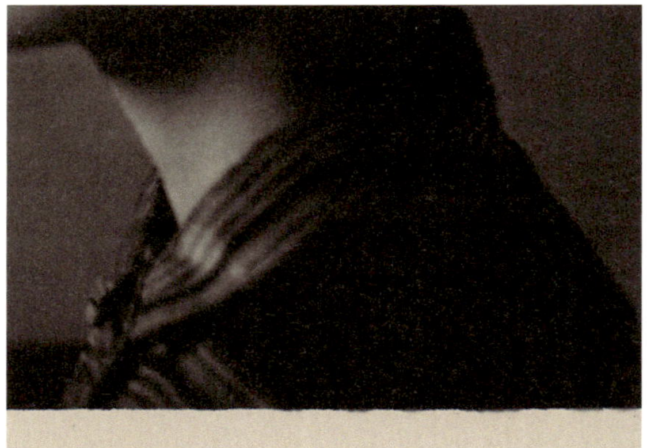

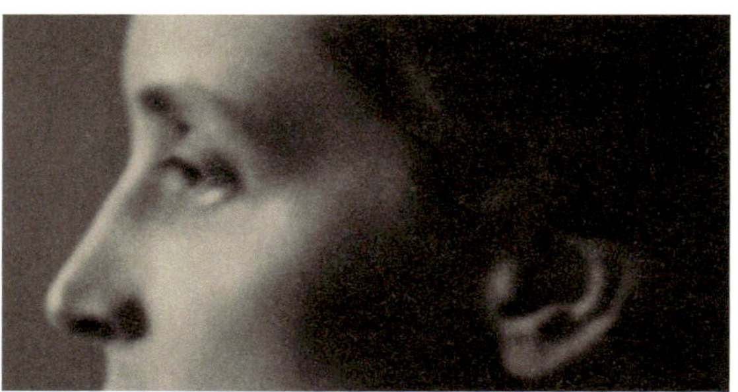

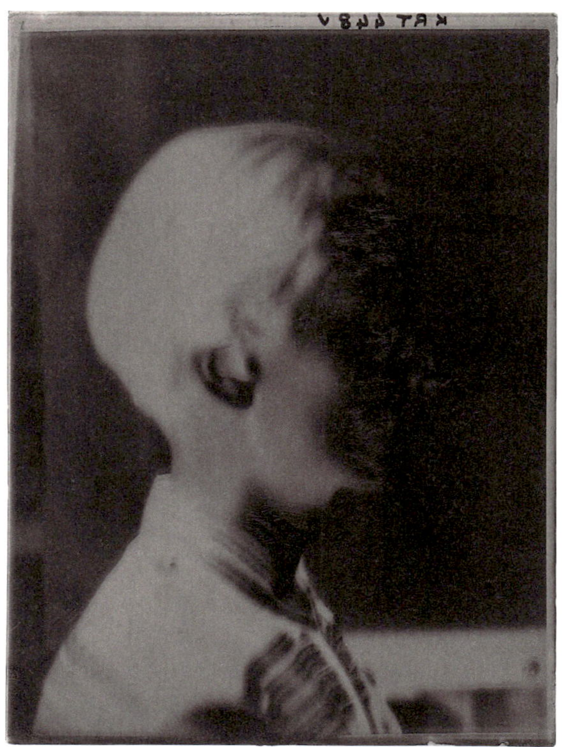

glossy). Kertész made *Fork* in 1928, the year he began to regularly contribute to numerous magazines and show his work in exhibitions.[25] It is also the year he purchased his first Leica camera and abandoned postcard paper altogether.

Later in Kertész's career, after his photographs had gained international recognition, his cartes postales attracted renewed attention from dealers and collectors actively seeking vintage works. In an interview recorded during research for the exhibition *André Kertész: Of Paris and New York*, the artist reminisced about the unique beauty of the material: "It was a beautiful paper," he said, "the nicest what I can find. But it existed only [in] carte postale form. I don't know why who made this

Fig. 5 Details and negative of *Anne-Marie Merkel*, 1926 (cat. 28). Upper left: Detail of irregular border caused by cropping with paper mask. Lower left: Detail of retouching on the face. Right: Glass-plate negative showing retouching on the face. André Kertész archive, Médiathèque de L'Architecture et du Patrimoine, Charenton-le-Pont, France.

don't made other size, only carte postale."[26] We now know that Guilleminot offered all its varieties of papers in a full range of sizes and that Kertész could have used his favorite line for enlargements if he so desired. During the same interview, when asked why he had abandoned printing on postcard paper, Kertész replied that it was because the paper he so much enjoyed had been discontinued. However, Guilleminot product catalogues show that at least until 1937 the manufacturer offered up to eight different types of carte postale papers, including Sédar, each in at least three to five grades of contrast, with multiple options for color support and surface finish. In addition to the postcard stock, ten other Sédar products were also available.[27] The onset of World War II and a decline in consumer interest in photographic postcards most likely led Guilleminot to cease production during the war or shortly after, long after Kertész had moved to New York. A 1951 product catalogue shows that the company no longer carried any type

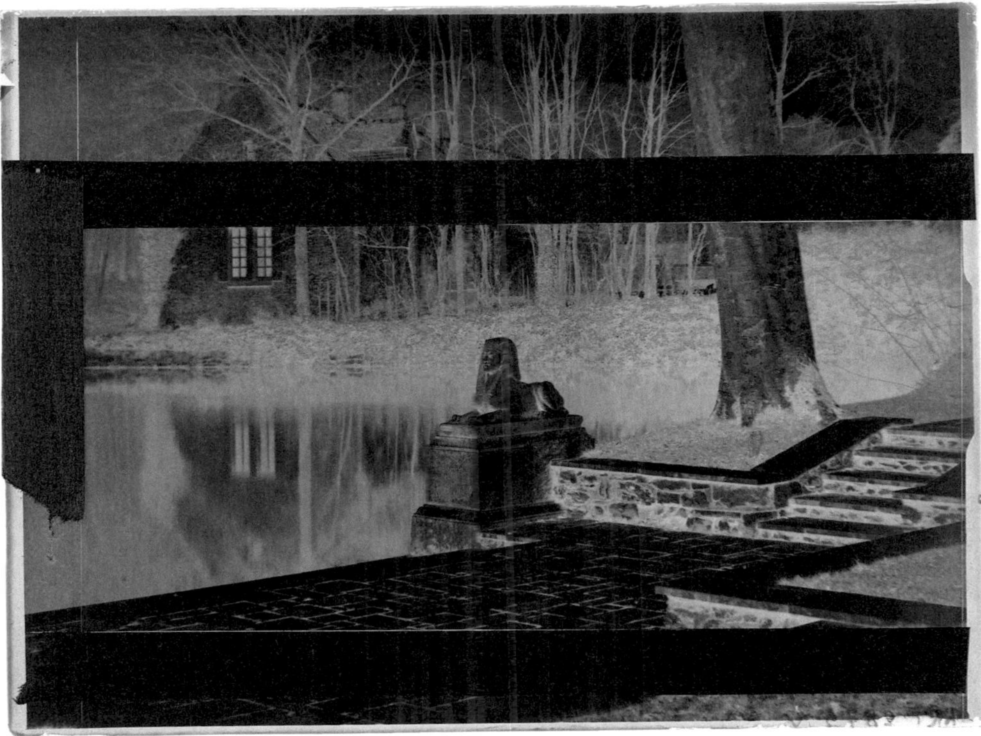

of carte postale paper and that Sédar emulsion products had also been discontinued.[28]

Historical and technical research for this exhibition have shown that Kertész printed most of his cartes postales on the same variety of paper and that his choice was probably influenced by a mix of aesthetic, artistic, economic, and practical motives. If there was one overarching reason he abandoned the postcard format, then it remains unclear. It seems possible, however, that he moved on from carte postale paper for the same mix of motives that led him to embrace it early in his Paris period. The year 1928 was a pivotal one for the photographer: he switched from 9-by-12-centimeter glass-plate negatives to 35mm film, started to receive regular assignments from magazines, and

exhibited his photographs internationally. The small negatives taken with his newly acquired Leica camera required enlargement, and the size and semigloss surface of the postcard prints were inappropriate for editorial work. Trends in straight photography accelerated the decline of interest in the platinum-print look. Photographer Edward Weston, considered by many to be the leader of this new aesthetic, noted in 1925 that "to use a tinted stock is a form of affectation near to 'artiness.'"[29] Perhaps Kertész was aware of these changing attitudes. Whatever led him to abandon printing on postcard paper, we can still revel in the rich tactile quality of the cartes postales as we imagine ourselves passing them around a table at the Dôme.

Fig. 6 Glass-plate negative of *Château de Sainte-Mesme*, 1926 (cat. 59), with black paper tape mask used to crop the final image. André Kertész archive, Médiathèque de L'Architecture et du Patrimoine, Charenton-le-Pont, France.

NOTES

I am grateful to the following people for their support in researching and writing this essay: Marie-Lou Beauchamp, Robert Gurbo, Paul Messier, Nancy Reinhold, Matthieu Rivallin, and Elizabeth Siegel. Funding for travel and research was generously provided by the Karen and Jim Frank Photograph Conservation Fund. All translations from French are my own.

1 Sandra S. Phillips, "The Photographic Work of André Kertész in France, 1925–1936: A Critical Essay and Catalogue" (PhD diss., City University of New York, 1985), I.261.

2 See, notably, Nancy Reinhold, "Exhibition in a Pocket: The Cartes Postales of André Kertész," in Mitra Abbaspour, Lee Ann Daffner, and Maria Morris Hambourg, eds., *Object:Photo. Modern Photographs: The Thomas Walther Collection 1909–1949. An Online Project of The Museum of Modern Art* (New York: Museum of Modern Art, 2014), moma.org/interactives/objectphoto/assets/essays/Reinhold.pdf.

3 Sarah Greenough and Robert Gurbo have made similar arguments about the calculated narrative Kertész crafted in his later years. See Sarah Greenough, "To Become a Virgin Again, 1925–1936," and Robert Gurbo, "La Réunion, 1962–1985," in Sarah Greenough, Robert Gurbo, and Sarah Kennel, *André Kertész*, exh. cat. (Washington, DC: National Gallery of Art; Princeton, NJ: Princeton University Press, 2005), 59–87 and 203–5.

4 Photocopies from a 1985 inventory of Kertész's estate show reproductions of six postcards that bear the logotype "K Ltd" in the stamp box. Little is known of this European (presumably German) manufacturer of photographic postcard stock that operated between 1918 and 1936.

5 See Françoise Denoyelle, *Le marché de la photographie, 1919–1939*, vol. 1 of *La lumière de Paris* (Paris: L'Harmattan, 1997), 60. Other smaller French manufacturers of photographic materials included Biot, Cellulose Planchon, Charles Martel, Compagnie Industrielle des Films, Ecu, Fotogen, Fresson, Jougla, Papeteries Photographiques de Colomb, and Simonot. The foreign manufacturers Agfa, Gevaert, Ilford, Kodak, and Wellington also operated in the French market.

6 R. Guilleminot, Bœspflug & Cie, *Caractéristiques, formules, modes d'emploi des plaques & papiers Guilleminot* (Paris: R. Guilleminot, Bœspflug, 1926), 25.

7 The expense book is in the holdings of the André Kertész archive, Médiathèque de L'Architecture et du Patrimoine, Charenton-le-Pont, France. Several entries in the book include purchases of 9-by-12-centimeter glass-plate negatives designated "SE." These entries refer most likely to Lumière SE orthochromatic (*SE* stands for *sans écran*, or screenless), anti-halo, glass-plate gelatin silver negatives. The plates were of moderate light sensitivity but with a good tolerance to exposure that resulted in suitable negatives in the most diverse circumstances. See *Société Lumière, Formulaire des plaques, pellicules, papiers, Produits photographiques*, 21st ed. (Lyon, France: Société Lumière, n.d. [c. 1931]), 20.

When specified, the entries related to photographic paper indicate the purchase of 18-by-24-centimeter sheets. Kertész identifies the brand of paper he bought on two occasions: November 5 ("Guill SR") and December 3 ("Lypa no 61"). The meaning of the November entry is unclear, since no referent for a Guilleminot paper called "SR" could be found. However, the manufacturer carried a bromide paper for enlargements called "S.F."; perhaps Kertész misspelled the paper's name. Lypa was a line of gelatin silver bromide developing papers offered by the Société Lumière. Lypa 61 was a single-weight paper with a glossy surface finish and regular contrast. Ibid., 44.

8 "Le papier 'Sedar' par MM. Guilleminot et Bœspflug et Cie," *Bulletin de la Société Française de Photographie* 25, no. 16 (1909): 308.

9 "News and Notes," *British Journal of Photography*, April 1, 1921, 190.

10 See Sarah Wagner, "Manufactured Platinum and Faux Platinum Papers, 1880s–1920s," in Constance McCabe, ed., *Platinum and Palladium Photographs: Technical History, Connoisseurship, and Preservation* (Washington, DC: American Institute for Conservation, 2017), 145–83.

11 Guilleminot, *Caractéristiques*, 16, 24.

12 See R. Guilleminot, Bœspflug & Cie, *Manuel Photographique Guilleminot,* 2nd ed. (Paris: Éditions Torcy, [1928]), 100.

13 Gloss was measured using a BYK micro-TRI-gloss glossmeter; reported gloss results are the average of four readings at the same location relative to the 60-degree geometry. Color was measured using an X-Rite eXact spectrophotometer; reported CIE L*a*b* values are the average of three readings at the same location in the white margins of the prints. Thickness was measured using a Mitutoyo Digimatic Micrometer Series 293; reported values are the average of four measurements made at different locations along one edge of the postcards.

14 Comparison with the aesthetic and physical characteristics of Kertész's cartes postales in the Thomas Walther Collection at The Museum of Modern Art, New York, revealed strong similarities with that group, reinforcing a sense of consistency in the artist's practice. Analysis of works in the Thomas Walther Collection can be found in Abbaspour, Daffner, and Hambourg, *Object:Photo* [online project], moma.org/interactives/objectphoto/artists/3072.html#photos. See also Reinhold, "Exhibition in a Pocket," 3.

15 See Paul Messier, "Image Isn't Everything: Revealing Affinities across Collections through the Language of the Photographic Print," in Abbaspour, Daffner, and Hambourg, *Object:Photo* [online project], moma.org/interactives/objectphoto/assets/essays/Messier.pdf.

"

16 The postcard samples studied here were acquired online and from the Lens Media Lab Reference Collection of Photographic Papers at Yale University, New Haven, CT.

17 The product lines were marked in the horsehead logo as follows: *H* (Chromex), *D* (Dinox), *E* (Etoile), *P* (Pirguil), *2* (Riviera), and star (Sédar). Aéro-Contraste is the only line of postcards for which there was no identifier below the horse's head. Although we could not find examples of postcards from Guilleminot's Bromure Rapide line, which was available between 1925 and 1928, we know that these cards were offered with only matte or glossy surface finishes and are therefore confident that Kertész did not print on them.

18 See Paul Messier, "Les émulsions industrielles au XXe siècle," in Anne Cartier-Bresson, ed., *Le vocabulaire technique de la photographie* (Paris: Marval, 2008), 454–56.

19 All sample cards known to have a chamois base displayed b* values above 15 on the verso, a characteristic shared by all of the Kertész's cards studied but only 35 percent of the random sample of Guilleminot postcards.

20 See Guilleminot, *Caractéristiques*, 16–17.

21 Messier, "Image Isn't Everything," 1.

22 See R. Guilleminot, Bœspflug & Cie, *Tarif des plaques, papiers, produits photographiques Guilleminot* (Paris: R. Guilleminot, Bœspflug, 1926), n.p.

23 On Kertész's photographic post-production, see Reinhold "Exhibition in a Pocket," 6–7.

24 See Michel Frizot and Annie-Laure Wanaverbecq, *André Kertész*, exh. cat. (Paris: Jeu de Paume, 2010), 328.

25 See Phillips, "The Photographic Work of André Kertész," I.435; and Frizot and Wanaverbecq, *André Kertész*, 328.

26 André Kertész, interview by Edwynn Houk, Nicholas Pritzker, and David Travis, New York, c. 1984, video courtesy of Nicholas Pritzker.

27 See R. Guilleminot, Bœspflug & Cie, *Formulaire Guilleminot: films, papiers, pellicules, plaques, produits photographiques* (Paris: R. Guilleminot, Bœspflug, 1937), 22–24. Interestingly, unlike previous catalogues, this 1937 catalogue makes no reference to platinum tone in its descriptions of the Sédar line of papers and cards.

28 R. Guilleminot, Bœspflug & Cie, *Formulaire général Guilleminot* (Paris: R. Guilleminot, Bœspflug, 1951), 40–46.

29 Edward Weston, *The Daybooks of Edward Weston*, vol. 1 (Millertown, NY: Aperture, 1973), 143.

Plates

ALL WORKS BY
ANDRÉ KERTÉSZ

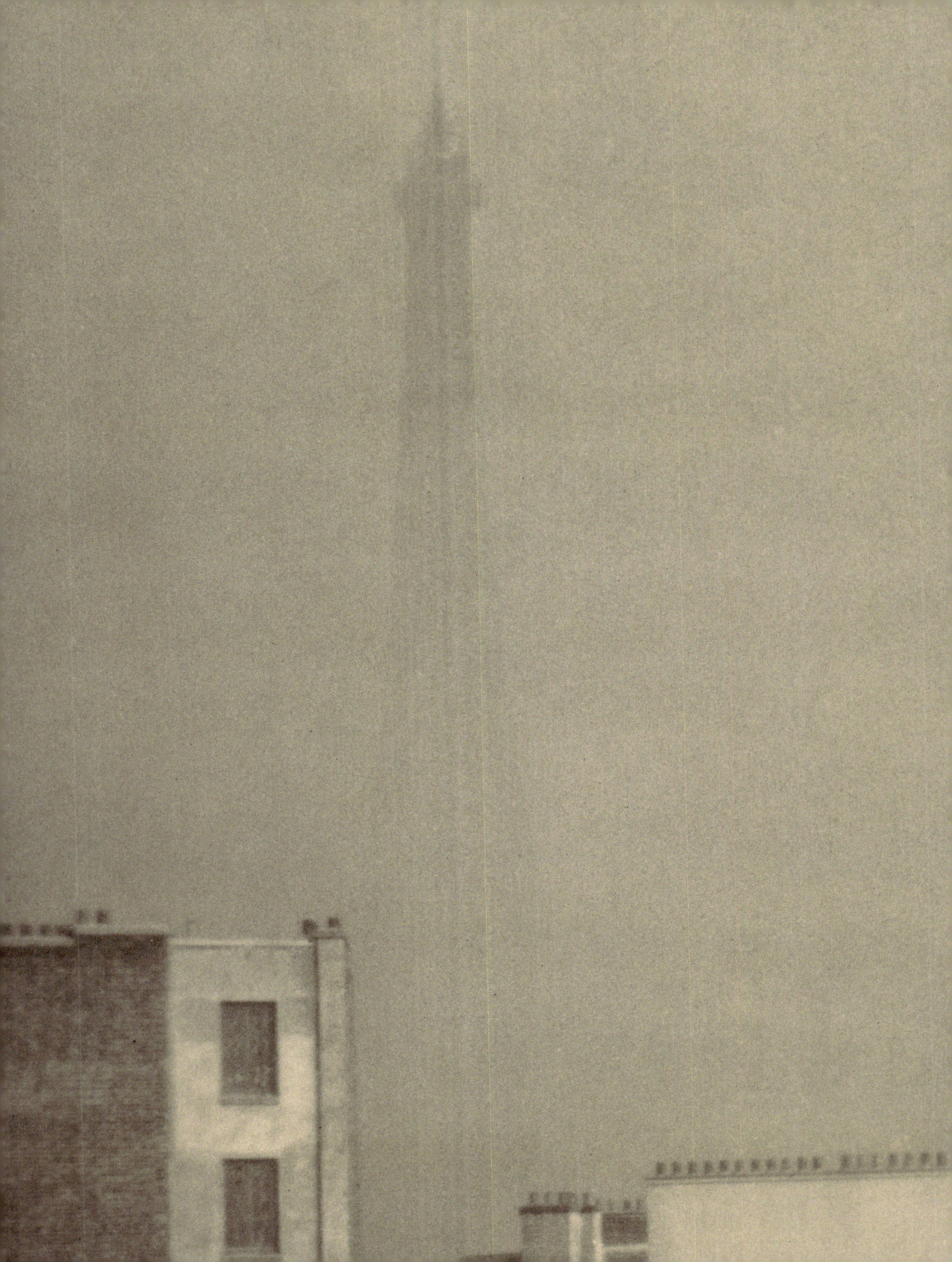

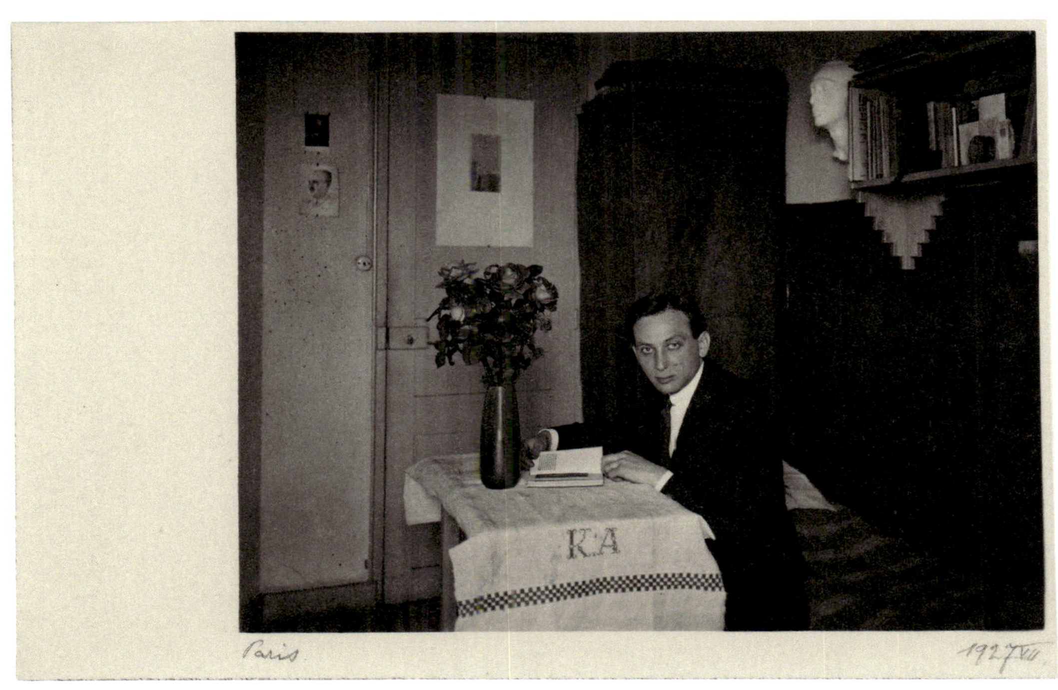

Paris
1927 VII

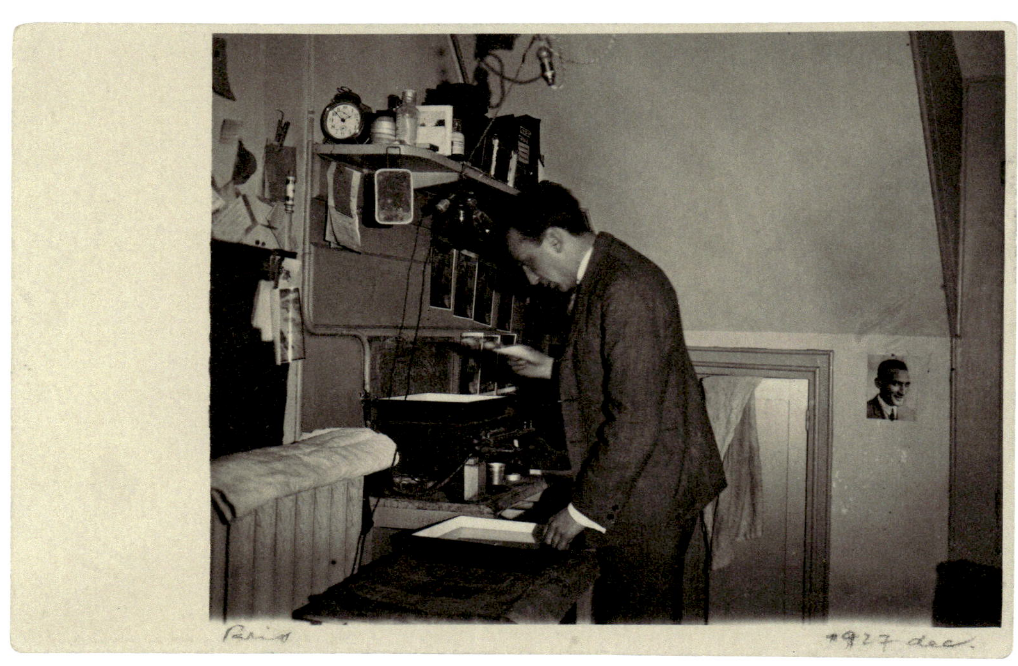

   Cat. 2 *Self-Portrait in Darkroom*, December 1927

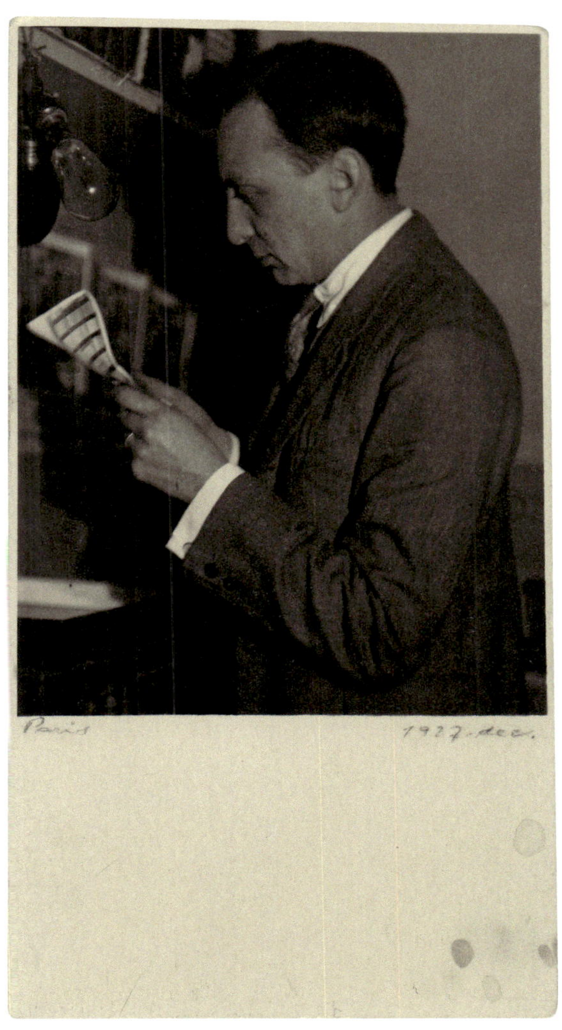

Paris
1927. dec.

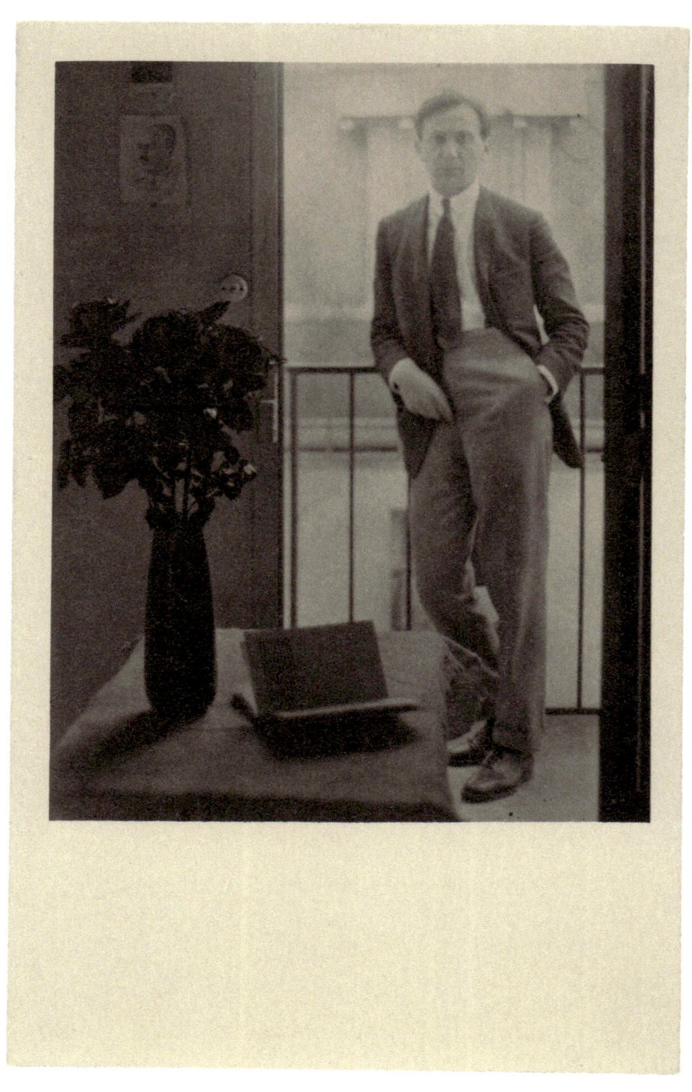

   Cat. 4 *Self-Portrait*, 1926–27

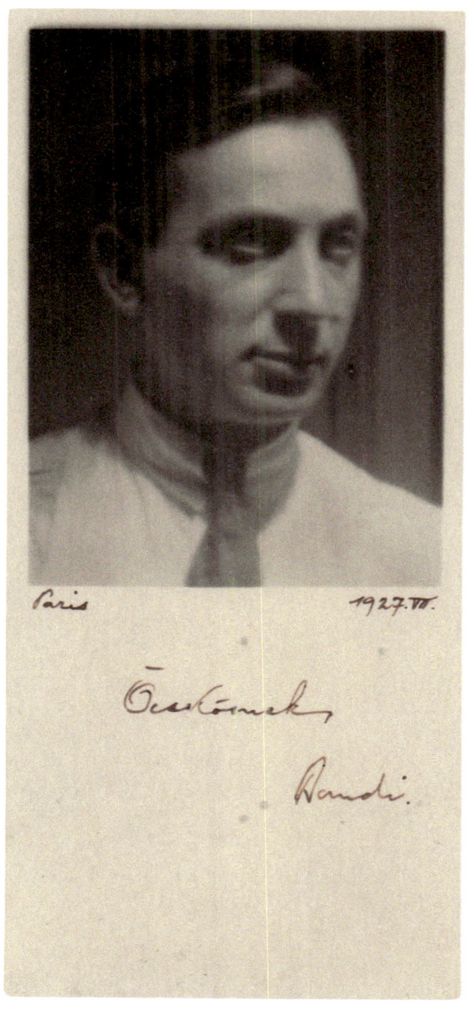

Paris   1927.VII.

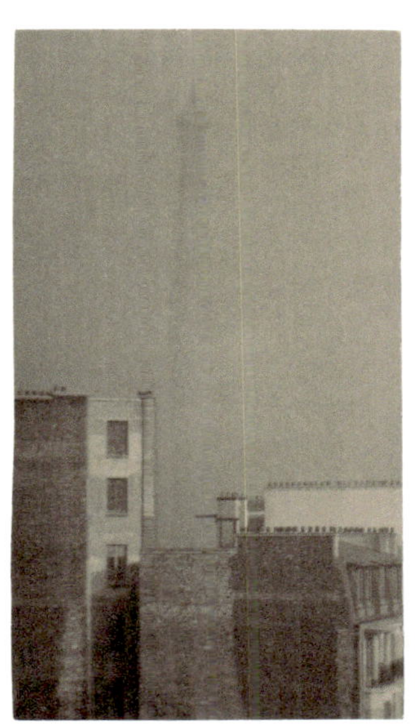

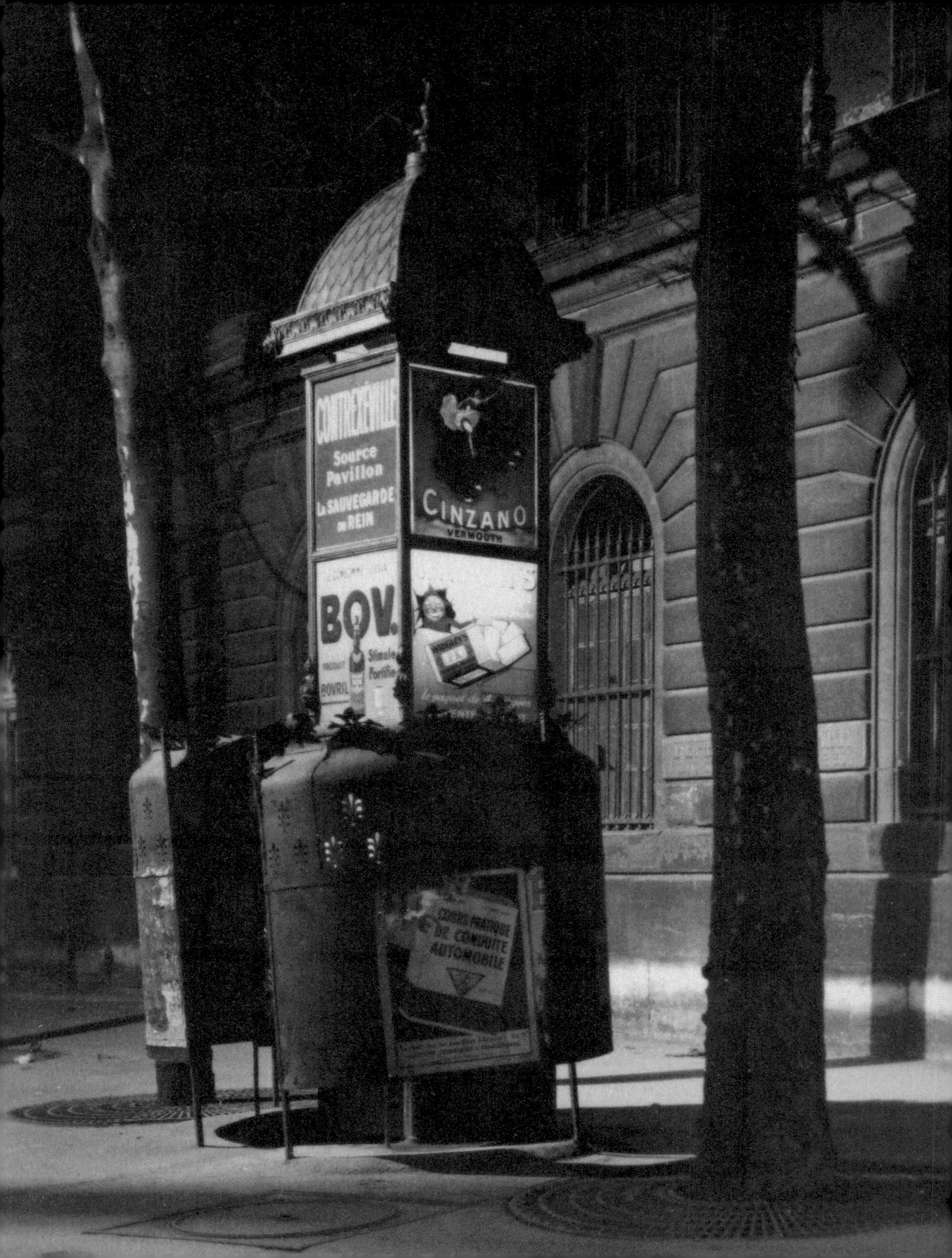
CONTREXEVILLE
Source Pavillon
La SAUVEGARDE du REIN
BOV.
PRODUIT Stimule
BOVRIL Fortifie
CINZANO
VERMOUTH
COURS PRATIQUE
DE CONDUITE
AUTOMOBILE

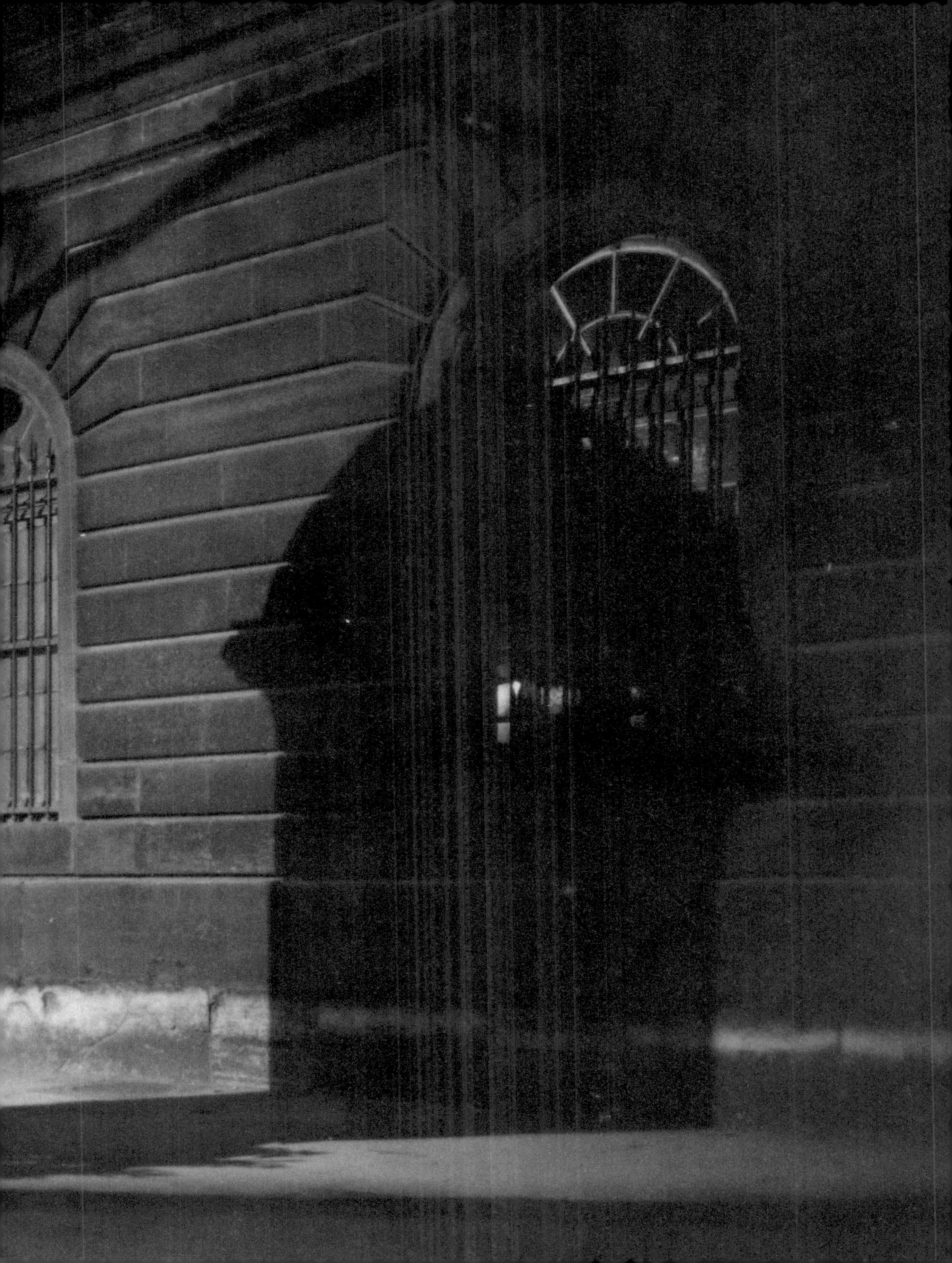

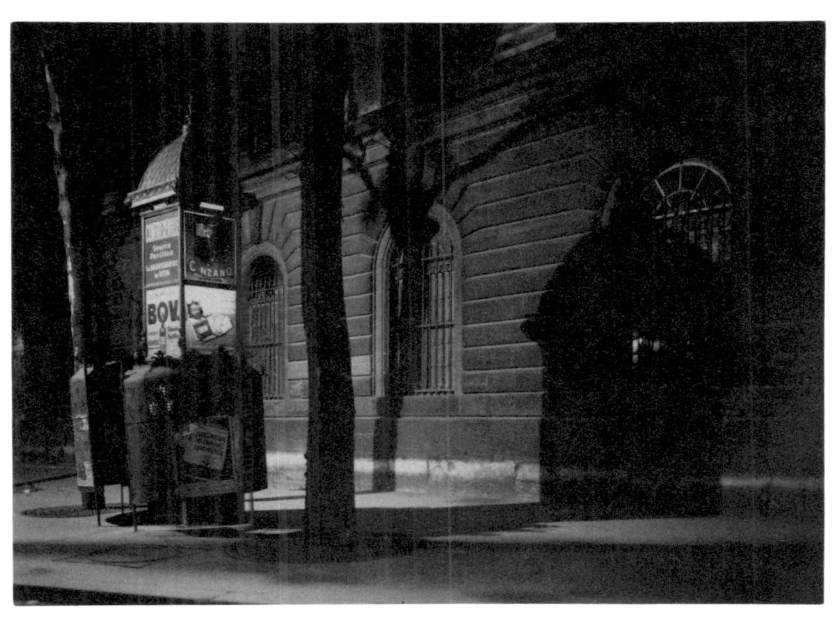

Cat. 7   *Behind the Hôtel de Ville*, 1925   **71**

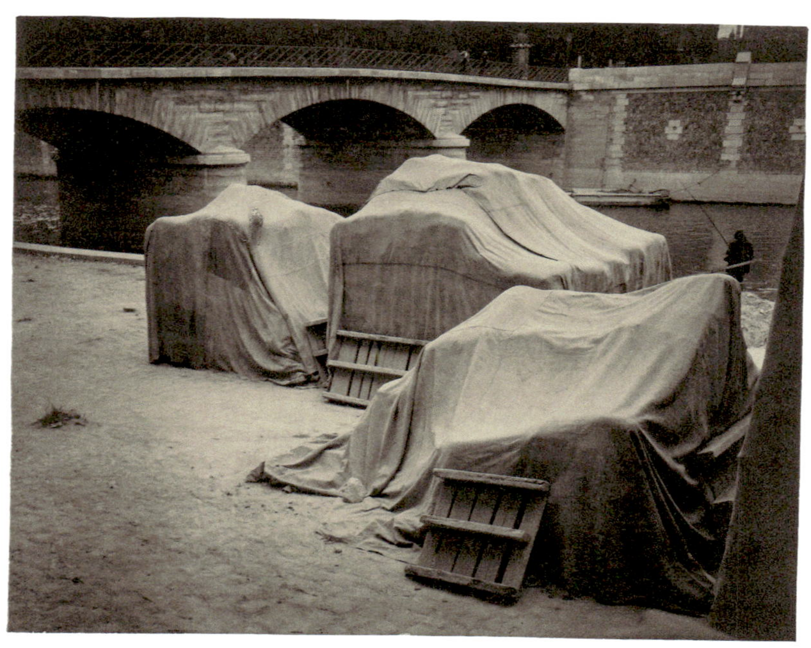

     Cat. 8   *Behind Notre-Dame*, 1925

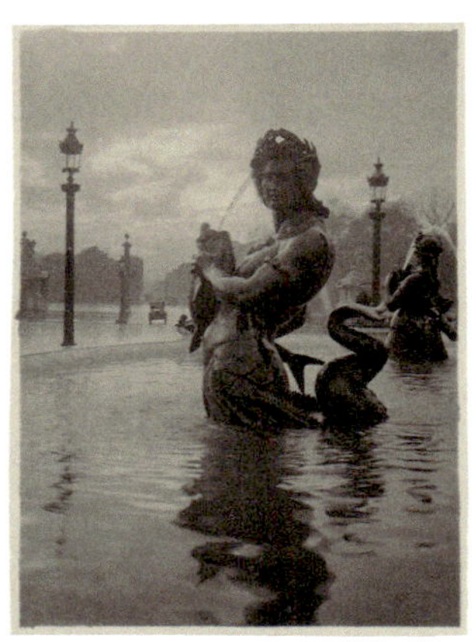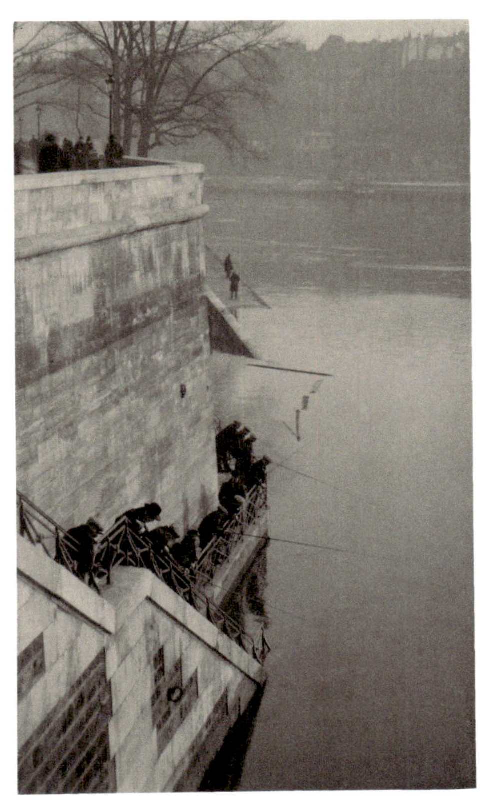

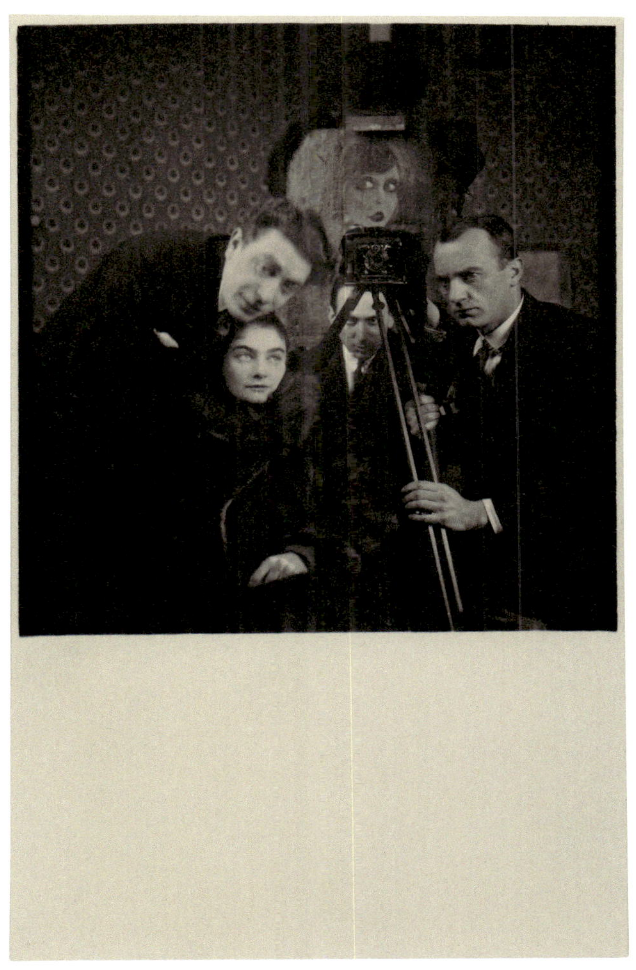

Cat. 11 *Self-Portrait with Friends,* 1925–28   **75**

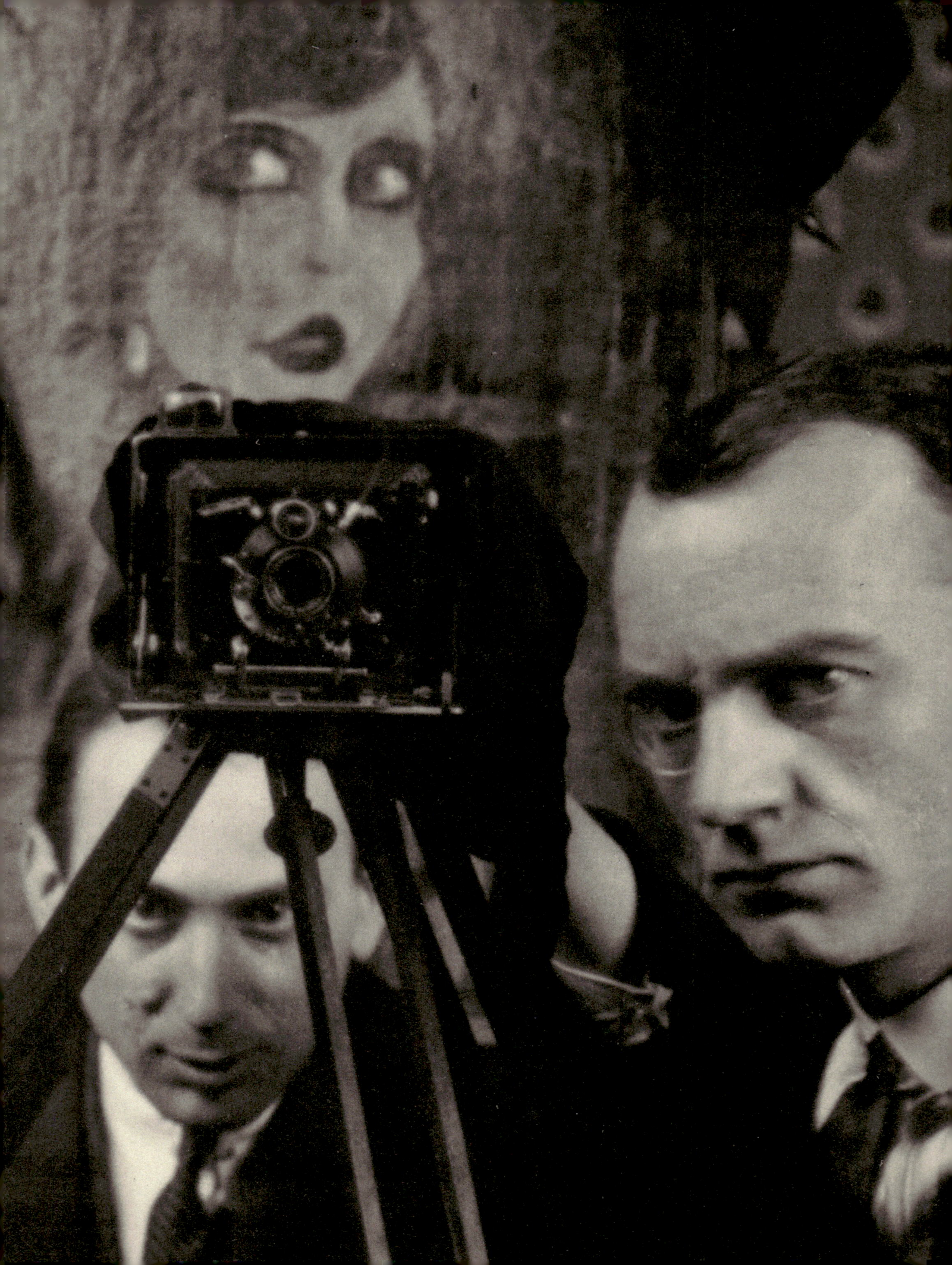

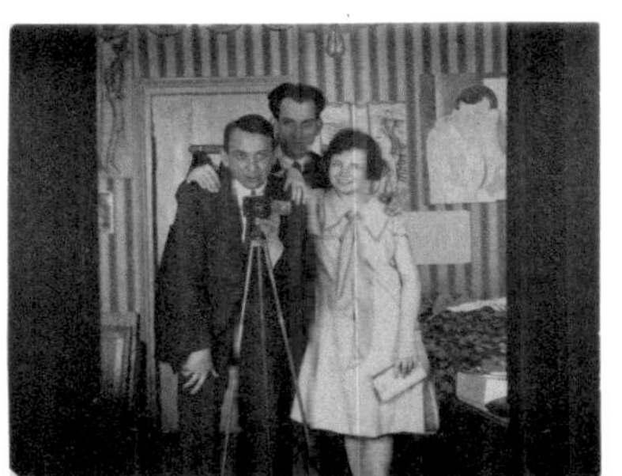

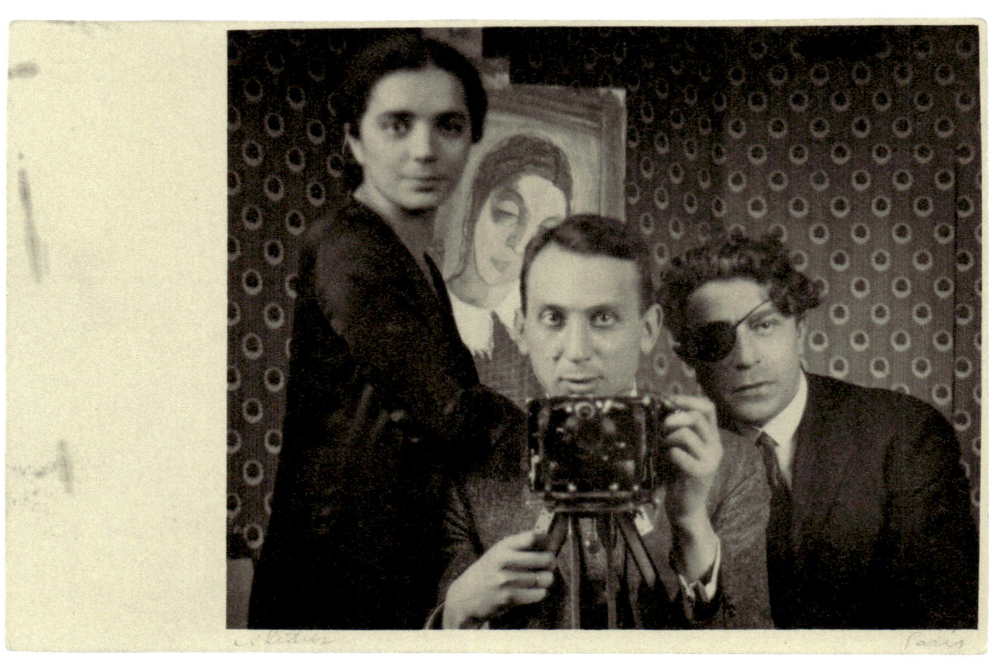

   Cat. 13 *Self-Portrait with Jean Jaffe and Frantisek Reichental,* December 1926

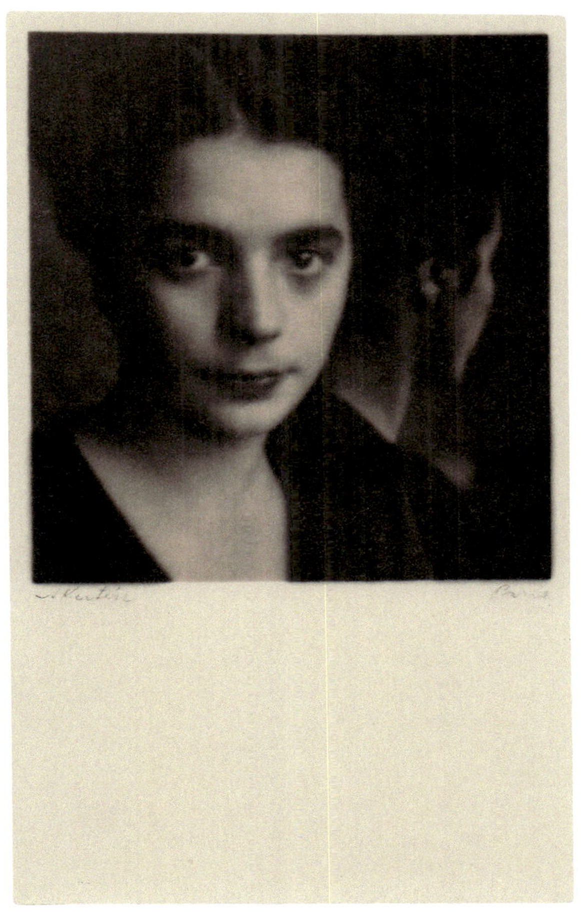

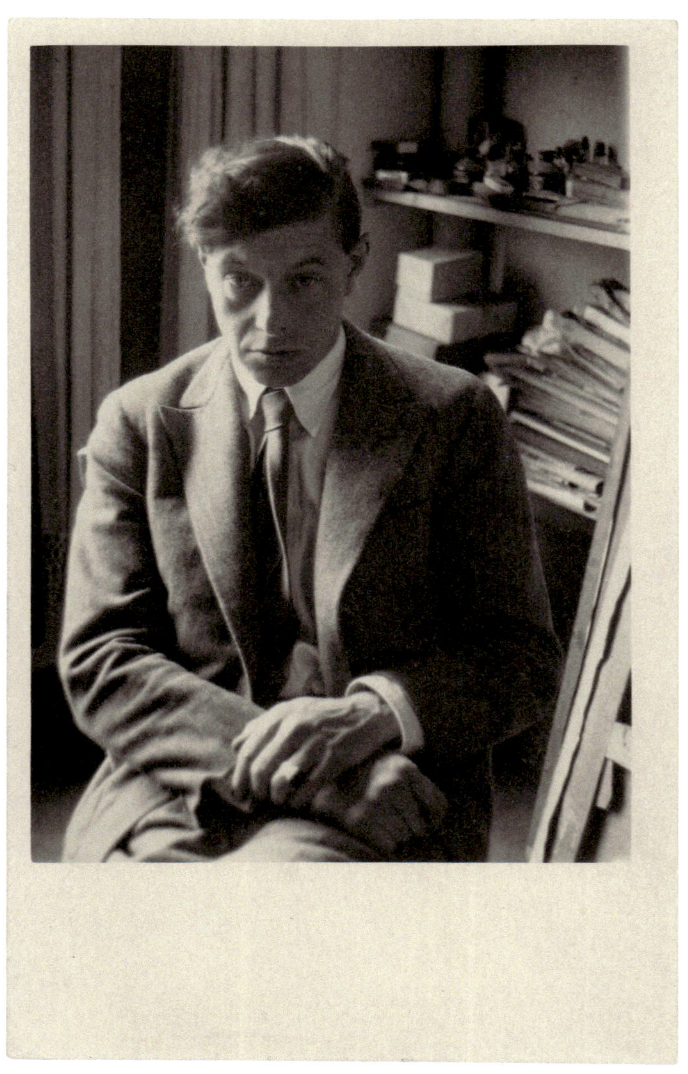

    Cat. 15 *Lajos Tihanyi*, 1926

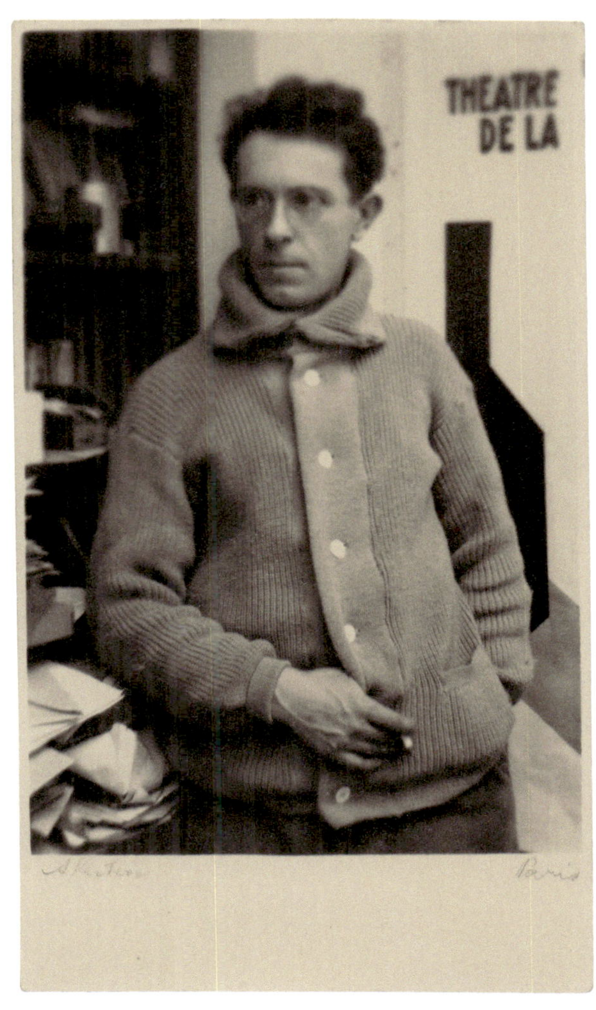

Cat 16 *Joseph Csáky*, 1926

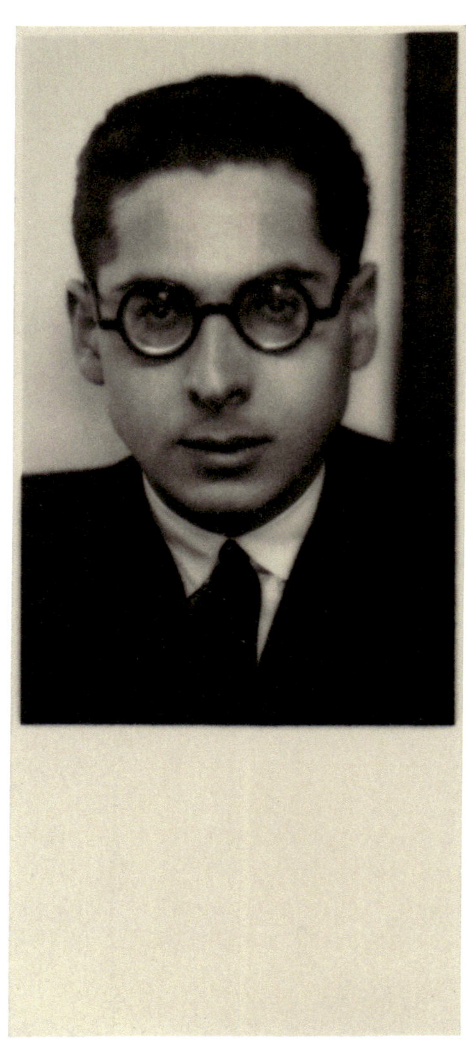

   Cat. 17 *Paul Arma*, 1928

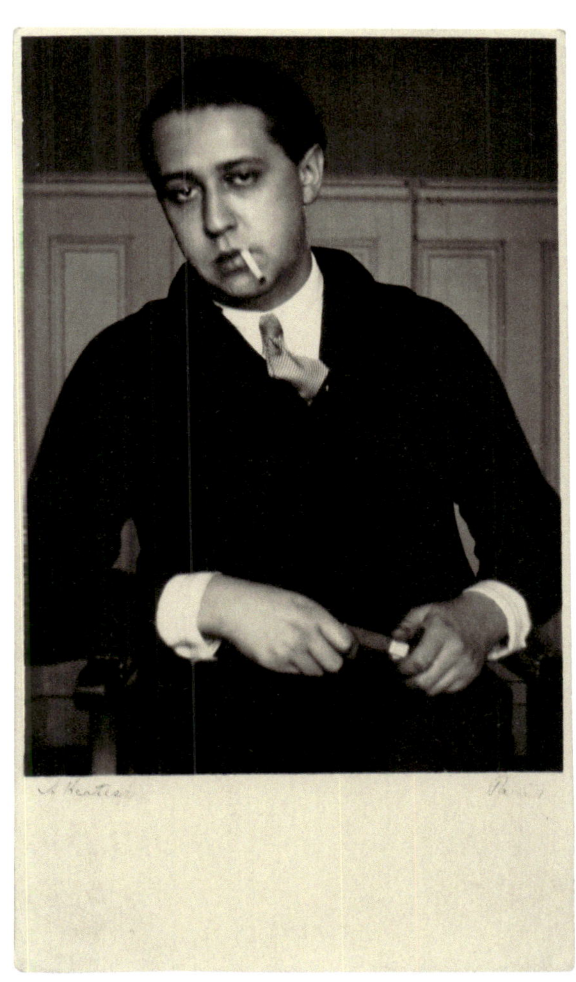

Cat. 18 *Sándor Márai*, 1925–28 **83**

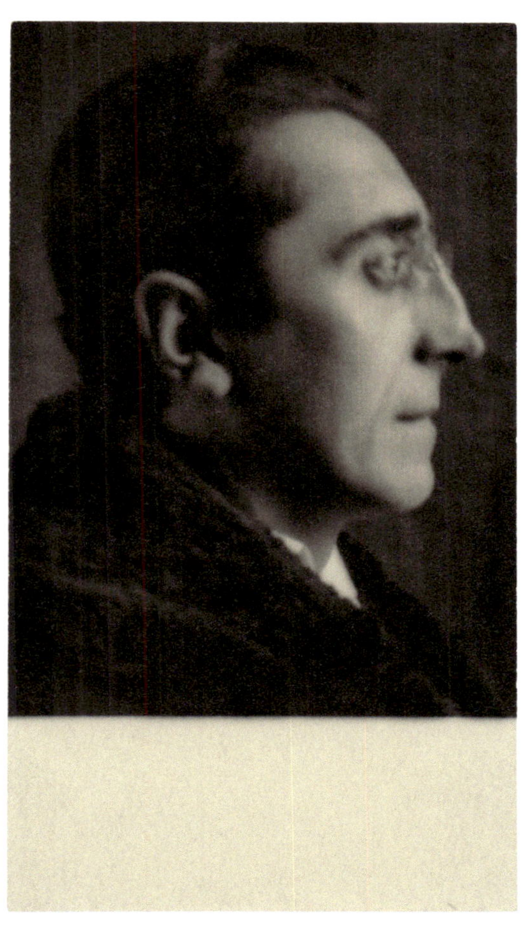

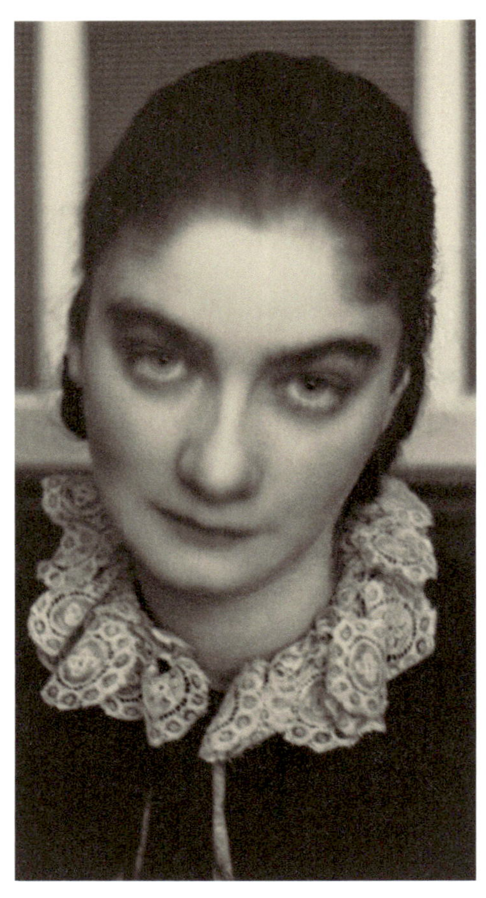

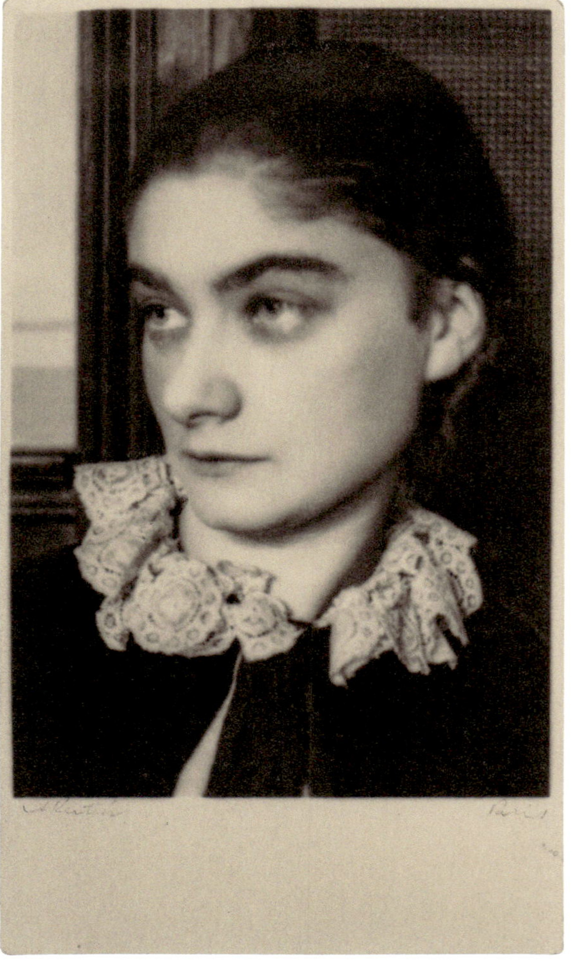

   Cat. 20 *Hilda Daus,* 1927 | Cat. 21 *Hilda Daus,* 1927

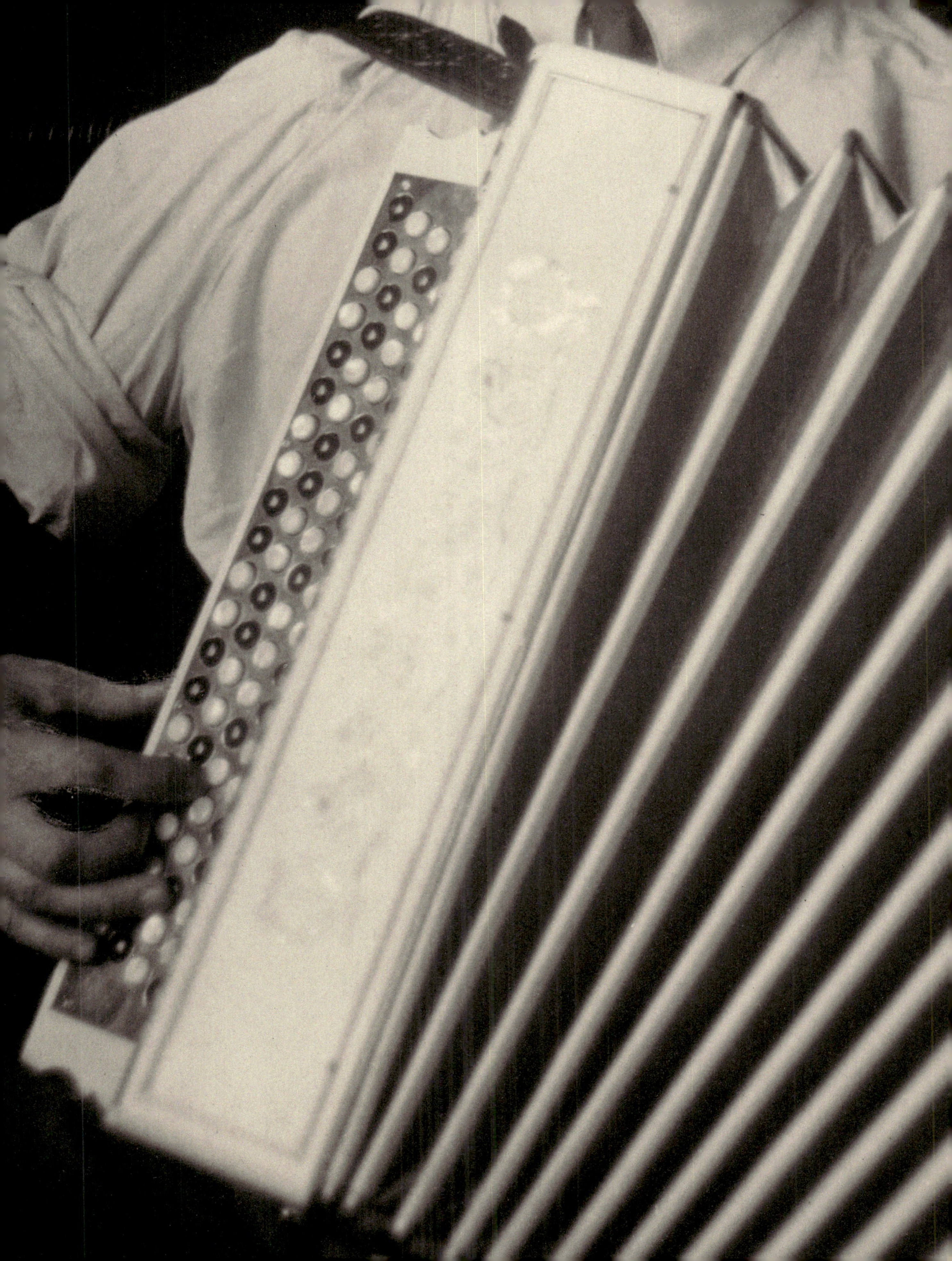

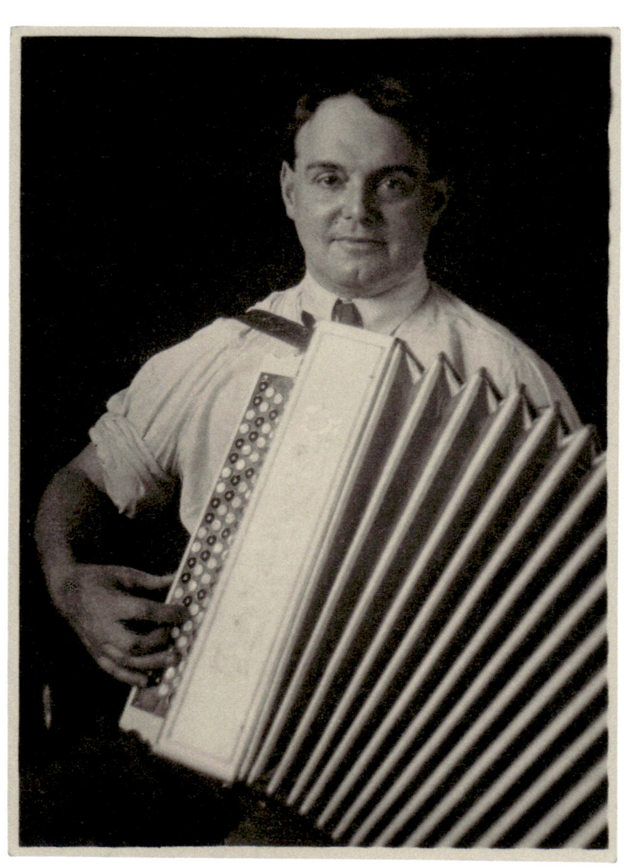

  Cat. 22 *Pierre Mac Orlan*, 1927

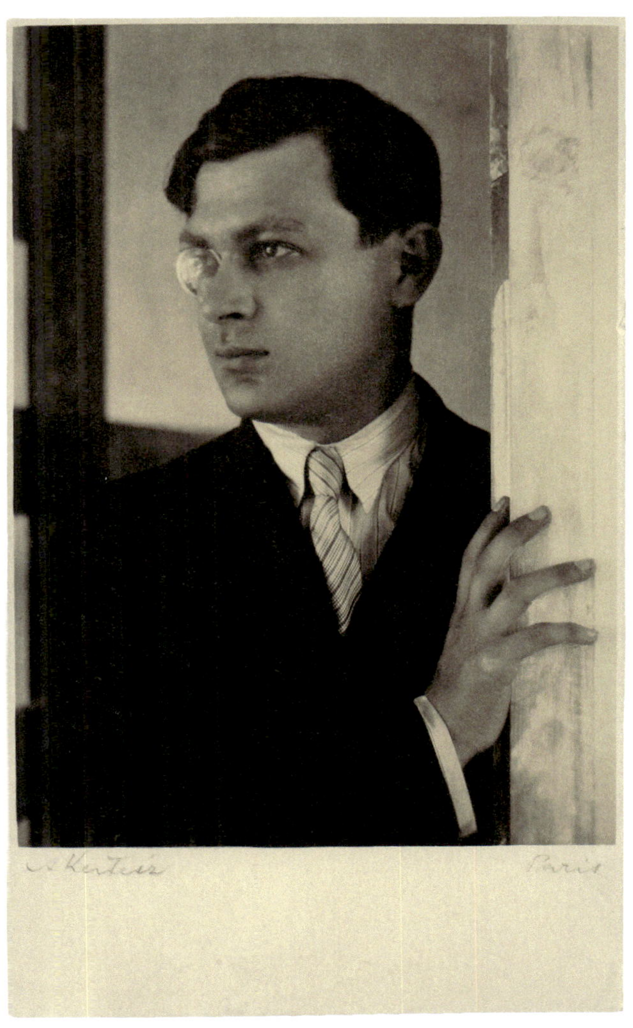

Cat. 23 *Tristan Tzara*, 1926 **89**

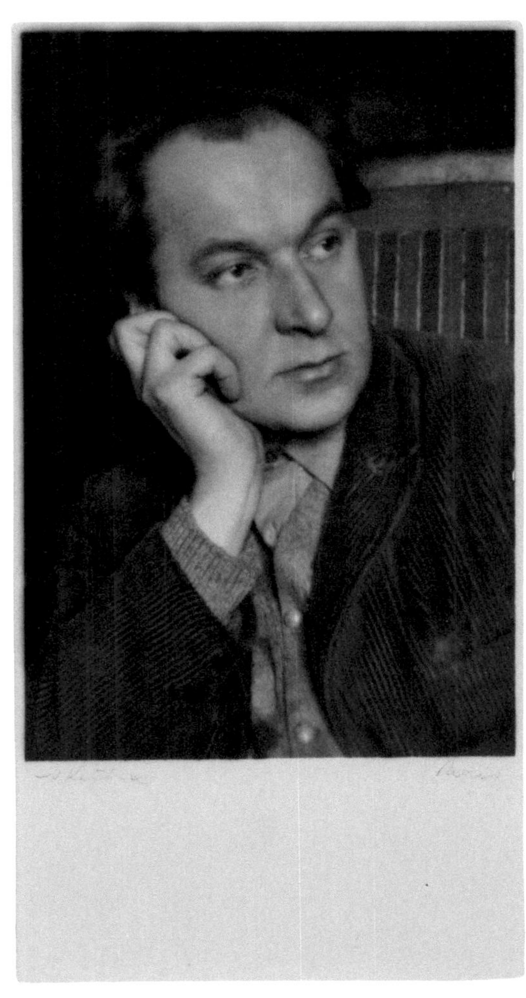

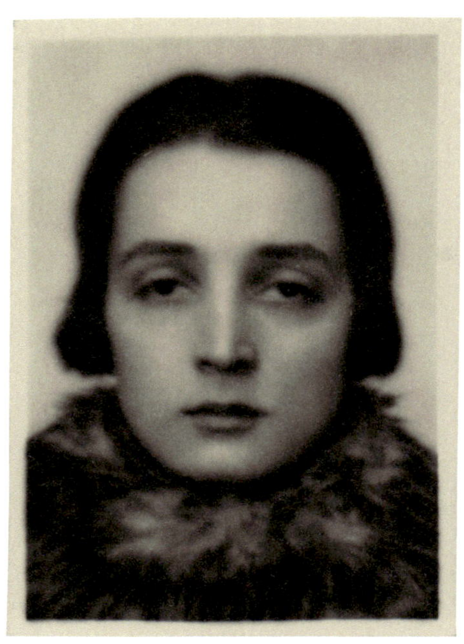

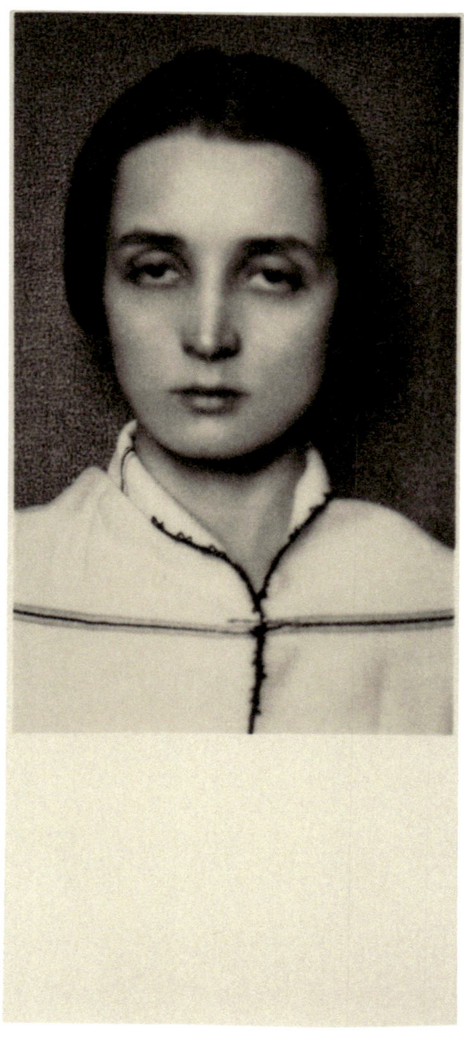

   Cat. 25 *Anne-Marie Merkel, 1926* | Cat. 26 *Anne-Marie Merkel, 1926*

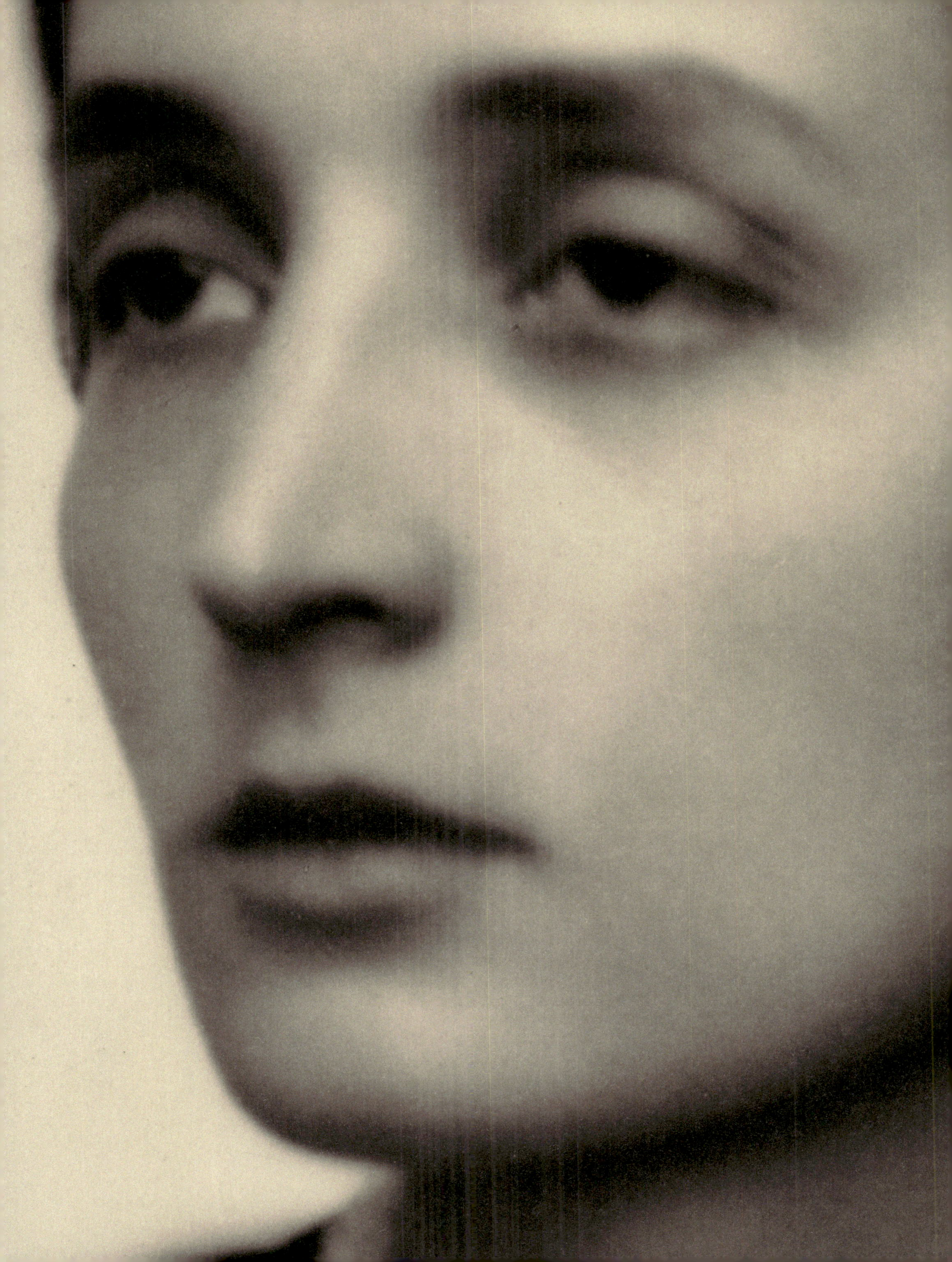

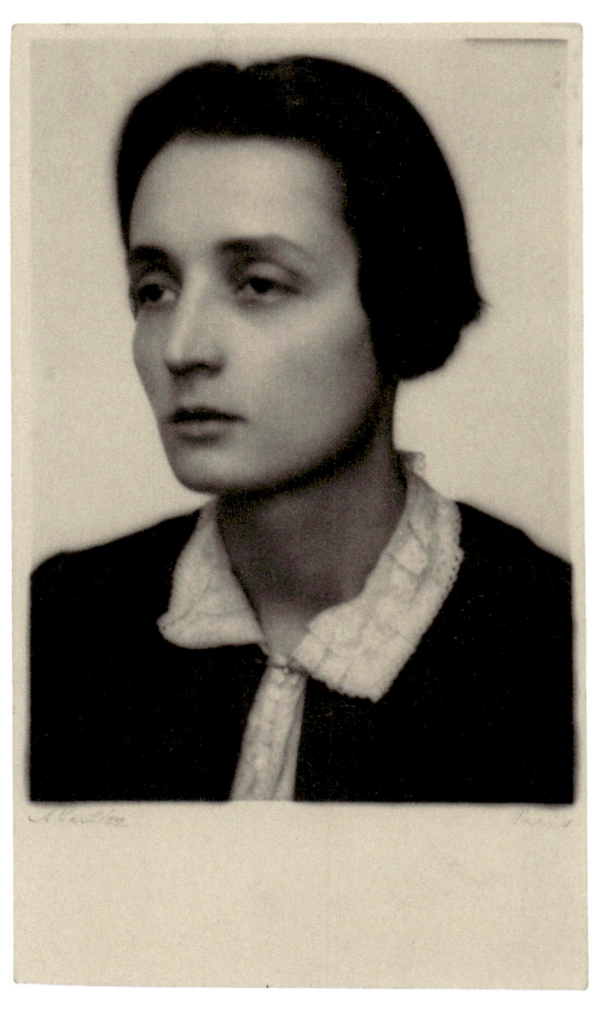

    Cat. 27 *Anne-Marie Merkel,* 1926

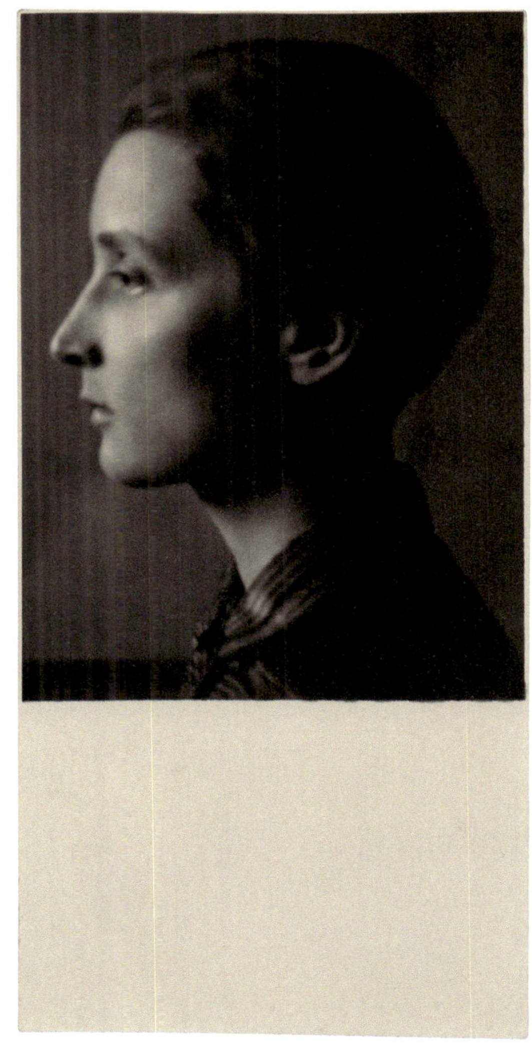

Cat. 28 *Anne-Marie Merkel, 1926*   **95**

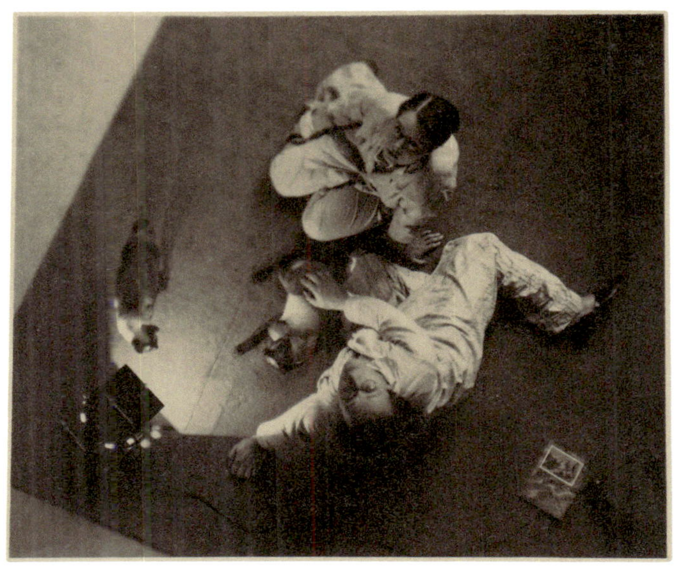

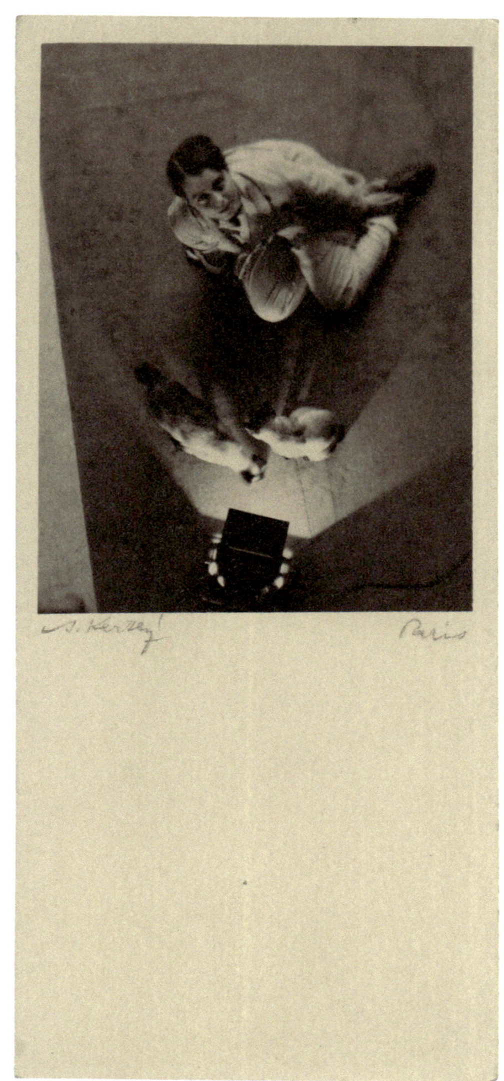

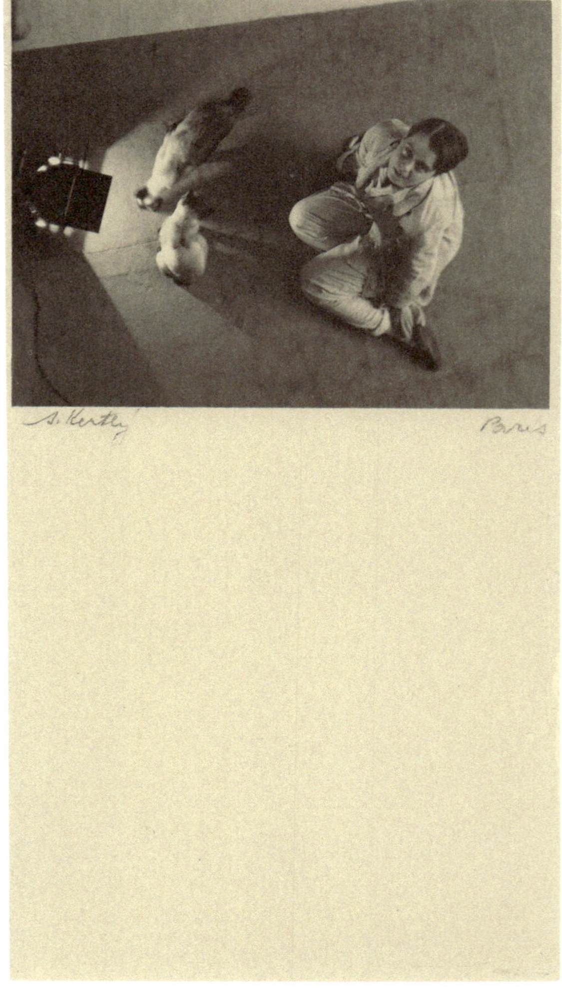

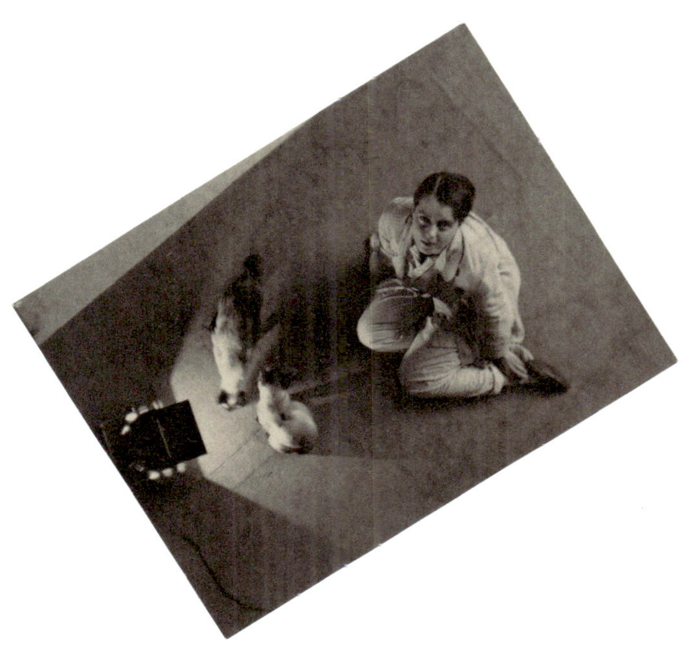

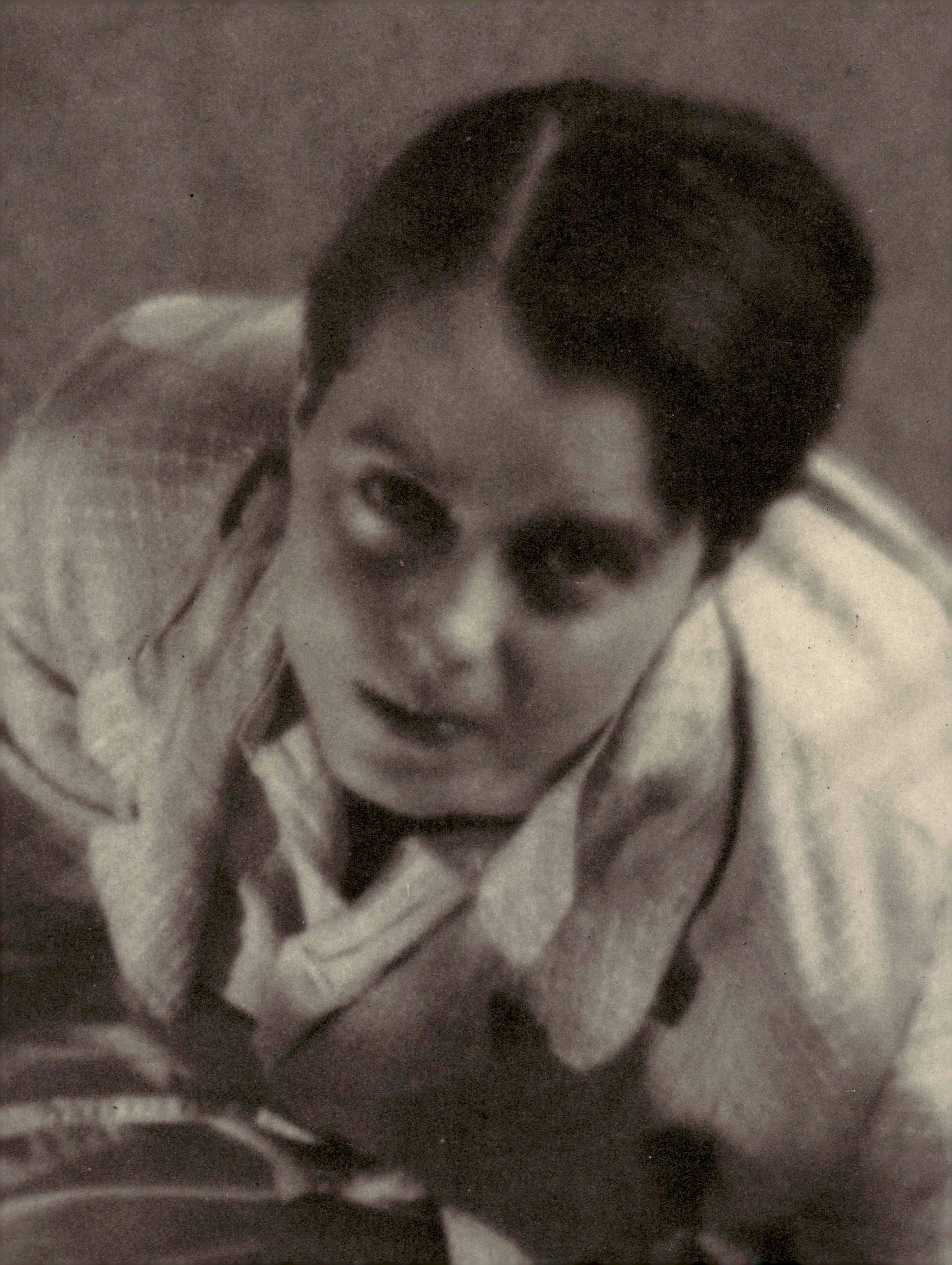

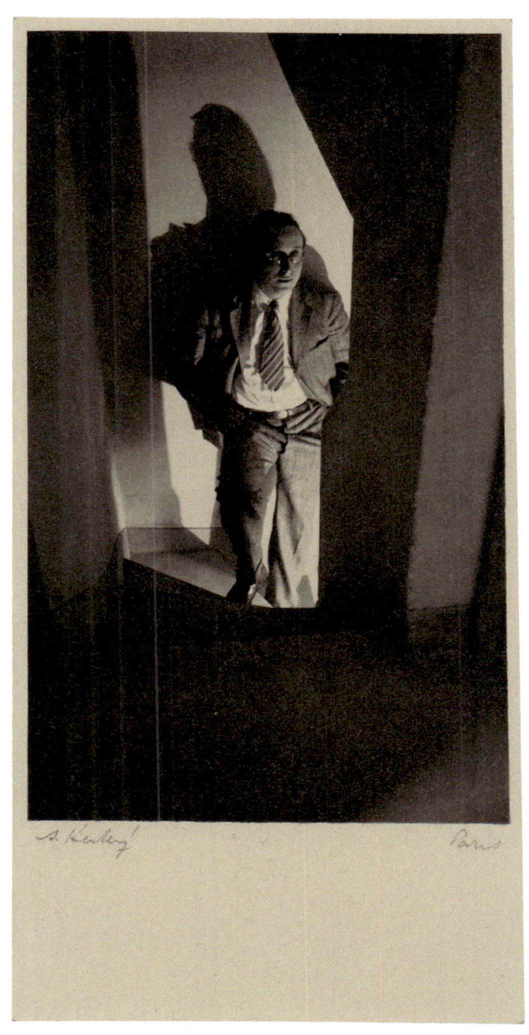
A. Kertész
Paris

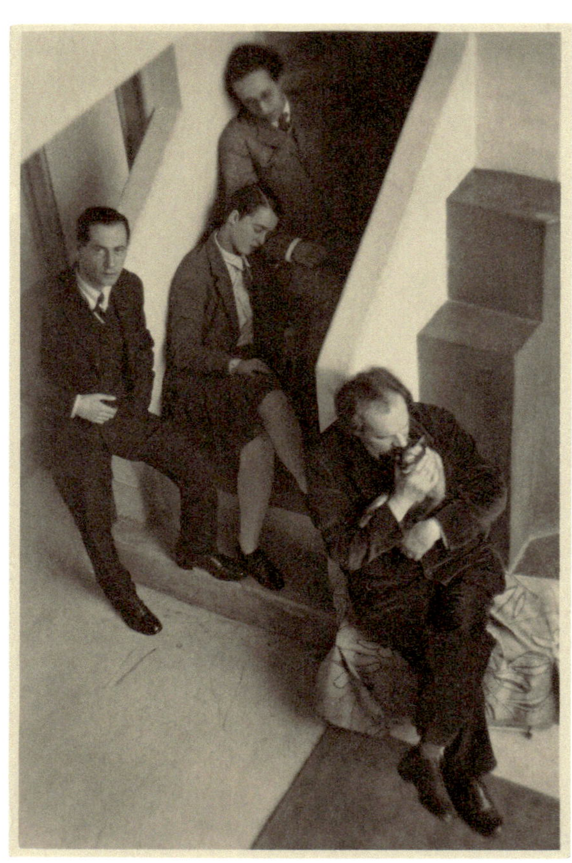

    Cat. 34   *Edwin and Peggy Rosskam, Jan Sliwinsky, and Friend*, 1927

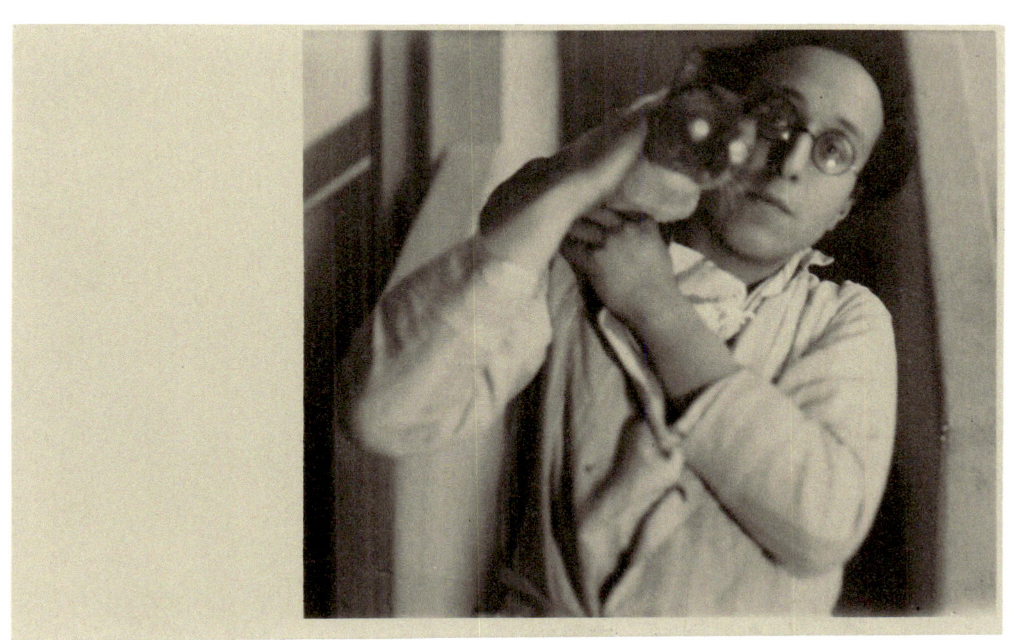

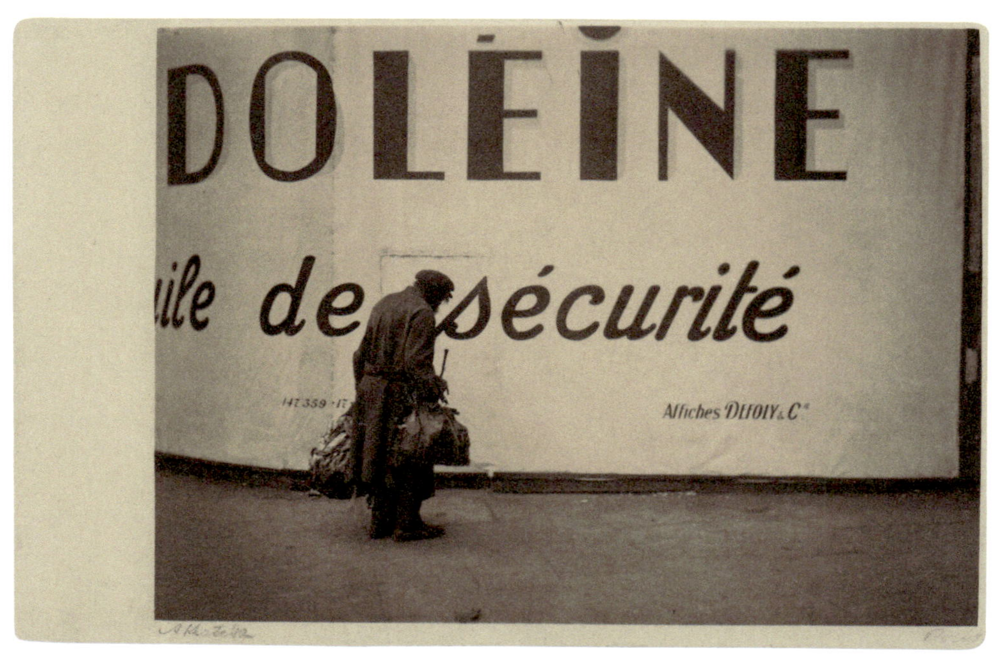

   Cat. 36   *"Sécurité,"* 1926–27

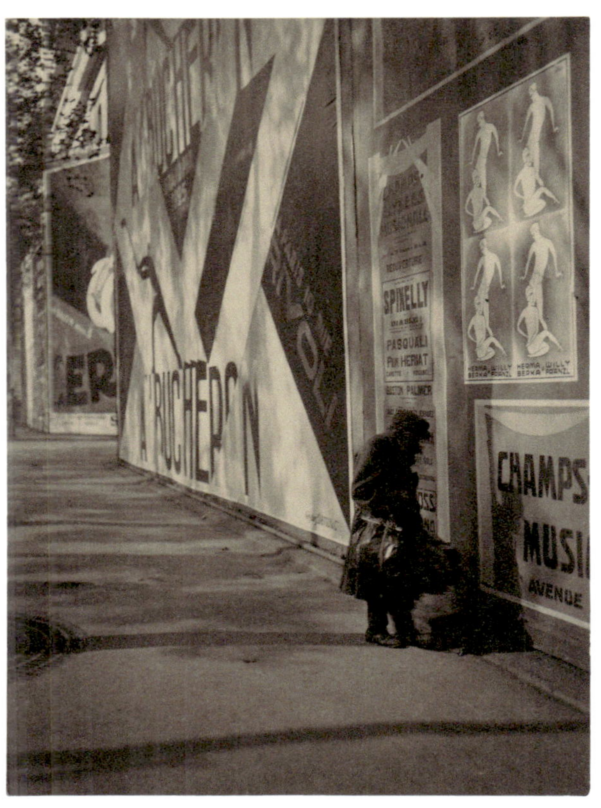
SPINELLY
PASQUALI
PUR HERMAT
BRUCHEPON
CHAMPS
MUSI
AVENUE

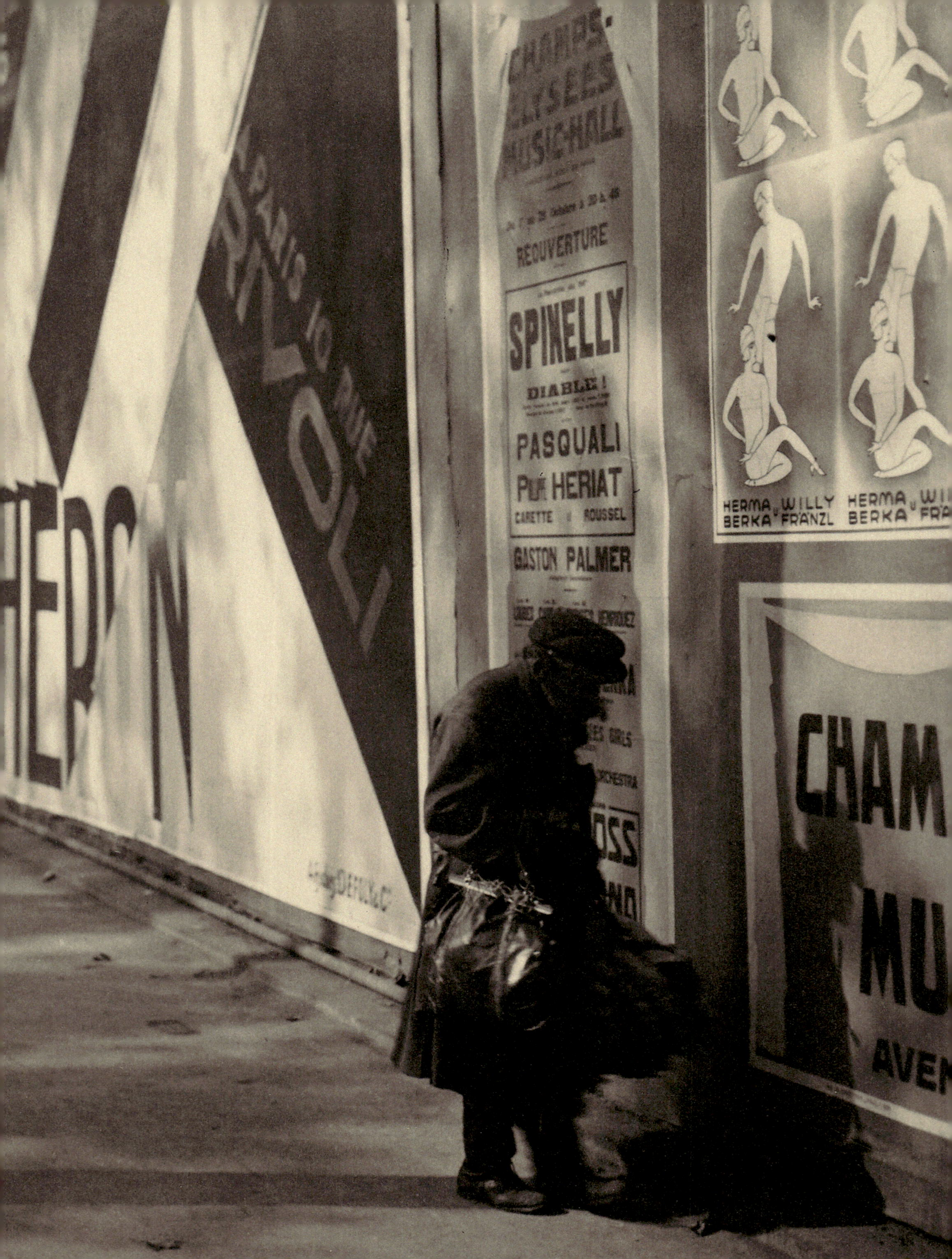

CHAMPS-
ELYSEES
MUSIC-HALL
REOUVERTURE
SPINELLY
DIABLE !
PASQUALI
Pie HERIAT
CARETTE ROUSSEL
GASTON PALMER
PARIS 10 RUE
HERMA u WILLY
BERKA FRÄNZL
HERMA u WILL
BERKA FRÄN
CHAM
MU
AVEN

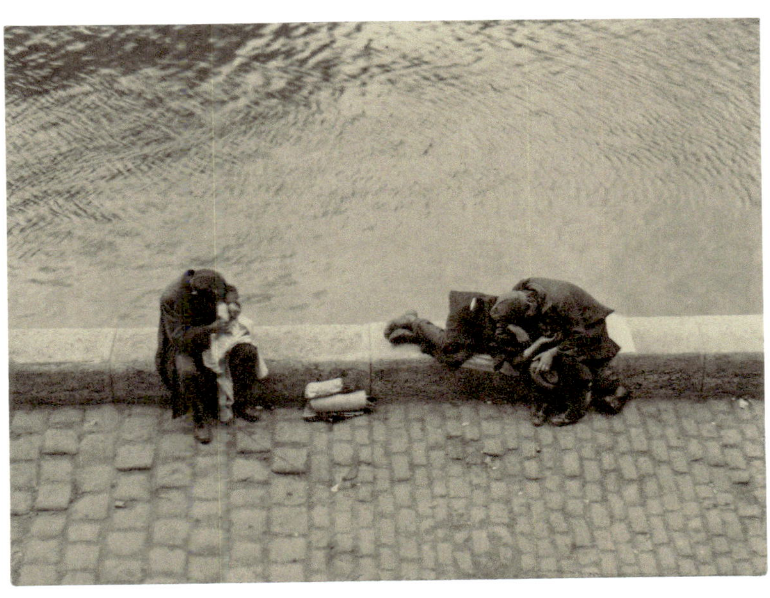

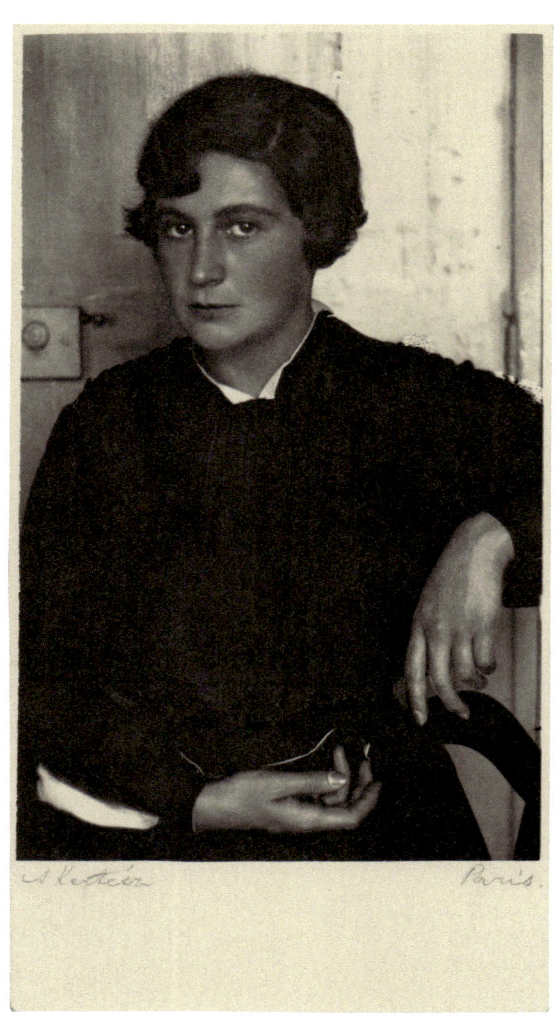

  Cat. 39 *Unidentified Sitter (Young German Doctor)*, 1926–27

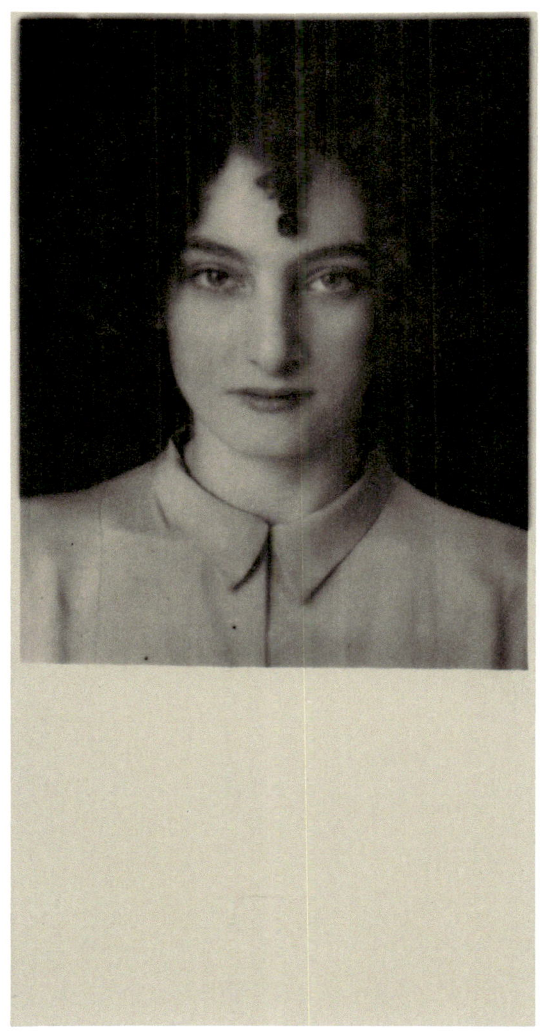

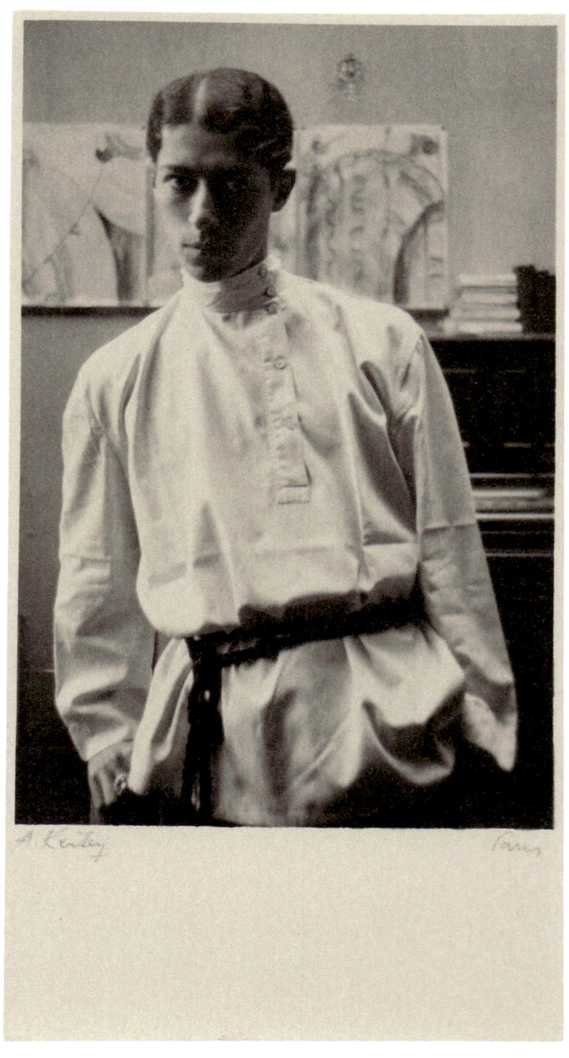

  Cat. 41 *Unidentified Sitter (Young Yugoslav Bibliophile)*, 1926–27

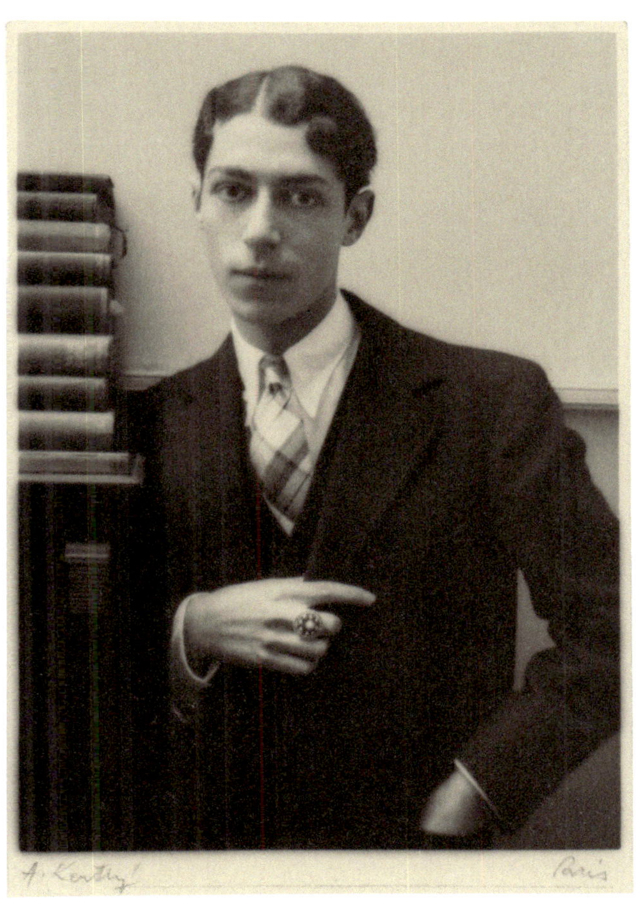

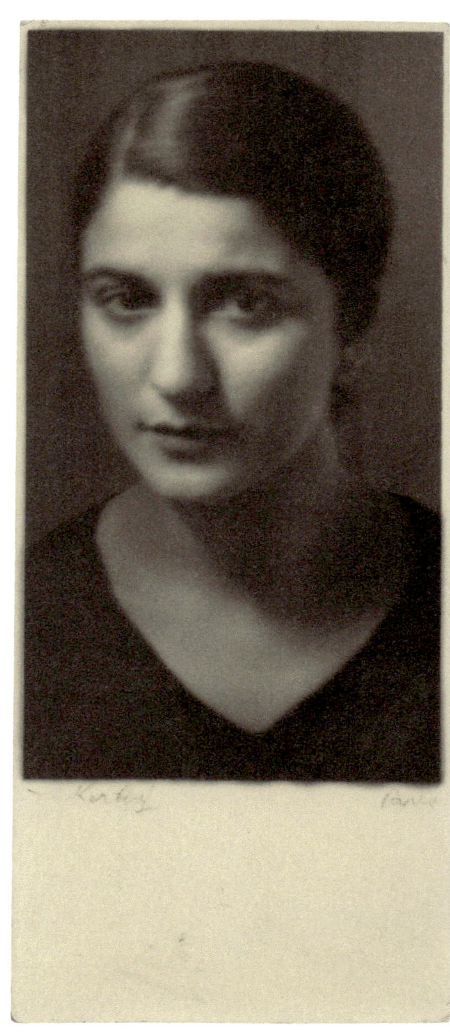

  Cat. 43 *Anita de Caro,* 1927

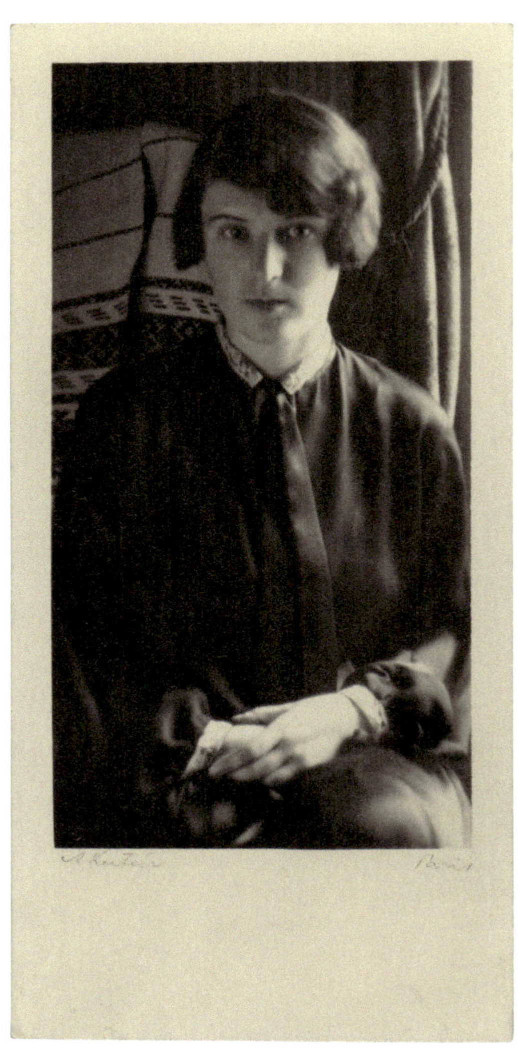

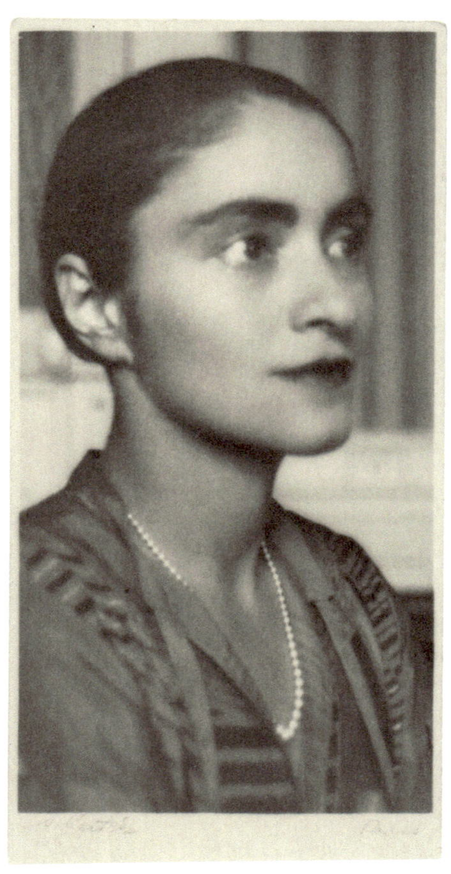

 Cat. 45 *Mrs. Wheeler,* 1928

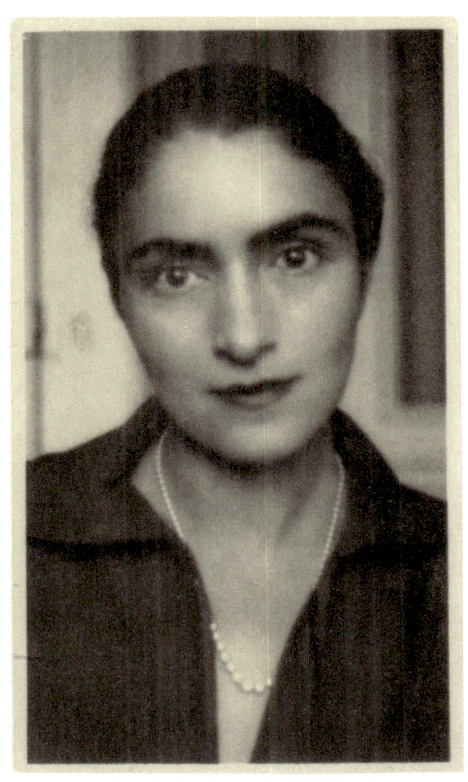

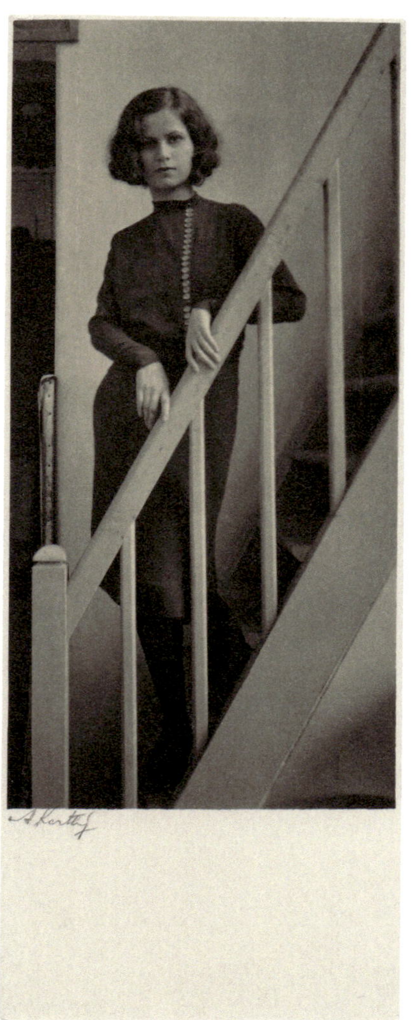

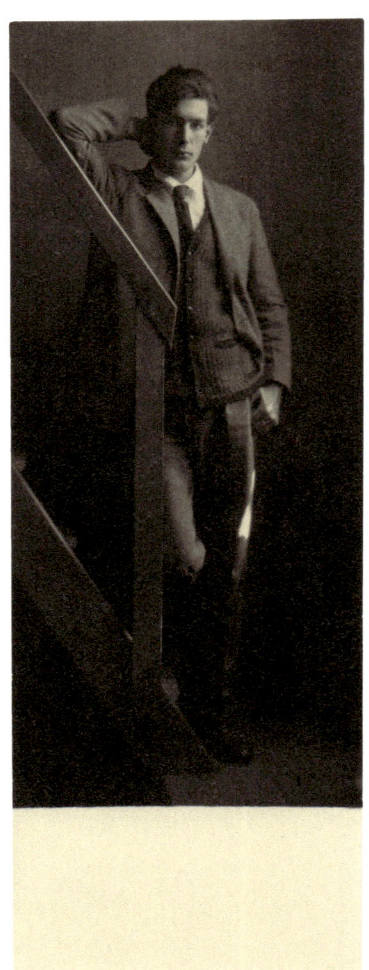

 Cat. 47 *Mr. Morgan, 1926–27* | Cat. 48 *Unidentified Sitter (Yugoslav Ballet Dancer), 1926–27*

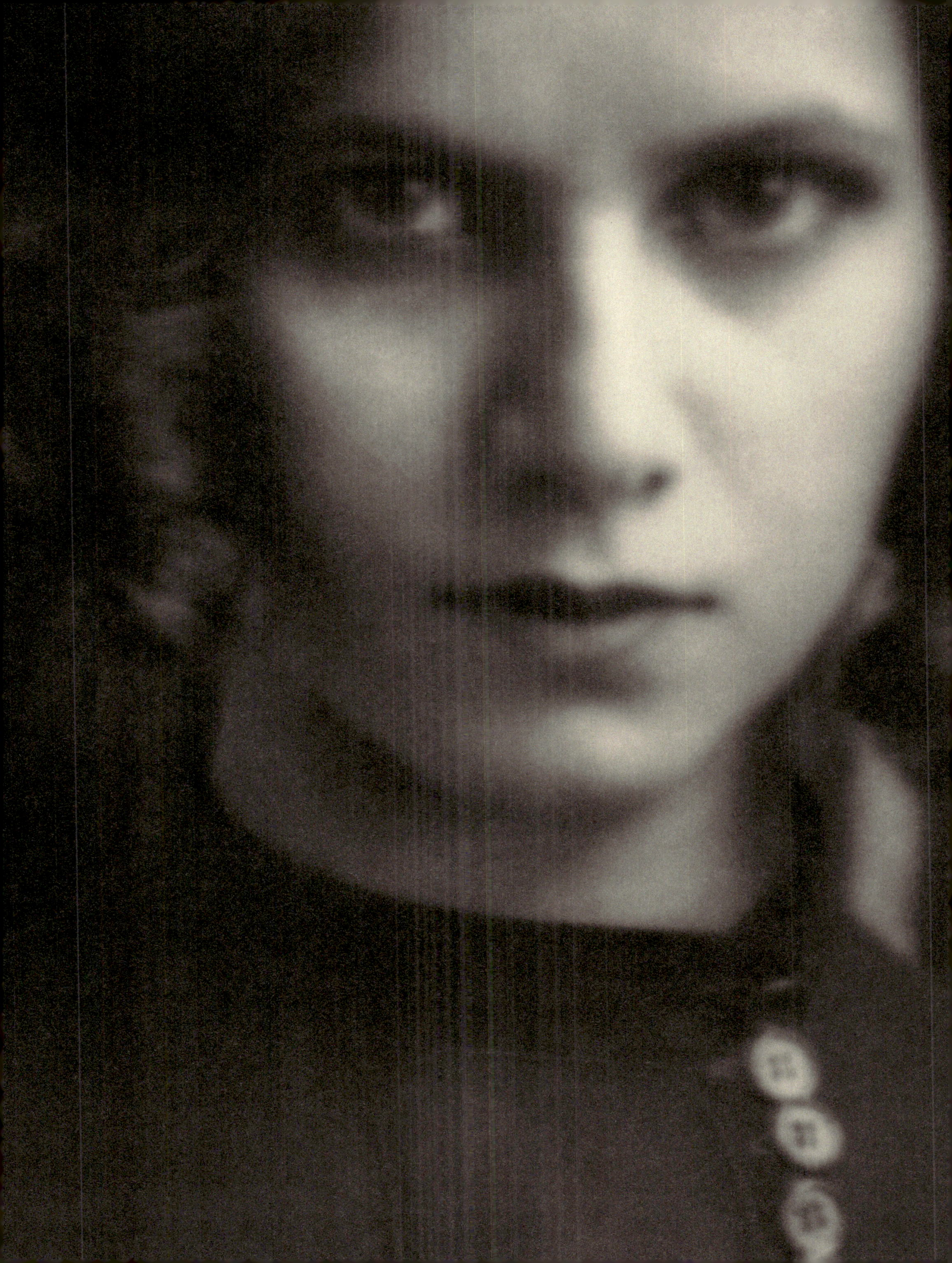

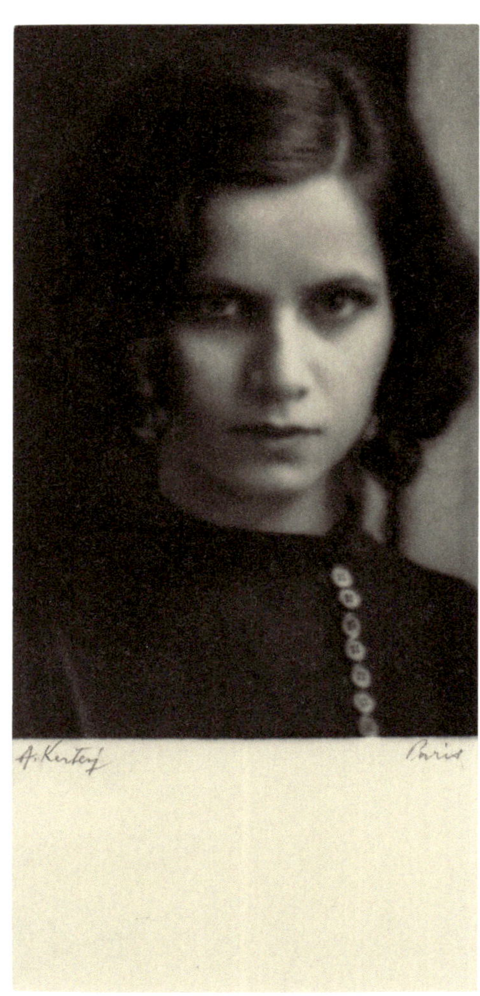

　　Cat. 49　*Unidentified Sitter (Yugoslav Ballet Dancer)*, 1926–27

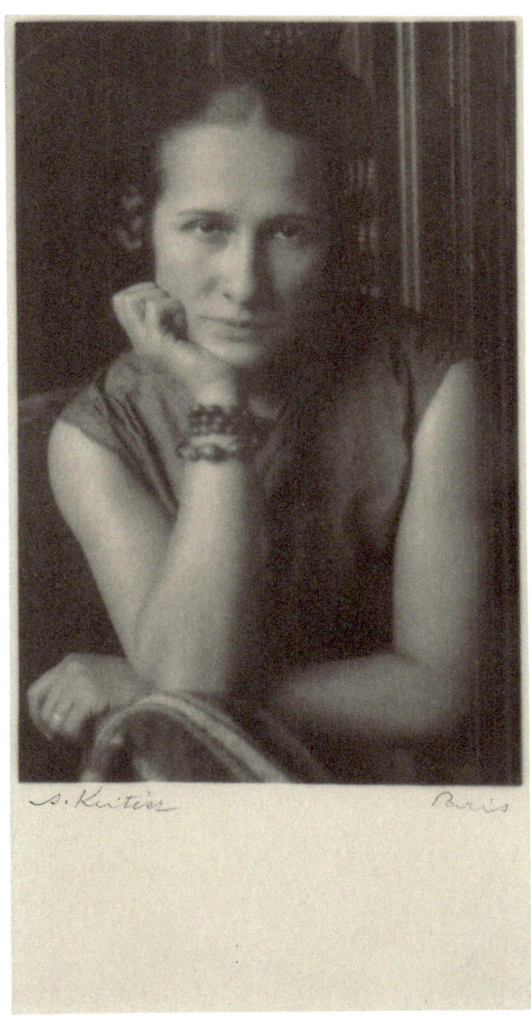

Cat. 50 *Madame Perret, 1927* **119**

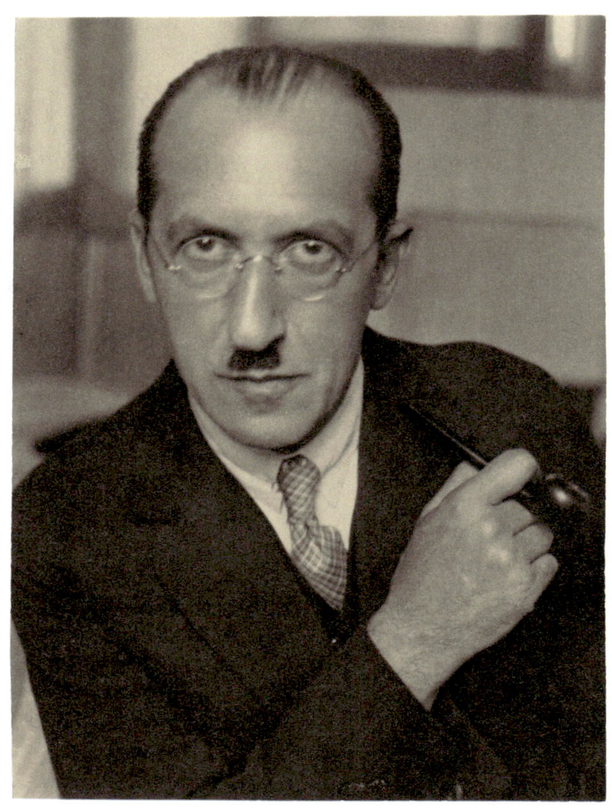

   Cat. 51 *Piet Mondrian*, 1926

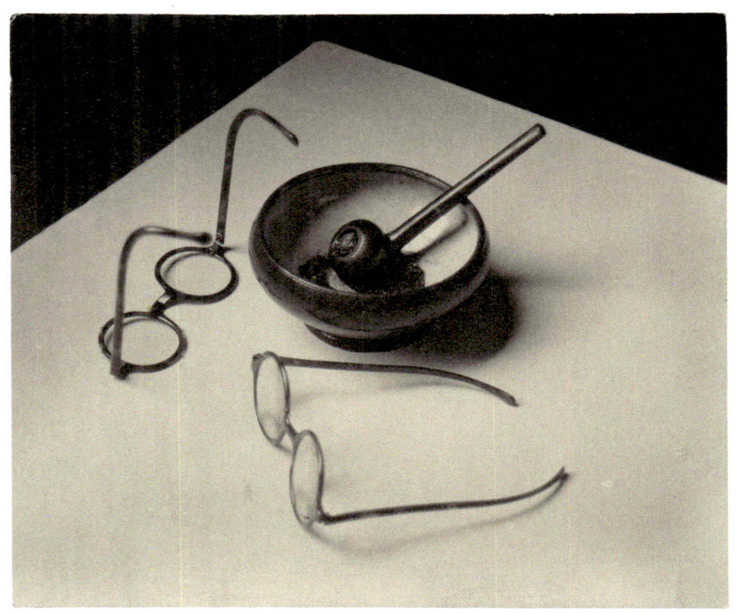

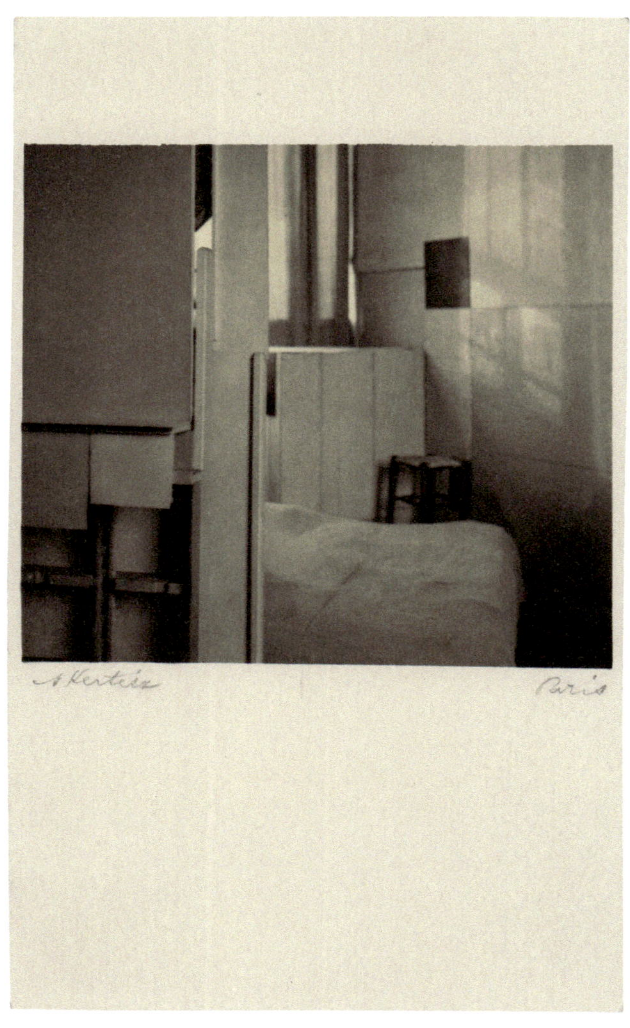

   Cat. 53 *Mondrian's Studio*, 1926

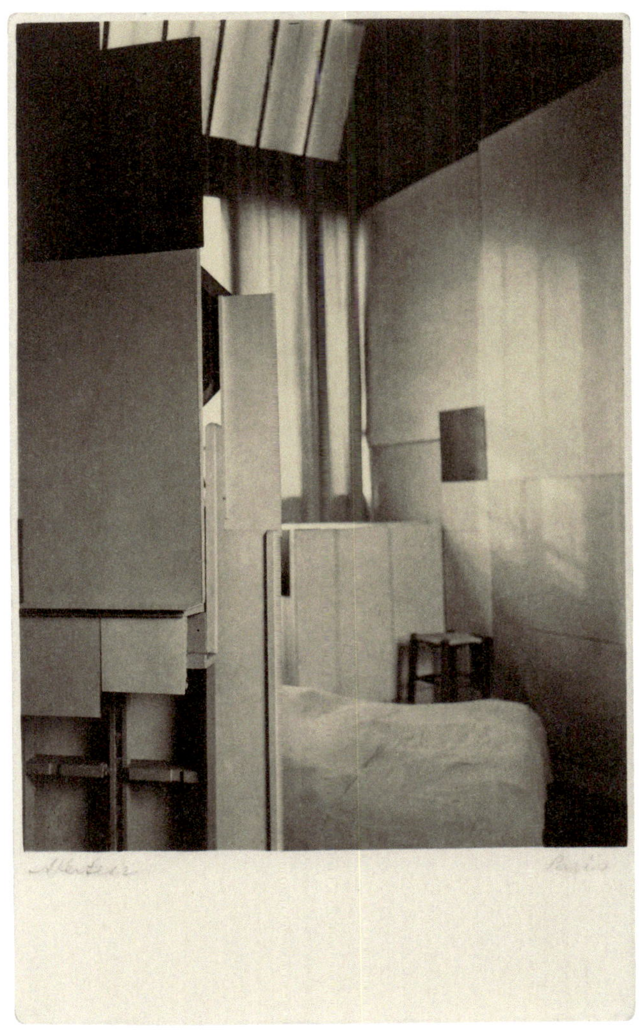

Cat. 54 *Mondrian's Studio*, 1926   **123**

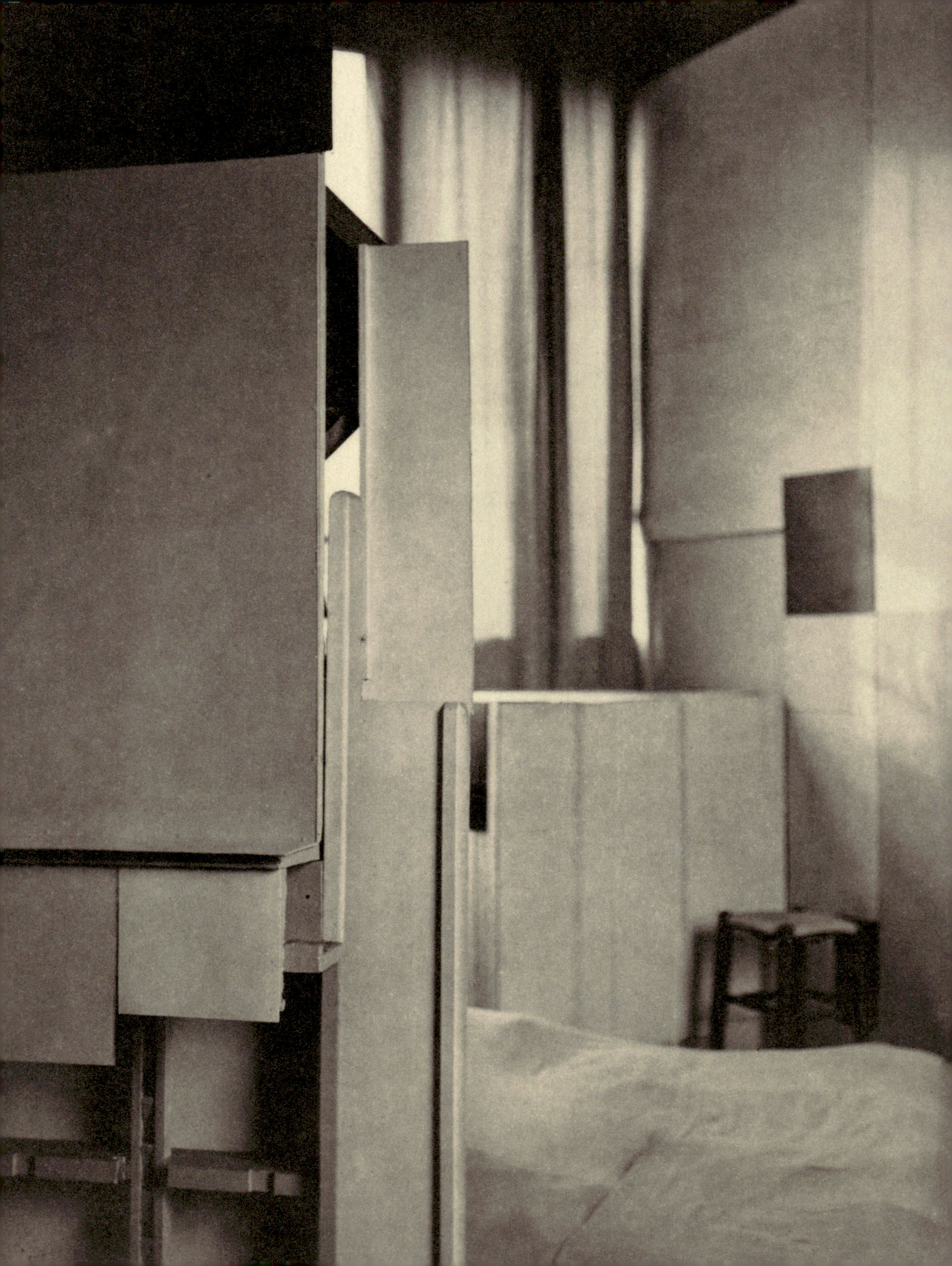

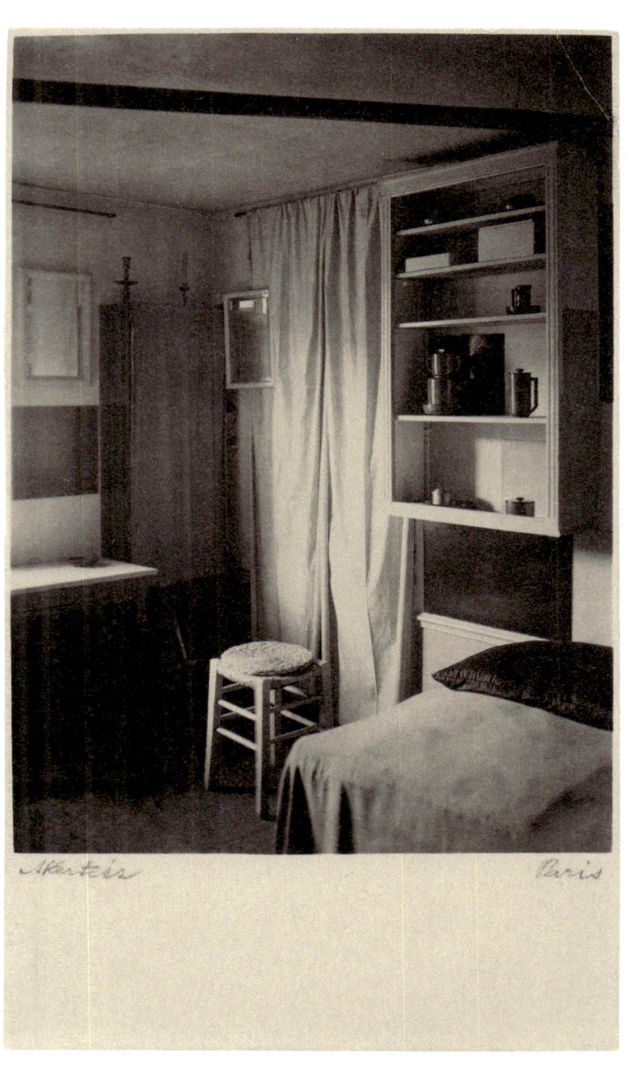

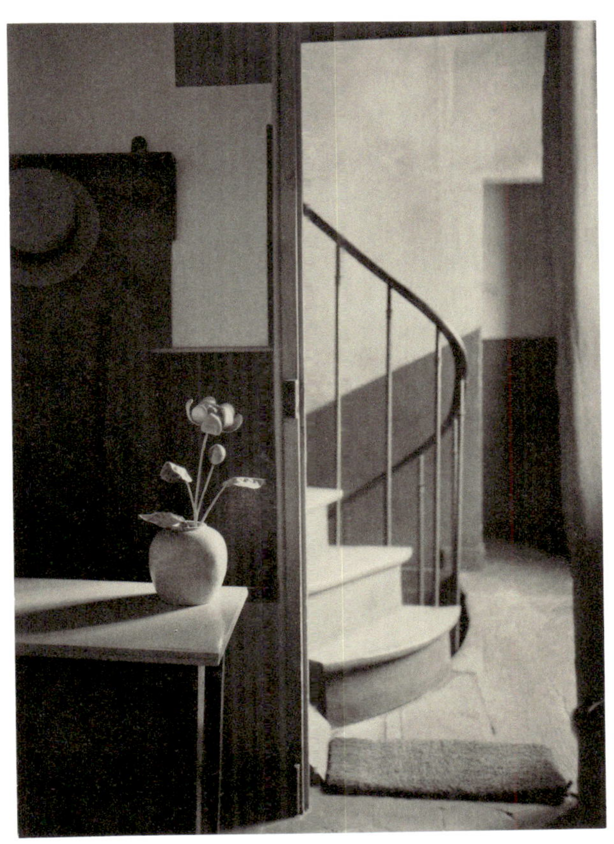

Cat. 56 *Chez Mondrian*, 1926

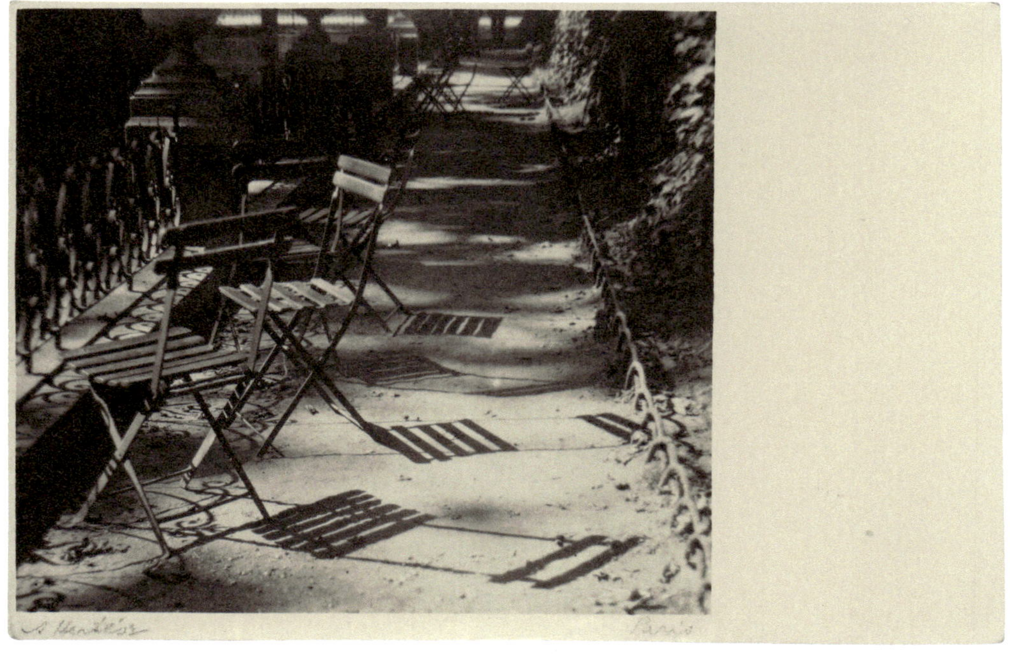

   Cat. 57 *Chairs at the Medici Fountain, Jardin du Luxembourg, 1925*

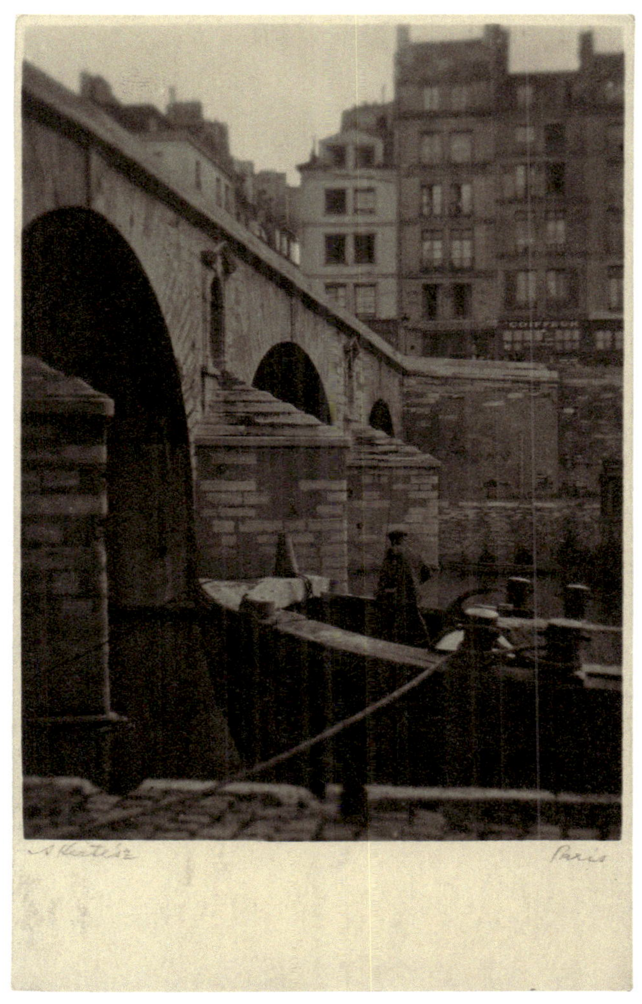

A Kertész
Paris

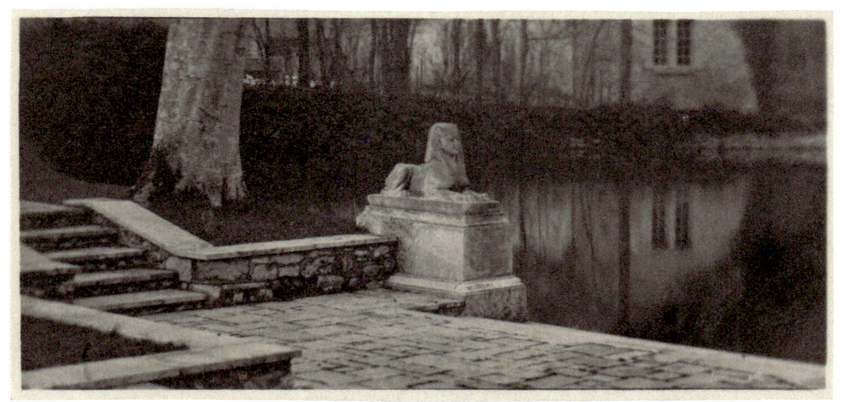

   Cat. 59   *Château de Sainte-Mesme*, 1926

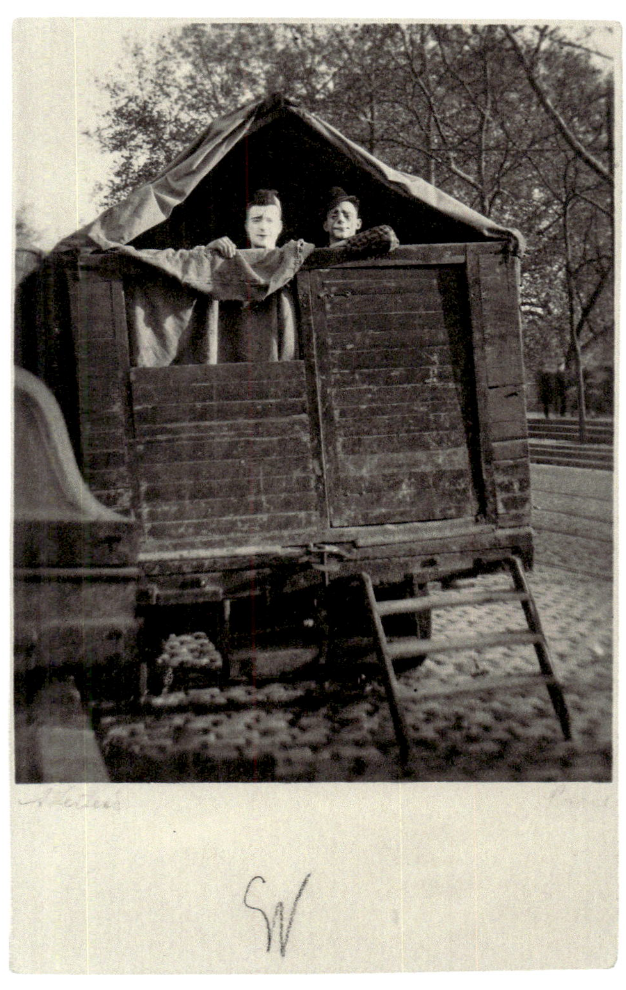

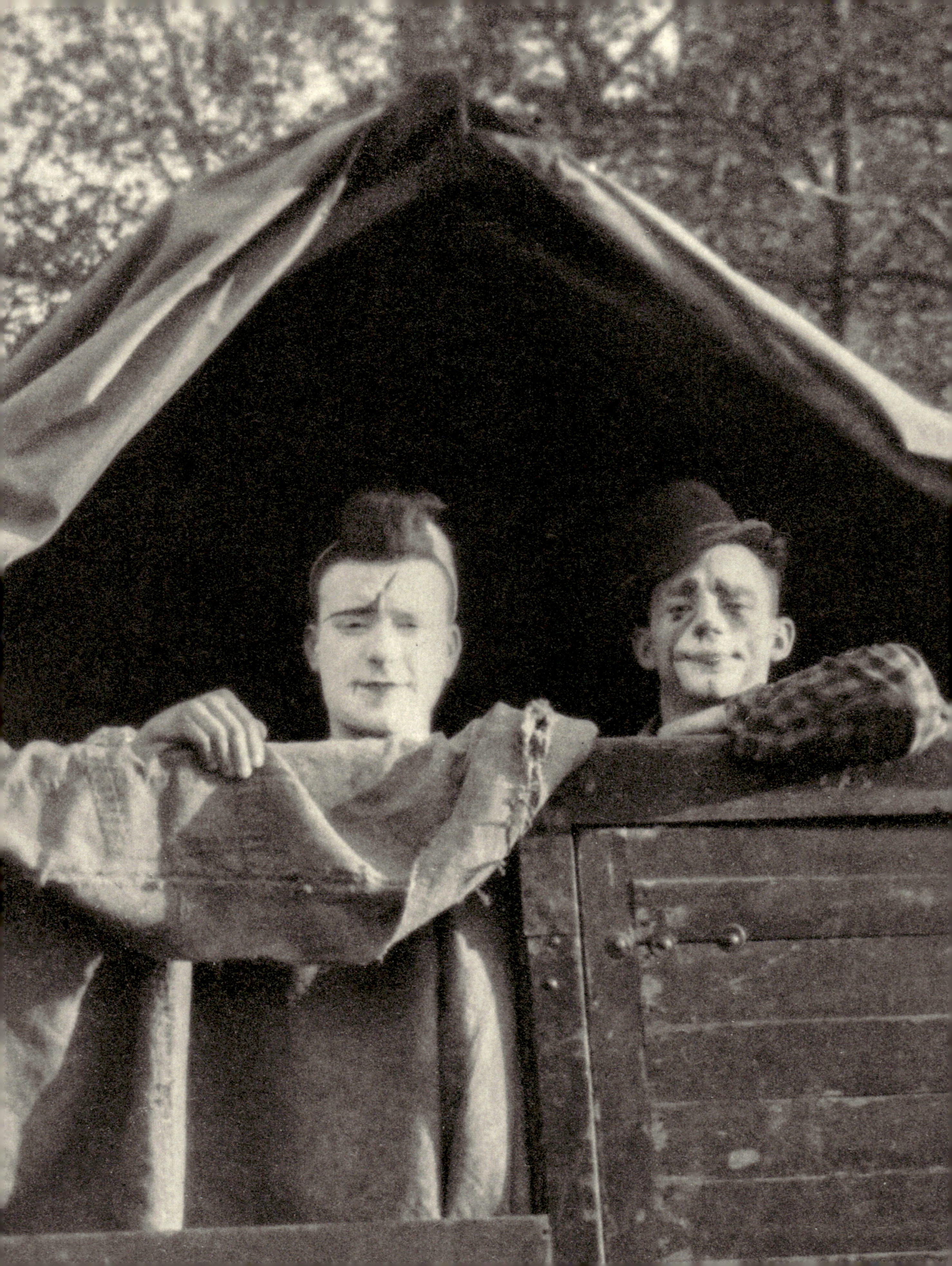

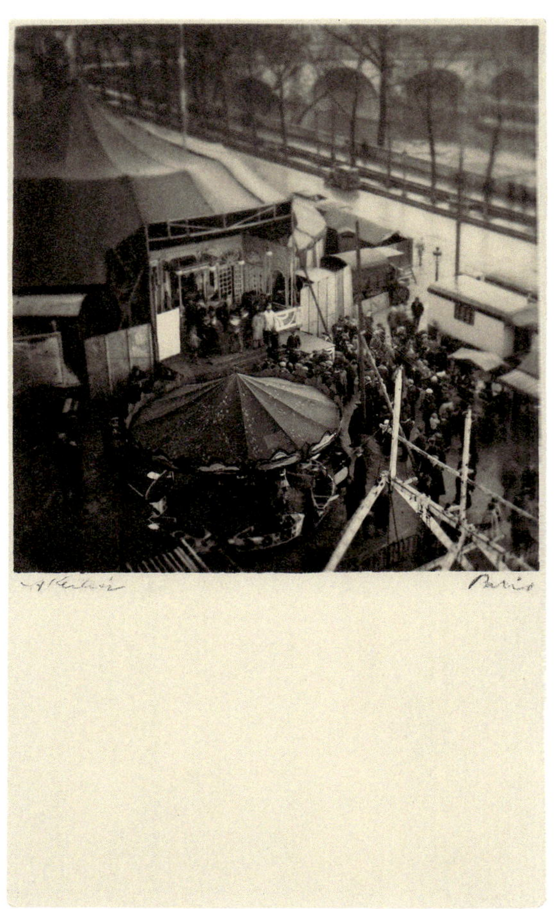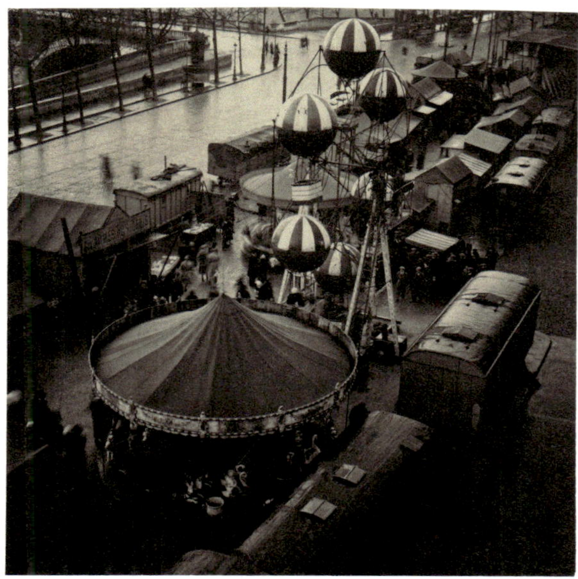

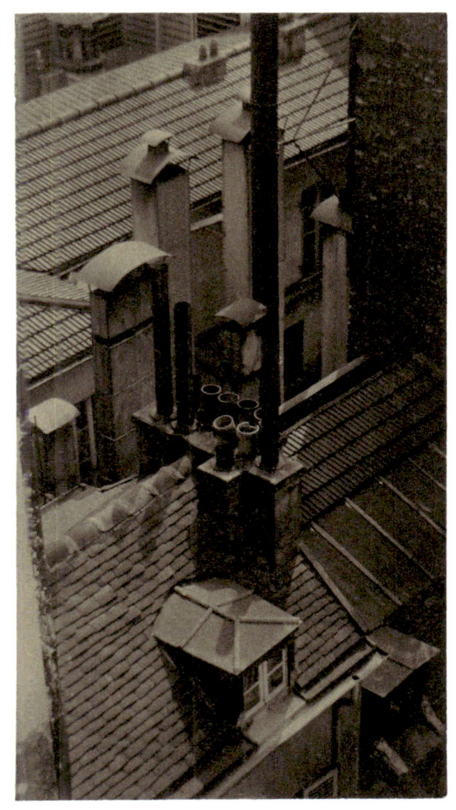

Cat. 63 *Rooftops and Chimneys*, 1927   **135**

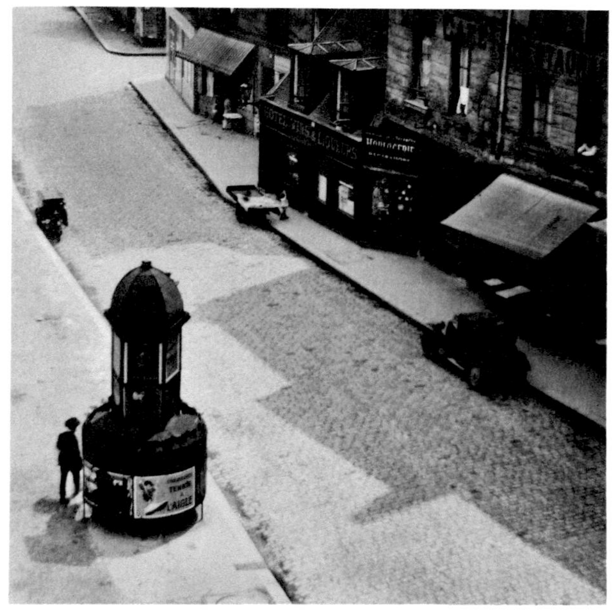

    Cat. 64   *Latin Quarter*, 1927

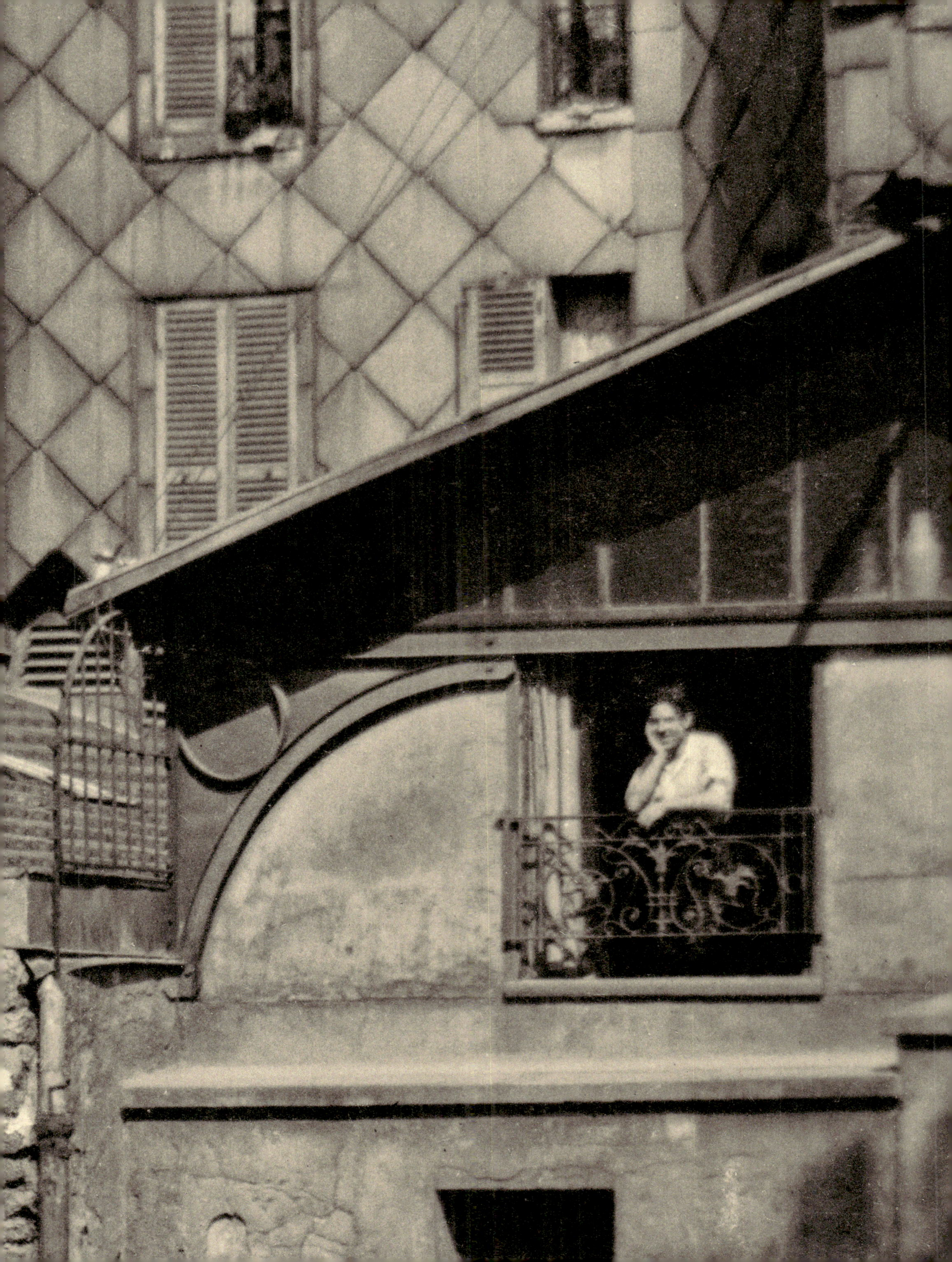

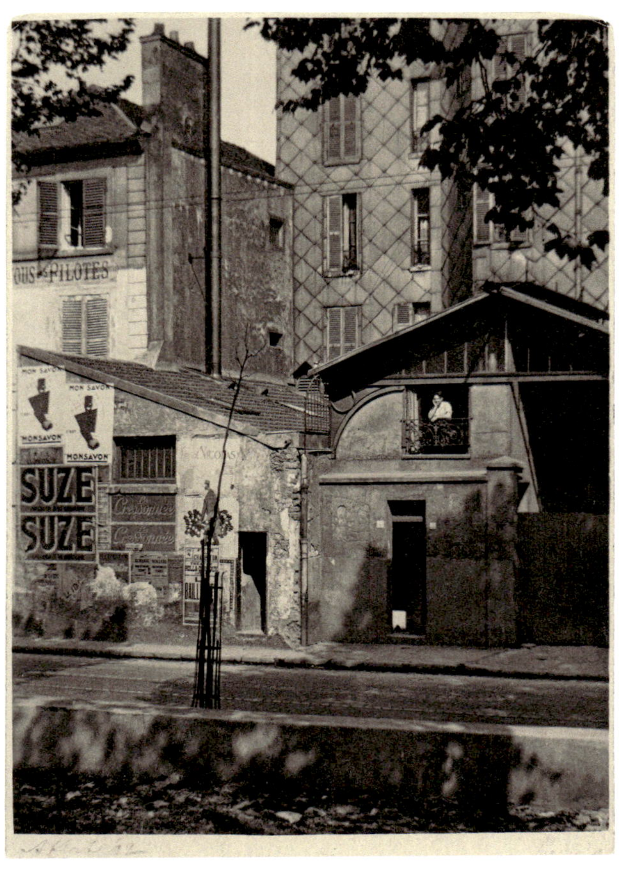

 Cat. 65   *Josep Llorens Artigas, 1926–28*

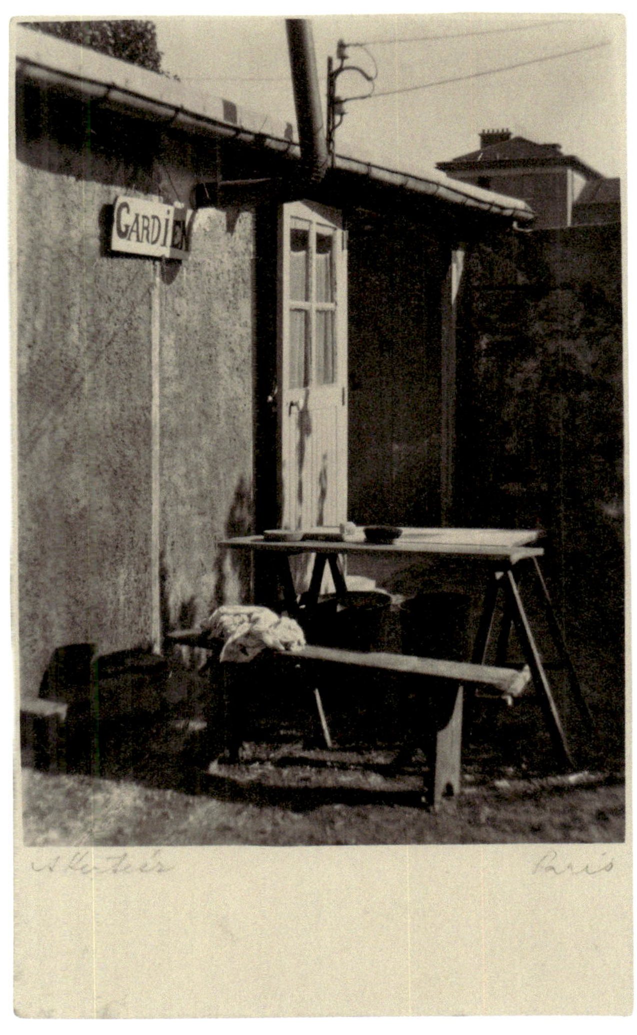

GARDIEN

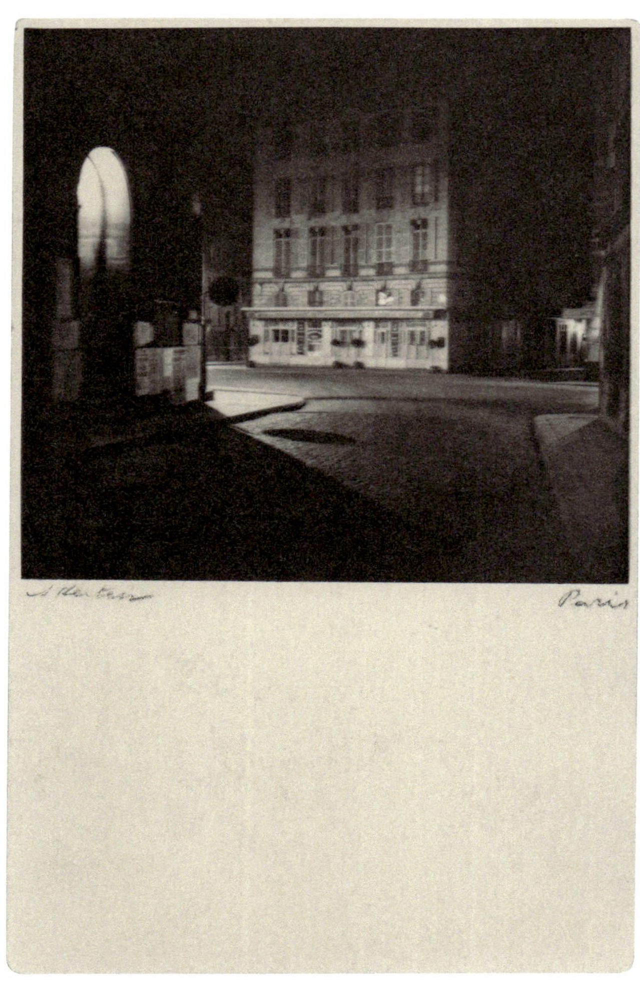

  Cat. 67 *Théâtre Odéon, 1925–28*

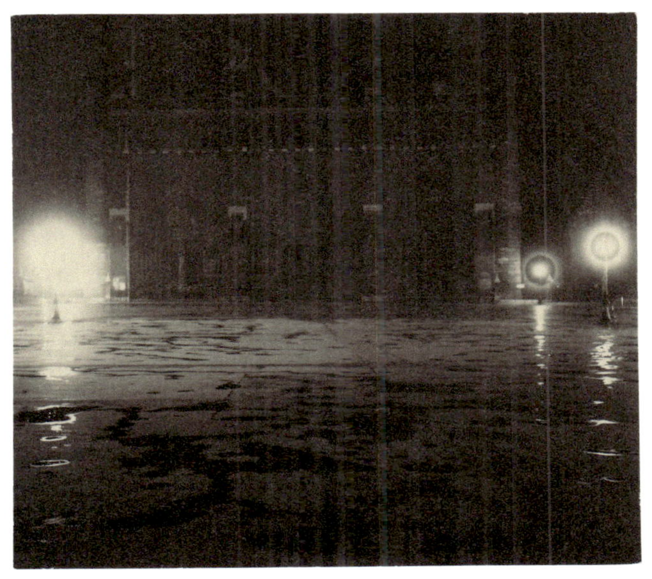

Cat. 68 *Notre-Dame at Night*, 1925

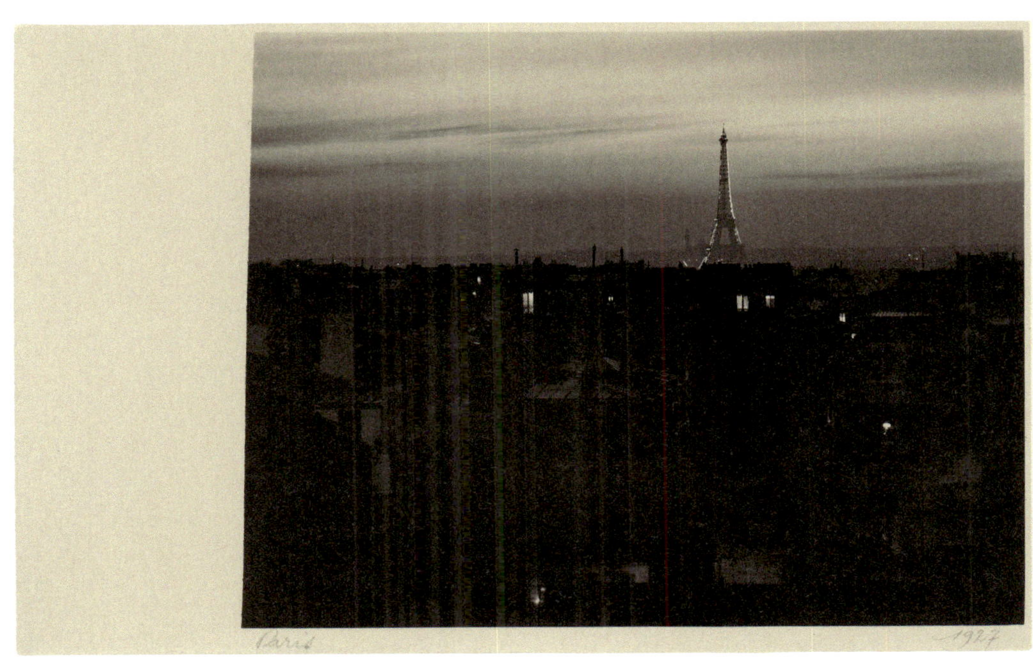

Paris
1927

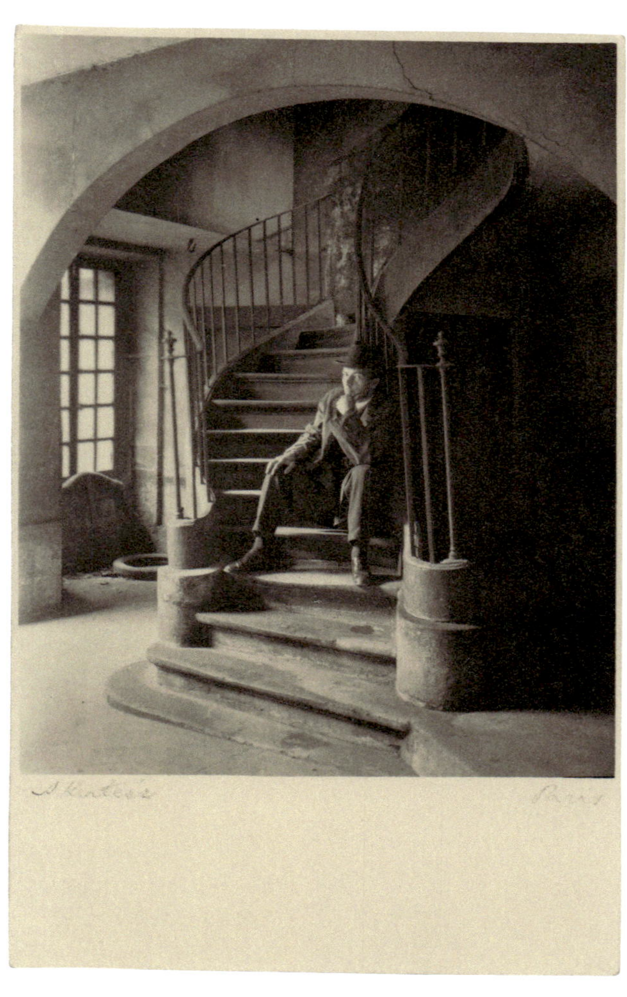

   Cat. 70   *Unidentified Sitter* (*Hungarian Woodcutter and Graphic Designer*), 1927

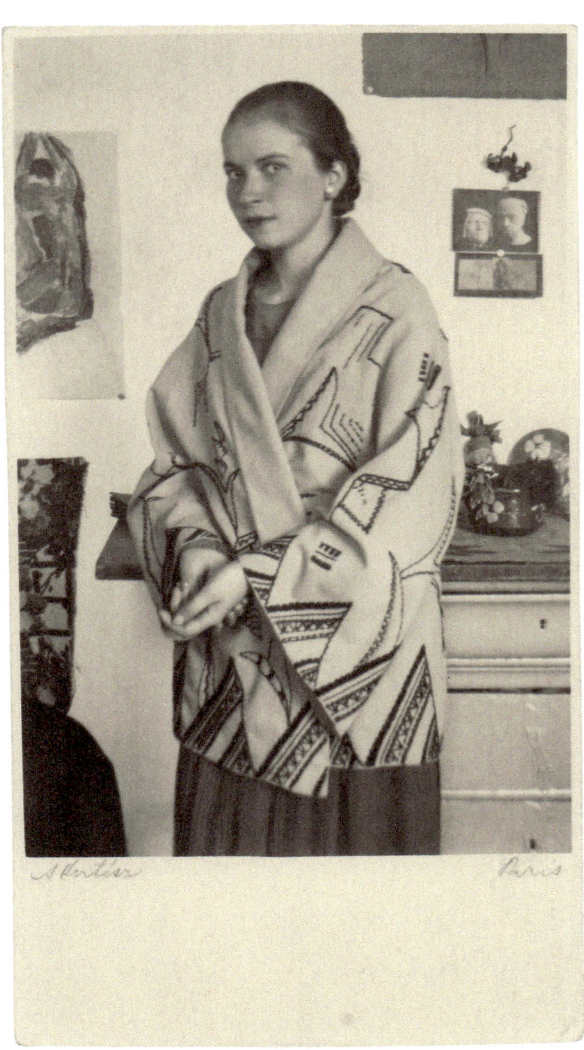

Cat 71 *Gundvor Berg in Her Studio*, August 1926   **145**

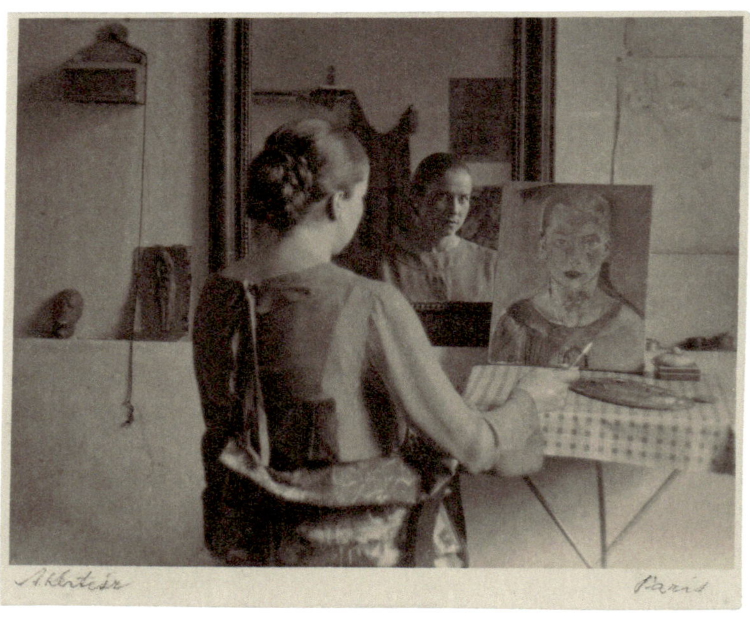

   Cat. 72 *Gundvor Berg*, 1926

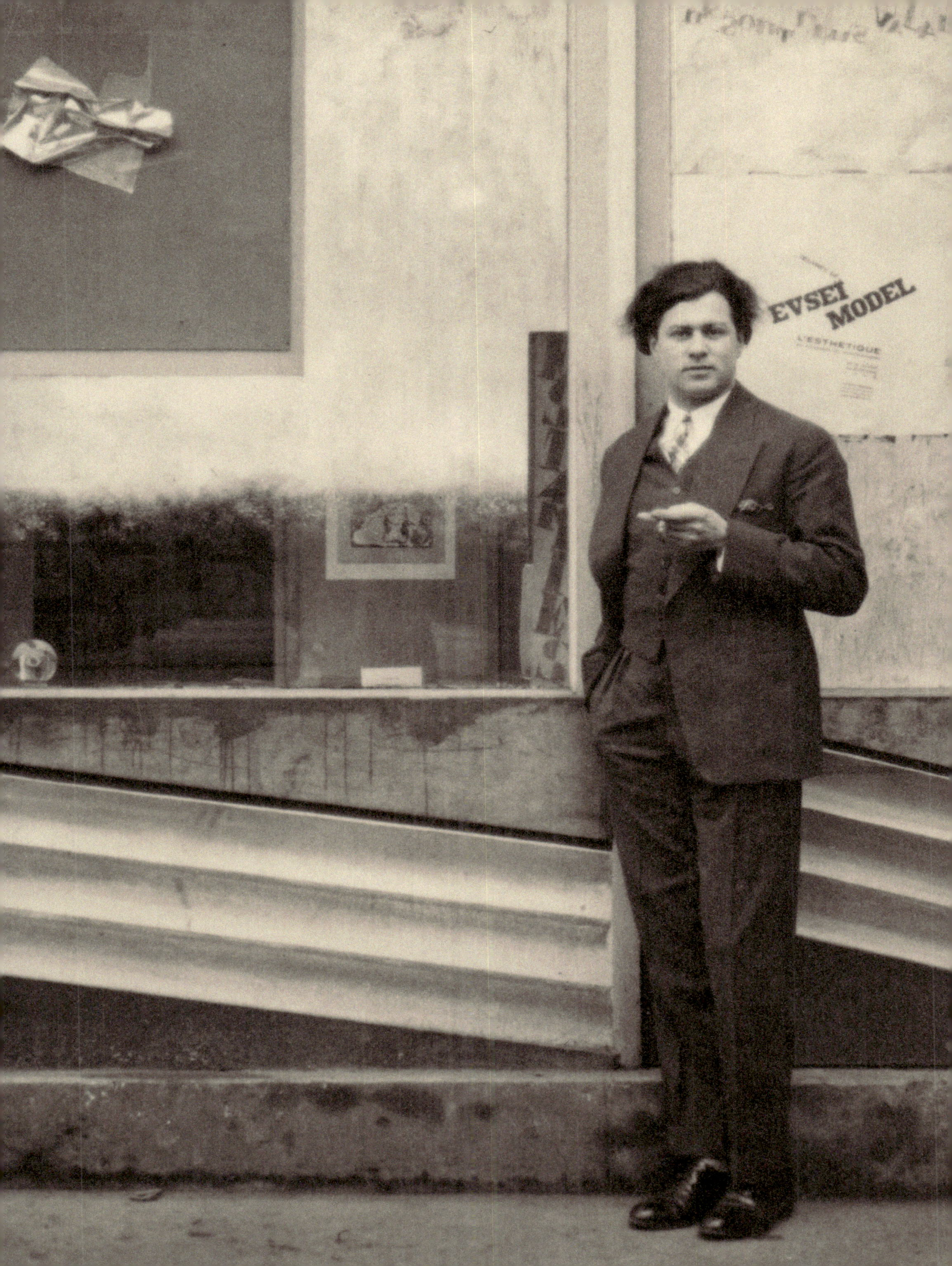
EVSEI
MODEL
L'ESTHETIQUE

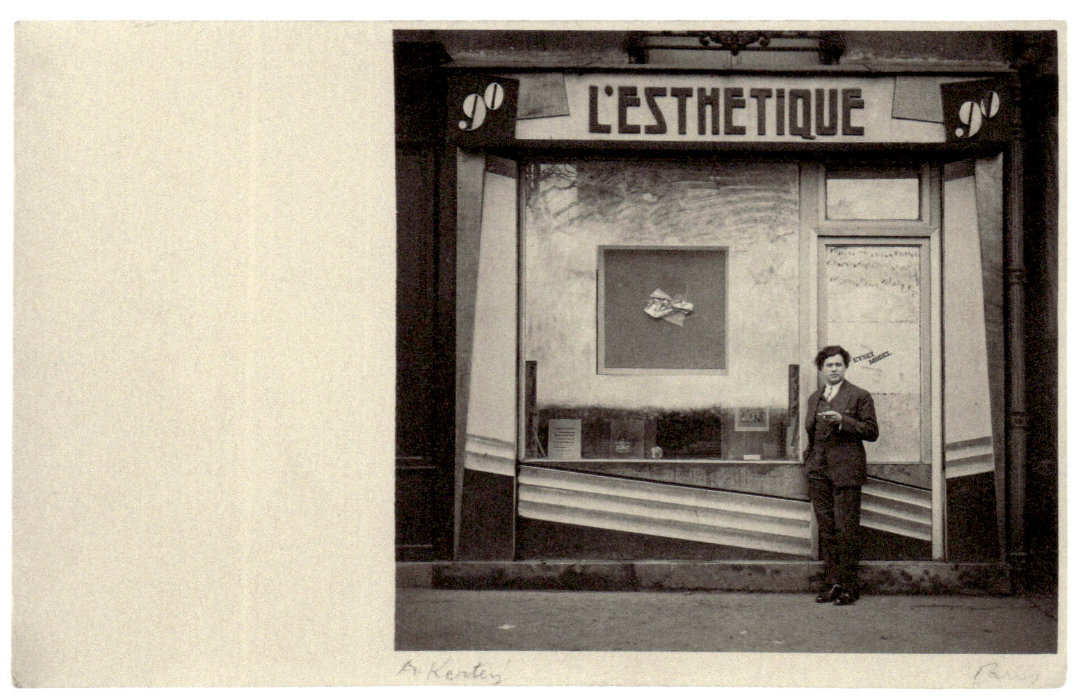

 Cat. 73 *Evsa Model in Front of L'Esthétique,* 1927

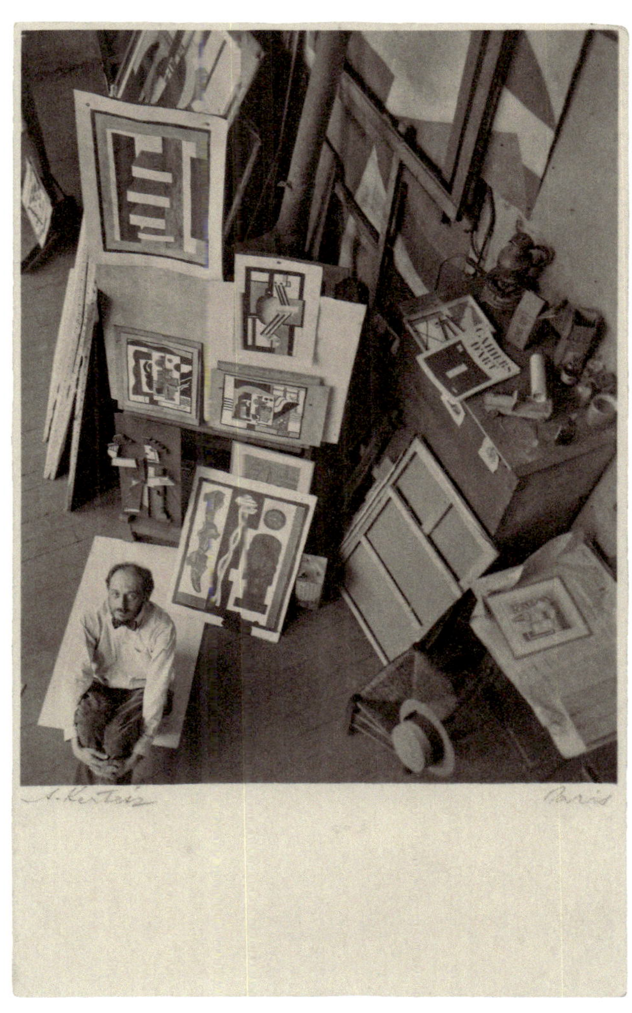

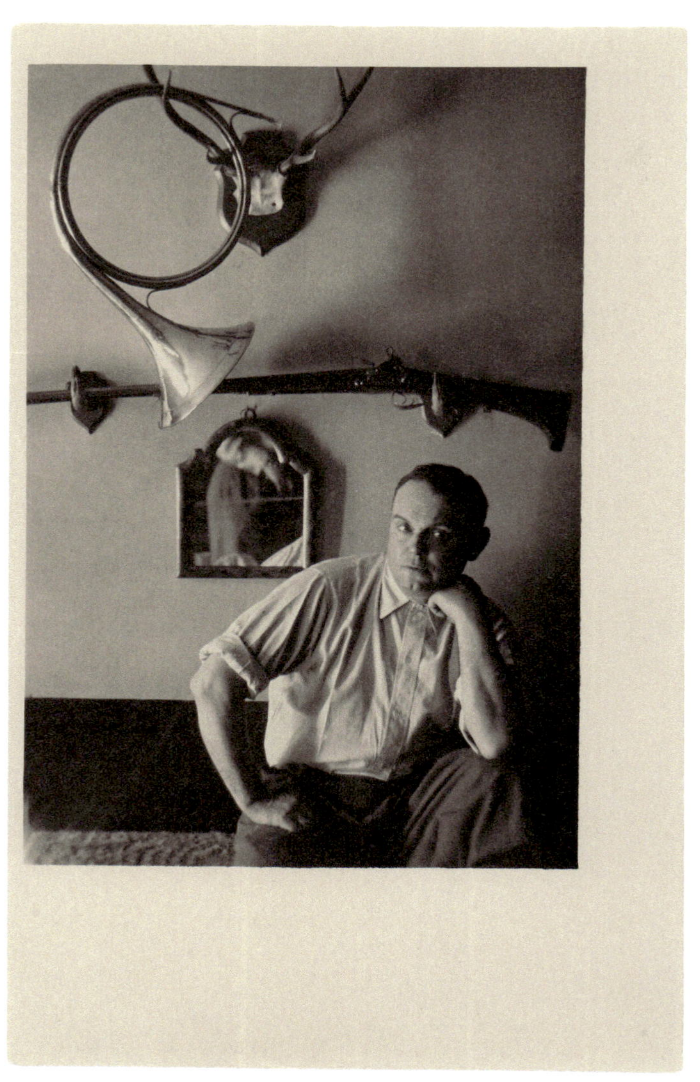

  Cat. 75 *Pierre Mac Orlan, 1928*

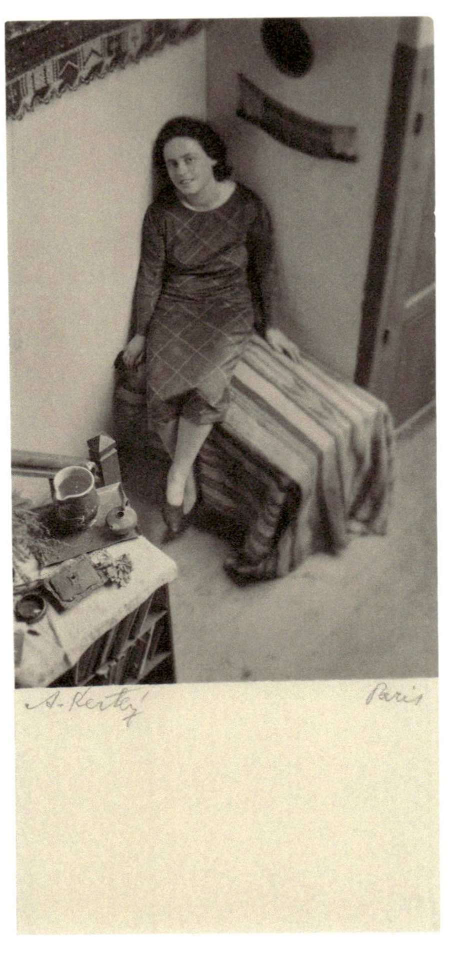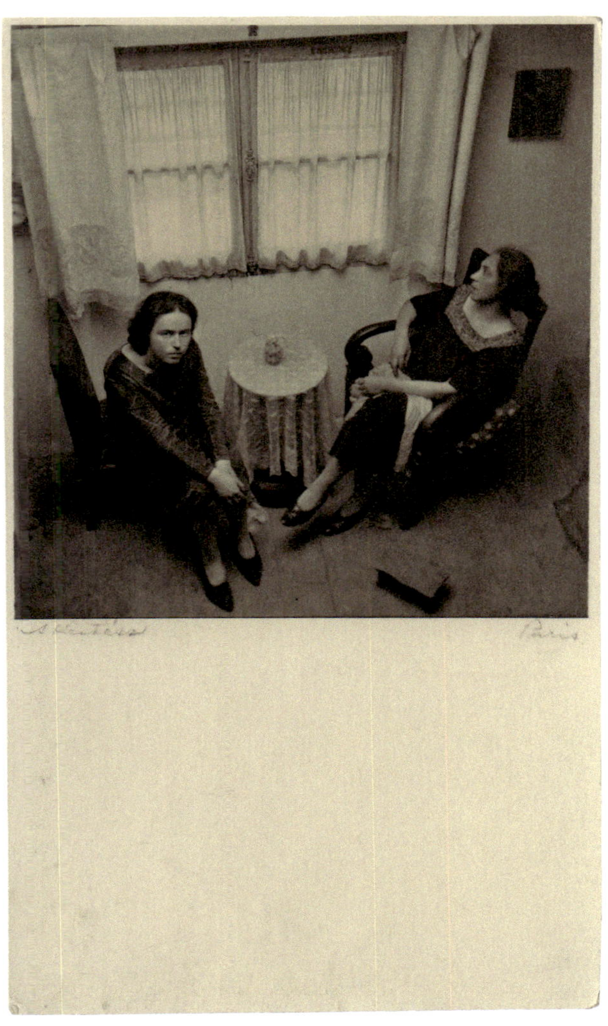

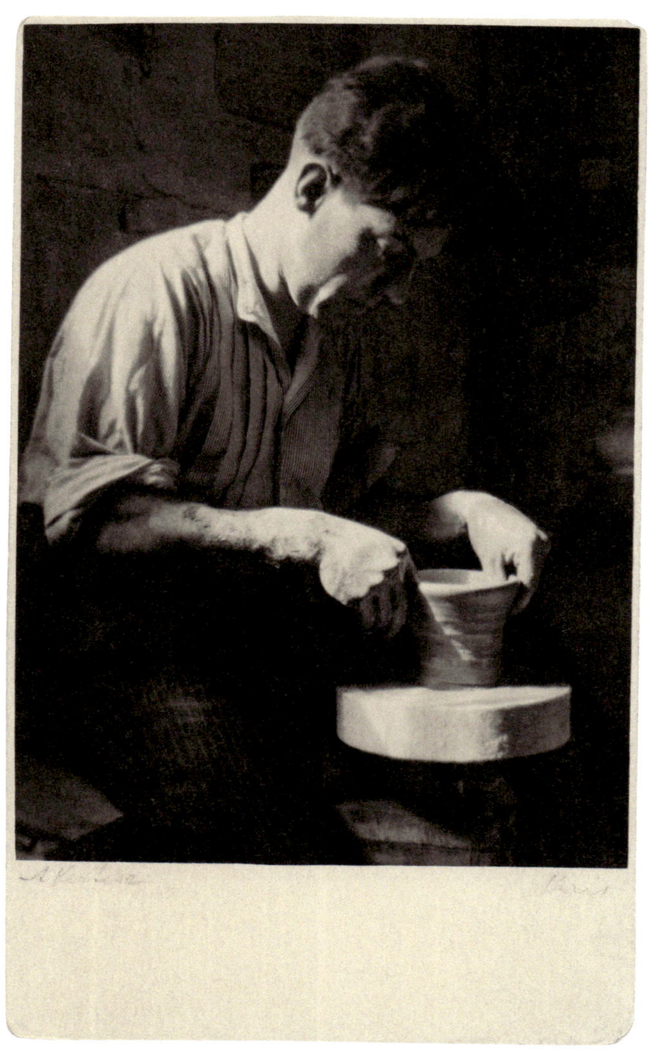

  Cat. 78 *Josep Llorens Artigas,* 1927

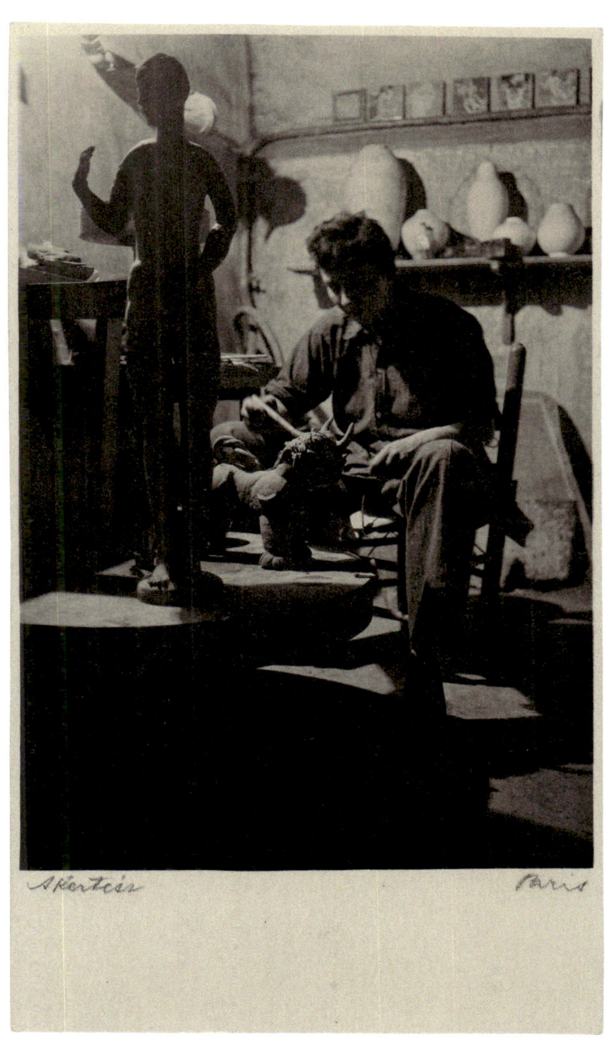

Cat. 79 *Vally Wiese'thier in Josep Llorens Artigas's Studio*, 1927   **153**

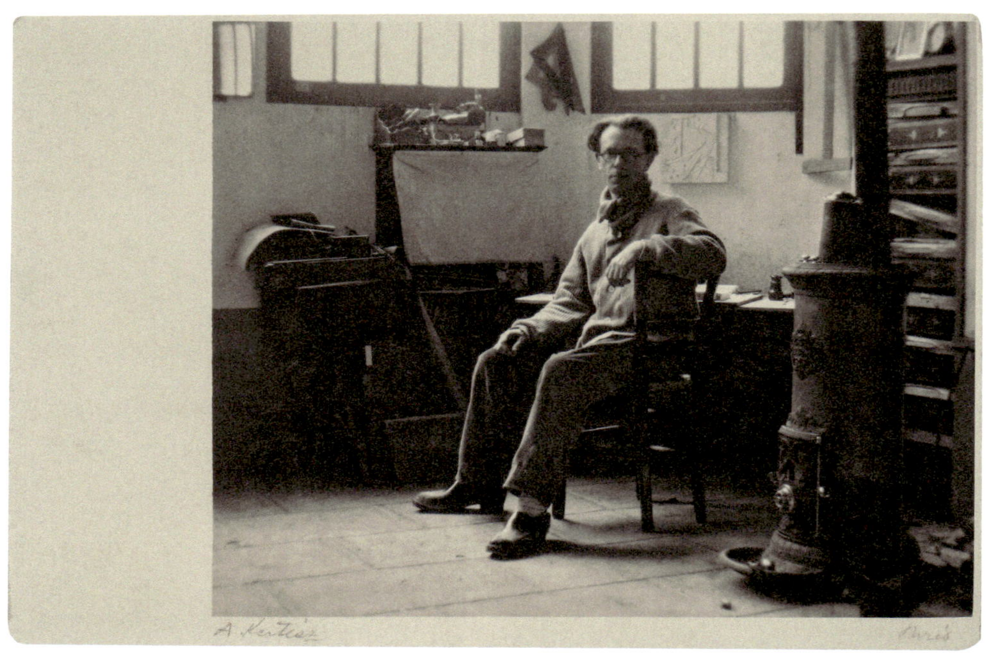

  Cat. 80 *Joseph Csáky*, 1926–28

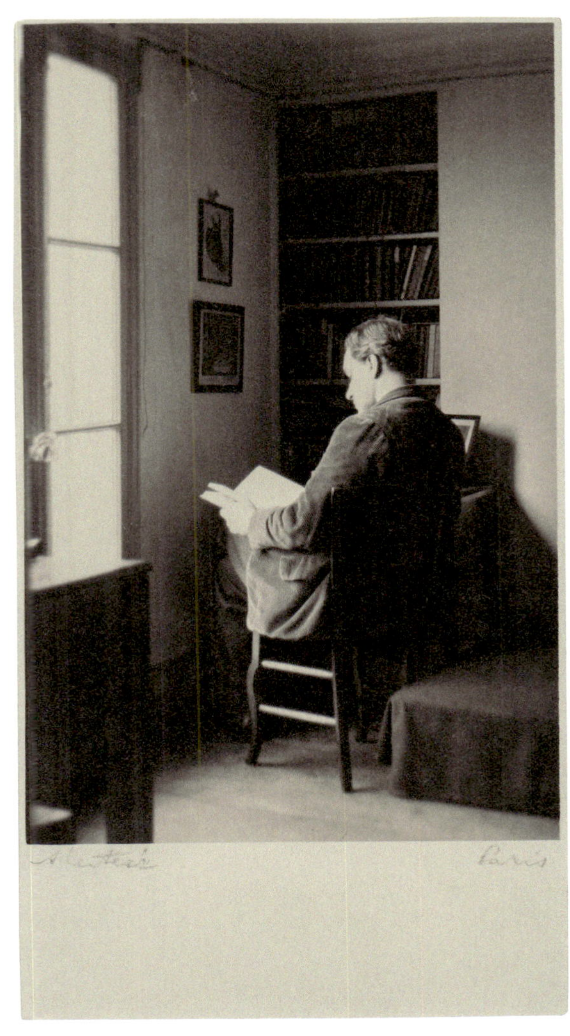

Cat. 81 *Jan Sliwinsky*, 1926–27   **155**

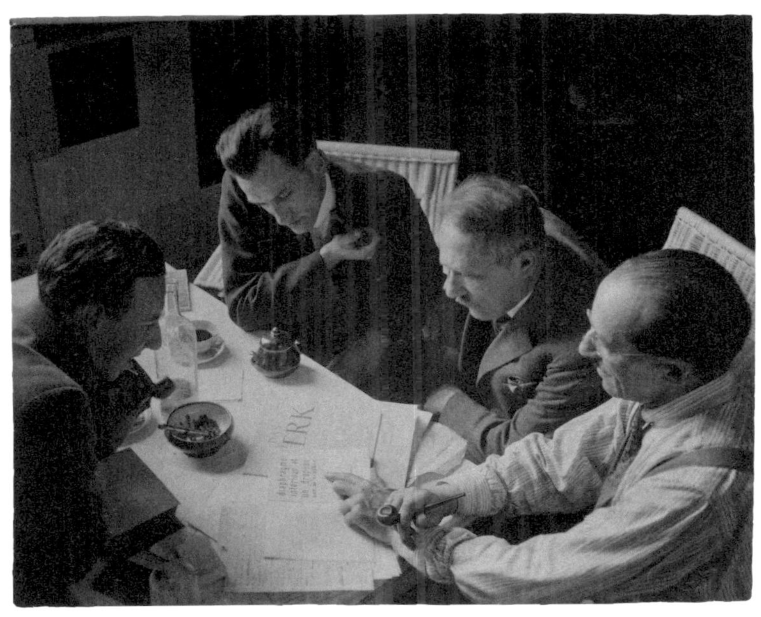

Cat. 82 *Michel Seuphor, Gyula Zilzer, a Dutch Constructivist, and Piet Mondrian in Mondrian's Studio*, 1926 **157**

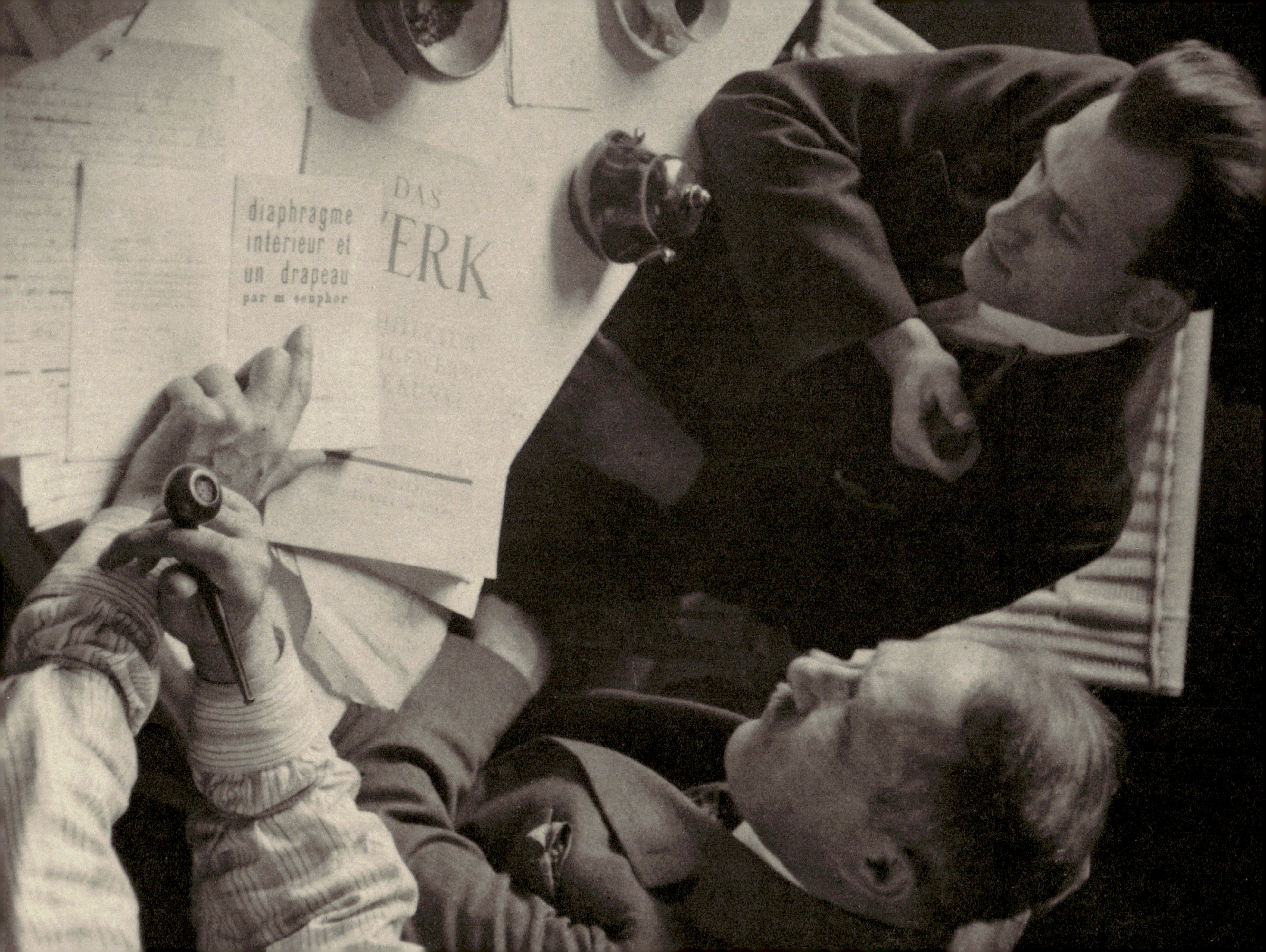
DAS 'ERK
diaphragme
intérieur et
un drapeau
par m. seuphor

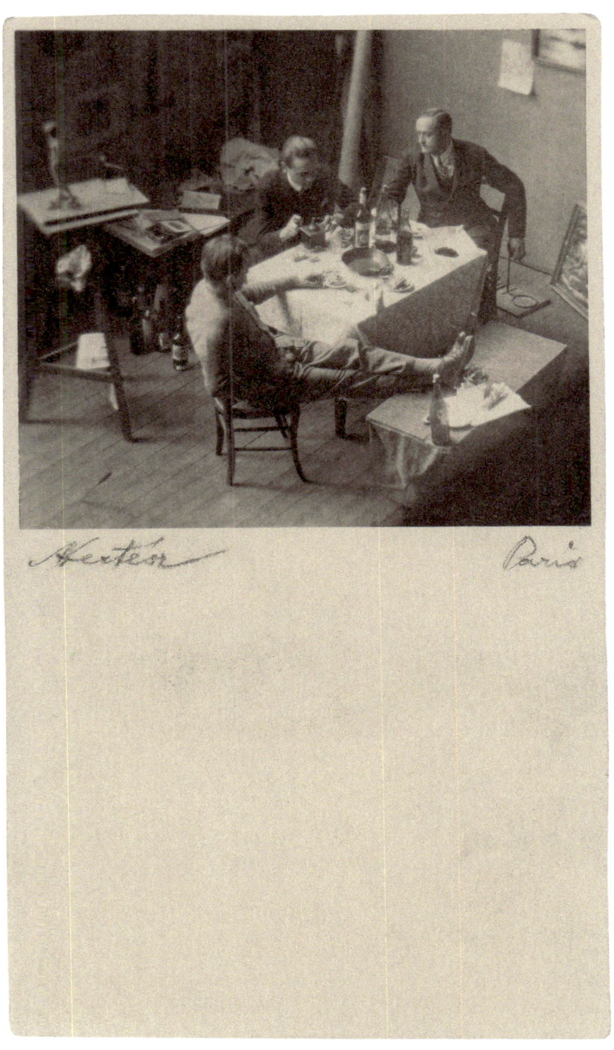

Hexter
Paris

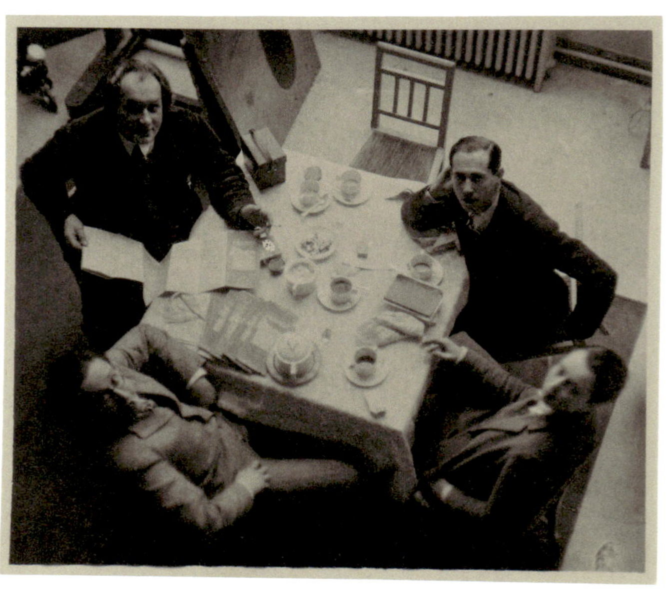

   Cat. 84   *Edwin Rosskam, Jan Sliwinsky, an American Journalist, and Peggy Rosskam in the Rosskams' Apartment, 1926–28*

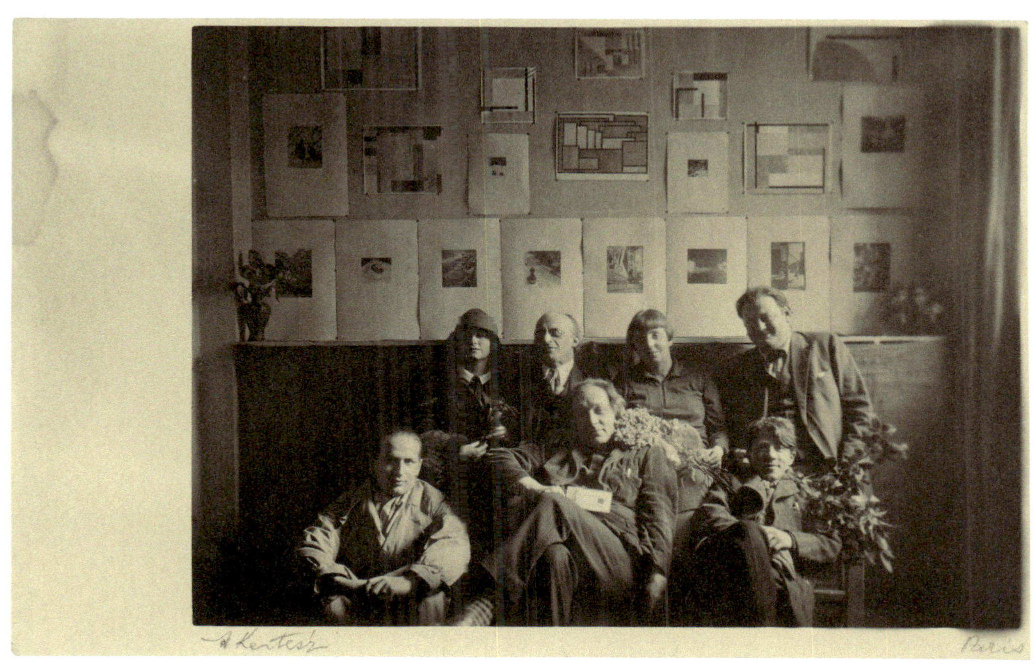

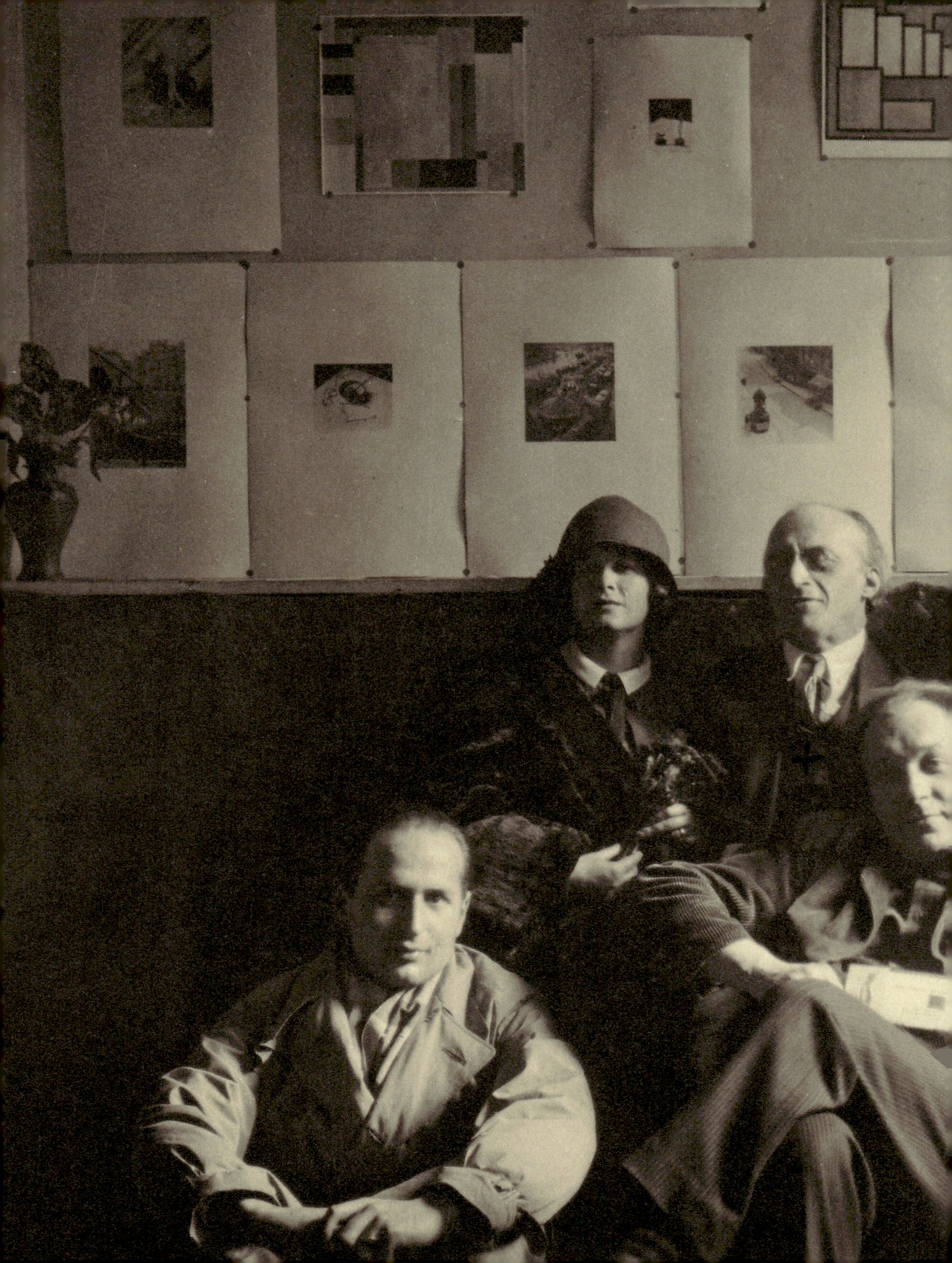

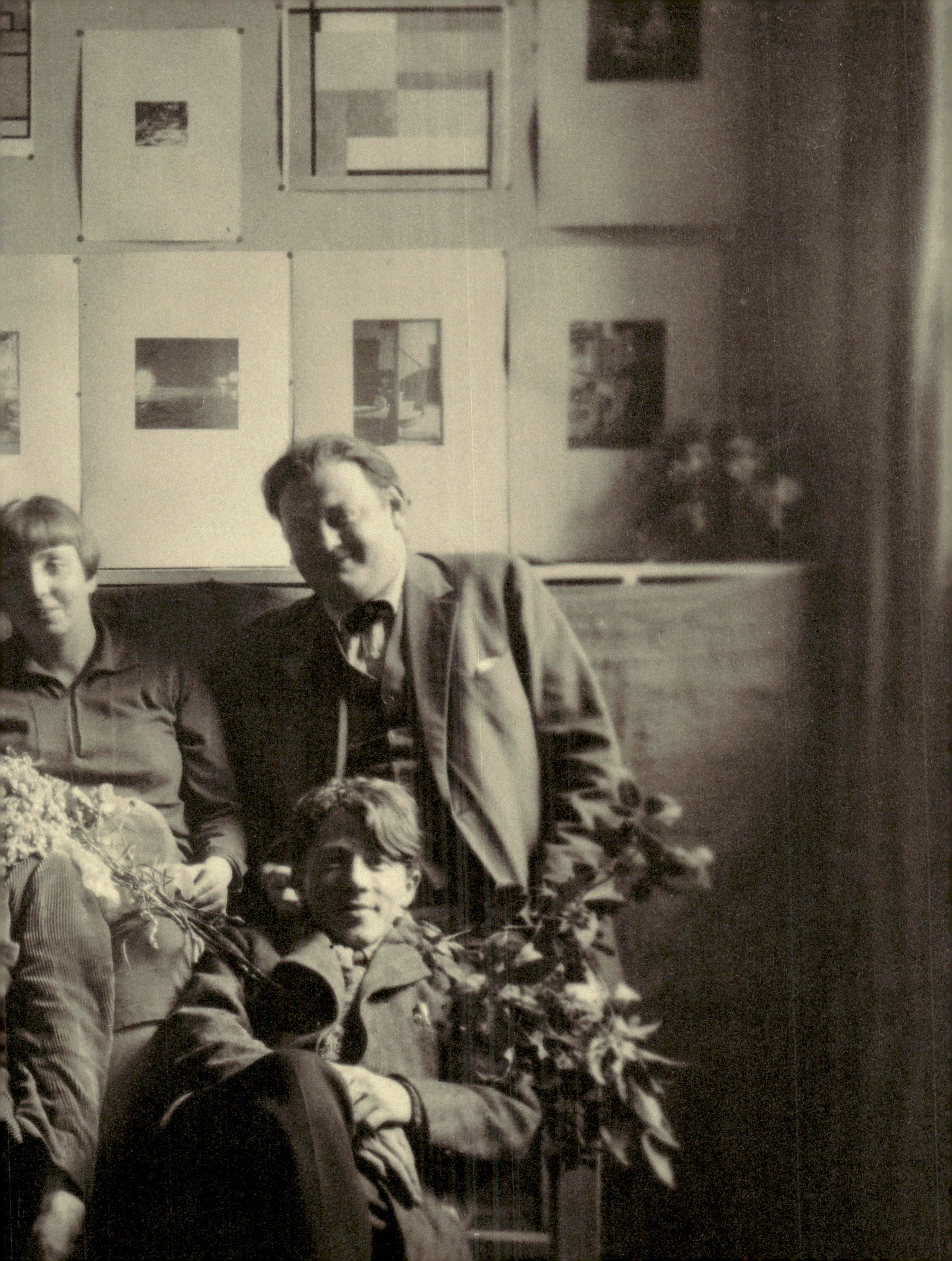

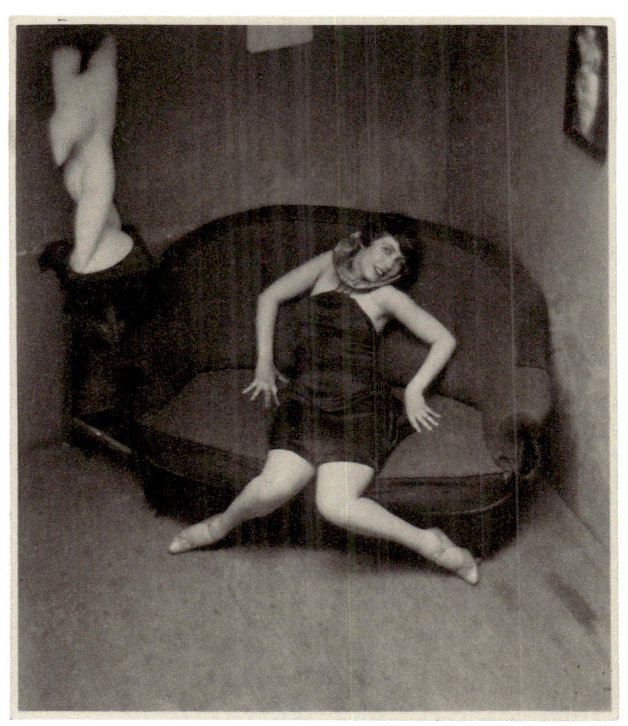

Cat. 86 *Satiric Dancer (Variant)*, 1927   **165**

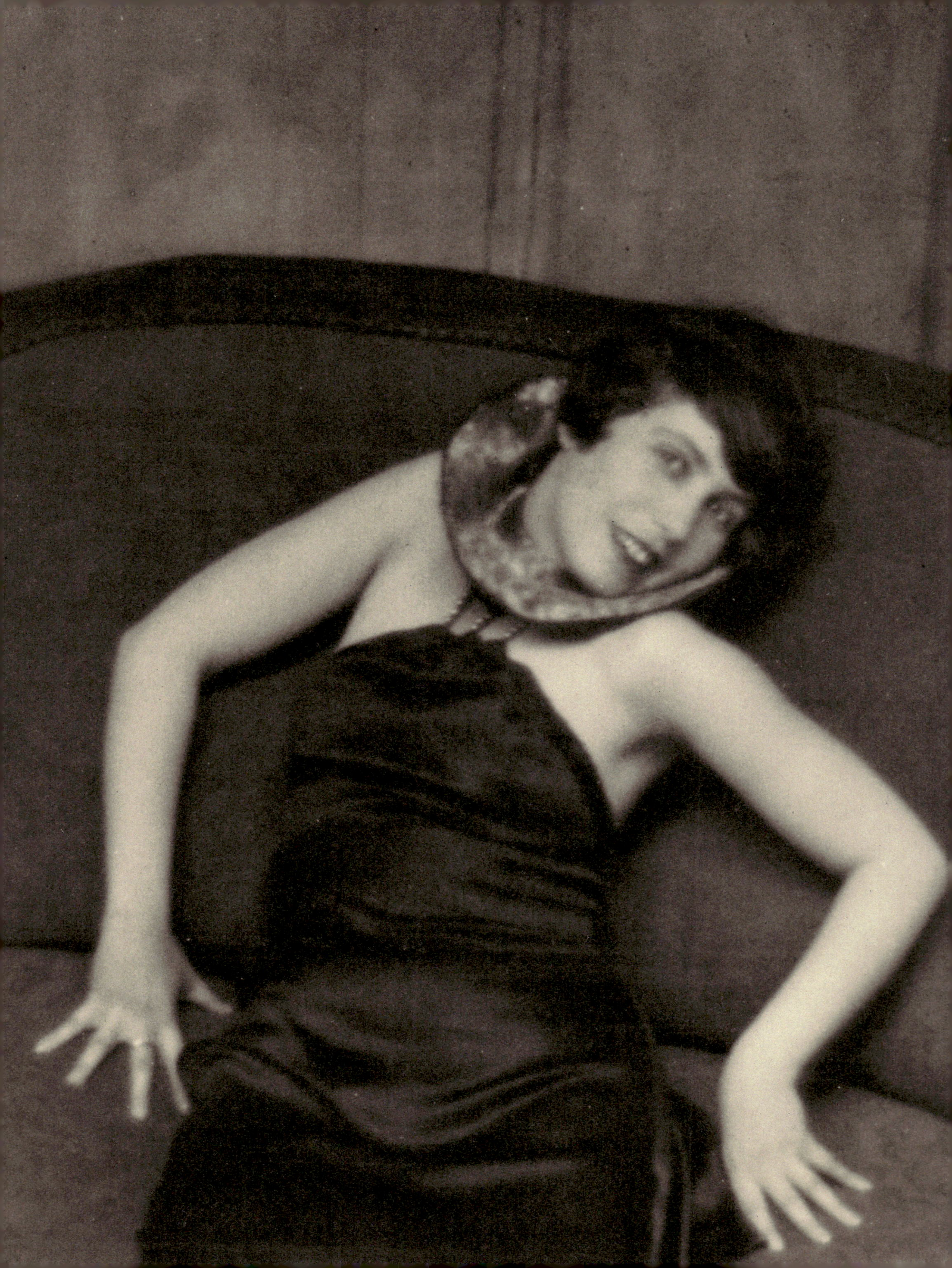

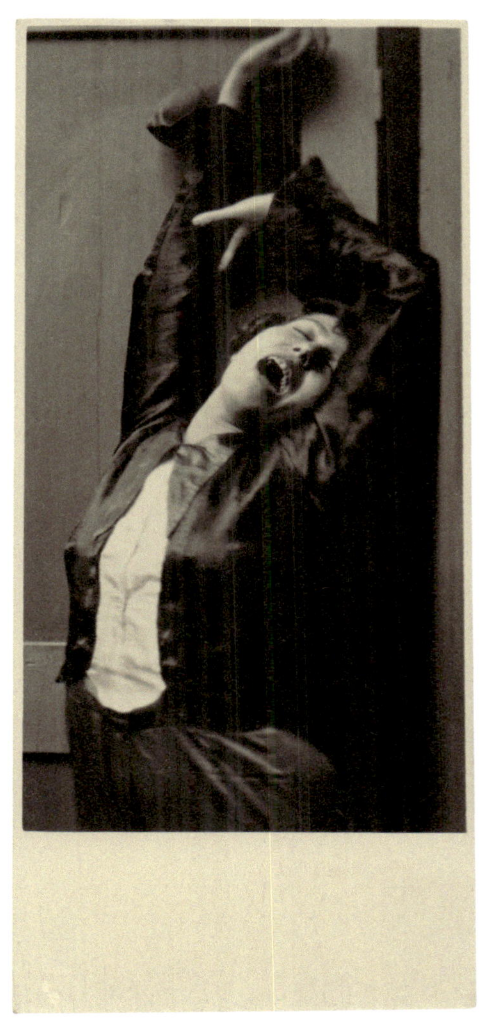

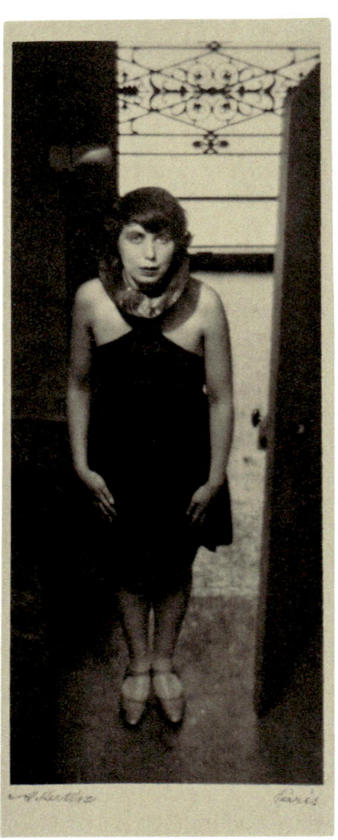

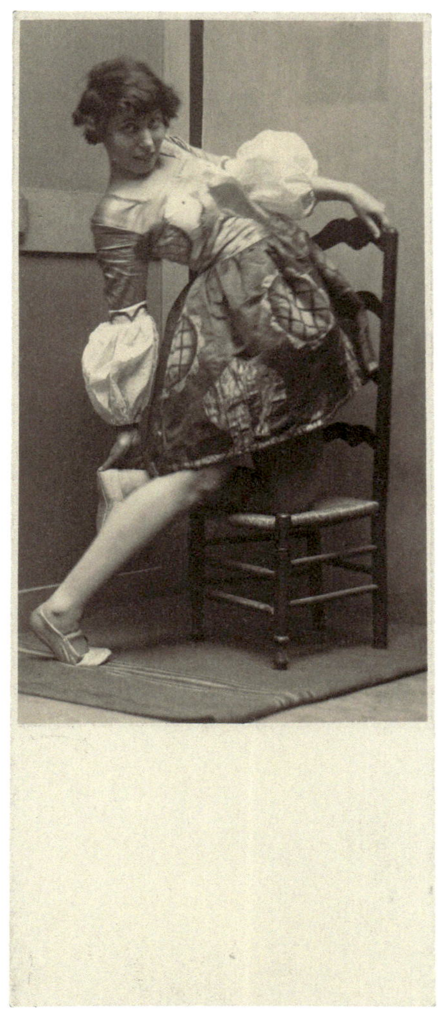

   Cat. 88 *Magda Förstner, 1927* | Cat. 89 *Magda Förstner, 1927*

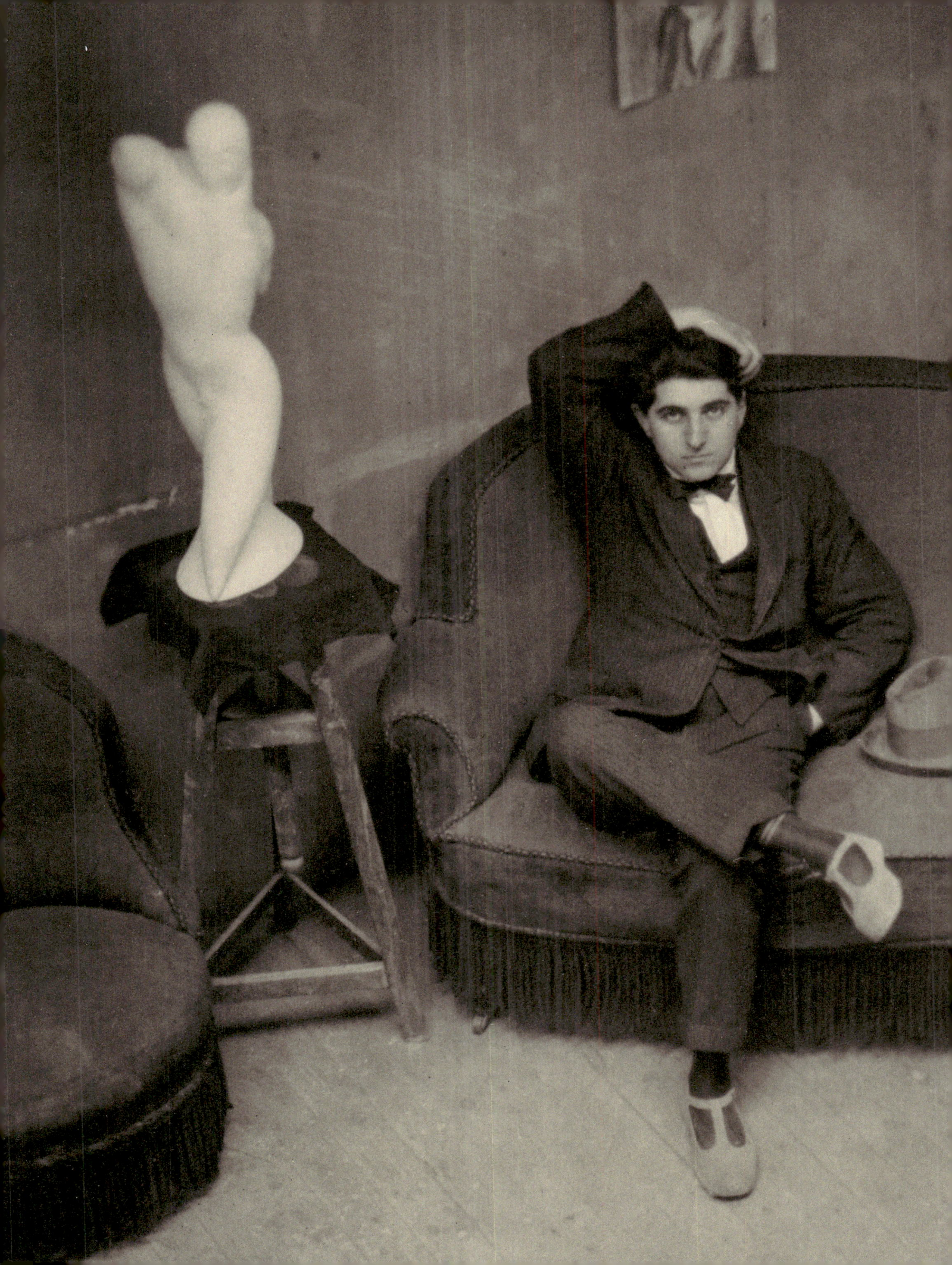

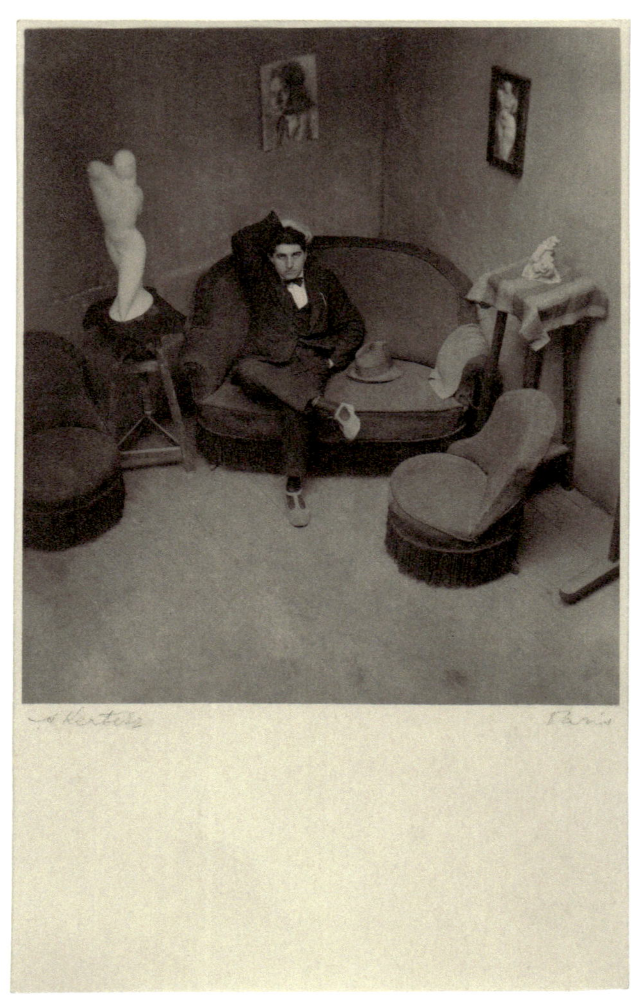

 Cat. 90 *Etienne Beöthy in His Studio,* 1928

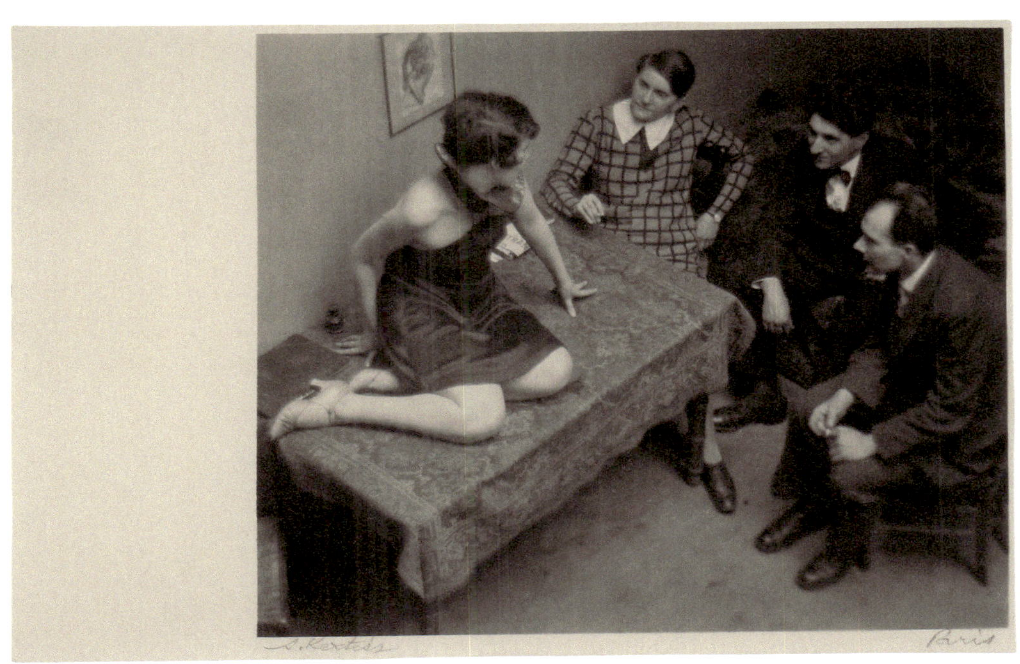

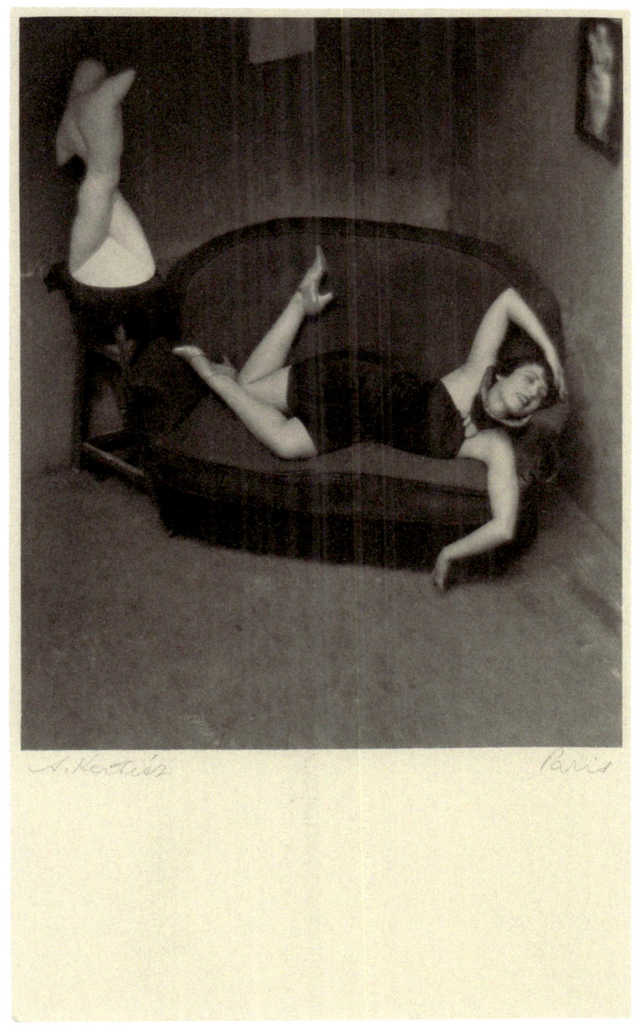

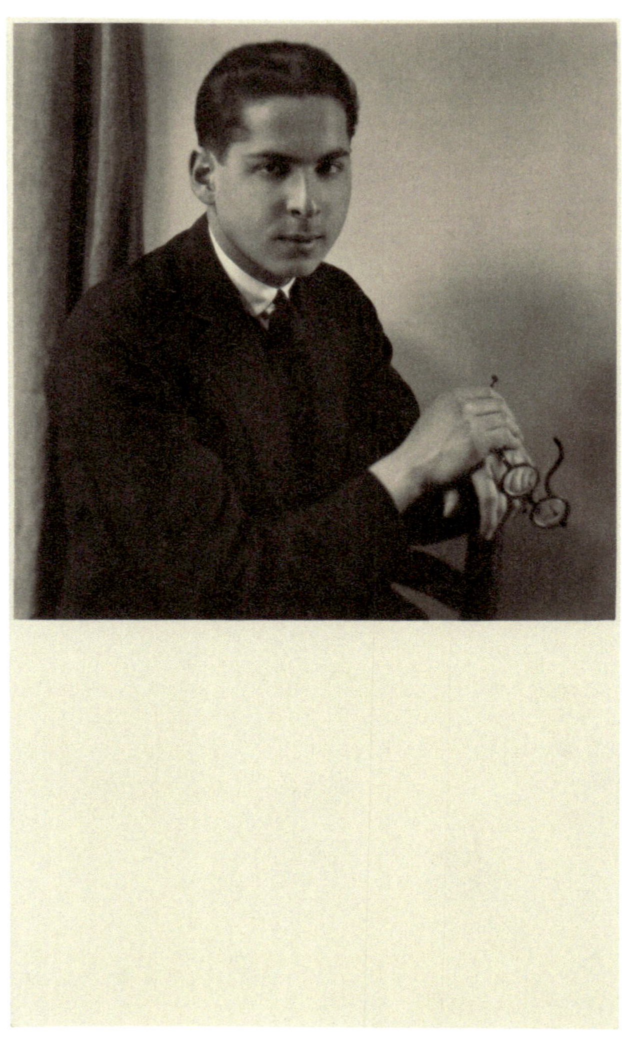

    Cat. 93 *Paul Arma*, 1928

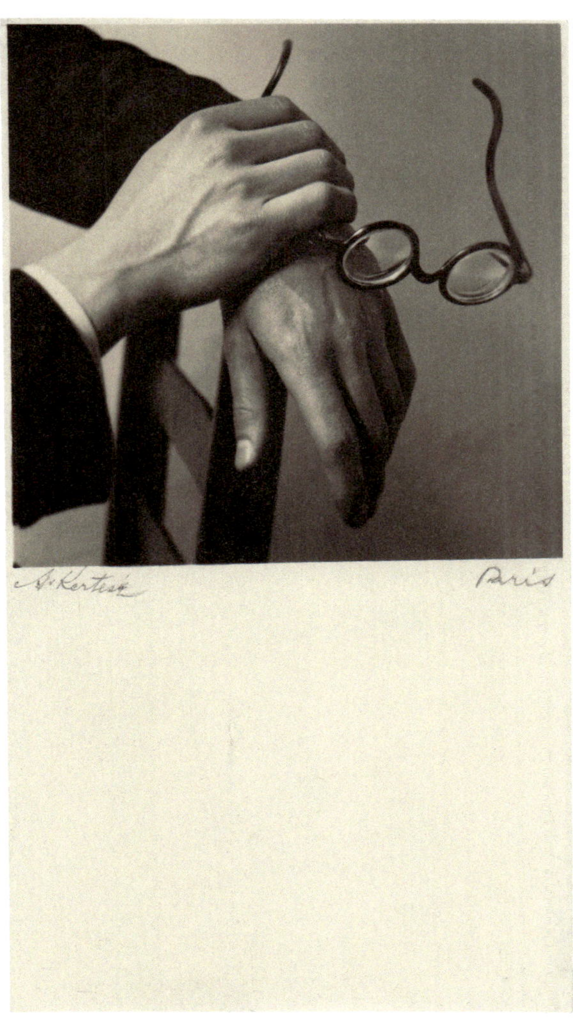

A. Kertész
Paris

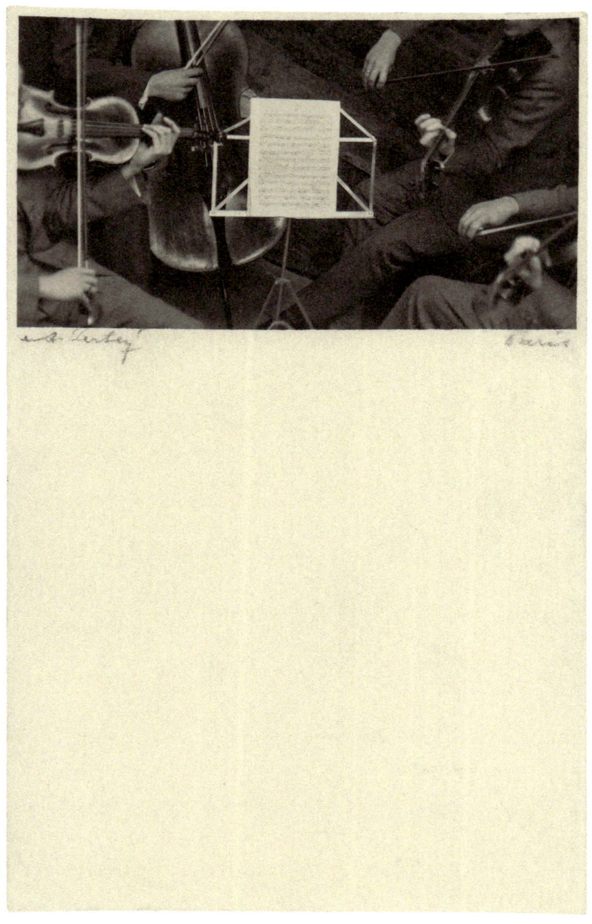

   Cat. 95   *Quartet*, 1926

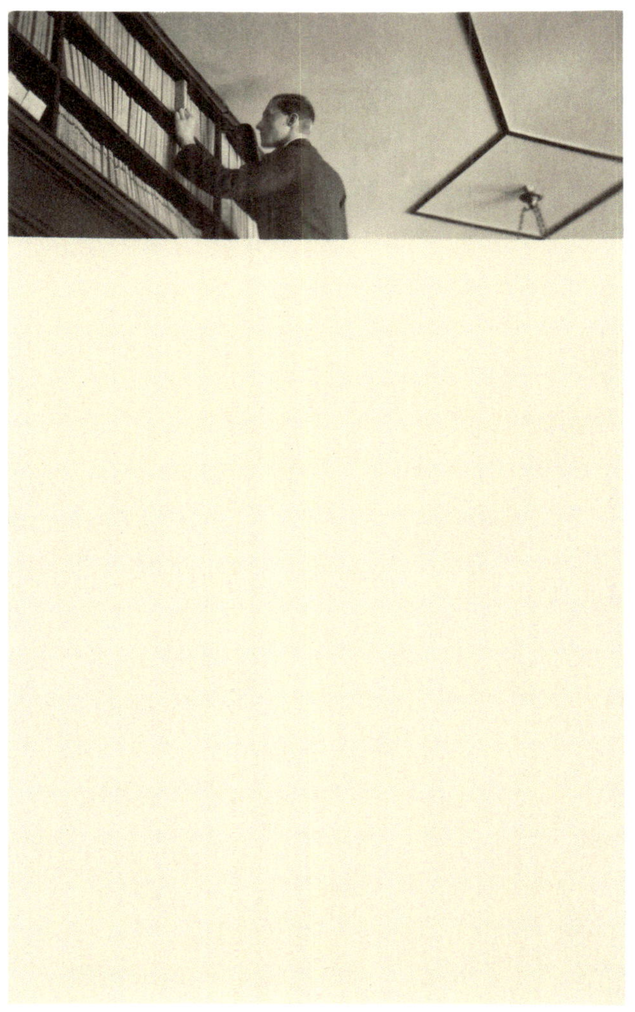

Cat. 96 *Le Soudier (Avant-Garde Bookstore)*, 1926–27   **177**

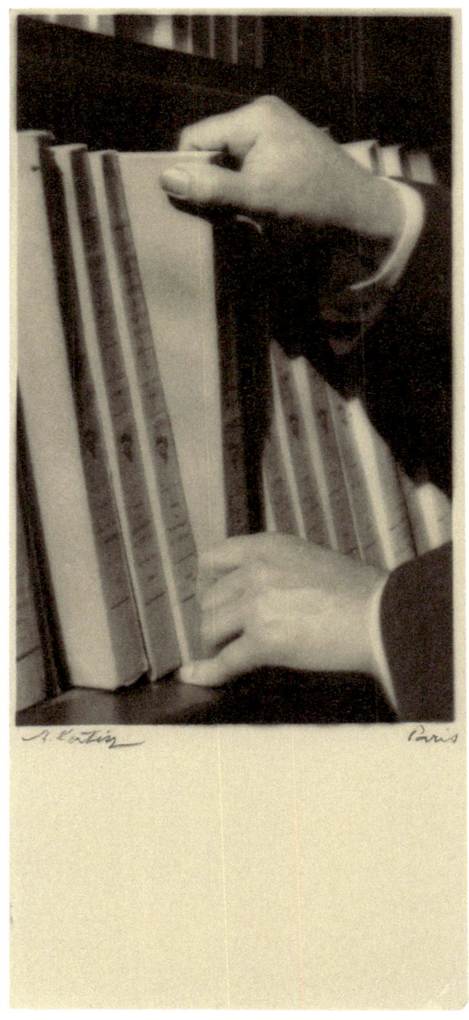

Cat. 97   *Le Soudier (Hands and Books)*, 1927   **179**

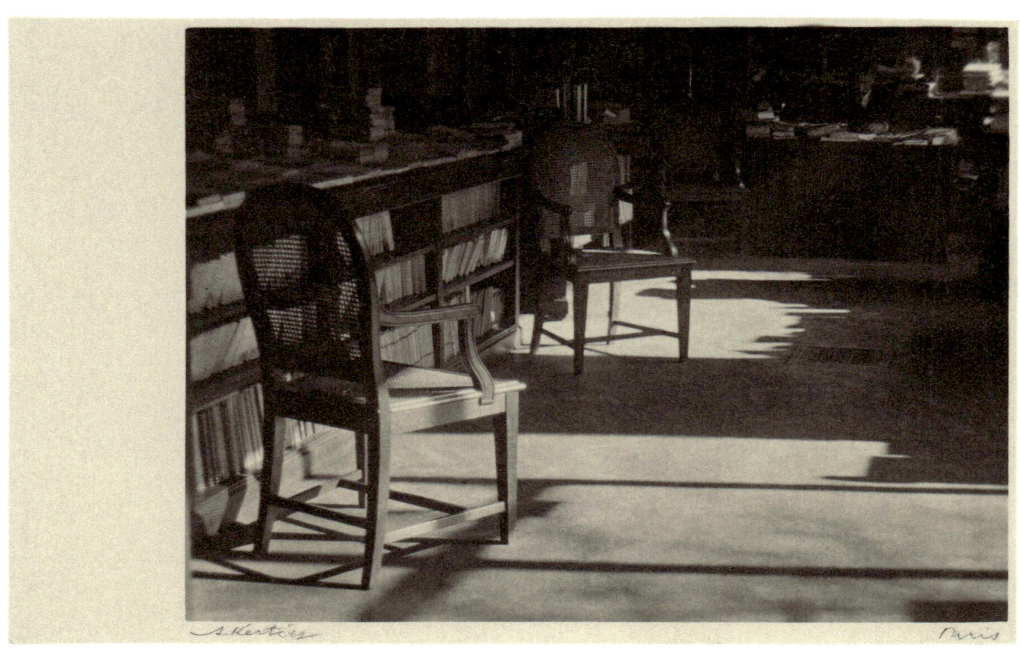

180 Cat. 98 *Library Chairs and Shadows*, 1927

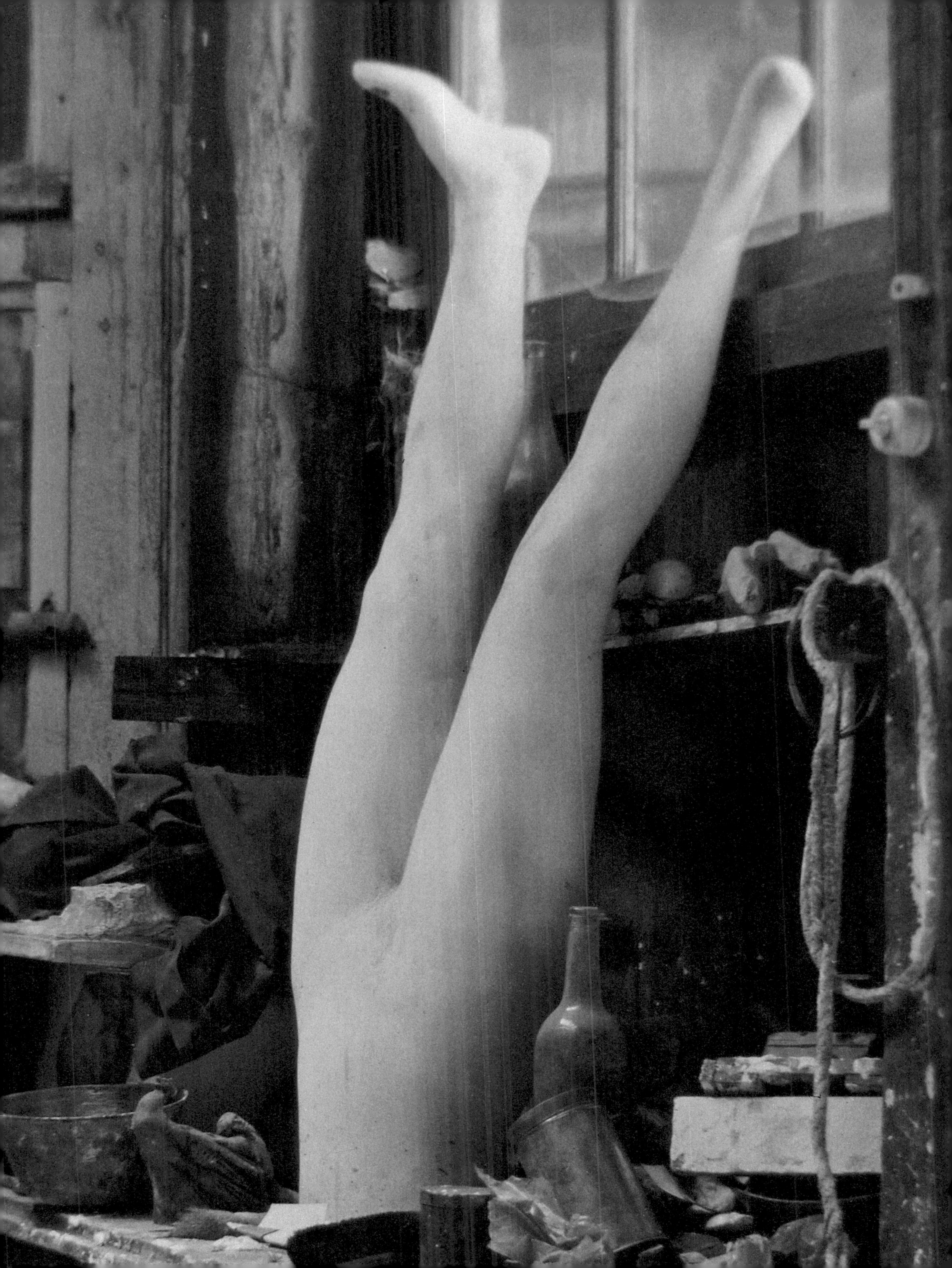

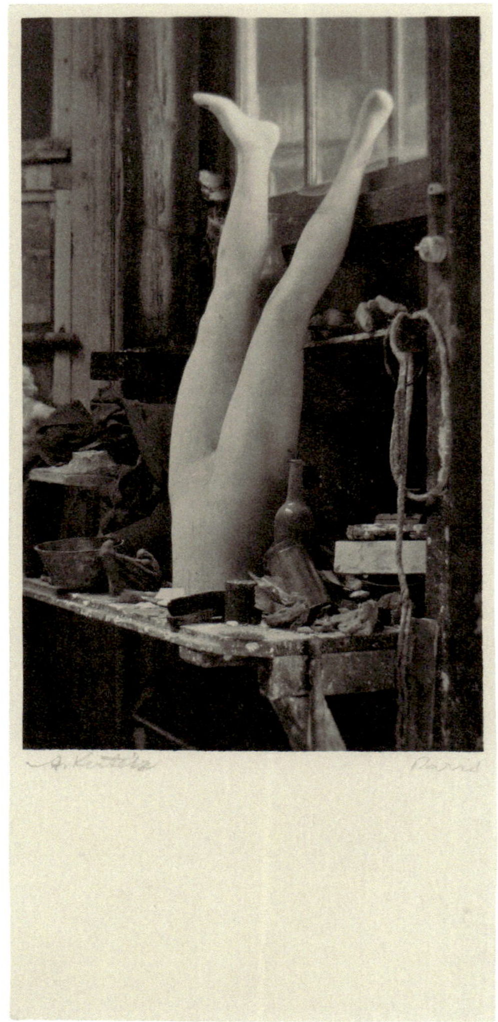

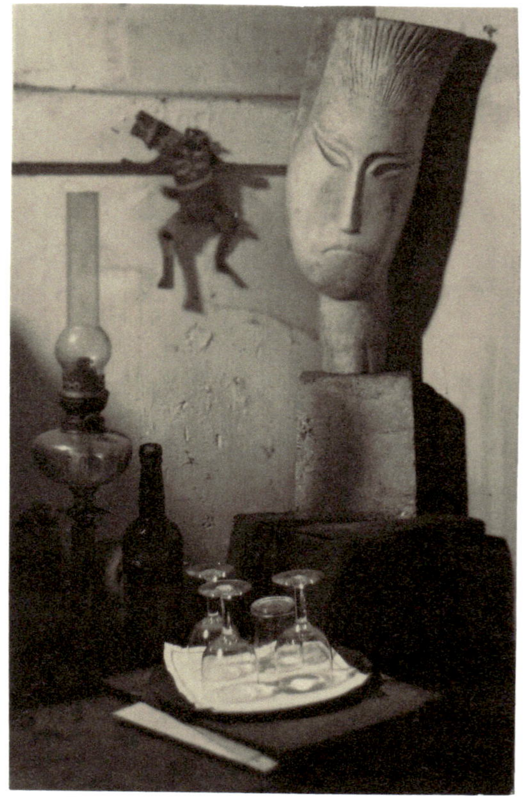

    Cat. 99 *Legs*, 1925 | Cat. 100 *Ossip Zadkine's Studio*, 1926

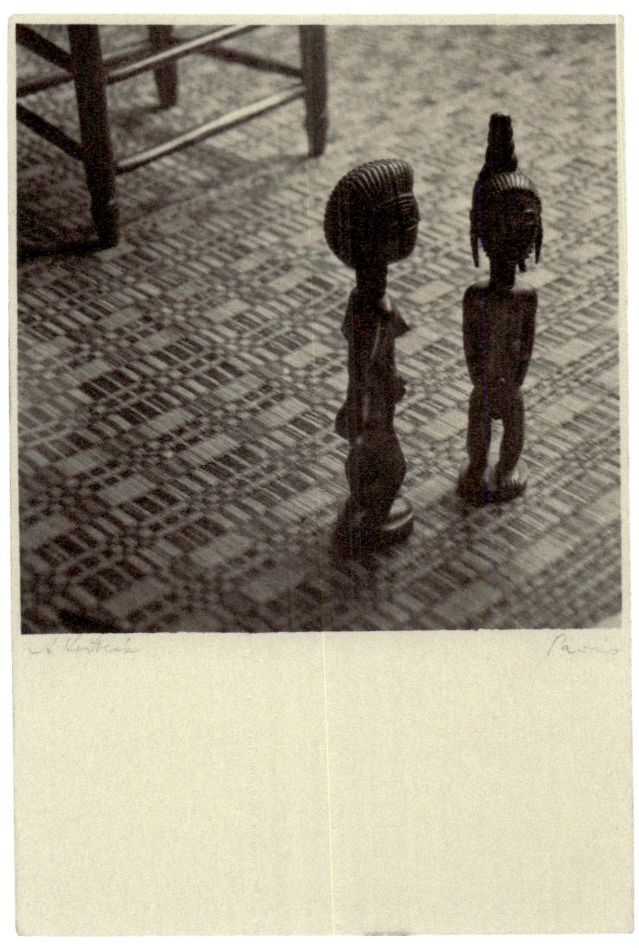

  183

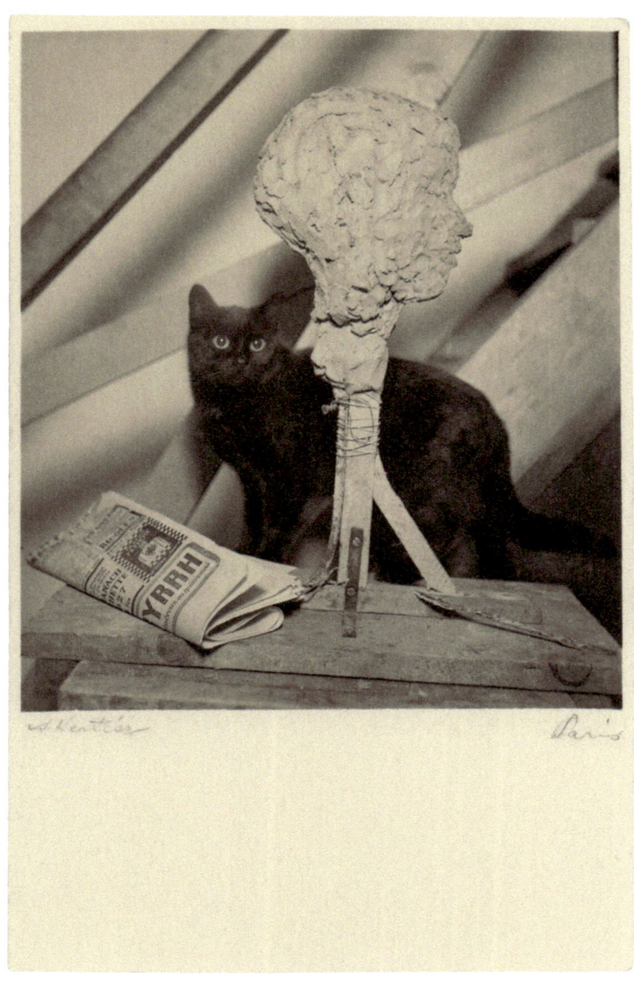

    Cat. 102   *The Studio Cat*, 1926–27

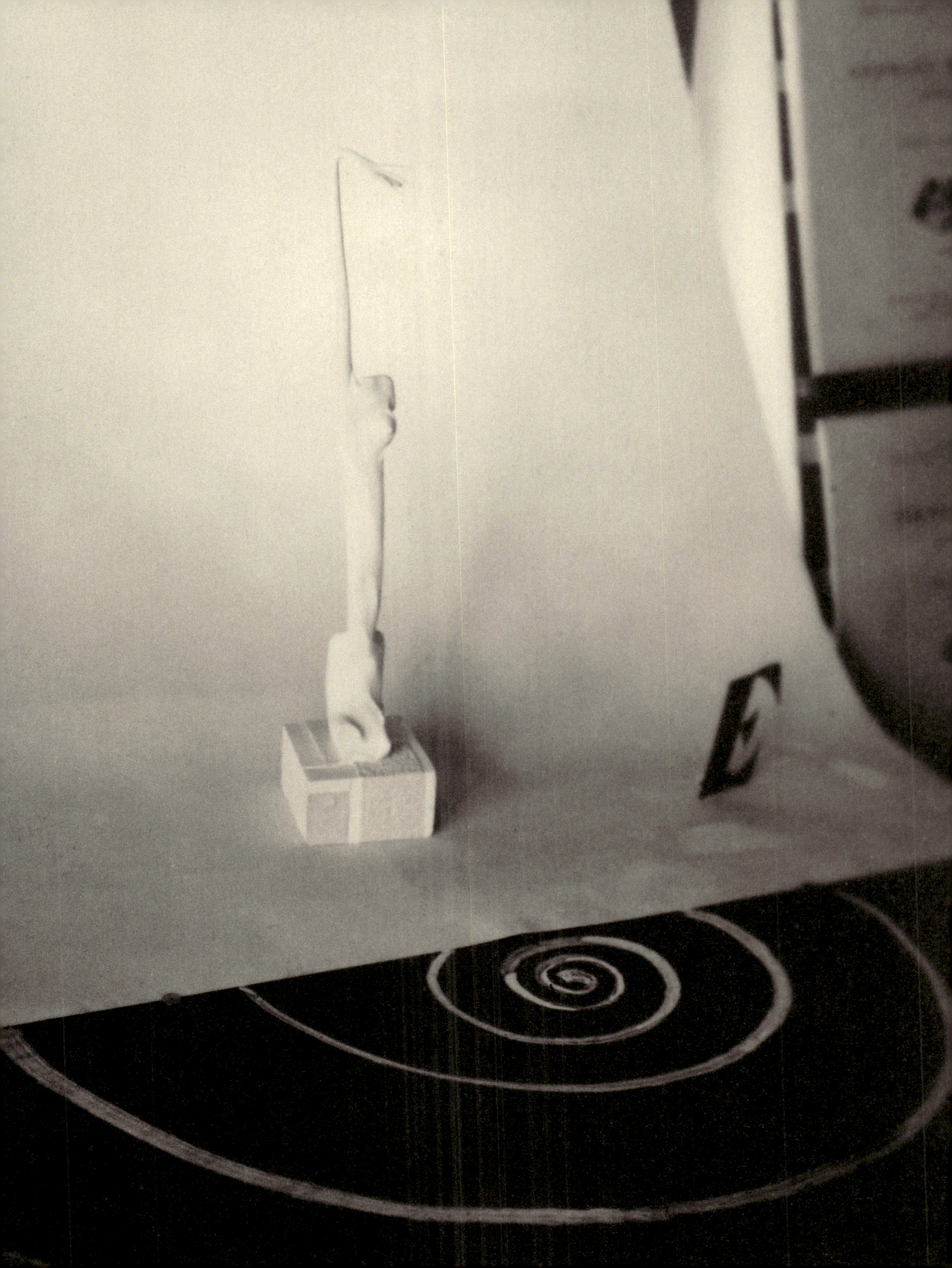

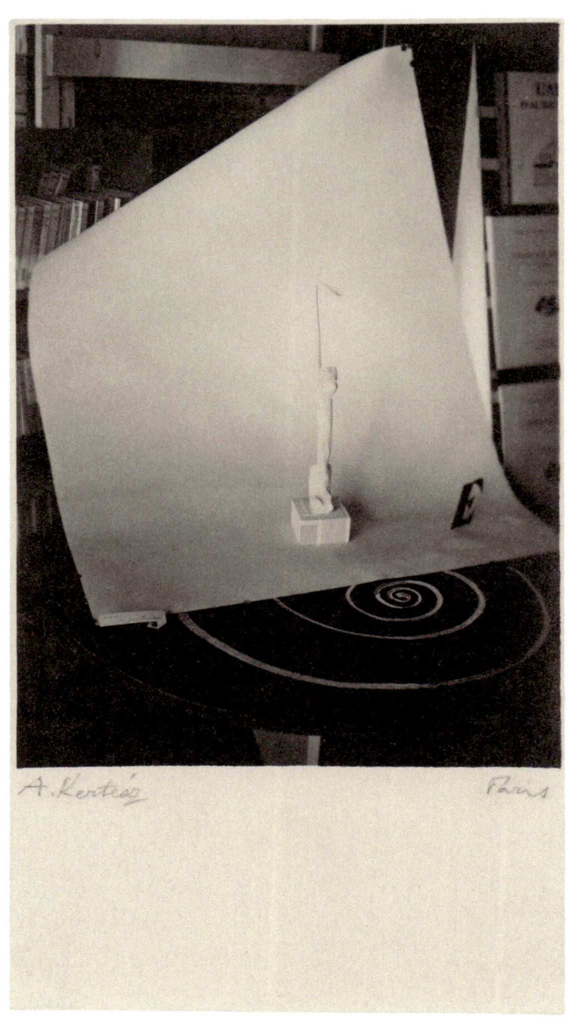

 Cat. 103 *Window, L'Esthétique*, 1927

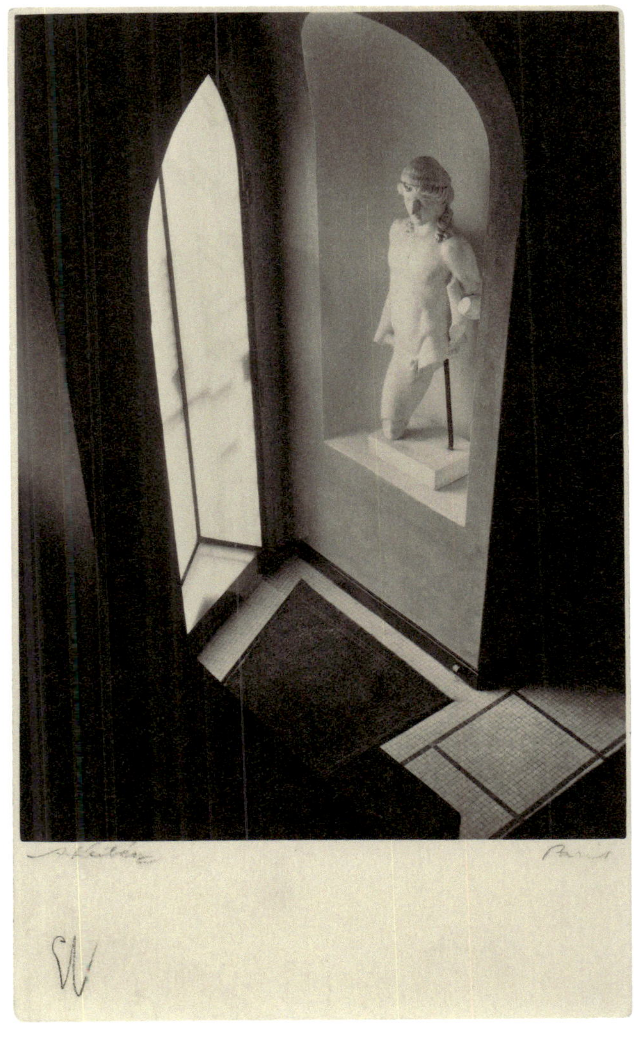

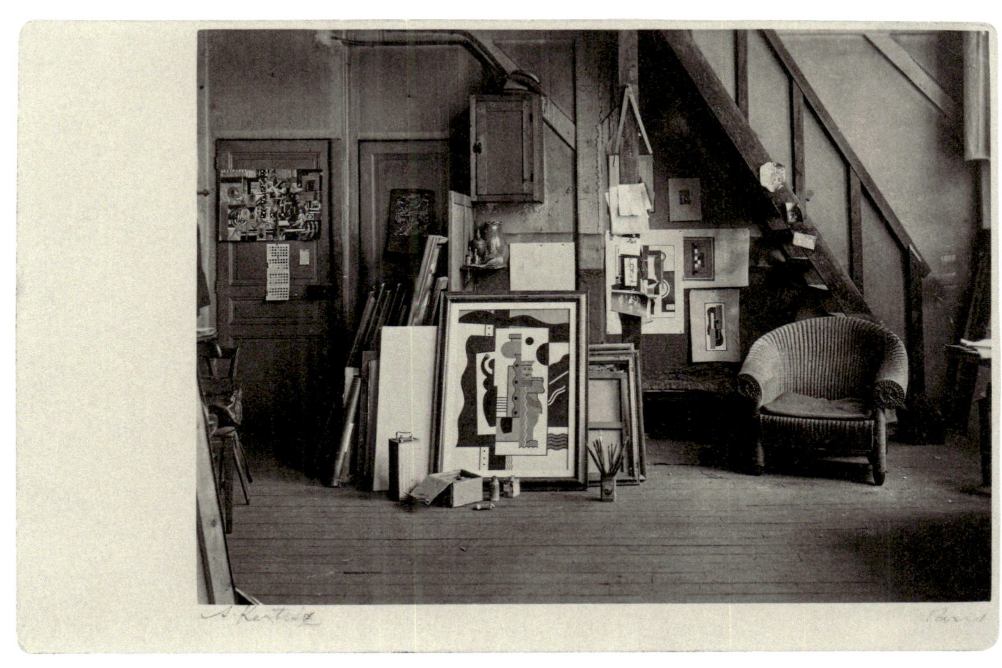

Cat. 105 *Fernand Léger's Studio, 1926–27*   **189**

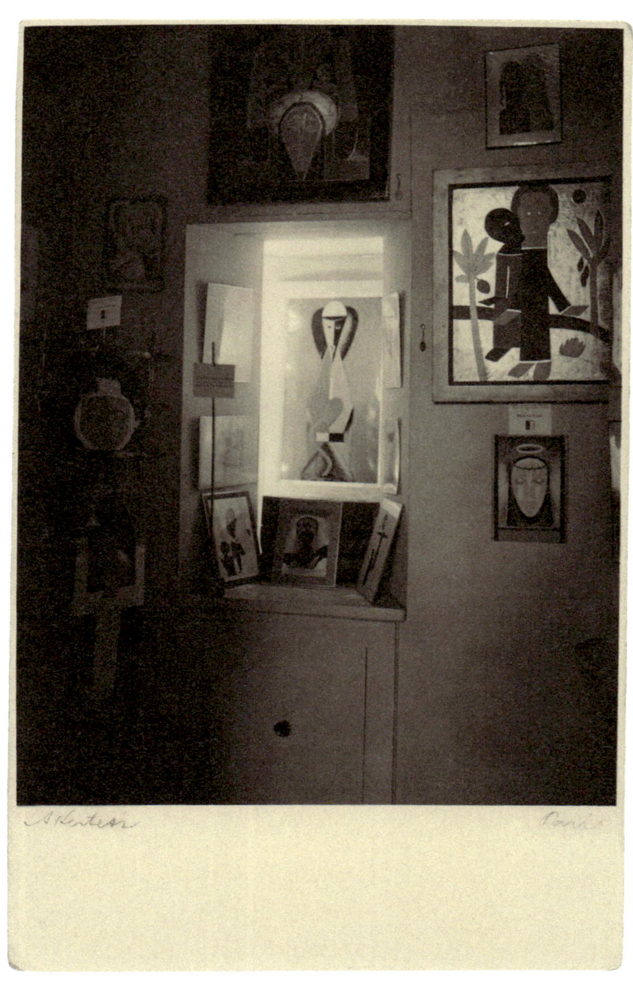

   Cat. 106 *Marie Vassilieff's Studio*, 1926

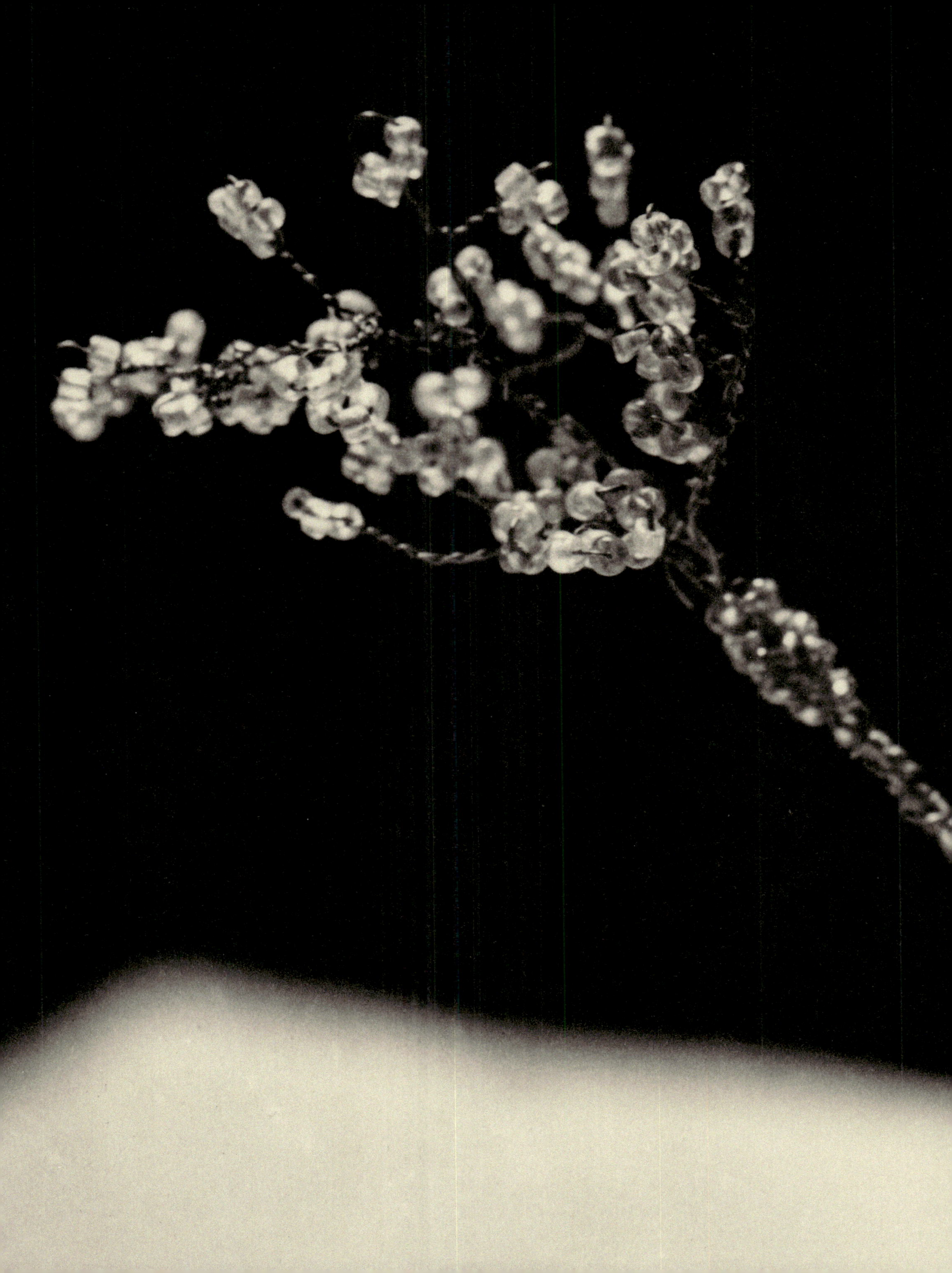

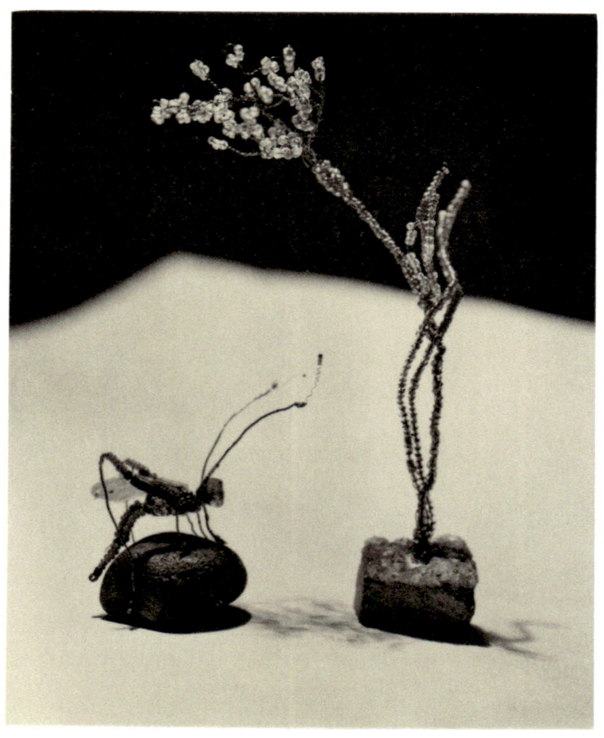

    Cat. 107 *Sculptures*, 1927

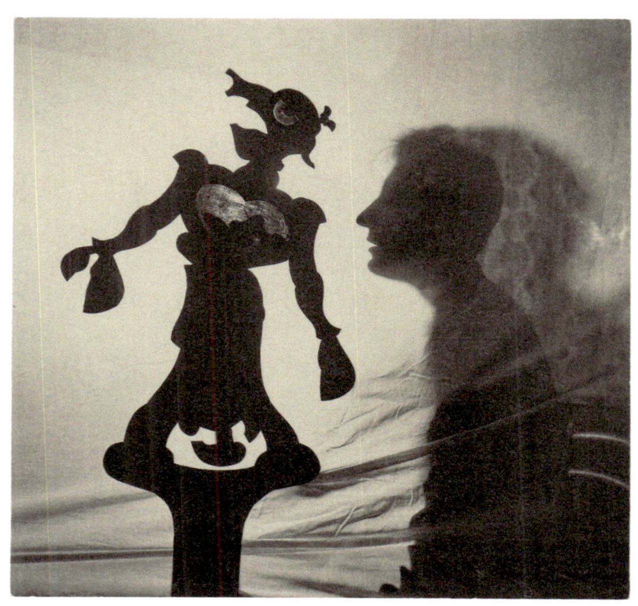

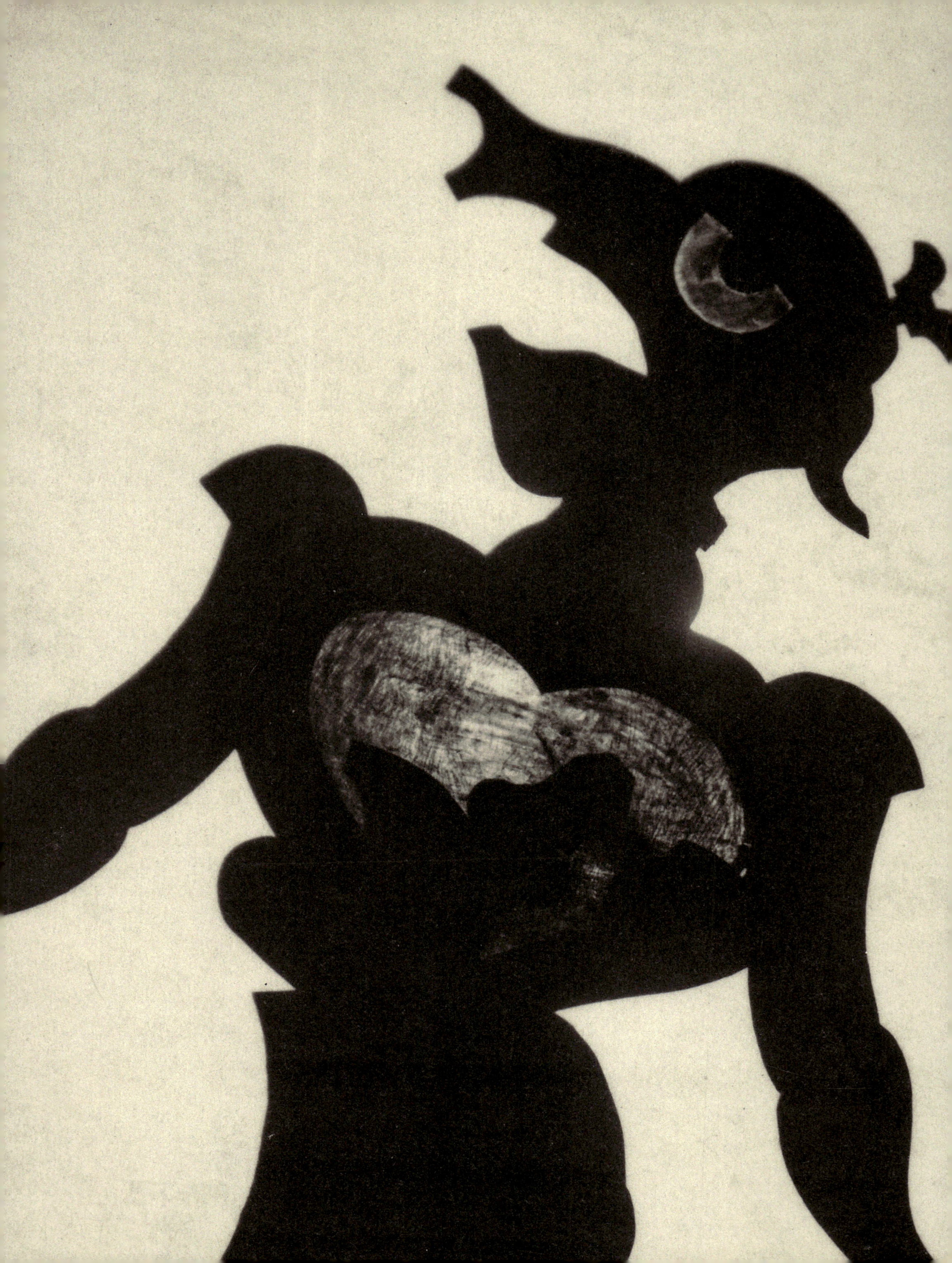

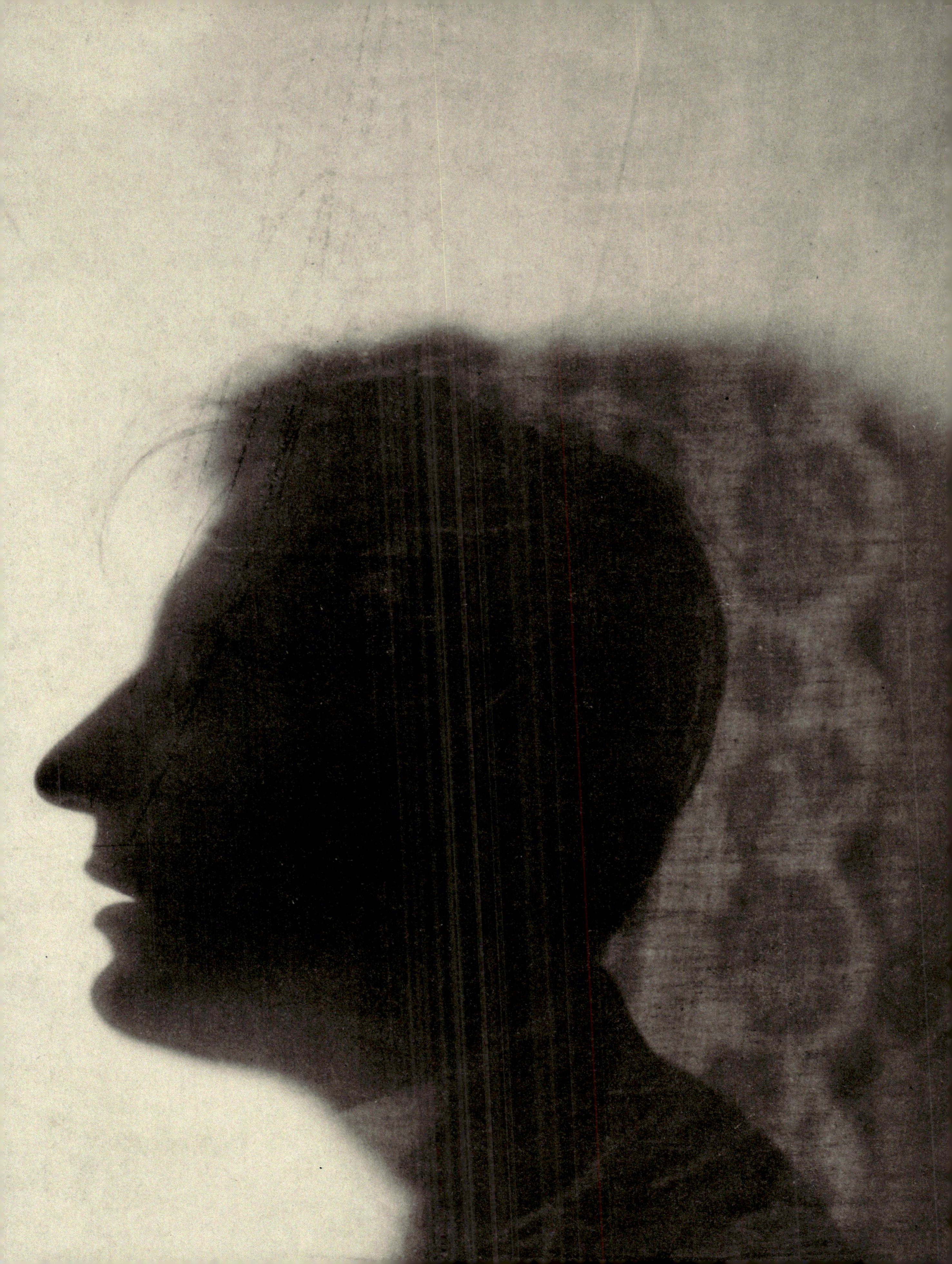

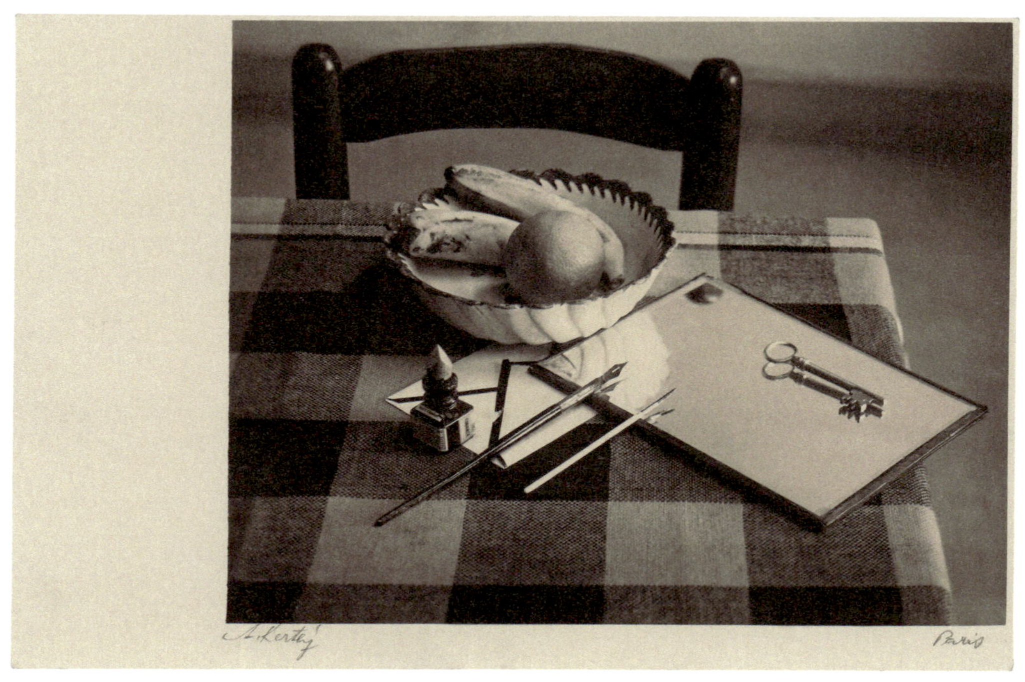

     Cat. 109 *Still Life*, 1926

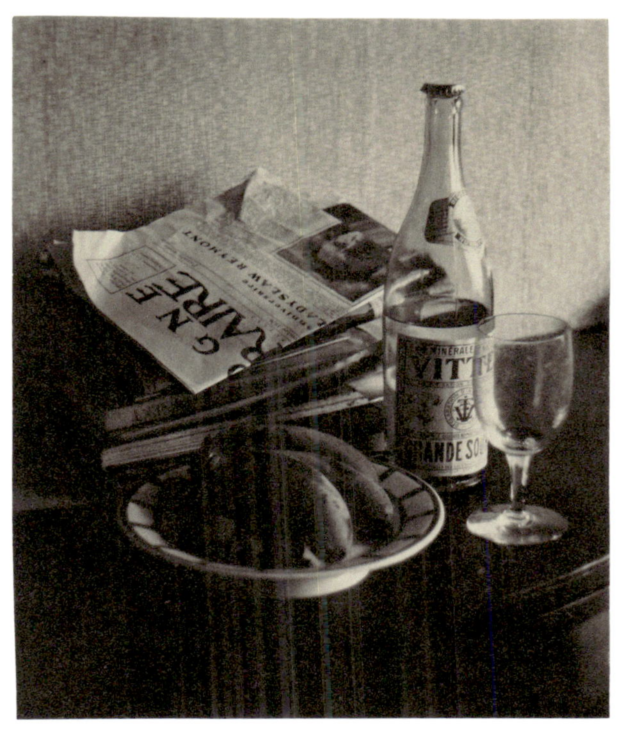

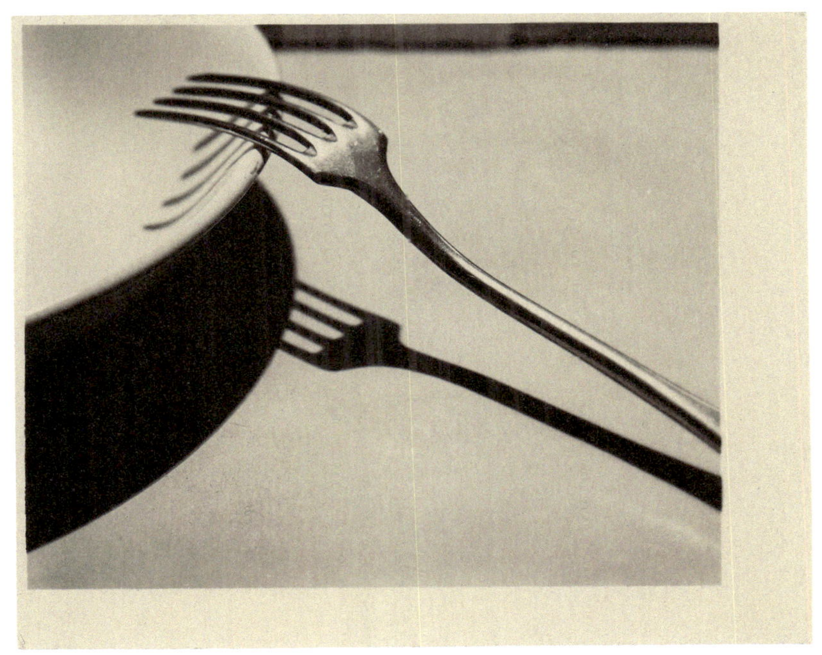

199

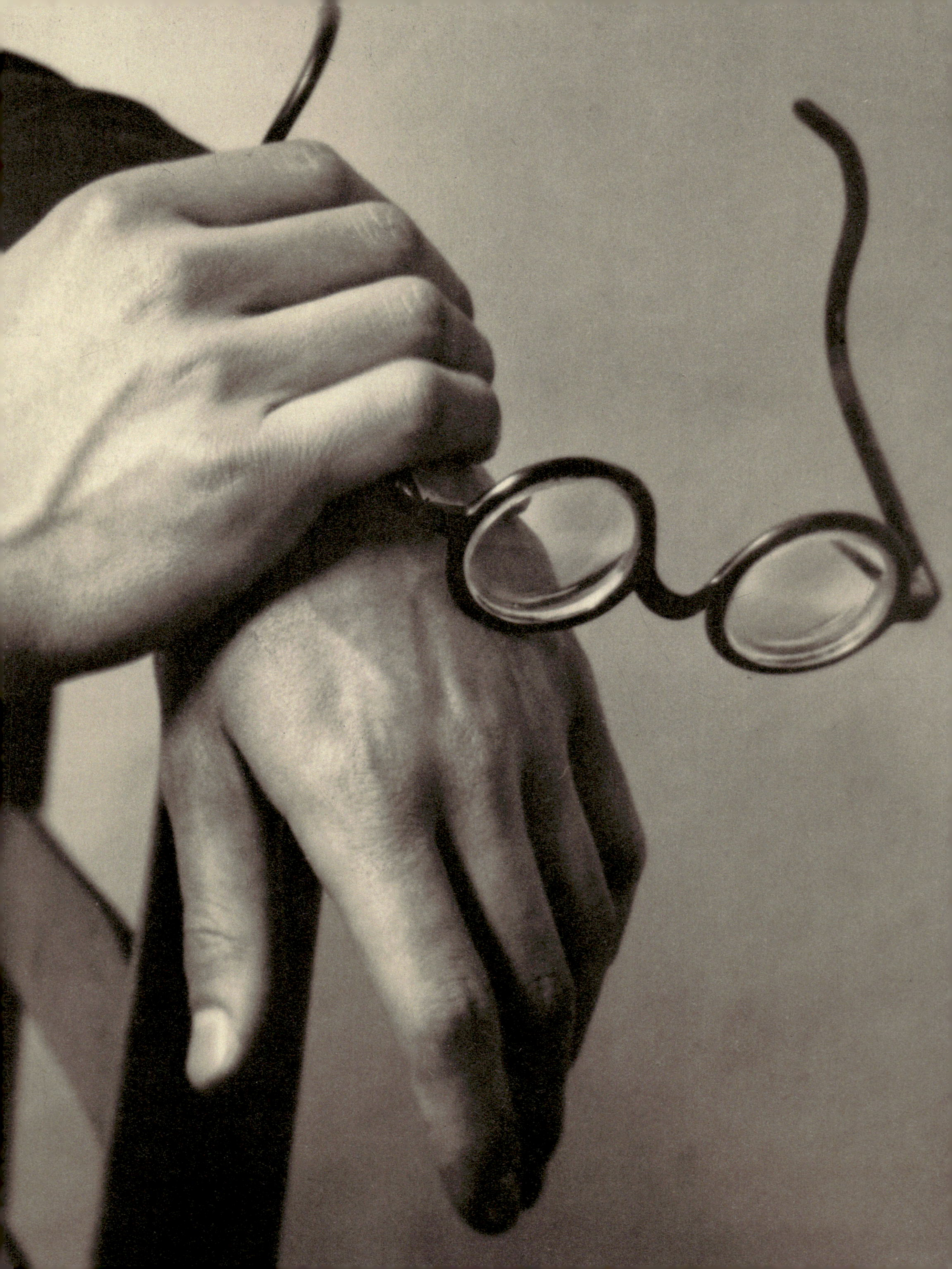

Catalogue

OF KNOWN
CARTE POSTALE
PRINTS

NOTES ON THE CATALOGUE

This catalogue provides a comprehensive list of known *carte postale* (postcard) prints made during Kertész's first three years in France and represents the best knowledge at the time of publication. It is divided into two parts: first, a checklist of the exhibition, with more complete object records, and second, a list of other images printed as cartes postales, with abbreviated entries. Images in the second section are listed in the following order: self-portraits, portraits of identified sitters (in alphabetical order), identified groups, unidentified sitters, unidentified groups, Paris, elsewhere in France, interiors, and still lifes. All works are gelatin silver contact prints on carte postale paper.

With photographs, it is often impossible to state definitively the number of prints made. Kertész typically produced only a small number of carte postale prints of each negative. Many of the works exist as unique carte postale prints; the most known carte postale prints for any single negative is eight (cat. 56, *Chez Mondrian*). Every effort has been made to accurately identify all extant carte postale prints made from a particular negative. (The language of "other known prints" and "only known print" refers exclusively to prints on carte postale paper, not to other period prints.) Research was conducted in institutional collections, auction records, and dealer inventories to locate prints. Comparing signatures, inscriptions, cropping, and trimming helped distinguish certain prints from others. Every work listed here was either viewed in person or verified by a digital image. When more than one print of an image exists, the accompanying thumbnail illustrates the print from the first collection listed. A handful of carte postale prints extant at one time (listed in auction catalogues or a 1985 inventory of Kertész's estate) that could not be located are not included.

Parameters for inclusion are deliberately conservative. The works are all prints on Kertész's favored Guilleminot paper (see Sylvie Pénichon's essay in this book), confirmed by the characteristic text and markings on the verso. Although Kertész experimented with at least two other postcard stocks, very few prints exist on those papers, and they are not included here. Works too small (made with his 4.5-by-6-centimeter camera) to have marks identifying Guilleminot as the manufacturer (see p. 20, fig. 5) have been omitted; consulted conservators noted that several of these were likely carte postale prints, but this could not be confirmed. Nor are contemporaneous prints made on similar double-weight paper included, although we know that Kertész occasionally contact-printed images on both carte postale and other papers. Additionally, this list includes only prints of negatives made in France, not later prints of earlier Hungarian negatives, nor of negatives made during a 1927 trip to Hungary.

Readers aware of additional prints or information are encouraged to email kertesz@artic.edu.

TITLES

Kertész rarely gave formal titles to his photographs. A few (*Chez Mondrian*, *Satiric Dancer*) came to be commonly used, including by the artist, over the years; others emerged from publications during his lifetime. When no published or customary title exists, a descriptive title is provided, occasionally with a post-humously accrued title in parentheses. First and last names of sitters are given when known; when not known, other identifying information inscribed or recalled by the artist (such as occupation or nationality) is used. The word *Paris* has been removed from all titles and is assumed to be the location unless otherwise indicated; more specific locations are given when known.

DATES

Although it is possible Kertész made a few carte postale prints in 1929, evidence suggests that their limited window of production was 1925–28; if the date of a work is unknown, that range is provided for the record. Otherwise, dates provided are based on prior research (see p. 30, note 3), inscriptions, contemporaneous exhibition records, Kertész's papers, and related works with known dates.

DIMENSIONS

Dimensions are provided for both the image and the card. Images around 4.5-by-6-centimeters or smaller generally indicate that Kertész used his smaller camera, whereas anything larger than that typically implies that he used his 9-by-12-centimeter camera. (A known exception is cat. 95, which was made with a 13-by-17-centimeter negative.) The standard size of a carte postale card is 9 by 14 centimeters; any departure from these dimensions indicates that Kertész trimmed the print, as he did with nearly all of his cartes postales.

MOUNTS

Kertész occasionally mounted his carte postale prints on larger, warm-toned, textured paper; these period mounts are noted for checklist objects, in the thumbnail reproductions and by the inclusion of mount dimensions.

SIGNATURES AND INSCRIPTIONS

Because a signature may indicate that Kertész considered the carte postale print a finished work of art, signatures are noted for checklist objects (most often, *A* [or *A.*] *Kertész / Paris* in graphite on the recto below the image). Kertész's own contemporaneous inscriptions on checklist objects (often written on the verso of works sent to his brother Jenő) are transcribed and translated, but inventory numbers, later stamps, Kertész's later inscriptions and signatures, and notes in any other hand are not given here. Eriksen Translations, New York, provided transcriptions and translations from Hungarian. Line breaks in inscriptions are illustrated when available but are not given in translations due to the grammatical differences between Hungarian and English.

Elizabeth Siegel

ABBREVIATIONS

In the list of other known prints, the following abbreviations are used for organizations with large holdings of Kertész's work:

AEKF	André and Elizabeth Kertész Foundation
AIC	The Art Institute of Chicago
EAK	Estate of André Kertész
JPGM	The J. Paul Getty Museum, Los Angeles
KM	Kassák Múzeum, Budapest
Met	The Metropolitan Museum of Art, New York
MFA Boston	Museum of Fine Arts, Boston
MFA Houston	The Museum of Fine Arts, Houston
MoMA	The Museum of Modern Art, New York
NGA	National Gallery of Art, Washington, DC
NOMA	New Orleans Museum of Art
SFMOMA	San Francisco Museum of Modern Art

CHECKLIST OF THE EXHIBITION

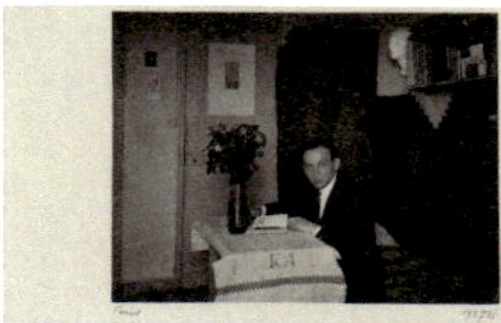

Cat. 1 *Self-Portrait*, July 1927
Image: 7.9 × 10.5 cm;
card: 8.7 × 13.6 cm
Inscribed, recto, in graphite:
Paris / 1927 VII
Estate of André Kertész,
courtesy of Stephen Bulger
Gallery, Toronto
Other known prints: EAK
(additional print); JPGM;
MoMA; NGA

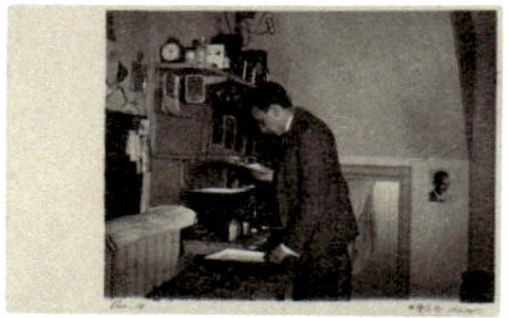

Cat. 2 *Self-Portrait in Darkroom*,
December 1927
Image: 7.9 × 10.5 cm;
card: 8.5 × 13.3 cm
Inscribed, recto, in graphite:
Paris / 1927 dec
Estate of André Kertész,
courtesy of Stephen Bulger
Gallery, Toronto
Other known prints: JPGM

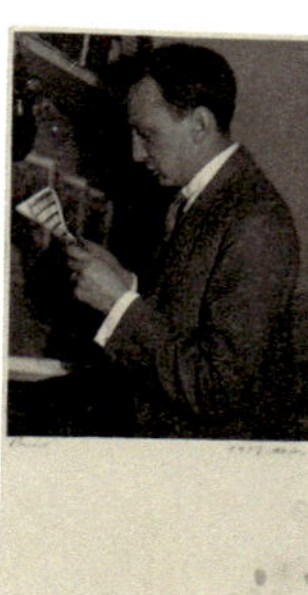

Cat. 3 *Self-Portrait in Darkroom*,
December 1927
Image: 9.2 × 7.1 cm;
card: 13.4 × 7.3 cm
Inscribed, recto, in graphite:
Paris / 1927 Dec
Estate of André Kertész,
courtesy of Stephen Bulger
Gallery, Toronto
Only known print

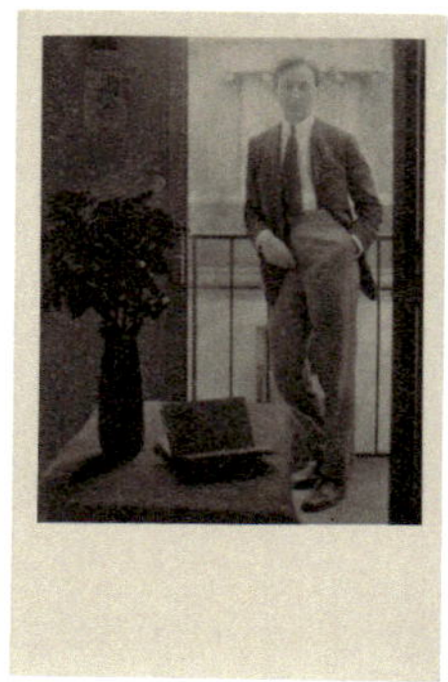

Cat. 4 *Self-Portrait*, 1926–27
Image: 10.9 × 7.9 cm;
card: 14 × 8.9 cm
The Metropolitan Museum of
Art, New York, gift of
Isaac Lagnado, in honor of
Edwynn Houk, 1997.515
Other known prints: Robert
Koch Gallery

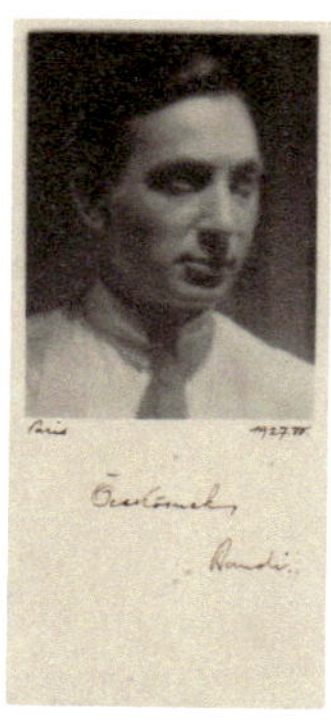

Cat. 5 *Self-Portrait*, July 1927
Image: 7.4 × 5.5 cm;
card: 13.2 × 6.1 cm
Inscribed, recto, in ink: *Paris /
1927 VII / Öcskösnek, /
Bandi* (Paris, July 1927.
To my younger brother, Bandi)
The Art Institute of Chicago,
gift of Nicholas and
Susan Pritzker, 2012.713
Other known prints: MoMA

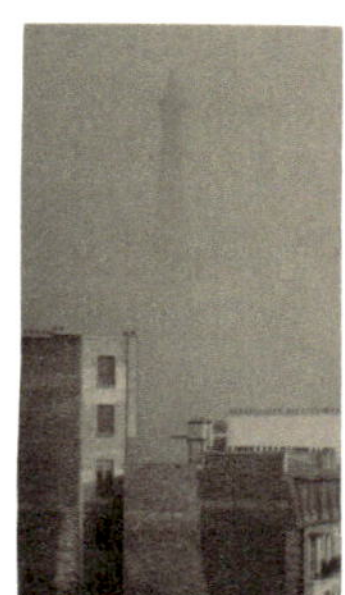

Cat. 6 *Eiffel Tower*, 1925
Image/card: 7.2 × 4.1 cm
Family Holdings of
Nicholas and Susan Pritzker
Only known print

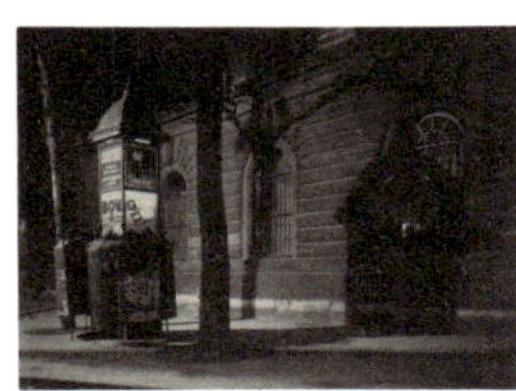

Cat. 7 *Behind the Hôtel de Ville,*
1925
Image/card: 7.8 × 10.8 cm
Family Holdings of
Nicholas and Susan Pritzker
Only known print

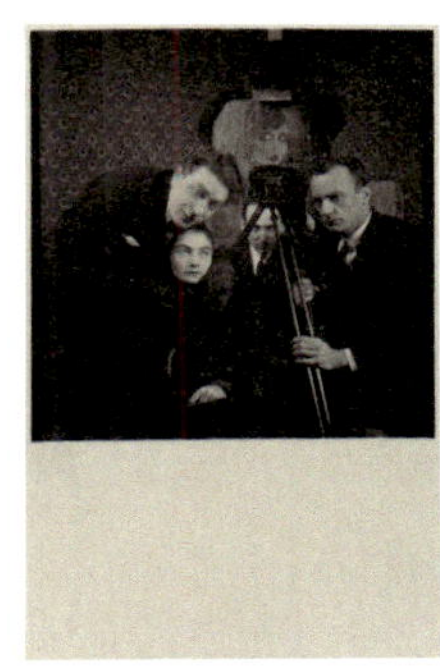

Cat. 11 *Self-Portrait with Friends,*
1925–28
Image: 8.2 × 8 cm;
card: 12.6 × 8.2 cm
Estate of André Kertész,
courtesy of Stephen Bulger
Gallery, Toronto
Other known prints: EAK
(additional print)

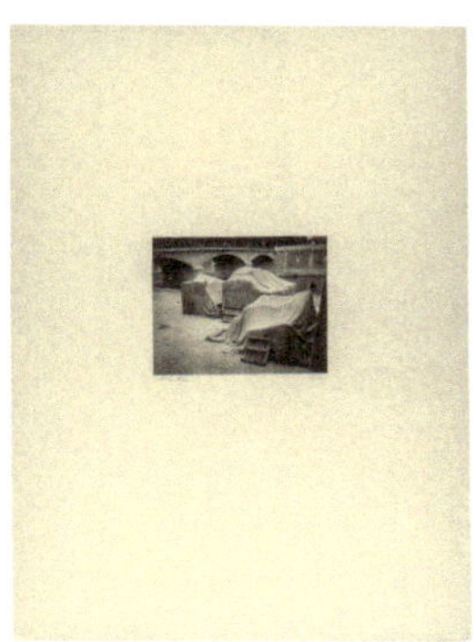

Cat. 8 *Behind Notre-Dame,*
1925
Image/card: 8.3 × 10.5 cm;
mount: 37.2 × 27.6 cm
Signed, mount, in graphite:
A. Kertész / Paris
Private collection, Canada
Only known print

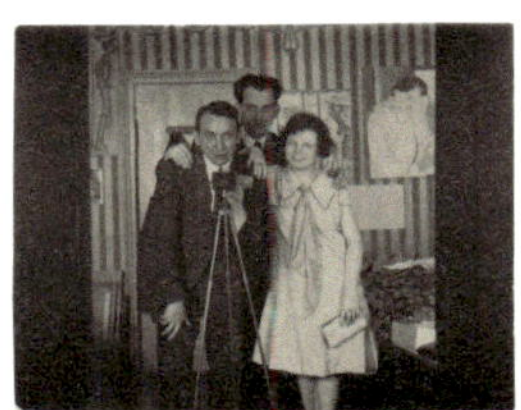

Cat. 12 *Self-Portrait with
Gyula Zilzer and Zilzer's
Girlfriend,* c. 1925
Image/card: 3.8 × 4.9 cm
Jane Corkin, Toronto
Only known print

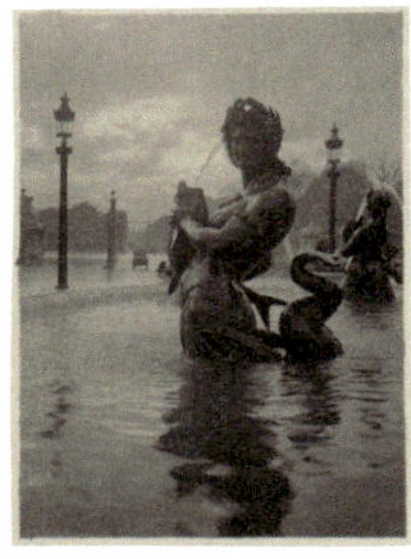

Cat. 9 *Place de la Concorde,*
1925
Image: 5.2 × 3.8 cm;
card: 5.4 × 4 cm
Inscribed, verso, in graphite:
Place de la Concorderól
(View of the Place
de la Concorde)
The J. Paul Getty Museum,
Los Angeles, 86.XM.706.1
Only known print

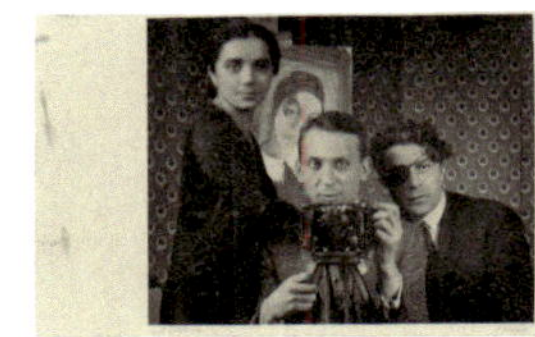

Cat. 13 *Self-Portrait with
Jean Jaffe and Frantisek Reichental,*
December 1926
Image: 8 × 9.9 cm;
card: 8.5 × 12.9 cm
Signed, recto, in graphite:
A Kertész / Paris; inscribed,
verso, in ink and graphite:
*Öcskösnek! / Bandid / Paris,
1926. dec. / Önarckép, egy a- /
merikai ujságíró- / nővel és egy
cseh / festővel.* (For my brother!
Your Bandi, Paris, December
1926. Self-portrait with
a female American journalist
and a Czech painter.)
The Art Institute of Chicago,
gift of Nicholas and
Susan Pritzker, 2012.717
Only known print

Cat. 10 *Fishermen behind
Notre-Dame, Quai d'Orléans,* 1925
Image/card: 10.2 × 6 cm;
mount: 36.8 × 27.3 cm
Signed, mount, in graphite:
A Kertész / Paris
National Gallery of Art,
Washington, DC, Corcoran
Collection, museum purchase,
Jacob and Charlotte Lehrman
Art Acquisition Endowment
Fund, 2014.136.165
Only known print

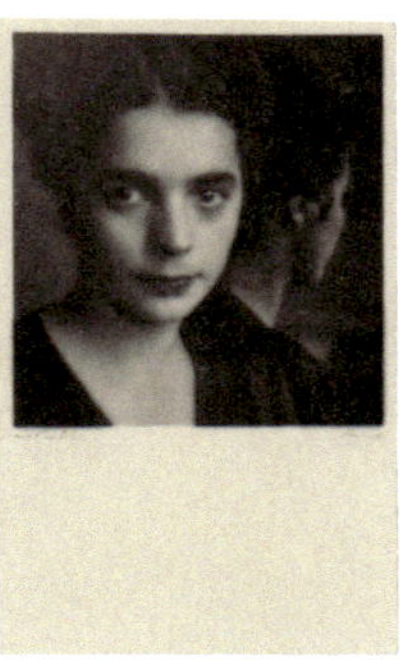

Cat. 14 *Jean Jaffe*, 1926
Image: 7.3 × 6.9 cm;
card: 11.9 × 7.5 cm
Signed, recto, in graphite:
A Kertész / Paris; inscribed, verso,
in graphite: *Mlle Jaffe / amerikai
ujságírónő, / a világ legnagyobb
jiddisch / lapjának, a Der Tag-nak /
munkatársnője.* (Miss Jaffe,
American journalist, contributor
to the world's largest
Yiddish paper, *Der Tag.*)
The Art Institute of Chicago,
gift of Nicholas and
Susan Pritzker, 2012.716
Other known prints: SFMOMA;
Stephen Daiter Gallery, Chicago;
Trish and Jan de Bont

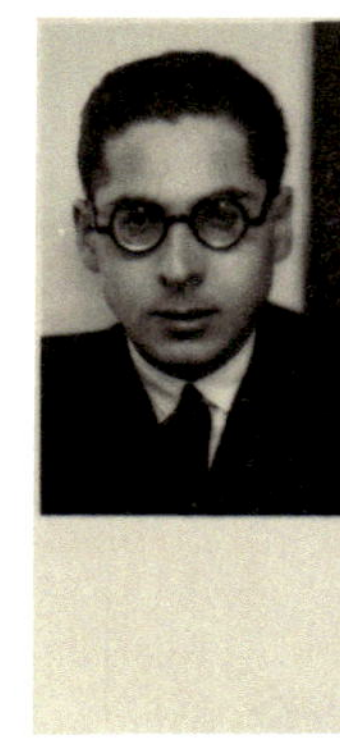

Cat. 17 *Paul Arma*, 1928
Image 9.2 × 5.7 cm;
card: 13.3 × 5.9 cm
Estate of André Kertész,
courtesy of Stephen Bulger
Gallery, Toronto
Only known print

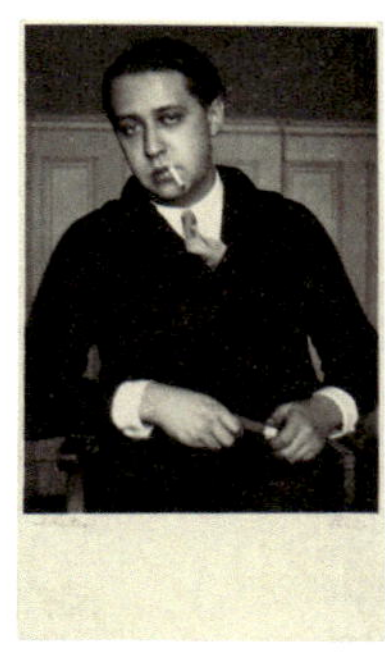

Cat. 18 *Sándor Márai*, 1925–28
Image: 9.8 × 7.1 cm;
card: 12.5 × 7.4 cm
Signed, recto, in graphite:
A Kertész / Paris
Estate of André Kertész,
courtesy of Stephen Bulger
Gallery, Toronto
Only known print

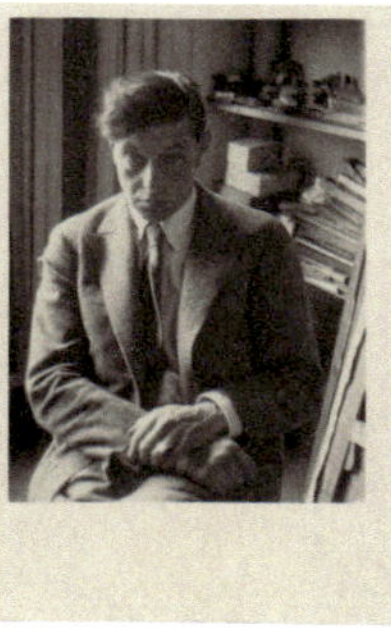

Cat. 15 *Lajos Tihanyi*, 1926
Image: 10.9 × 7.9 cm;
card: 14 × 8.9 cm
The Art Institute of Chicago,
Ada Turnbull Hertle Fund,
1984.544
Only known print

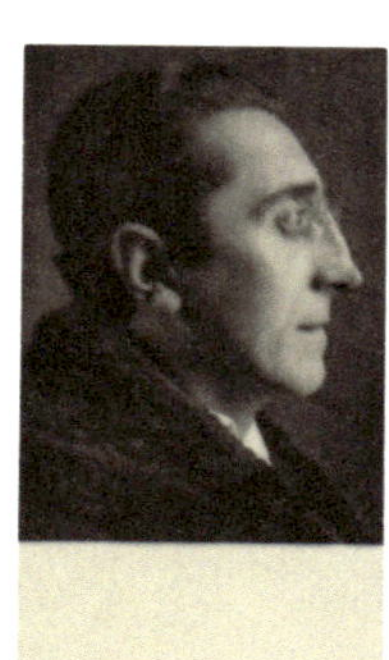

Cat. 19 *Paul Dermée*, 1927
Image: 9.3 × 6.8 cm;
card: 11.9 × 6.8 cm
The Art Institute of Chicago,
gift of Nicholas and
Susan Pritzker, 2012.712
Only known print

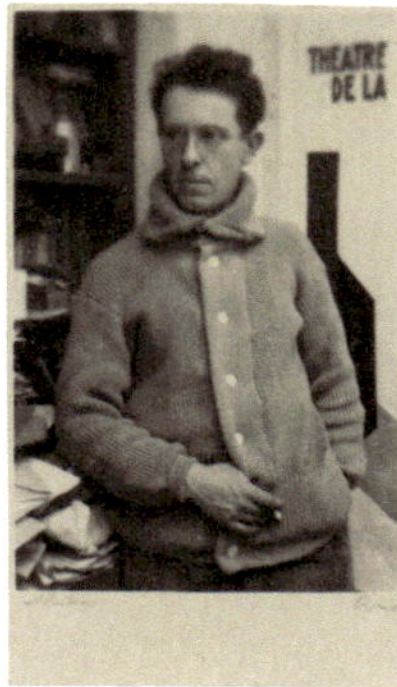

Cat. 16 *Joseph Csáky*, 1926
Image: 10.9 × 7.2 cm;
card: 12.9 × 7.6 cm
Signed, recto, in graphite:
A Kertész / Paris; inscribed,
verso, in graphite: *Csáky, most
már / nemzetközileg elismert /
szobrász.* (Csáky, a sculptor of
international renown by now.)
The Art Institute of Chicago,
gift of Nicholas and
Susan Pritzker, 2012.709
Other known prints:
private collection

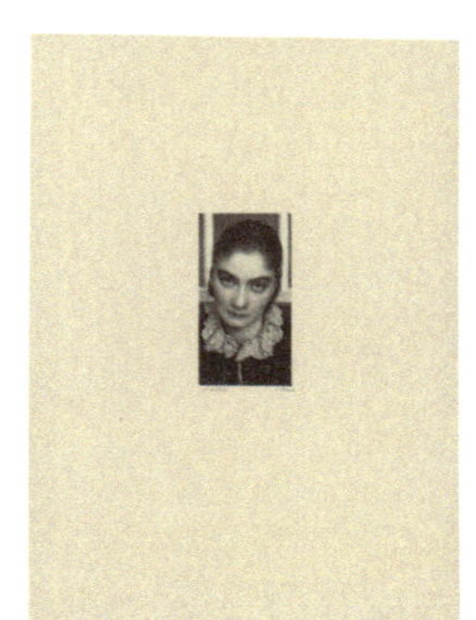

Cat. 20 *Hilda Daus*, 1927
Image/card: 11.2 × 6.1 cm;
mount: 37 × 27.4 cm
Signed, mount, in graphite:
A. Kertész / Paris
Jane Corkin, Toronto
Only known print

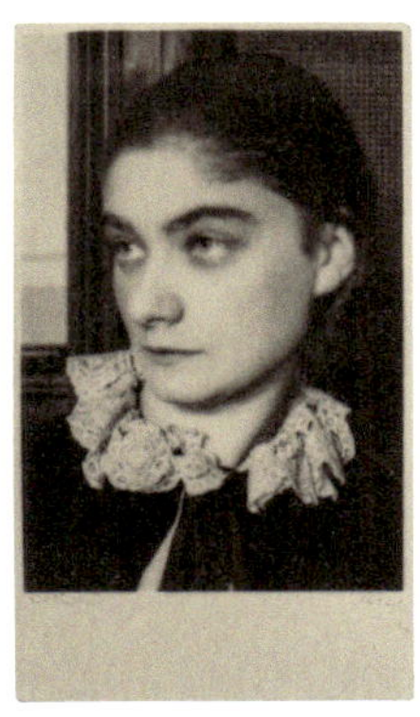

Cat. 21 *Hilda Daus*, 1927
Image: 10.5 × 7 cm;
card: 12.7 × 7.5 cm
Signed, recto, in graphite:
A Kertész / Paris
New Orleans Museum of Art,
museum purchase,
Women's Volunteer
Committee Fund, 73.179
Only known print

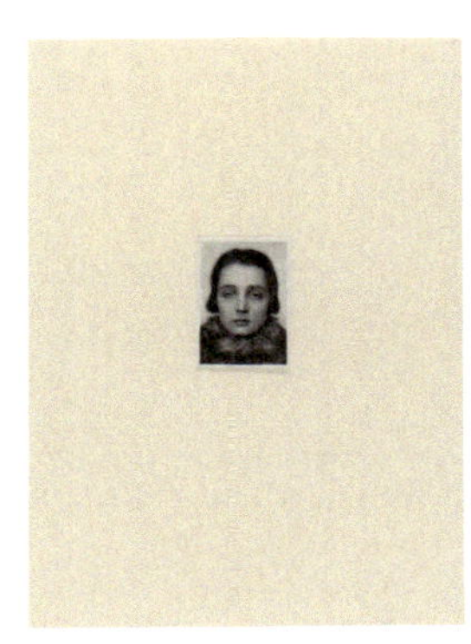

Cat. 25 *Anne-Marie Merkel*, 1926
Image: 7.6 × 5.4 cm;
card: 8.3 × 5.7 cm;
mount: 37 × 27.4 cm
Collection of Stephen Brown,
courtesy of Corkin
Gallery, Toronto
Only known print

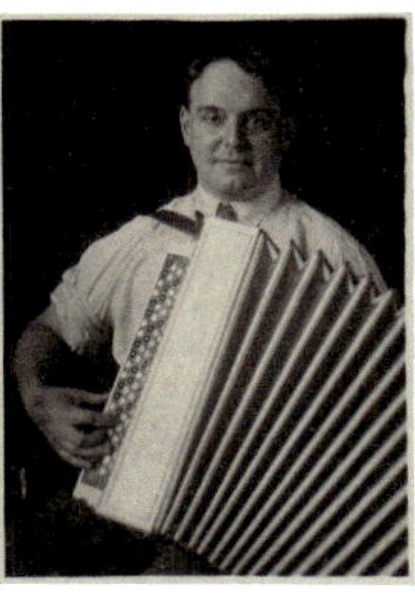

Cat. 22 *Pierre Mac Orlan*, 1927
Image: 10.8 × 7.8 cm;
card: 11.1 × 8.1 cm
The Art Institute of Chicago,
Wirt D. Walker Fund, 1984.532
Only known print

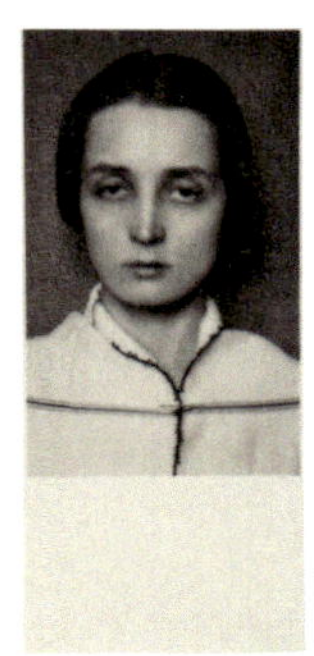

Cat. 26 *Anne-Marie Merkel*, 1926
Image: 9.3 × 5.8 cm;
card: 14.2 × 6.9 cm
Städel Museum, Frankfurt,
Eigentum des Städelschen
Museums-Vereins e.V., St.F.107
Only known print

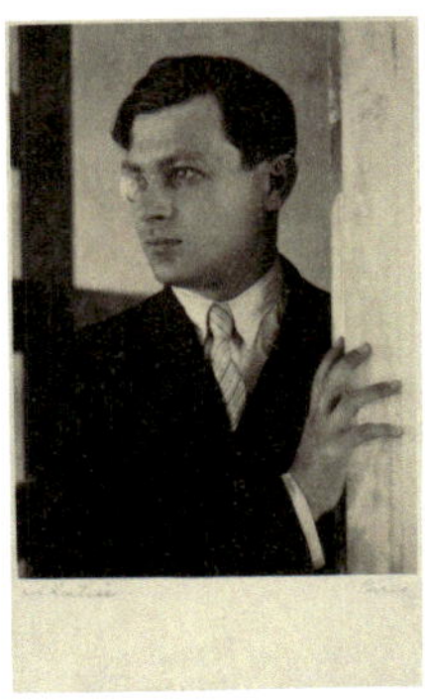

Cat. 23 *Tristan Tzara*, 1926
Image: 11 × 8 cm;
card: 13.3 × 8.3 cm
Signed, recto, in graphite:
A Kertész / Paris
Ubu Gallery, New York
Only known print

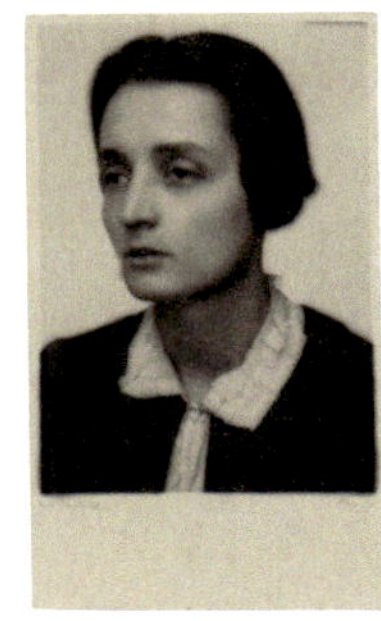

Cat. 27 *Anne-Marie Merkel*, 1926
Image: 10.2 × 7.2 cm;
card: 12.9 × 7.7 cm
Signed, recto, in graphite:
A Kertész / Paris; inscribed,
verso, in graphite: *Mme Repsz
(német)* (Mme Repsz [German])
The Art Institute of Chicago,
gift of Nicholas and
Susan Pritzker, 2012.699
Other known prints: JPGM;
Nelson-Atkins Museum of Art,
Kansas City, MO

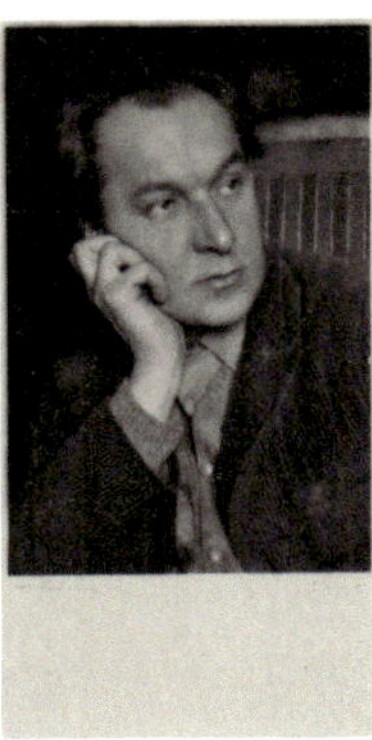

Cat. 24 *Jan Sliwinsky*, 1927
Image: 9.8 × 6.5 cm;
card: 12.8 × 6.8 cm
Signed, recto, in graphite:
A. Kertész / Paris
Museum of Fine Arts, Boston,
gift of Patricia Corkin Kennedy
and John Kennedy in honor of
Jane Corkin, 2009.5262
Only known print

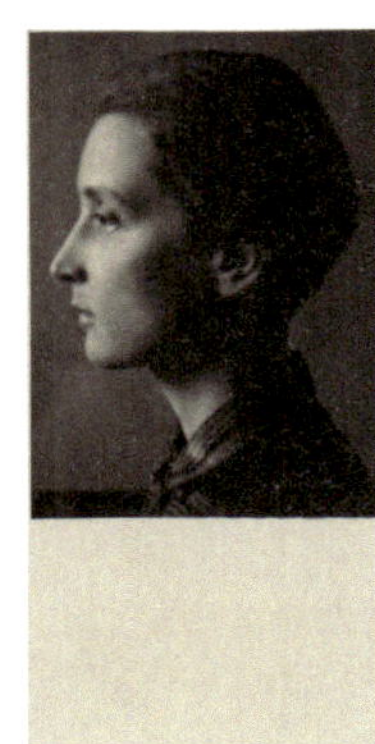

Cat. 28 *Anne-Marie Merkel*, 1926
Image: 9.1 × 6.6 cm;
card: 13.7 × 6.8 cm
The Art Institute of Chicago,
Wirt D. Walker Fund, 1984.533
Only known print

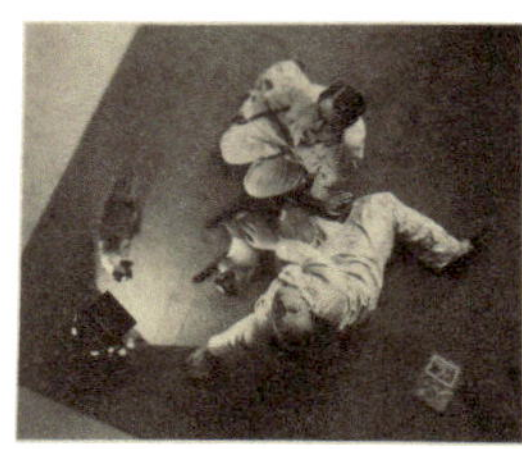

Cat. 29 *Edwin and Peggy Rosskam*, 1927
Image/card: 7.3 × 8.7 cm
New Orleans Museum of Art, museum purchase, Women's Volunteer Committee Fund, 73.175
Other known prints: Bruce Silverstein Gallery, New York; Family Holdings of Nicholas and Susan Pritzker

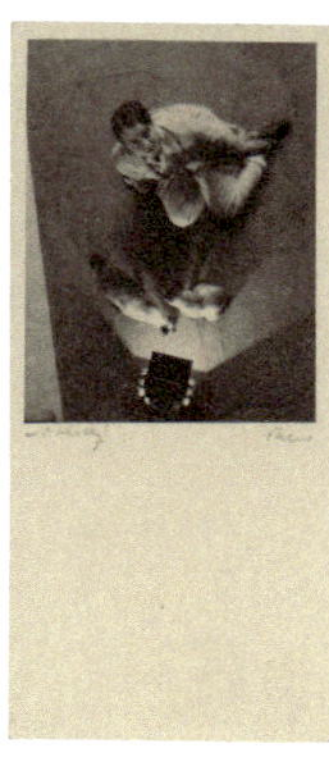

Cat. 30 *Peggy Rosskam*, 1927
Image: 7.4 × 6.1 cm;
card: 13 × 6.4 cm
Signed, recto, in graphite:
A Kertész / Paris
Bruce Silverstein Gallery, New York
Other known prints: AIC (cat. 32); JPGM (cat. 31); Steven and Claudia Schwartz

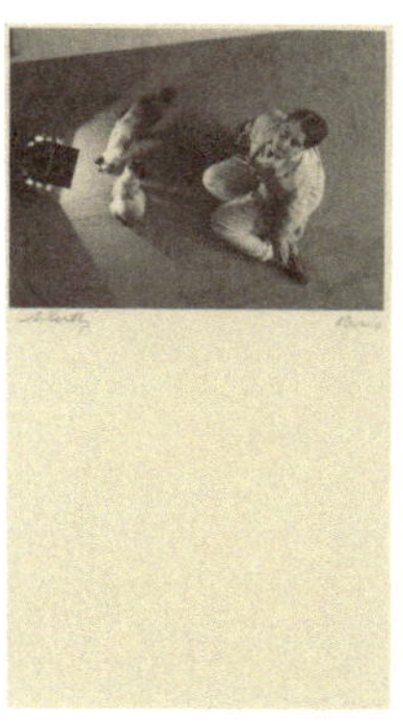

Cat. 31 *Peggy Rosskam*, 1927
Image: 5.4 × 7 cm;
card: 13.2 × 7.3 cm
Signed, recto, in graphite:
A. Kertész / Paris
The J. Paul Getty Museum, Los Angeles, 86.XM.706.12
Other known prints: AIC (cat. 32); Bruce Silverstein Gallery, New York (cat. 30); Steven and Claudia Schwartz

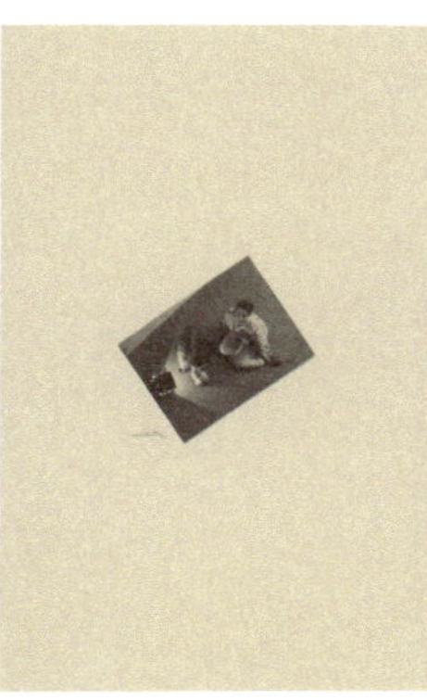

Cat. 32 *Peggy Rosskam*, 1927
Image/card: 5.3 × 7.1 cm; mount (possibly later): 19.5 × 9.6 cm
Signed, mount, in graphite:
A. Kertész
The Art Institute of Chicago, restricted gift of Mrs. Leigh B. Block, 1980.43
Other known prints: JPGM (cat. 31); Bruce Silverstein Gallery, New York (cat. 30); Steven and Claudia Schwartz

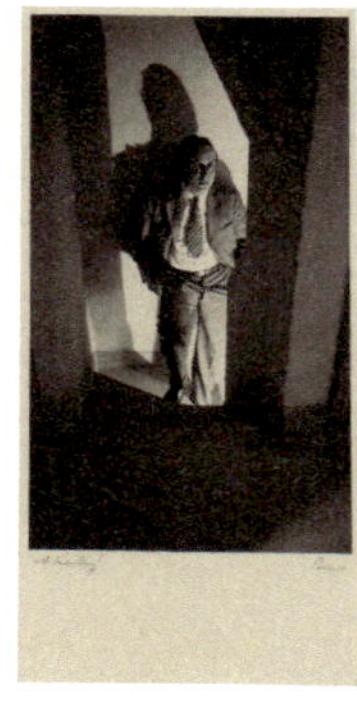

Cat. 33 *Edwin Rosskam*, 1927
Image: 10.5 cm × 6.4 cm;
card: 13.4 × 6.8 cm
Signed, recto, in graphite:
A. Kertész / Paris
Family Holdings of Nicholas and Susan Pritzker
Other known prints: NOMA; Susan Herzig and Paul Hertzmann, Paul M. Hertzmann, Inc., San Francisco; Hans P. Kraus, Jr. Fine Photographs, New York

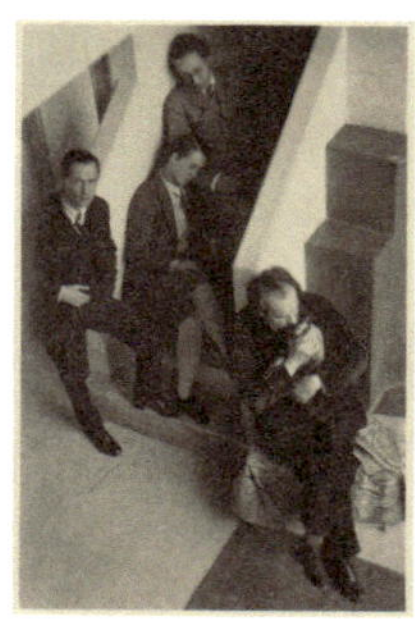

Cat. 34 *Edwin and Peggy Rosskam, Jan Sliwinsky, and Friend*, 1927
Image: 10.9 × 7.1 cm;
card: 11.1 × 7.5 cm
The J. Paul Getty Museum, Los Angeles, 85.XM.371.2
Only known print

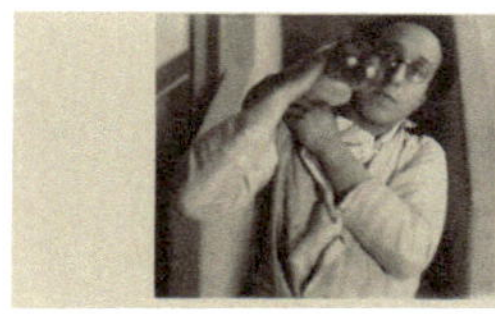

Cat. 35 *Edwin Rosskam*, 1927
Image: 7.9 × 9.4 cm;
card: 8.4 × 13.5 cm
San Francisco Museum of Modern Art, Helen Crocker Russell Memorial Fund purchase, 84.30
Other known prints: private collection

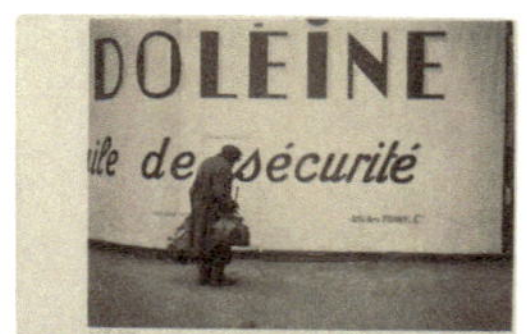

Cat. 36 *"Sécurité,"* 1926–27
Image: 7.8 × 10.9 cm;
card: 8.4 × 12.9 cm
Signed, recto, in graphite:
A Kertész / Paris
The Museum of Modern Art, New York, Thomas Walther Collection, gift of Thomas Walther, 1728.2001
Other known prints: KM

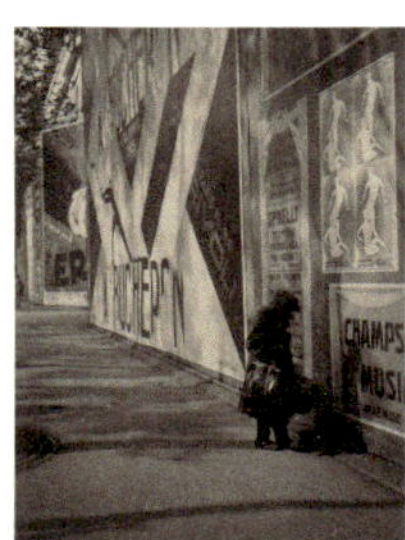

Cat. 37 *Wall of Posters*, 1926
Image/card: 10.3 × 7.7 cm
The Museum of Fine Arts,
Houston, museum purchase
funded by the Caroline Wiess
Law Accessions Endowment
Fund, The Manfred Heiting
Collection, 2002.257
Other known prints: NOMA;
Betsy Karel

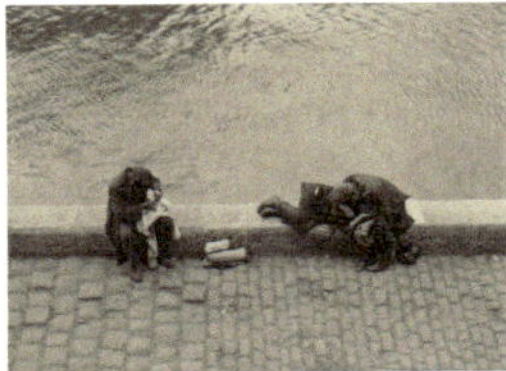

Cat. 38 *Clochards on the Quay*,
1925
Image/card: 7.4 × 10 cm
The J. Paul Getty Museum,
Los Angeles, 85.XM.259.1
Other known prints: KM;
The Gilman and Gonzalez-Falla
Arts Collection

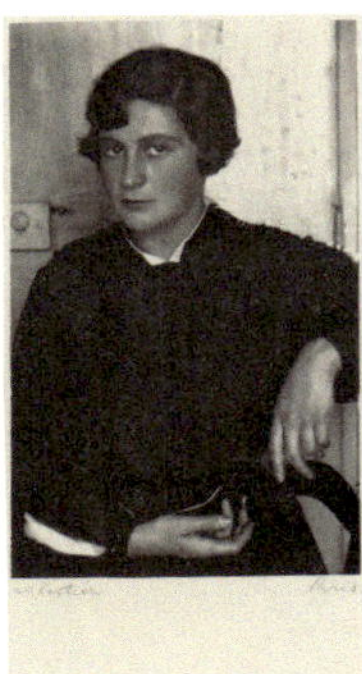

Cat. 39 *Unidentified Sitter*
(*Young German Doctor*), 1926–27
Image: 10.9 × 6.9 cm;
card: 13.1 × 7.1 cm
Signed, recto, in graphite:
A Kertész / Paris
The Art Institute of Chicago,
Wirt D. Walker Fund, 1984.538
Other known prints: AEKF
(two prints); JPGM;
private collection

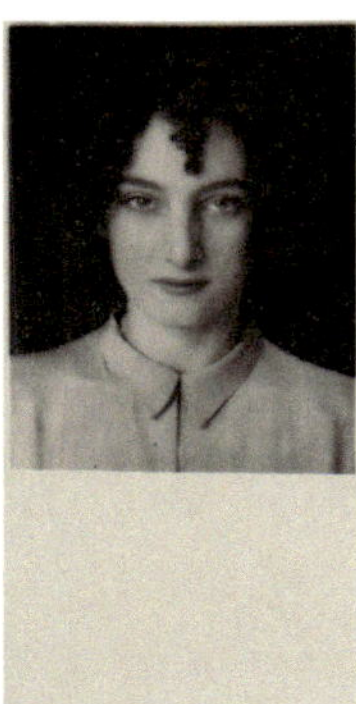

Cat. 40 *Unidentified Sitter*
(*Young Woman with a Curl of
Hair*), 1926–27
Image: 8.6 × 6.8 cm;
card: 13.5 × 7 cm
The Art Institute of Chicago,
Wirt D. Walker Fund, 1984.546
Only known print

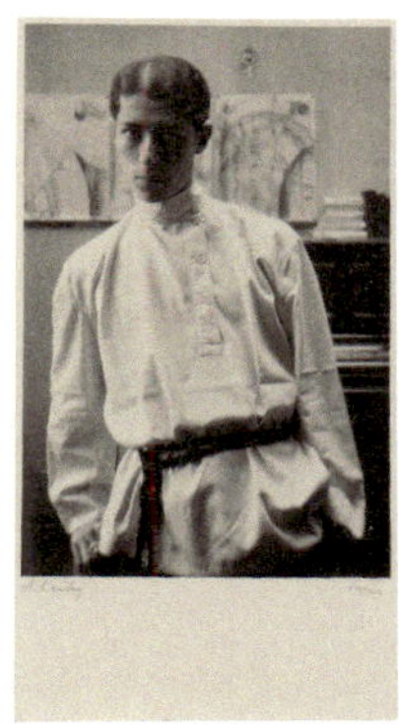

Cat. 41 *Unidentified Sitter*
(*Young Yugoslav Bibliophile*),
1926–27
Image: 10.6 × 7 cm;
card: 13.7 × 7.3 cm
Signed, recto, in graphite:
A. Kertész / Paris
San Francisco Museum of
Modern Art, gift of Lisa and
John Pritzker, 2016.158
Only known print

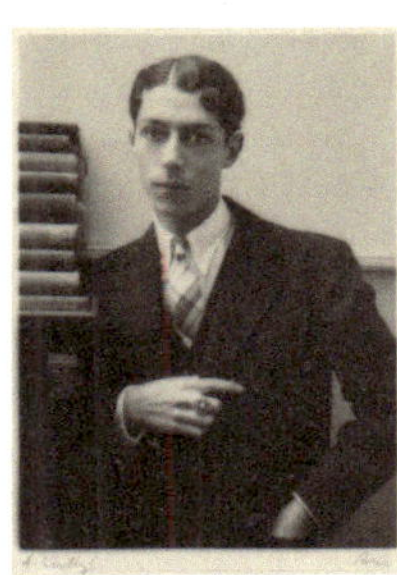

Cat. 42 *Unidentified Sitter*
(*Young Yugoslav Bibliophile*),
1926–27
Image: 10.9 × 8 cm;
card: 11.7 × 8.3 cm
Signed, recto, in graphite:
A Kertész / Paris
The Art Institute of Chicago,
Wirt D. Walker Fund, 1984.545
Only known print

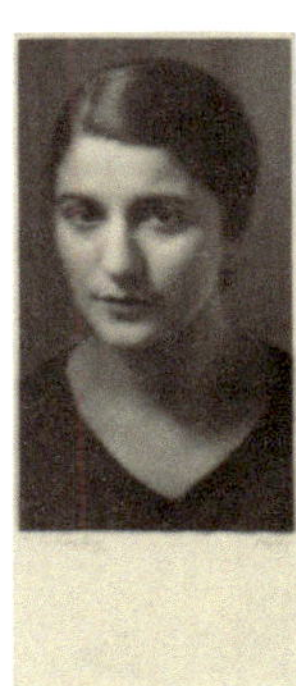

Cat. 43 *Anita de Caro*, 1927
Image: 10 × 5.6 cm;
card: 13.3 × 5.9 cm
Signed, recto, in graphite:
A. Kertész / Paris
The J. Paul Getty Museum,
Los Angeles, 85.XM.259.3
Other known prints:
Weston Gallery,
Carmel-by-the-Sea, CA

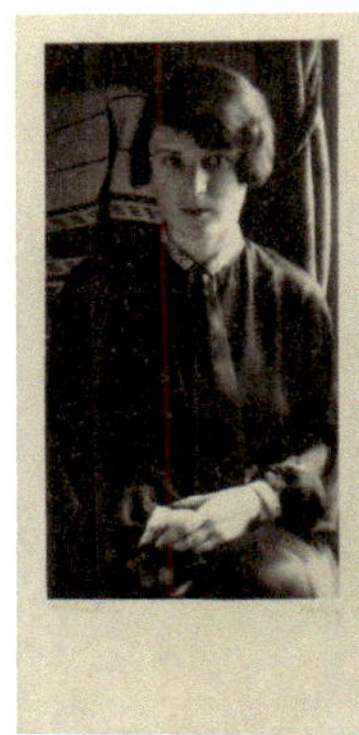

Cat. 44 *Elizabeth Pfeiffer at 30*,
1926
Image: 10.3 × 5.5 cm;
card: 13.4 × 6.6 cm
Signed, recto, in graphite:
A Kertész / Paris
Estate of André Kertész,
courtesy of Stephen Bulger
Gallery, Toronto
Other known prints: Collection of
Ann and Jürgen Wilde, Cologne

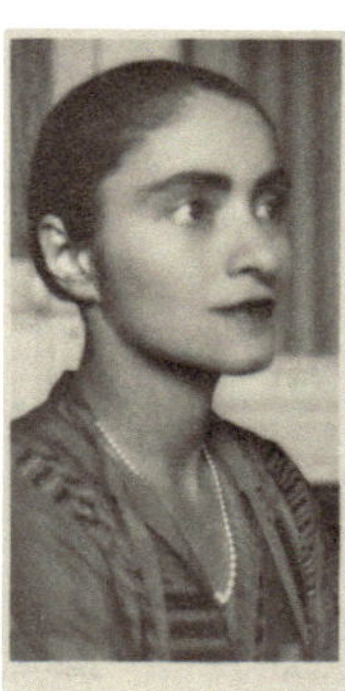

Cat. 45 *Mrs. Wheeler*, 1928
Image: 10.5 × 5.6 cm;
card: 11.4 × 5.8 cm
Signed, recto, in graphite:
A. Kertész / Paris
San Francisco Museum of
Modern Art, gift of Lisa and
John Pritzker, 2016.148
Only known print

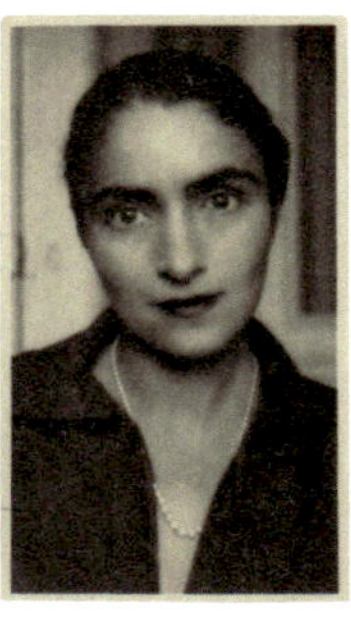

Cat. 46 *Mrs. Wheeler*, 1928
Image: 9.8 × 5.7 cm;
card: 10 × 6 cm
Stephen Daiter Gallery, Chicago
Only known print

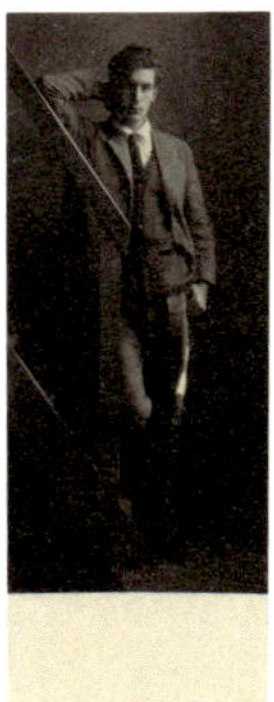

Cat. 47 *Mr. Morgan*, 1926–27
Image: 11.5 × 4.7 cm;
card: 12.8 × 4.7 cm
National Gallery of Art,
Washington, DC, gift of the
André and Elizabeth Kertész
Foundation, 1997.123.6
Only known print

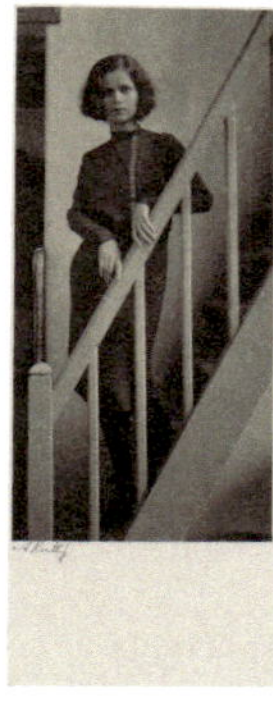

Cat. 48 *Unidentified Sitter*
(*Yugoslav Ballet Dancer*),
1926–27
Image: 11.4 × 5.1 cm;
card: 13.4 × 5.3 cm
Signed, recto, in graphite:
A Kertész
National Gallery of Art,
Washington, DC, gift of the
André and Elizabeth Kertész
Foundation, 1997.123.4
Only known print

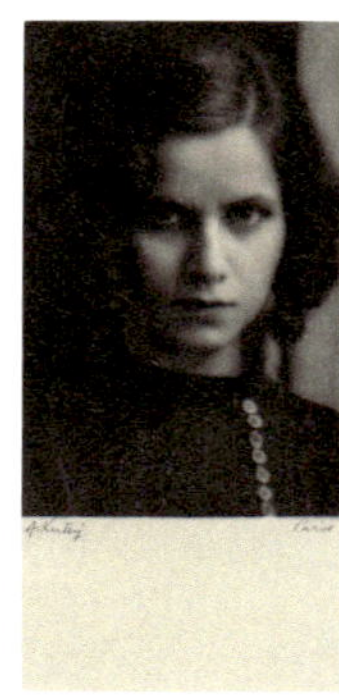

Cat. 49 *Unidentified Sitter*
(*Yugoslav Ballet Dancer*),
1926–27
Image: 9.5 × 6.1 cm;
card: 12.9 × 6.2 cm
Signed, recto, in graphite:
A. Kertész / Paris
National Gallery of Art,
Washington, DC, the Herbert
and Nannette Rothschild
Memorial Fund in memory of
Judith Rothschild, 1997.45.1
Only known print

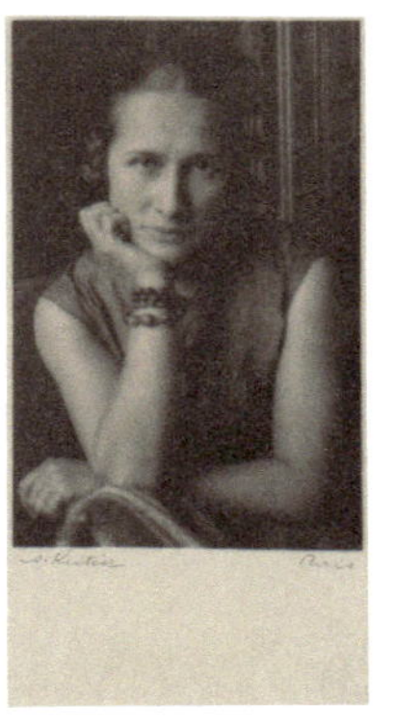

Cat. 50 *Madame Perret*, 1927
Image: 10.3 × 6.7 cm;
card: 13.3 × 7 cm
Signed, recto, in graphite:
A. Kertész / Paris
The Museum of Fine Arts,
Houston, museum purchase
funded by the Caroline Wiess
Law Accessions Endowment
Fund, The Manfred Heiting
Collection, 2002.1424
Only known print

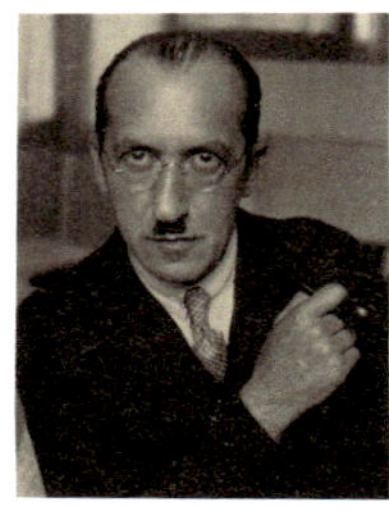

Cat. 51 *Piet Mondrian*, 1926
Image/card: 10.4 × 7.9 cm
Family Holdings of
Nicholas and Susan Pritzker
Other known prints: Bruce
Silverstein Gallery, New York

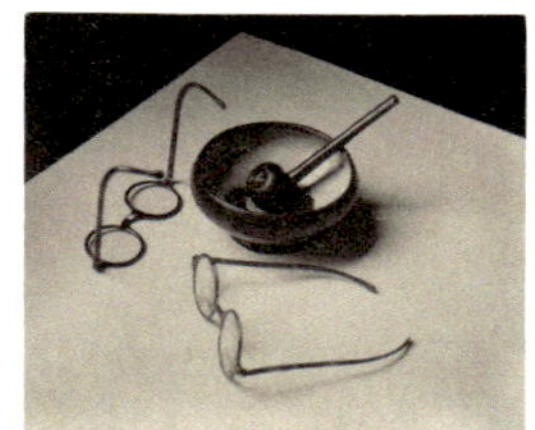

Cat. 52 *Mondrian's Pipe
and Glasses*, 1926
Image/card: 7.9 × 9.5 cm
Family Holdings of
Nicholas and Susan Pritzker
Other known prints: MoMA;
Edwynn Houk Gallery,
New York; The Sir Elton John
Photography Collection;
private collection

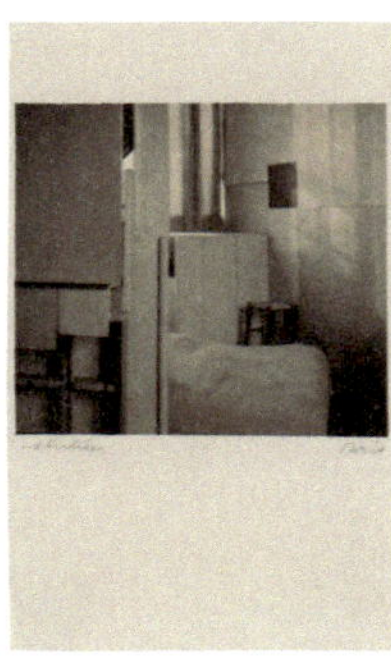

Cat. 53 *Mondrian's Studio*, 1926
Image: 7 × 7.9 cm;
card: 13.8 × 8.4 cm
Signed, recto, in graphite:
A Kertész / Paris
Family Holdings of
Nicholas and Susan Pritzker
Other known prints: Met;
MoMA; Edwynn Houk
Gallery, New York (cat. 54);
private collection

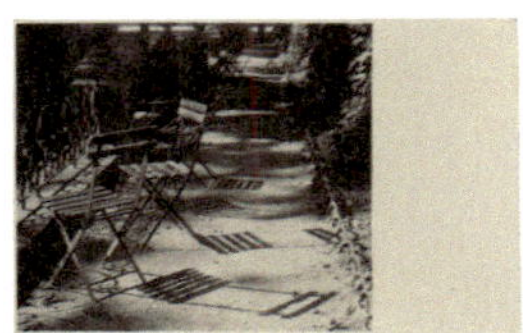

Cat. 57 *Chairs at the Medici
Fountain, Jardin du Luxembourg*, 1925
Image: 8 × 9.2 cm;
card: 8.5 × 13 cm
Signed, recto, in graphite:
A Kertész / Paris
Bruce Silverstein Gallery,
New York, and Edwynn Houk
Gallery, New York
Other known prints: Collection of
Ann and Jürgen Wilde, Cologne;
private collection

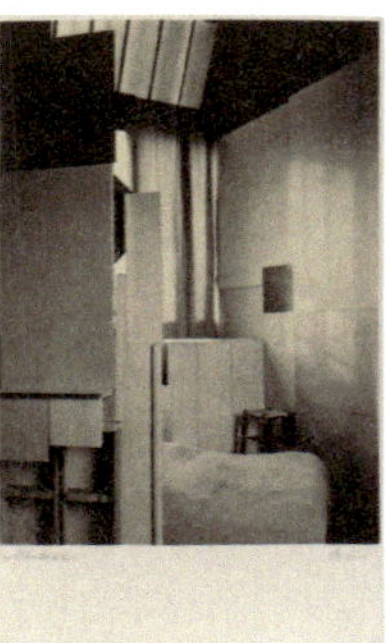

Cat. 54 *Mondrian's Studio*, 1926
Image: 10.9 × 7.9 cm;
card: 13.3 × 8.2 cm
Signed, recto, in graphite:
A Kertész / Paris
Edwynn Houk Gallery,
New York
Other known prints: Met;
MoMA; Family Holdings of
Nicholas and Susan Pritzker
(cat. 53); private collection

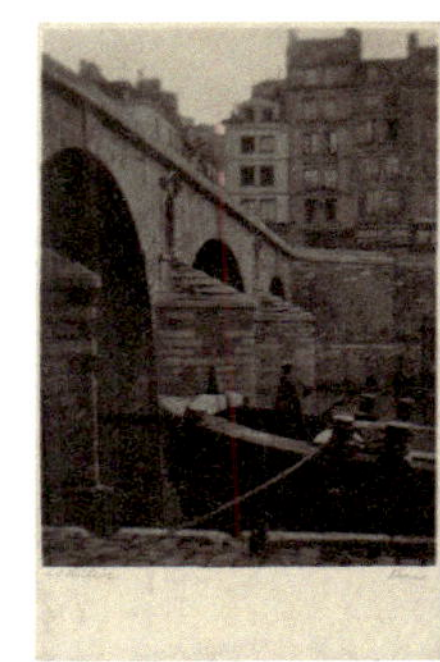

Cat. 58 *Pont Marie*, 1926–27
Image: 10.9 × 8 cm;
card: 13 × 8.2 cm
Signed, recto, in graphite:
A Kertész / Paris
The Museum of Fine Arts,
Houston, museum purchase
funded by the Caroline Wiess
Law Accessions Endowment
Fund, The Manfred Heiting
Collection, 2002.261
Other known prints:
MFA Boston

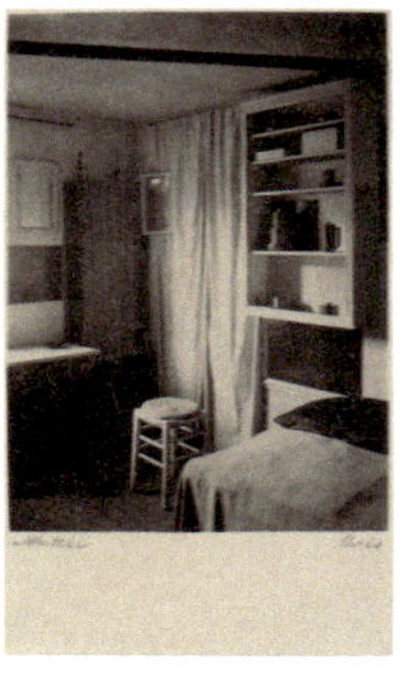

Cat. 55 *Mondrian's Studio*, 1926
Image: 10.9 × 8 cm;
card: 13.7 × 8.2 cm
Signed, recto, in graphite:
A Kertész / Paris
The Metropolitan Museum of
Art, New York, gift of
Harry Holtzman, 1986.1225 2
Only known print

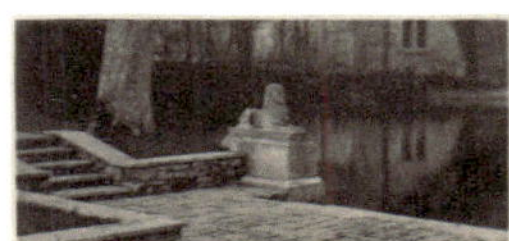

Cat. 59 *Château de
Sainte-Mesme*, 1926
Image: 4.9 × 10.6 cm;
card: 5.2 × 10.9 cm
National Gallery of Art,
Washington, DC, gift of the
André and Elizabeth Kertész
Foundation, 1997.123.2
Only known print

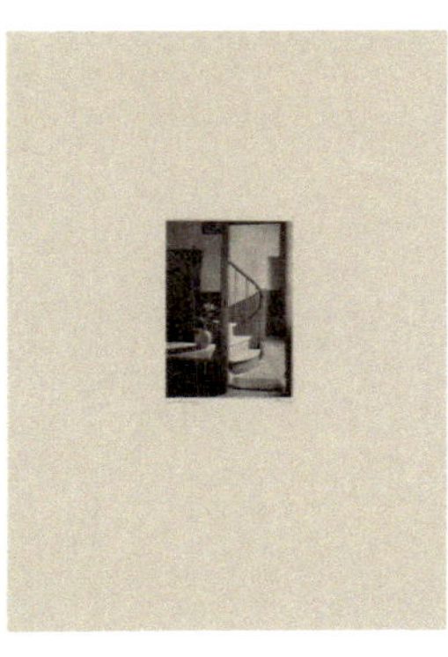

Cat. 56 *Chez Mondrian*, 1926
Image/card: 10.8 × 7.9 cm;
mount: 37.2 × 27.4 cm
Signed, mount, in graphite:
A Kertész / Paris
The Art Institute of Chicago,
Julien Levy Collection, gift of
Jean and Julien Levy, 1975.1136
Other known prints: JPGM;
Met; MFA Boston; MoMA;
Edwynn Houk Gallery,
New York; Family Holdings of
Nicholas and Susan Pritzker;
private collection

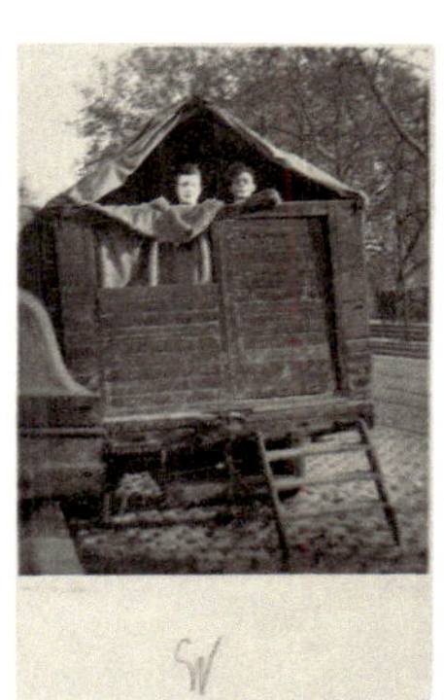

Cat. 60 *Fairground*, 1926
Image: 10.1 × 7.9 cm;
card: 12.7 × 8.1 cm
Signed, recto, in graphite:
A Kertész / Paris
New Orleans Museum of Art,
museum purchase,
Women's Volunteer
Committee Fund, 73.171
Only known print

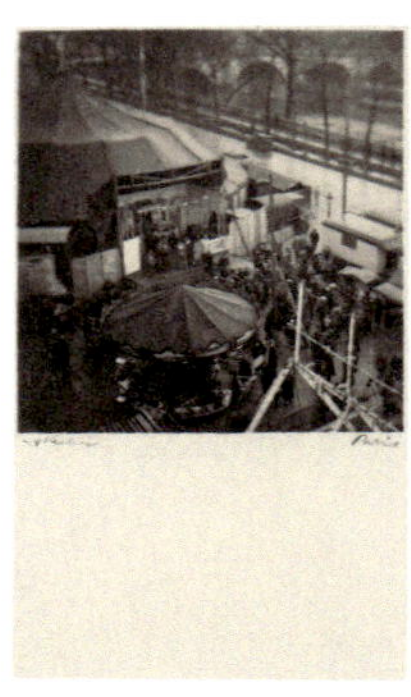

Cat. 61 *Fairground*, 1926
Image: 7.5 × 7.1 cm;
card: 21.1 × 7.3 cm
Signed, recto, in graphite:
A Kertész / Paris; inscribed,
verso, in graphite:
Typikus parisi / búcsú
(A typical Parisian fair)
Lookout Dove Partners,
courtesy of Stephen Bulger
Gallery, Toronto
Only known print

Cat. 62 *Fairground, Quai de
l'Hôtel de Ville*, 1926
Image/card: 7.7 × 7.7 cm;
mount: 37.1 × 27.4 cm
Signed, mount, in graphite:
A. Kertész / Paris
Collection of Stephen Brown,
courtesy of Corkin
Gallery, Toronto
Only known print

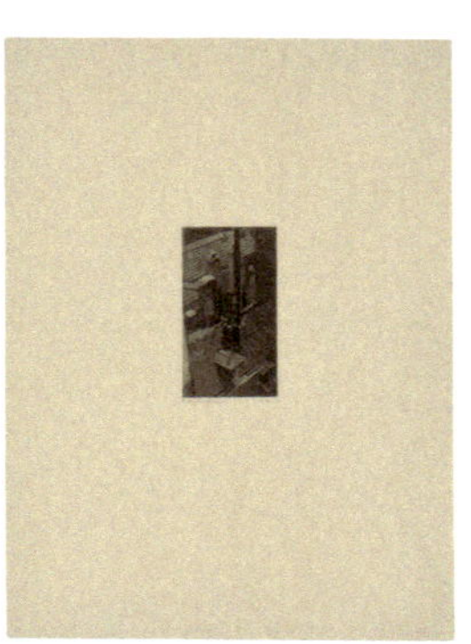

Cat. 63 *Rooftops and Chimneys*,
1927
Image/card: 10.5 × 5.7 cm;
mount: 36.8 × 27.3 cm
Signed, mount, in graphite:
A. Kertész / Paris
Private collection, San Francisco
Other known prints: Collection of
Ann and Jürgen Wilde, Cologne

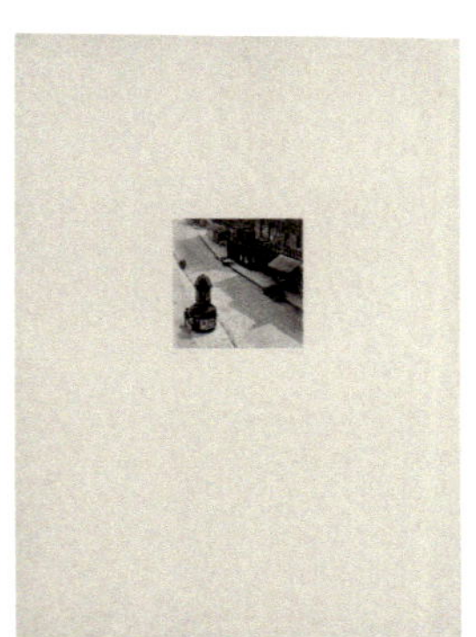

Cat. 64 *Latin Quarter*, 1927
Image/card: 7.9 × 7.9 cm;
mount: 37.1 × 27.3 cm
Signed, mount, in graphite:
A. Kertész / Paris
Joy of Giving Something, Inc.
Only known print

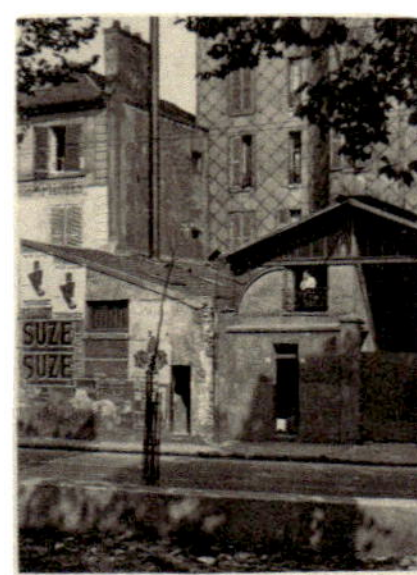

Cat. 65 *Josep Llorens Artigas*,
1926–28
Image: 10.8 × 7.9 cm;
card: 11.3 × 8.1 cm
Signed, recto, in graphite:
A Kertész / Paris
New Orleans Museum of Art,
museum purchase,
Women's Volunteer
Committee Fund, 73.172
Other known prints: Collection of
Ann and Jürgen Wilde, Cologne;
private collection

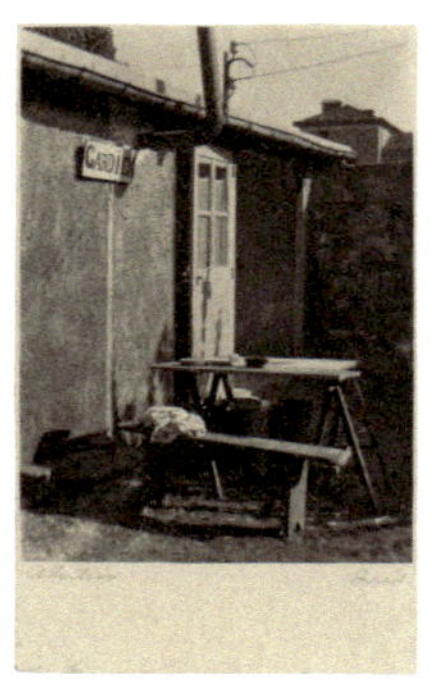

Cat. 66 *"Gardien,"* 1926
Image: 10.9 × 7.9 cm;
card: 13.2 × 8.2 cm
Signed, recto, in graphite:
A Kertész / Paris
The Art Institute of Chicago,
gift of Nicholas and
Susan Pritzker, 2012.710
Other known prints: AEKF
(two prints); Amanda and
Don Mullen; Collection of
Paul Sack, promised gift to
the San Francisco Museum of
Modern Art

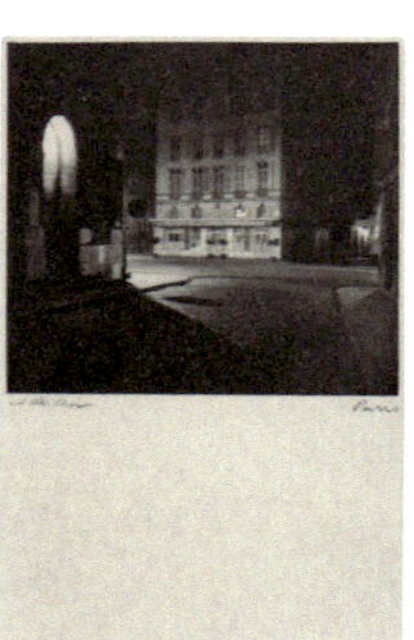

Cat. 67 *Théatre Odéon*, 1925–28
Image: 7.3 × 7.9 cm;
card: 12.7 × 8.3 cm
Signed, recto, in graphite:
A Kertész / Paris
New Orleans Museum of Art,
museum purchase,
Women's Volunteer
Committee Fund, 73.170
Other known prints: Joy of
Giving Something, Inc.

Cat. 68 *Notre-Dame at Night*,
1925
Image/card: 7.3 × 8.3 cm;
mount: 36.8 × 27.3 cm
Signed, mount, in graphite:
A. Kertész / Paris
Bruce Silverstein Gallery,
New York
Only known print

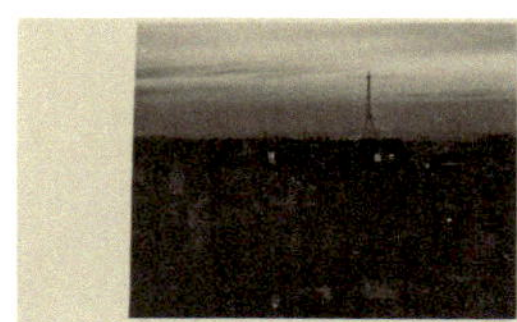

Cat. 69 *Eiffel Tower at Night*, 1927
Image: 7.9 × 10.3 cm;
card: 8.4 × 13.5 cm
Inscribed, recto, in graphite:
Paris / 1927; inscribed, verso,
in graphite: *Estefelé a [. . .]
ablakából, Bandi* (Evening from
the window in the [. . .], Bandi)
The J. Paul Getty Museum,
Los Angeles, 86.XM.706.13
Other known prints: AIC

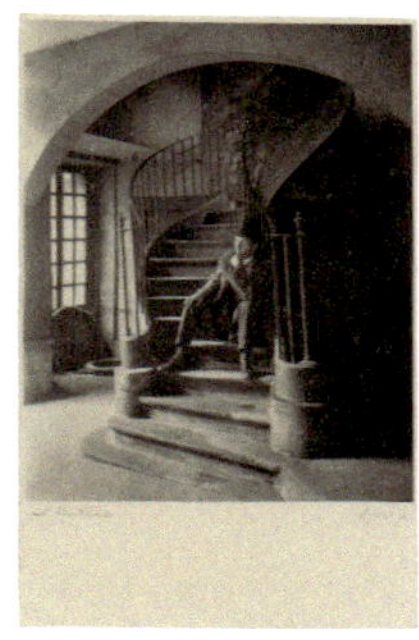

Cat. 70 *Unidentified Sitter
(Hungarian Woodcutter and
Graphic Designer)*, 1927
Image: 9.8 × 7.9 cm;
card: 12.6 × 8.2 cm
Signed, recto, in graphite:
A Kertész / Paris; inscribed,
verso, in graphite: *Ez inkább
mozi, mint / fotografia, de akit /
ábrázol, az így karakterisztikus.
A / gyönyörű lépcsőház az / én
felfedezésem.* (This is more like
a movie than a photograph,
but it is typical of the person
depicted. The gorgeous stairwell
is my discovery.)
The Art Institute of Chicago,
gift of Nicholas and
Susan Pritzker, 2012.703
Other known prints: MoMA

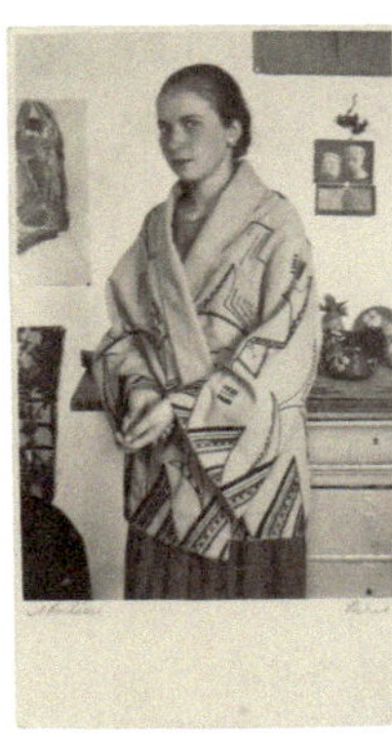

Cat. 71 *Gundvor Berg in
Her Studio*, August 1926
Image: 10.9 × 7.2 cm;
card: 13.6 × 7.7 cm
Signed, recto, in graphite:
A Kertész / Paris; inscribed,
verso, in graphite: *VIII/30 / Ezt
a nőt úgy hívják, hogy / Gunvor
Berg. / (Günvornak olvasssák és
ez a keresztneve)* (August 30.
This woman's name is Gunvor
Berg [It is pronounced as Günvor,
and that's her first name])
The Art Institute of Chicago,
gift of Nicholas and
Susan Pritzker, 2012.700
Only known print

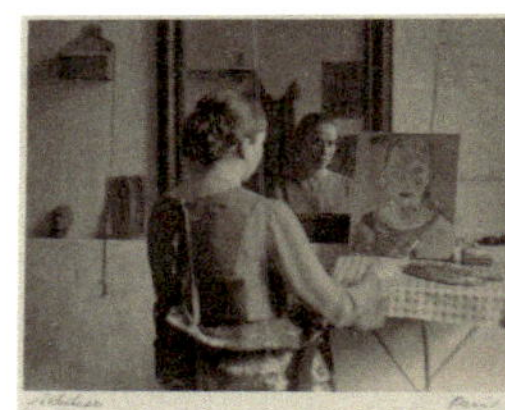

Cat. 72 *Gundvor Berg*, 1926
Image: 7.3 × 9.6 cm;
card: 8 × 9.9 cm
Signed, recto, in graphite:
A. Kertész / Paris
The Art Institute of Chicago,
gift of Nicholas and
Susan Pritzker, 2012.720
Only known print

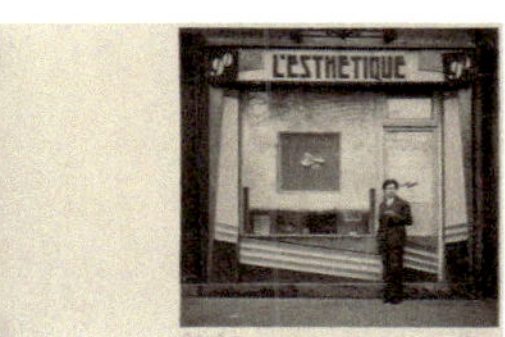

Cat. 73 *Evsa Model in Front
of L'Esthétique*, 1927
Image: 8 × 8.5 cm;
card: 9 × 14 cm
Signed, recto, in graphite:
A Kertész / Paris
Gary S. Davis Collection
Only known print

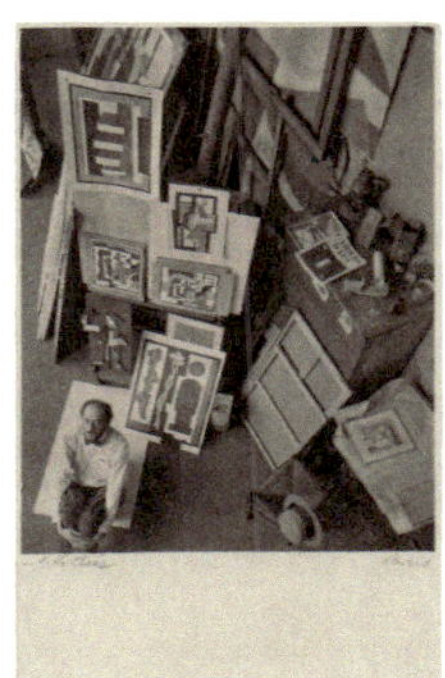

Cat. 74 *Otto Carlsund, Fernand
Léger's Assistant, in Léger's Studio*,
1926–27
Image: 10.1 × 7.9 cm;
card: 13.1 × 8.2 cm
Signed, recto, in graphite:
A. Kertész / Paris
The Art Institute of Chicago,
gift of Nicholas and
Susan Pritzker, 2012.707
Other known prints: NOMA

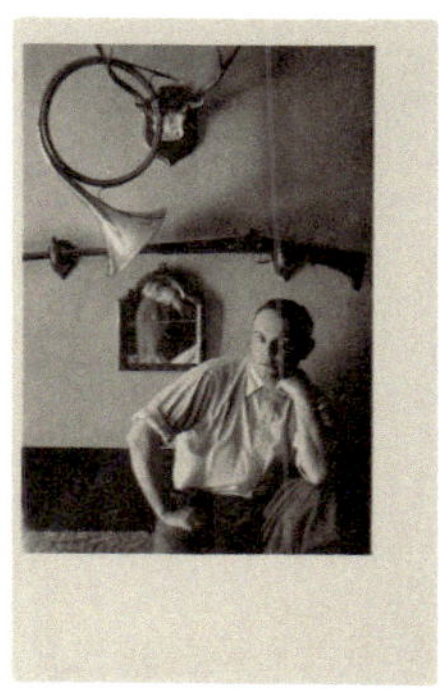

Cat. 75 *Pierre Mac Orlan*, 1928
Image: 10.7 × 7.4 cm,
card: 14 × 9 cm
Princeton University Art Museum,
Princeton, NJ, gift of Patricia and
Franklin S. Kolodny, x1990-126
Only known print

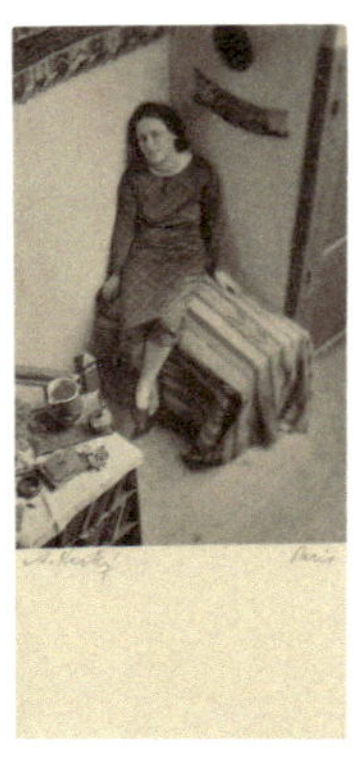

Cat. 76 *Eva Révai in
Her Studio*, 1927
Image: 9 × 5.8 cm;
card: 12.2 × 5.8 cm
Signed, recto, in graphite:
A. Kertész / Paris
The J. Paul Getty Museum,
Los Angeles, 85.XM.259.6
Other known prints:
Jane Corkin, Toronto;
Robert Yoskowitz

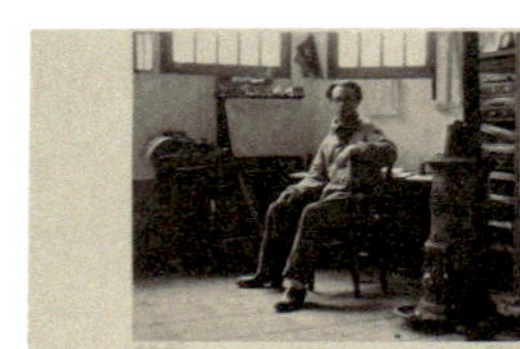

Cat. 80 *Joseph Csáky*, 1926–28
Image: 7.8 × 10.2 cm;
card: 8.4 × 12.9 cm
Signed, recto, in graphite:
A. Kertész / Paris
New Orleans Museum of Art,
museum purchase,
Women's Volunteer
Committee Fund, 73.176
Only known print

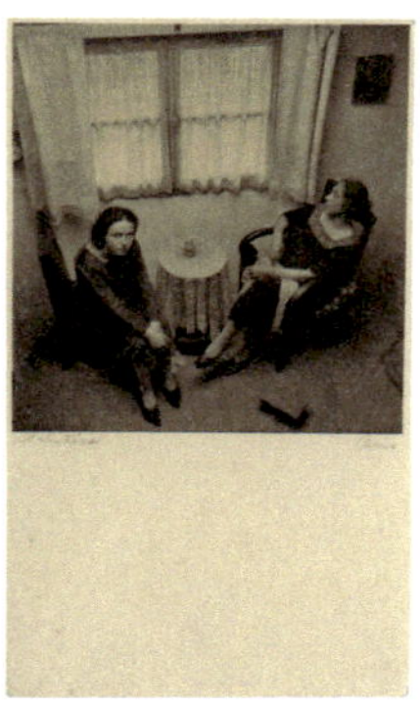

Cat. 77 *Eva and Ilka Révai*, 1927
Image: 8 × 7.5 cm;
card: 13.3 × 7.9 cm
Signed, recto, in graphite:
A Kertész / Paris
Collection of Michael P. Mattis
and Judith G. Hochberg
Other known prints:
Hungarian Museum of
Photography, Kecskemét

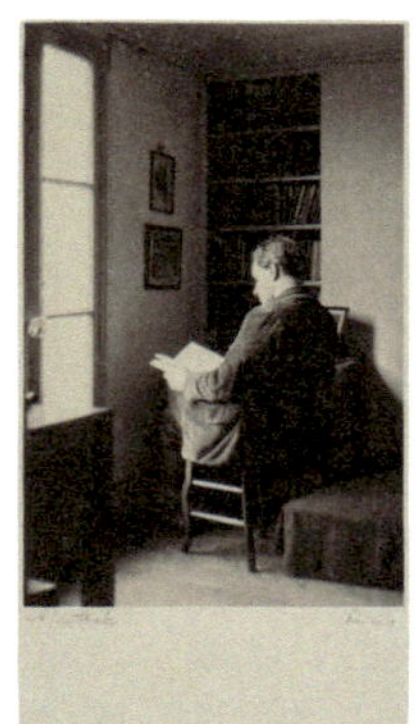

Cat. 81 *Jan Sliwinsky*, 1926–27
Image: 11 × 7.1 cm;
card: 13.3 × 7.3 cm
Signed, recto, in graphite:
A Kertész / Paris
New Orleans Museum of Art,
museum purchase,
Women's Volunteer
Committee Fund, 73.182
Only known print

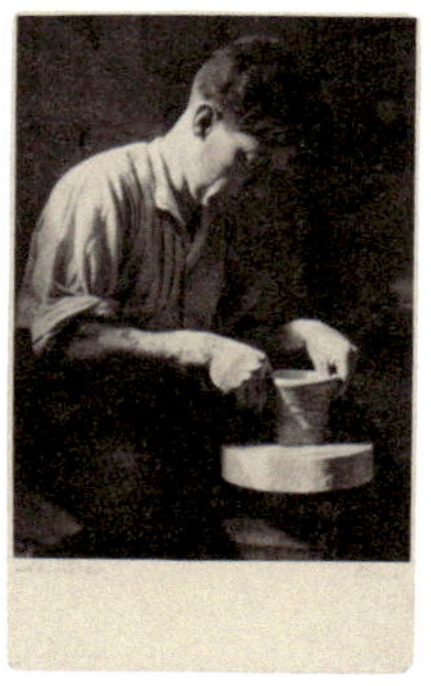

Cat. 78 *Josep Llorens Artigas*,
1927
Image: 10.8 × 7.9 cm;
card: 13.5 × 8.4 cm
Signed, recto, in graphite:
A Kertész / Paris
San Francisco Museum of
Modern Art, gift of Lisa and
John Pritzker, 2016.159
Other known prints: AEKF

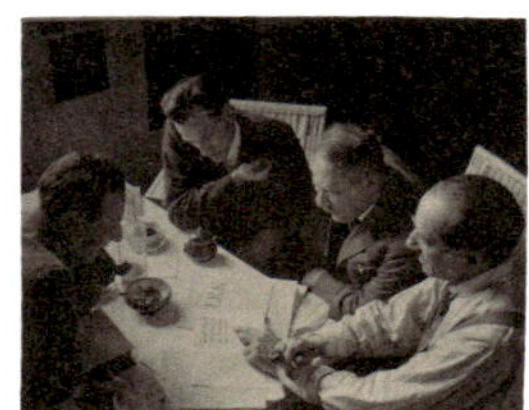

Cat. 82 *Michel Seuphor,
Gyula Zilzer, a Dutch
Constructivist, and Piet Mondrian
in Mondrian's Studio*, 1926
Image/card: 7.9 × 9.8 cm
Richard and Ellen Sandor
Family Collection
Other known prints: NOMA;
private collection, New York

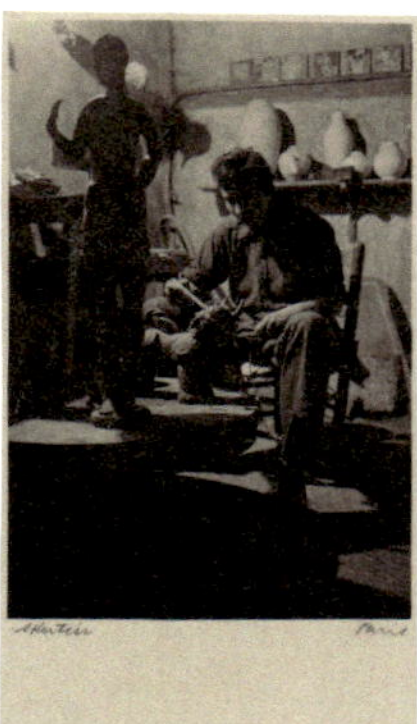

Cat. 79 *Vally Wieselthier
in Josep Llorens Artigas's
Studio*, 1927
Image: 10.9 × 7.4 cm;
card: 13.5 × 7.7 cm
Signed, recto, in graphite:
A Kertész / Paris
André and Elizabeth Kertész
Foundation, courtesy of
Stephen Bulger Gallery,
Toronto
Only known print

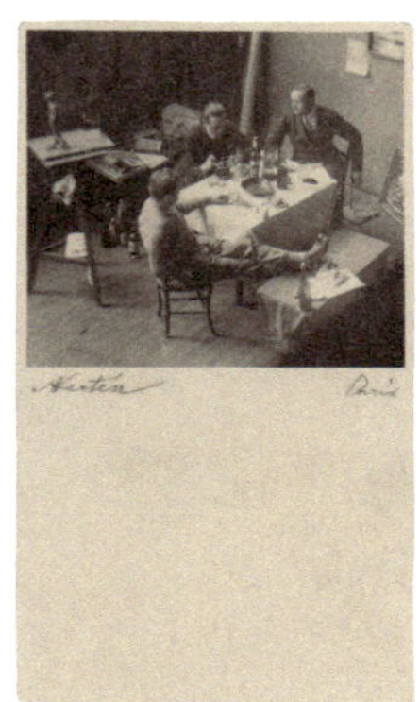

Cat. 83 *Károly Kernstok's
Studio*, 1925
Image: 6.6 × 7.5 cm;
card: 13.5 × 8 cm
Signed, recto, in graphite:
A Kertész / Paris
The Art Institute of Chicago,
gift of Nicholas and
Susan Pritzker, 2012.705
Other known prints: AEKF; AIC
(additional print)

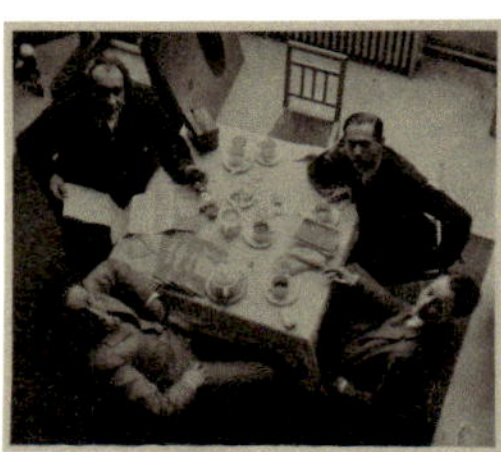

Cat. 84 *Edwin Rosskam,
Jan Sliwinsky, an American
Journalist, and Peggy Rosskam
in the Rosskams' Apartment,*
1926–28
Image: 7.3 × 8.6 cm;
card: 7.6 × 8.7
New Orleans Museum of Art,
museum purchase,
Women's Volunteer
Committee Fund, 73.131
Only known print

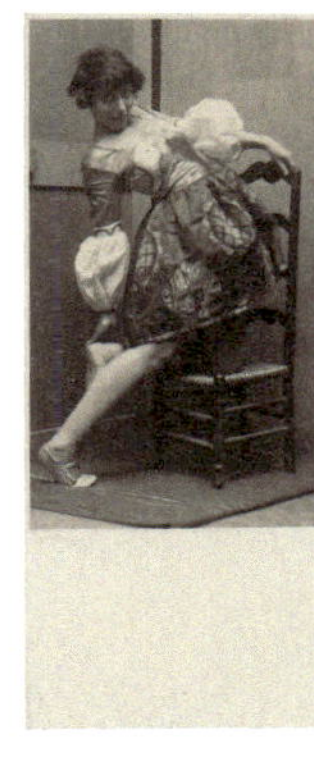

Cat. 88 *Magda Förstner,* 1927
Image: 9.2 × 5.5 cm;
card: 13.4 × 5.7 cm
Family Holdings of
Nicholas and Susan Pritzker
Only known print

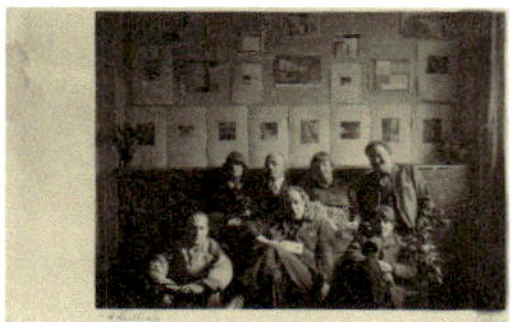

Cat. 85 *Jan Sliwinsky,
Herwarth Walden, and Friends
at Au Sacre du Printemps,*
March 1927
Image: 7.9 × 11 cm;
card: 8.4 × 13.5 cm
Signed, recto, in graphite:
A Kertész / Paris
The J. Paul Getty Museum,
Los Angeles, 86.XM.706.7
Other known prints:
Jane Corkin, Toronto

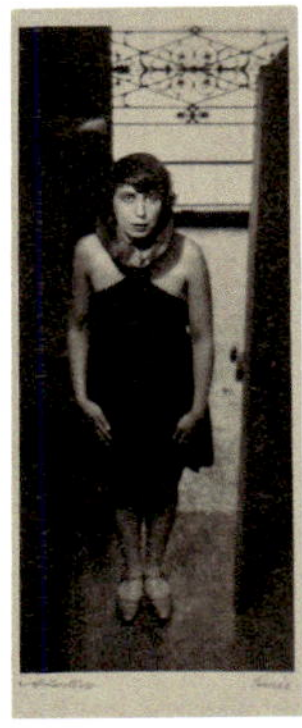

Cat. 89 *Magda Förstner,* 1927
Image: 9 × 3.8 cm;
card: 10.1 × 4.1 cm
Signed, recto, in graphite:
A. Kertész / Paris
New Orleans Museum of Art,
museum purchase,
Women's Volunteer
Committee Fund, 73.165
Other known prints: MoMA

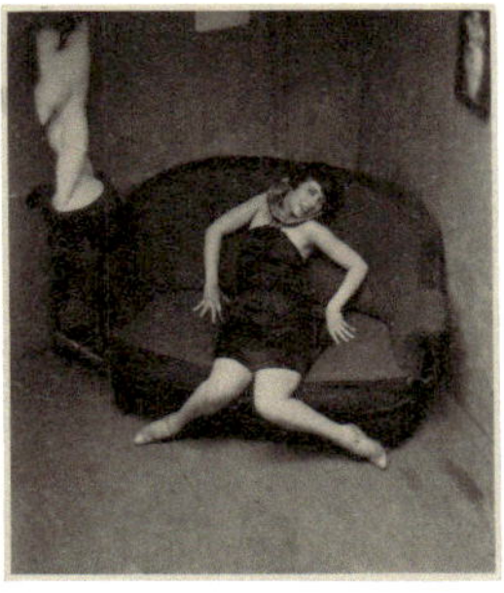

Cat. 86 *Satiric Dancer
(Variant),* 1927
Image: 9 × 7.8 cm;
card: 9.5 × 8.1 cm
The Art Institute of Chicago,
gift of Nicholas and
Susan Pritzker, 2009.646
Only known print

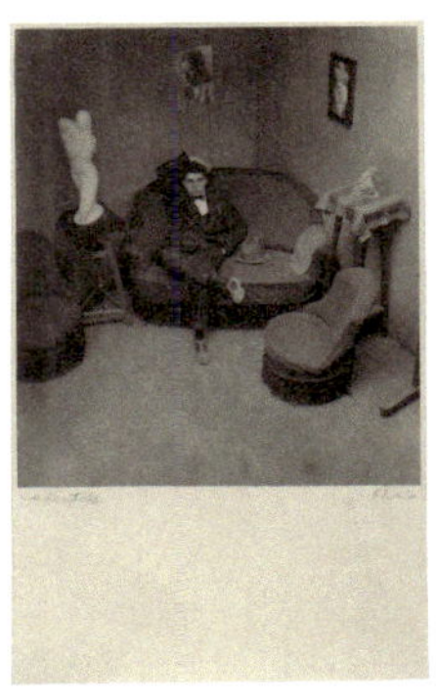

Cat. 90 *Etienne Beöthy in
His Studio,* 1928
Image: 9.1 × 7.9 cm;
card: 13 × 8.2 cm
Signed, recto, in graphite:
A Kertész / Paris
The Museum of Modern Art,
New York, Thomas Walther
Collection, Grace M. Mayer
Fund, 1729.2001
Only known print

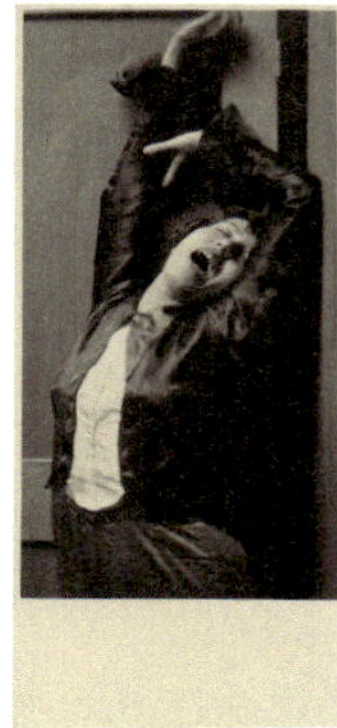

Cat. 87 *Magda Förstner,* 1927
Image: 10.9 × 5.9 cm;
card: 13.3 × 6.2 cm
The J. Paul Getty Museum,
Los Angeles, 85.XM.371.1
Only known print

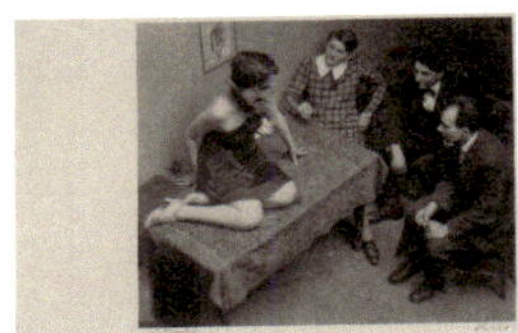

Cat. 91 *Magda Förstner,
Rogi André, Etienne Beöthy,
and Friend,* 1927
Image: 7.9 × 9.8 cm;
card: 8.4 × 13.2 cm
Signed, recto, in graphite:
A. Kertész / Paris
The Museum of Modern Art,
New York, Thomas Walther
Collection, gift of
Thomas Walther, 1732.2001
Only known print

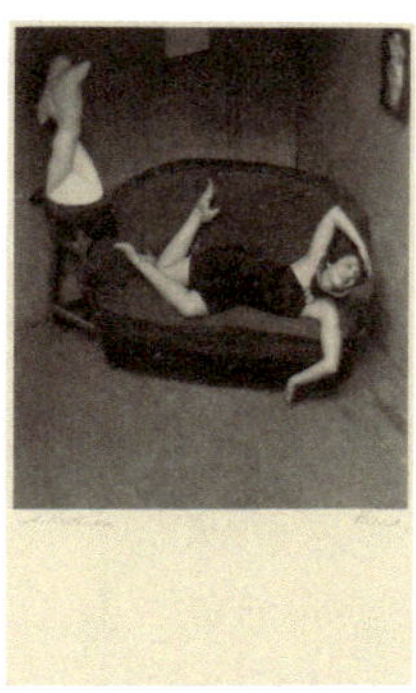

Cat. 92 *Satiric Dancer*, 1927
Image: 10.5 cm × 7.9;
card: 13.5 × 8.2 cm
Signed, recto, in graphite:
A. Kertész / Paris; inscribed,
verso, in graphite:
*Förstner Magda, / a pesti
groteszk / táncosnő*
(Magda Förstner, grotesque
dancer from Pest)
Family Holdings of
Nicholas and Susan Pritzker
Other known prints:
private collection

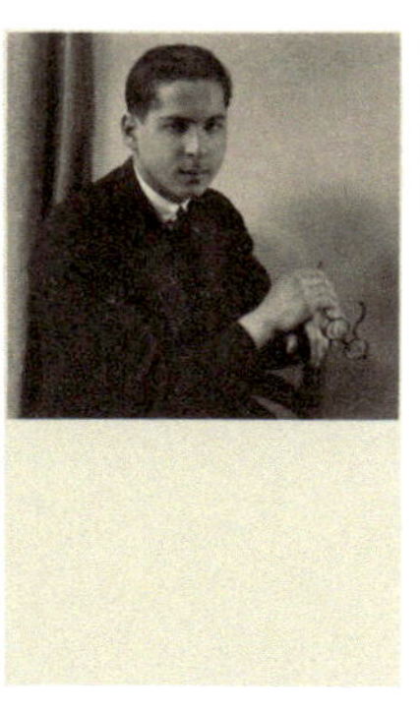

Cat. 93 *Paul Arma*, 1928
Image: 7.9 × 7.9 cm;
card: 13.5 × 8.1 cm
The Art Institute of Chicago,
Wirt D. Walker Fund, 1984.534
Only known print

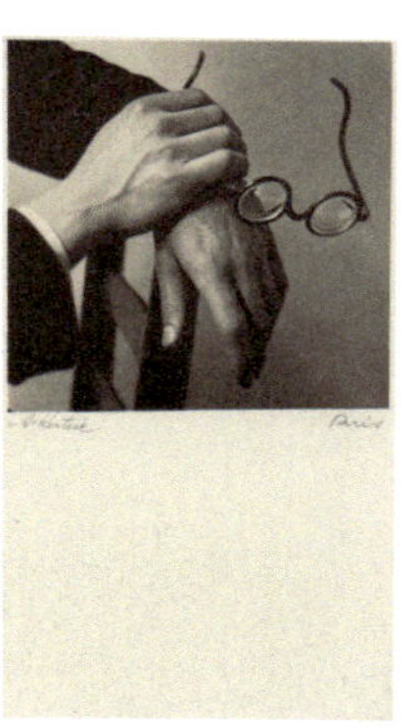

Cat. 94 *Paul Arma's Hands*,
1928
Image: 7.2 × 7.2 cm;
card: 13.1 × 7.5 cm
Signed, recto, in graphite:
A. Kertész / Paris
Family Holdings of
Nicholas and Susan Pritzker
Only known print

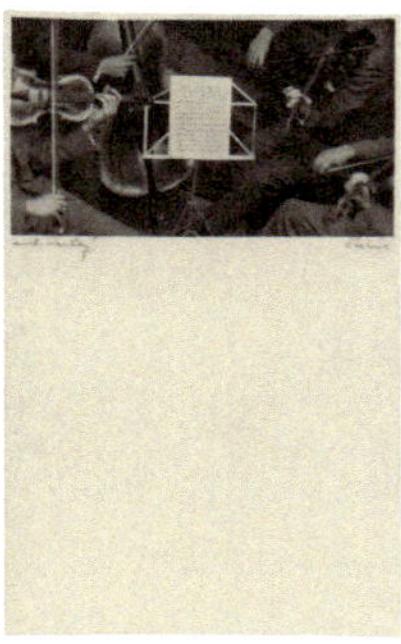

Cat. 95 *Quartet*, 1926
Image: 4 × 7.3 cm;
card: 11.8 × 7.6 cm
Signed, recto, in graphite:
A. Kertész / Paris
The Art Institute of Chicago,
gift of Nicholas and
Susan Pritzker, 2012.711
Only known print

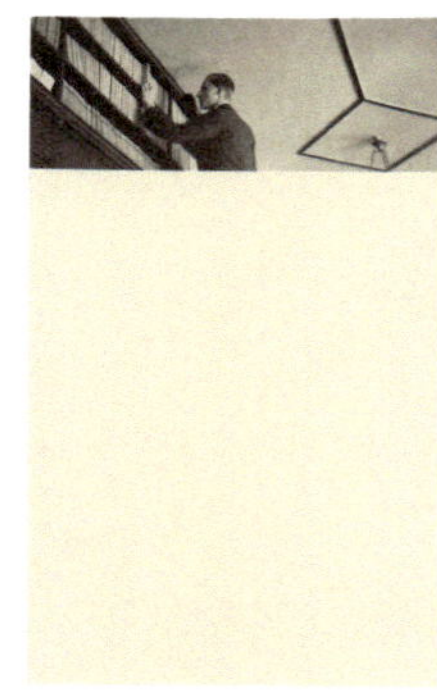

Cat. 96 *Le Soudier
(Avant-Garde Bookstore)*,
1926–27
Image: 3 × 8.1 cm;
card: 13.3 × 8.2 cm
Family Holdings of
Nicholas and Susan Pritzker
Other known prints: JPGM;
private collection, Paris

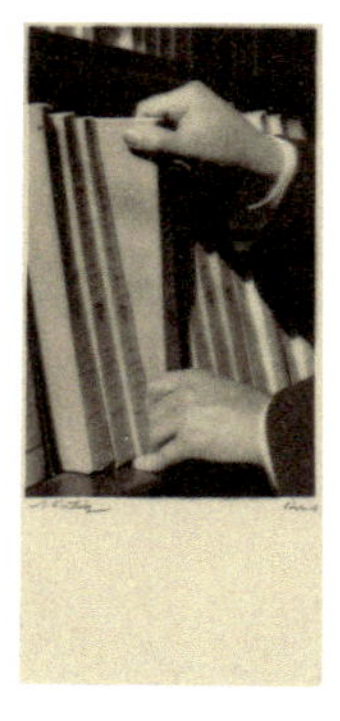

Cat. 97 *Le Soudier
(Hands and Books)*, 1927
Image: 9.5 × 5.7 cm;
card: 13.4 × 6 cm
Signed, recto, in graphite:
A. Kertész / Paris
The J. Paul Getty Museum,
Los Angeles, 86.XM.706.11
Other known prints:
Israel Museum, Jerusalem;
The Sir Elton John
Photography Collection

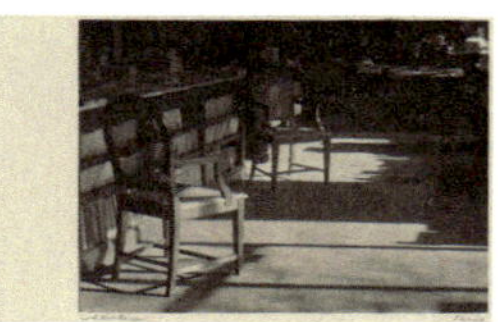

Cat. 98 *Library Chairs and
Shadows*, 1927
Image: 7.9 × 10.9 cm;
card: 8.4 × 13.4 cm
Signed, recto, in graphite:
A. Kertész / Paris
Family Holdings of
Nicholas and Susan Pritzker
Only known print

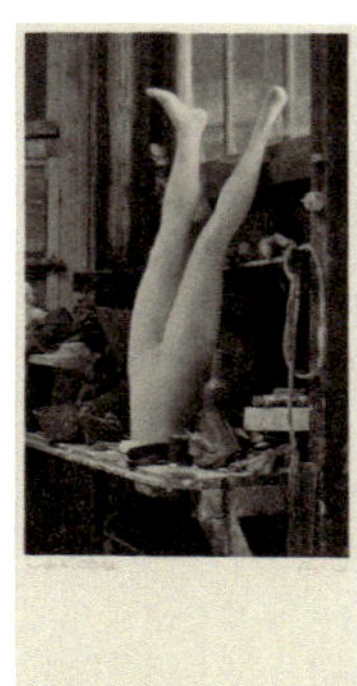

Cat. 99 *Legs*, 1925
Image: 9.8 × 6.2 cm;
card: 13.6 × 6.5 cm
Signed, recto, in graphite:
A. Kertész / Paris; inscribed,
verso, in graphite: *Érdekes véletlen.
Ráfog- / ják, hogy szürrealista
/ legyen, ha az embereknek úgy
jobb.* (Interesting coincidence.
They claim it as being surrealistic,
if it suits people better.)
Family Holdings of
Nicholas and Susan Pritzker
Only known print

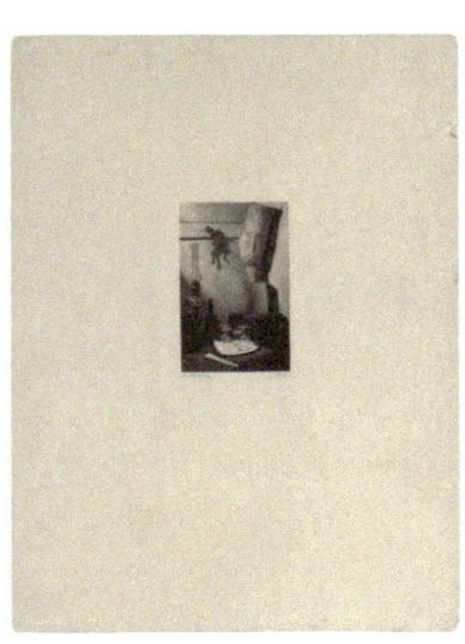

Cat. 100 *Ossip Zadkine's Studio*, 1926
Image/card: 10.5 × 6.7 cm; mount: 37 × 27.7 cm
Signed, mount, in graphite: *A. Kertész / Paris*
The Museum of Modern Art, New York, Thomas Walther Collection, Grace M. Mayer Fund, 1724.2001
Other known prints: Amsab-Institute of Social History, Ghent

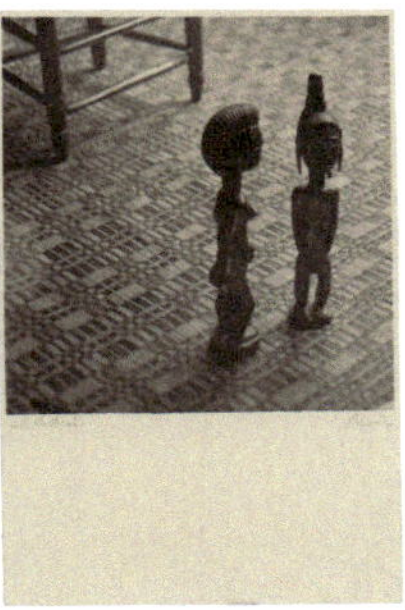

Cat. 101 *African Sculptures*, 1927
Image: 8.1 × 7.9 cm; card: 12.3 × 8.2 cm
Signed, recto, in graphite *A Kertész / Paris*; inscribed, verso, in graphite: *Kicsit sötét képen / néger szobrok.* (Negro sculptures on a somewhat dark picture.)
The Art Institute of Chicago, gift of Nicholas and Susan Pritzker, 2012.708
Other known prints: Jane Corkin, Toronto; Collection of Ealan and Melinda Wingate

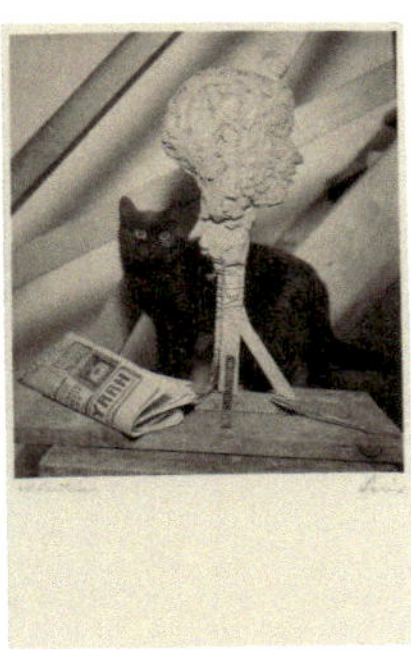

Cat. 102 *The Studio Cat*, 1926–27
Image: 9.1 × 8 cm; card: 12.8 × 8.3 cm
Signed, recto, in graphite: *A Kertész / Paris*; inscribed, verso, in graphite: *Blitzlicht* (magnesium light)
The Art Institute of Chicago, gift of Nicholas and Susan Pritzker, 2012.718
Other known prints: KM; Israel Museum, Jerusalem; Jill Quasha, New York

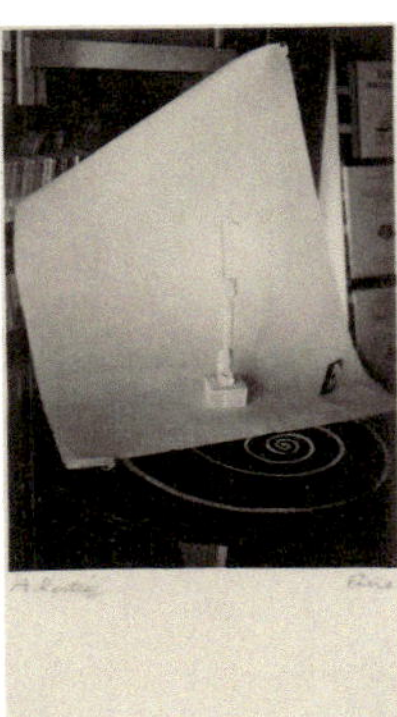

Cat. 103 *Window, L'Esthétique*, 1927
Image: 10 × 6.5 cm; card: 13.3 × 7.3 cm
Signed, recto, in graphite: *A. Kertész / Paris*
Collection of Ealan and Melinda Wingate
Only known print

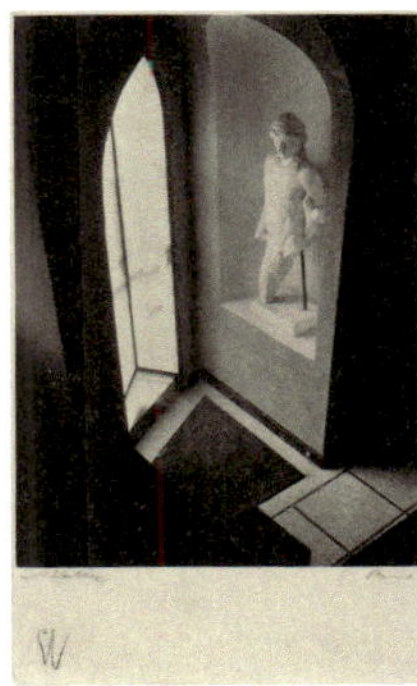

Cat. 104 *Interior with Sculpture*, 1927
Image: 10.9 × 7 cm; card: 13.4 × 8.2 cm
Signed, recto, in graphite: *A. Kertész / Paris*
The Metropolitan Museum of Art, New York, Gilman Collection, purchase, Mr. and Mrs. Henry R. Kravis Gift, 2005.100.367
Only known print

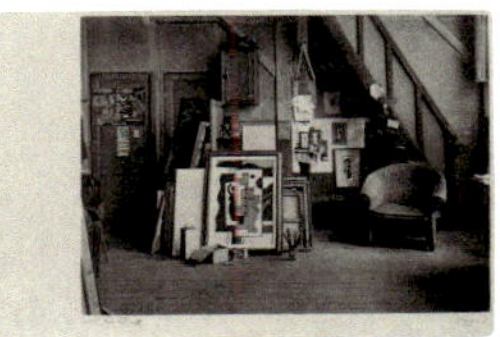

Cat. 105 *Fernand Léger's Studio*, 1926–27
Image: 7 × 10.5 cm; card: 7.3 × 12.7 cm
Signed, recto, in graphite: *A. Kertész / Paris*
New Orleans Museum of Art, museum purchase, Women's Volunteer Committee Fund, 73.169
Only known print

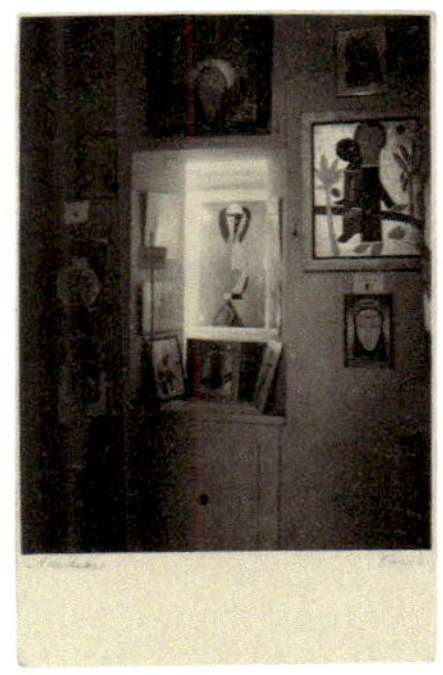

Cat. 106 *Marie Vassilieff's Studio*, 1926
Image: 10.6 × 8.3 cm; card: 12.7 × 8.4 cm
Signed, recto, in graphite: *A. Kertész / Paris*
The J. Paul Getty Museum, Los Angeles, 86.XM.614.1
Only known print

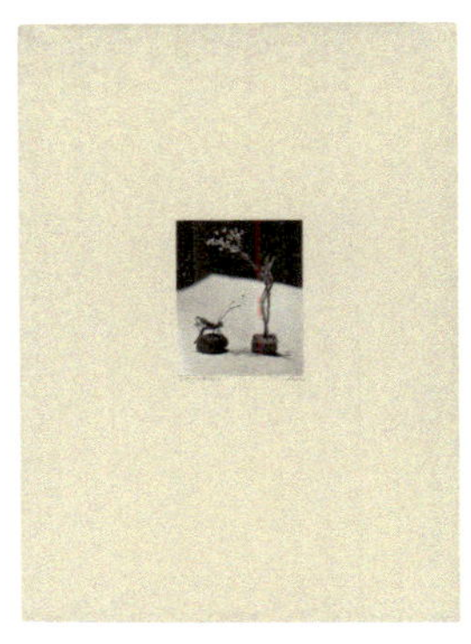

Cat. 107 *Sculptures*, 1927
Image/card: 9.5 × 7.5 cm; mount: 37 × 27.3 cm
Signed, mount, in graphite: *A. Kertész / Paris*
Museum of Fine Arts, Boston, gift of Patricia Corkin Kennedy and John Kennedy in honor of Jane Corkin, 2009.5263
Other known prints: JPGM; KM

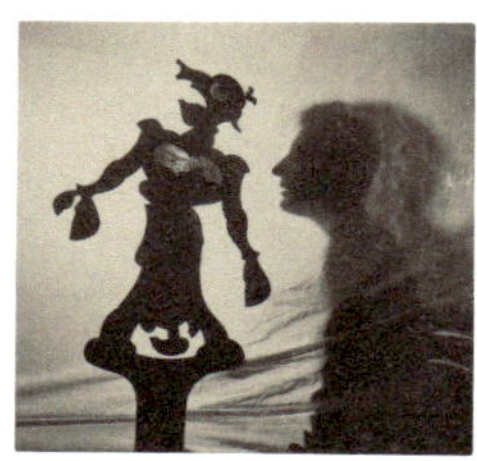

Cat. 108 *Géza Blattner and Puppet*, 1925
Image/card: 7.7 × 8.2 cm
The Museum of Modern Art,
New York, Thomas Walther
Collection, gift of
Thomas Walther, 1716.2001
Only known print

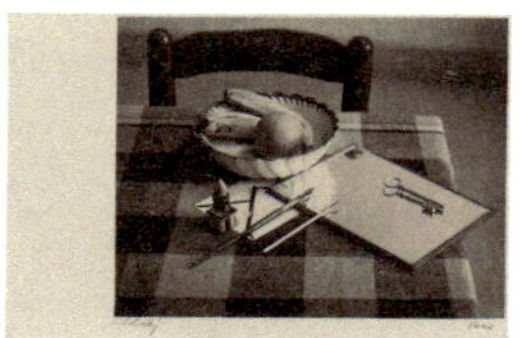

Cat. 109 *Still Life*, 1926
Image: 7.9 × 10.5 cm;
card: 8.7 × 13.3 cm
Signed, recto, in graphite:
A. Kertész / Paris
Family Holdings of
Nicholas and Susan Pritzker
Only known print

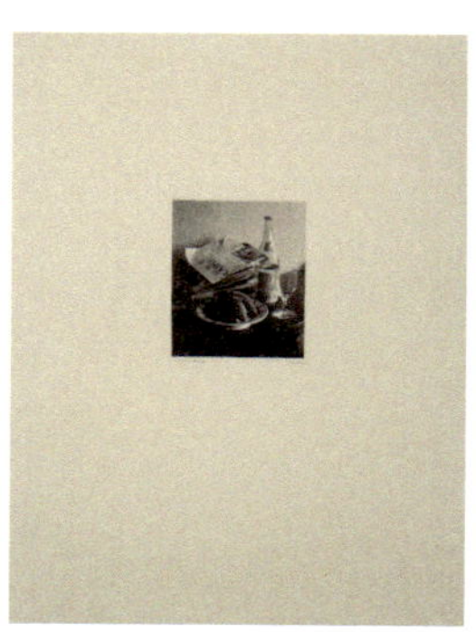

Cat. 110 *Still Life*, 1926
Image/card: 9.4 × 7.8 cm;
mount: 34.9 × 26.7 cm
Signed, mount, in graphite:
A Kertész / Paris
The J. Paul Getty Museum,
Los Angeles, 86.XM.614.3
Other known prints: Collection of
Ann and Jürgen Wilde, Cologne

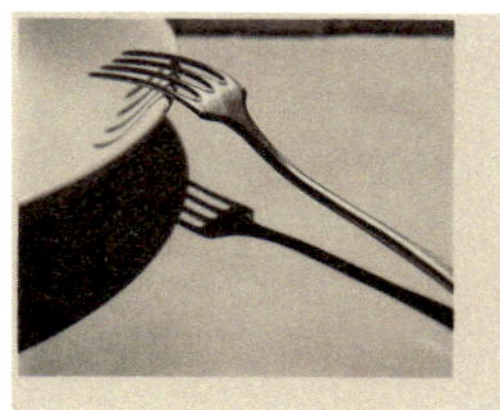

Cat. 111 *Fork*, 1928
Image: 7.5 × 9.2 cm;
card: 8.5 × 10.6 cm
National Gallery of Canada,
Ottawa, purchased 1978, 31336
Only known print

OTHER KNOWN PRINTS

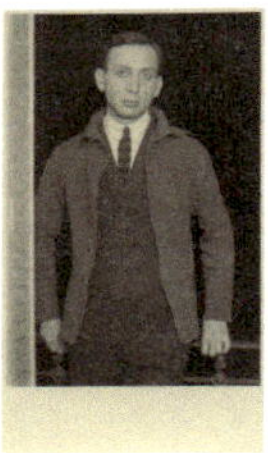

Cat. 112 *Self-Portrait*, 1926
Estate of André Kertész
Other known prints: EAK
(two additional prints);
SFMOMA

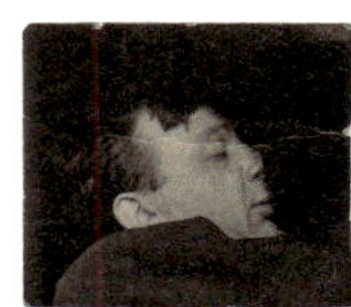

Cat. 117 *Self-Portrait*, 1925–28
Estate of André Kertész
Only known print

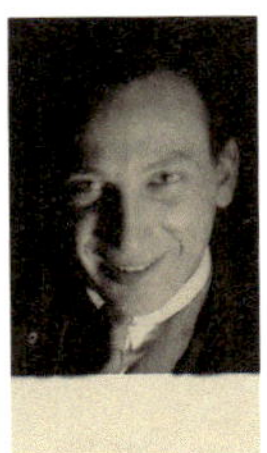

Cat. 113 *Self-Portrait*, 1926–27
The J. Paul Getty Museum,
Los Angeles, 93.XM.21.2
Only known print

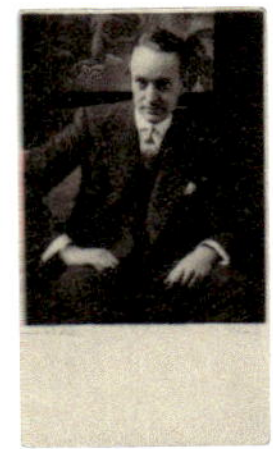

Cat. 118 *William Aguet*, 1926–27
Estate of André Kertész
Only known print

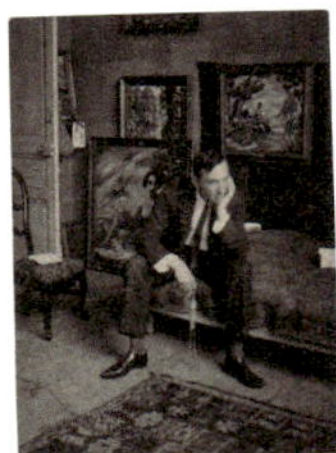

Cat. 114 *Self-Portrait*, 1925–28
Estate of André Kertész
Other known prints: EAK
(two additional prints)

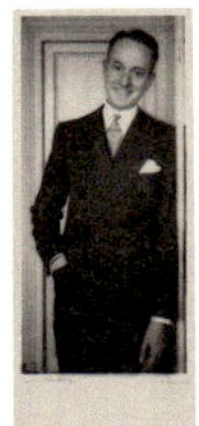

Cat. 119 *William Aguet*, 1927
Richard and Ellen Sandor
Family Collection
Only known print

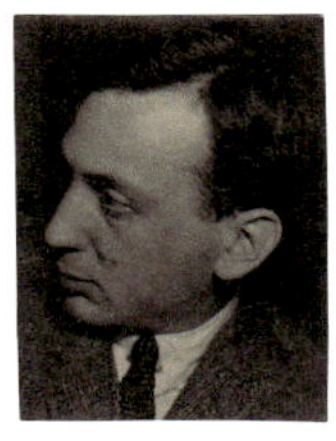

Cat. 115 *Self-Portrait*, 1925–28
Estate of André Kertész
Only known print

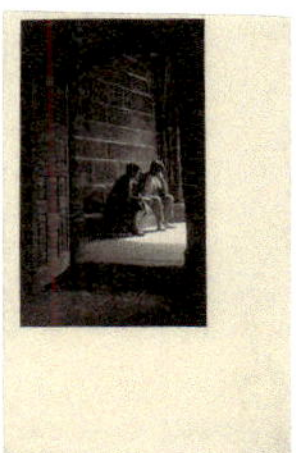

Cat. 120 *Rogi André and
Etienne Beöthy*, 1926
Estate of André Kertész
Only known print

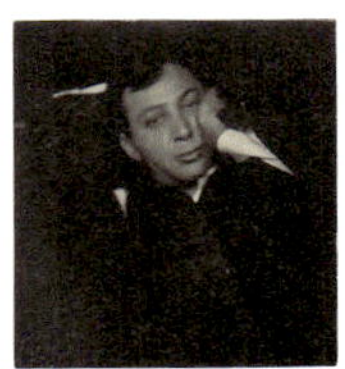

Cat. 116 *Self-Portrait*, 1925–28
Estate of André Kertész
Other known prints: EAK
(additional print)

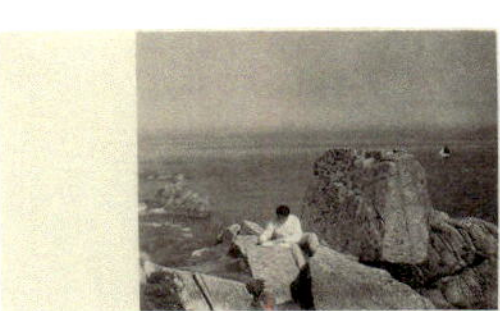

Cat. 121 *Etienne Beöthy,
Brittany*, 1927
Collection of Ann and
Jürgen Wilde, Cologne
Only known print

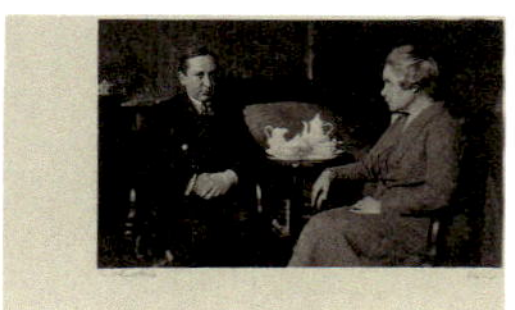

Cat. 122 *György and Itóka Bölöni*, c. 1928
Petőfi Literary Museum, Budapest, F.10931
Only known print

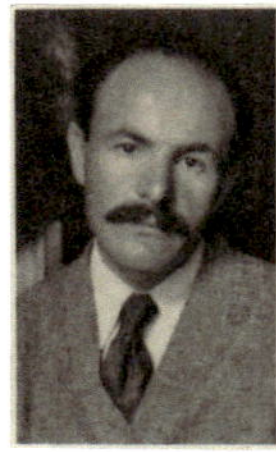

Cat. 128 *Hugo Gellert*, 1925–28
Estate of André Kertész
Only known print

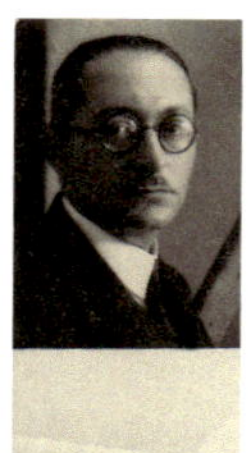

Cat. 123 *Wolfgang Born*, 1925–28
Estate of André Kertész
Only known print

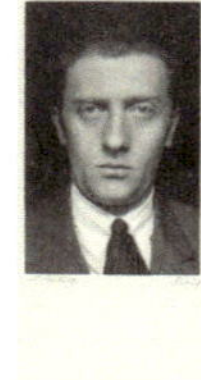

Cat. 129 *Tibor Harsányi*, 1925–28
Petőfi Literary Museum, Budapest, F.15079
Only known print

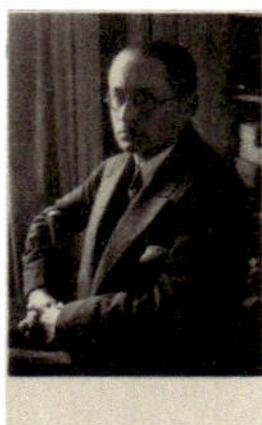

Cat. 124 *Wolfgang Born*, 1925–28
Estate of André Kertész
Only known print

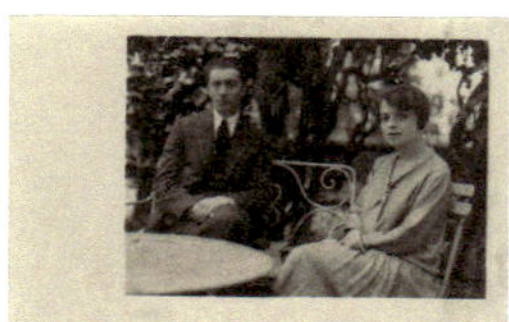

Cat. 130 *Tibor Harsányi and Friend*, 1925–28
Estate of André Kertész
Only known print

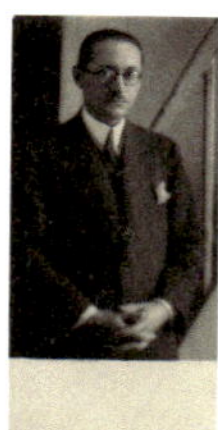

Cat. 125 *Wolfgang Born*, 1925–28
Estate of André Kertész
Only known print

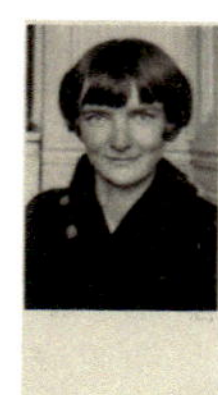

Cat. 131 *Miss Johnson*, 1927
Stephen Daiter Gallery, Chicago
Only known print

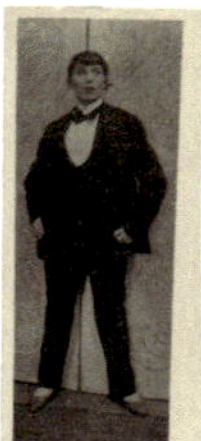

Cat. 126 *Magda Förstner*, 1927
Corkin Gallery, Toronto
Only known print

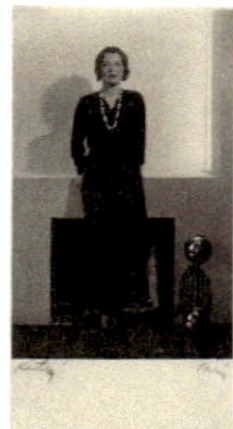

Cat. 132 *Catherine Károlyi*, 1927
Magyar Nemzeti Múzeum Historical Photographic Collection, Budapest
Only known print

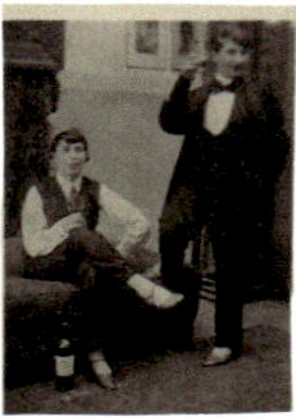

Cat. 127 *Magda Förstner and "Lidi,"* 1927
Corkin Gallery, Toronto
Only known print

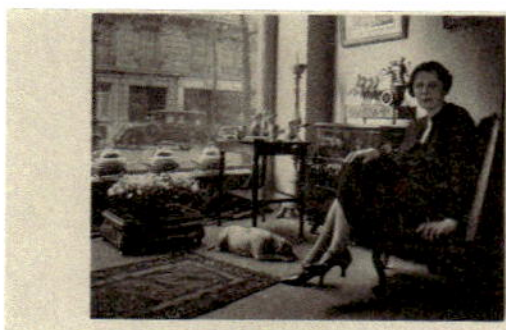

Cat. 133 *Catherine Károlyi*, 1927
Estate of André Kertész
Only known print

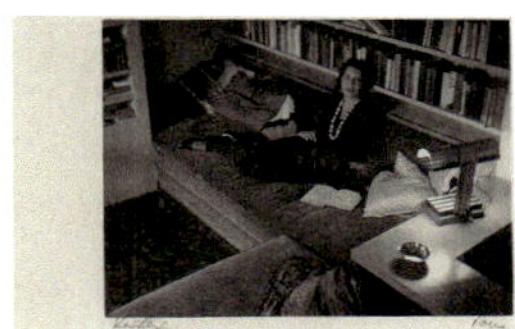

Cat. 134 *Catherine Károlyi*, 1927
Petőfi Literary Museum
Budapest, F.15598
Only known print

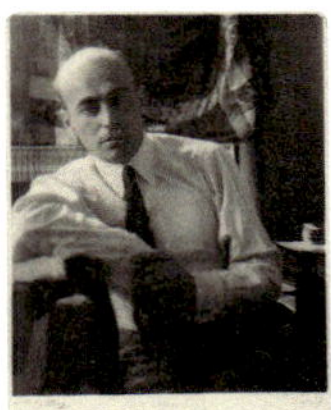

Cat. 140 *Jean Lurçat*, c. 1928
San Francisco Museum of
Modern Art, gift of Lisa and
John Pritzker, 2016.157
Only known print

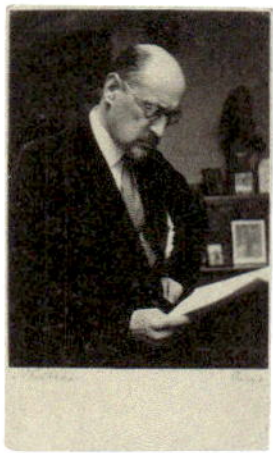

Cat. 135 *Mihály Károly*, 1927
Kassák Múzeum, Budapest,
KM-F.86.554
Only known print

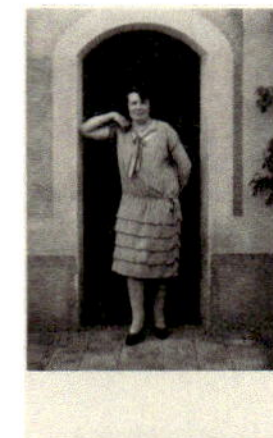

Cat. 141 *Marguerite Mac Orlan*,
1925–28
Estate of André Kertész
Only known print

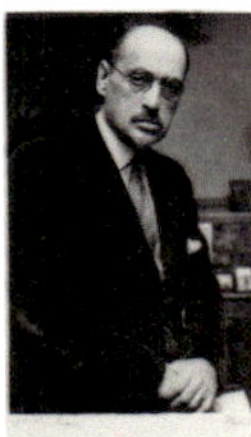

Cat. 136 *Mihály Károlyi*, 1927
Gallery Fifty One, Antwerp
Only known print

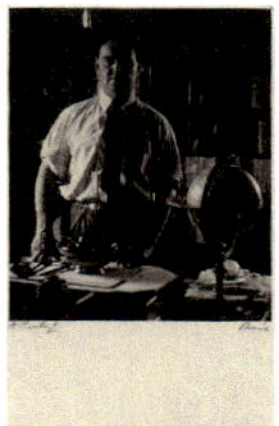

Cat. 142 *Pierre Mac Orlan*, 1928
André and Elizabeth Kertész
Foundation
Only known print

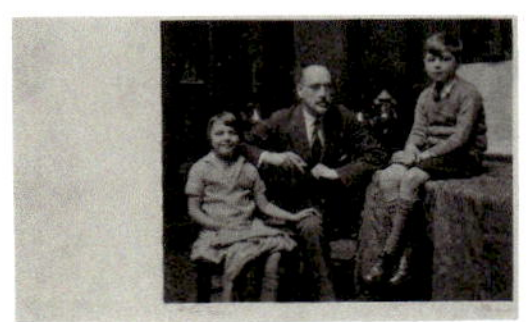

Cat. 137 *Mihály Károlyi with
His Children*, 1927
Petőfi Literary Museum,
Budapest, F.2786
Only known print

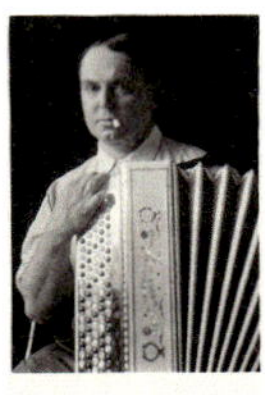

Cat. 143 *Pierre Mac Orlan*, 1927
San Francisco Museum of
Modern Art, gift of Lisa and
John Pritzker, 2016.149
Only known print

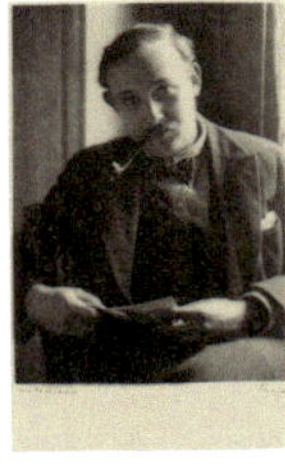

Cat. 138 *Manuel Komroff*, 1928
The J. Paul Getty Museum,
Los Angeles, 85.XM.176.1
Other known prints: AEKF

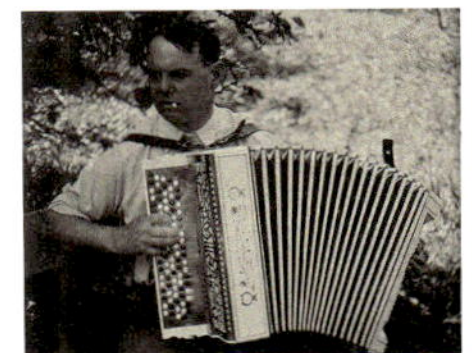

Cat. 144 *Pierre Mac Orlan*, 1927
Collection of Nion McEvoy
Only known print

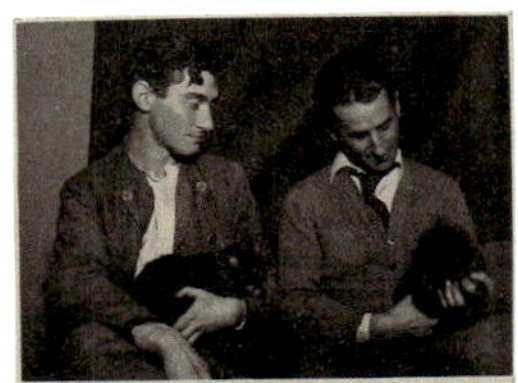

Cat. 139 *Vincent Korda and
a Swiss Sculptor*, 1926
Estate of André Kertész
Only known print

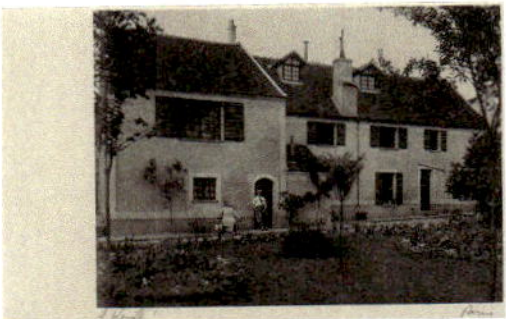

Cat. 145 *Marguerite and
Pierre Mac Orlan in Front of
Their House*, 1928
Estate of André Kertész
Only known print

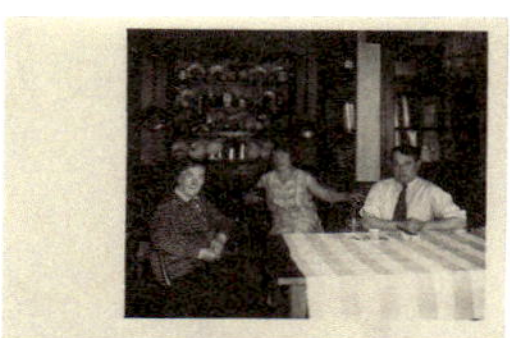

Cat. 146 *Marguerite and Pierre Mac Orlan with His Mother*, 1926–28
Estate of André Kertész
Only known print

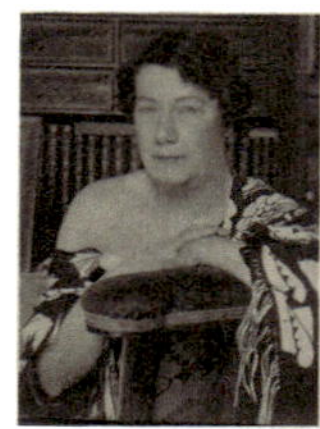

Cat. 152 *Princess Murat*, 1927
André and Elizabeth Kertész Foundation
Only known print

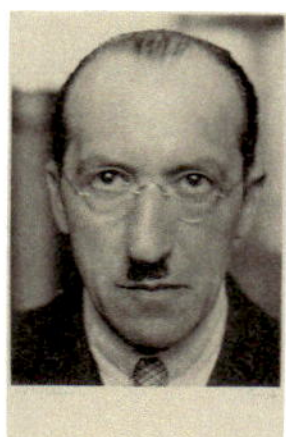

Cat. 147 *Piet Mondrian*, 1926
The Museum of Modern Art, New York, Thomas Walther Collection, gift of Thomas Walther, 1720.2001
Other known prints:
private collection, Paris, courtesy of Galerie Françoise Paviot, Paris

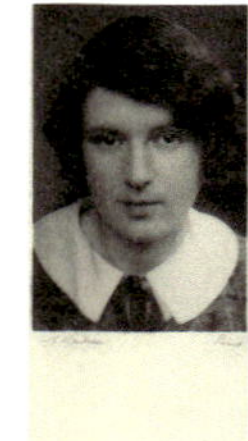

Cat. 153 *Elizabeth Pfeiffer*, 1927
Collection of Ann and Jürgen Wilde, Cologne
Only known print

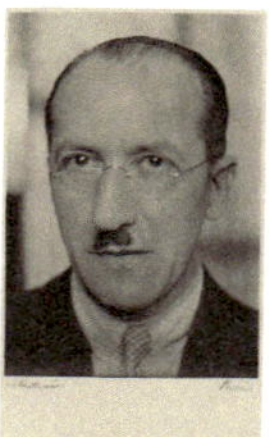

Cat. 148 *Piet Mondrian*, 1926
The J. Paul Getty Museum, Los Angeles, 93.XM.21.1
Only known print

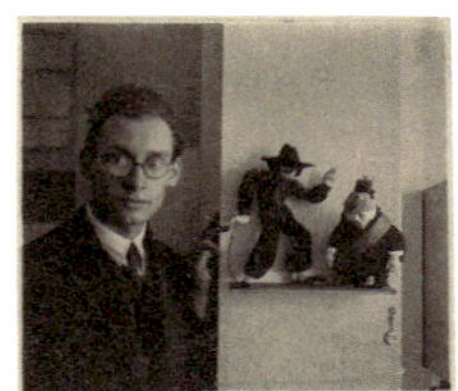

Cat. 154 *Etienne Raik*, 1925–28
Estate of André Kertész
Only known print

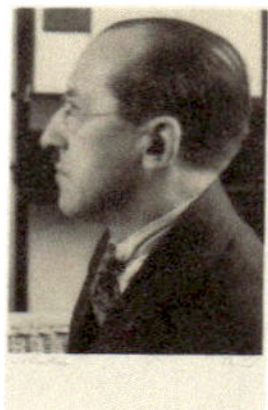

Cat. 149 *Piet Mondrian*, 1926
Estate of André Kertész
Only known print

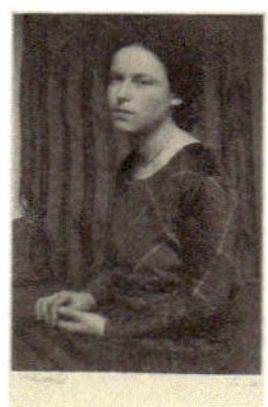

Cat. 155 *Eva Révai*, 1927
Vintage Works, Ltd., Chalfont, PA
Only known print

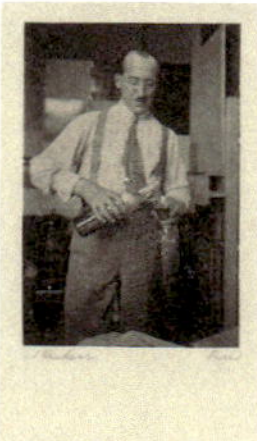

Cat. 150 *Piet Mondrian*, 1926
Collection of Ann and Jürgen Wilde, Cologne
Only known print

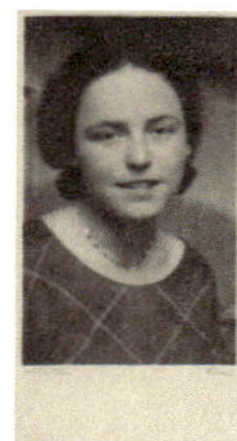

Cat. 156 *Eva Révai*, 1927
Vintage Works, Ltd., Chalfont, PA
Only known print

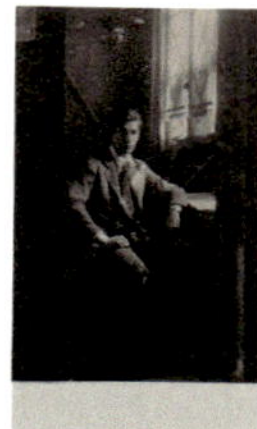

Cat. 151 *Mr. Morgan*, 1927
Weston Gallery, Carmel-by-the-Sea, CA
Only known print

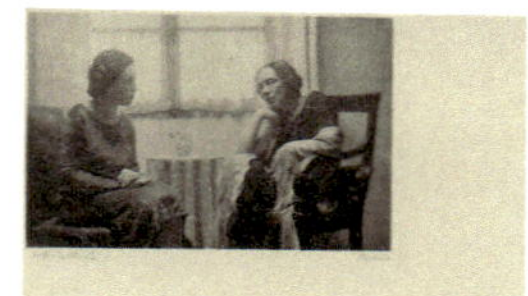

Cat. 157 *Eva and Ilka Révai*, 1927
Hungarian Museum of Photography, Kecskemét, 183/2000
Other known prints:
Bernard Bouche, Paris

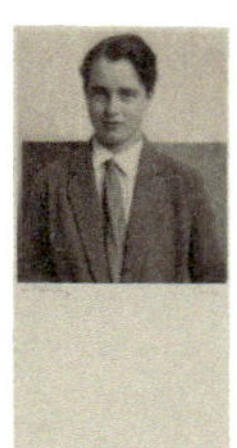

Cat. 158 *Peggy Rosskam*, 1927
Bruce Silverstein Gallery,
New York
Other known prints:
Christopher G. Cardozo
Collection

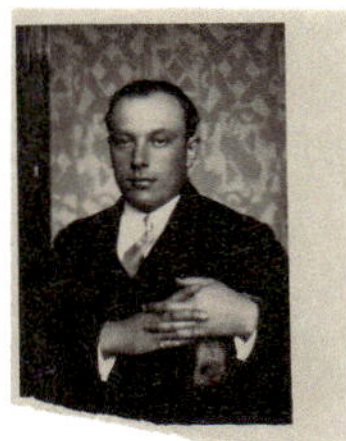

Cat. 159 *Philippe de Rothschild*,
1927
Estate of André Kertész
Only known print

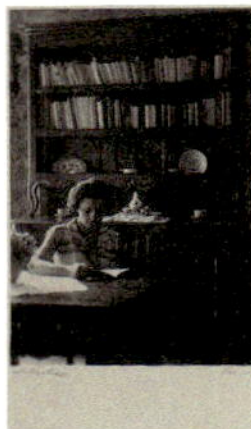

Cat. 160 *Ibi Salgo*, 1925–28
Collection of Jeanne
Salgo Aboudrar
Only known print

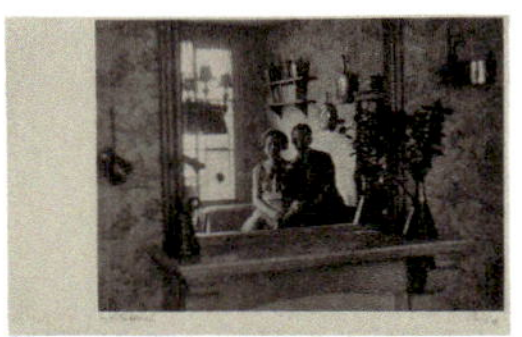

Cat. 161 *Ibi and Nicolas Salgo*,
1925–28
Collection of Jeanne
Salgo Aboudrar
Only known print

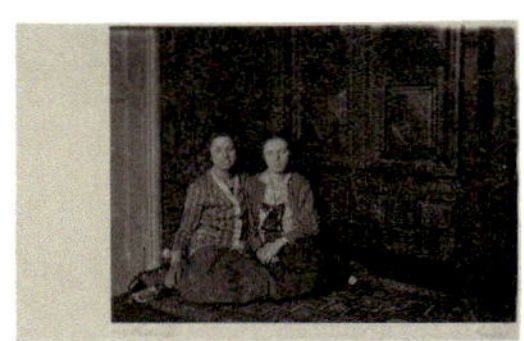

Cat. 162 *Ibi Salgo and
Margarit Varga*, 1925–28
Collection of Jeanne
Salgo Aboudrar
Only known print

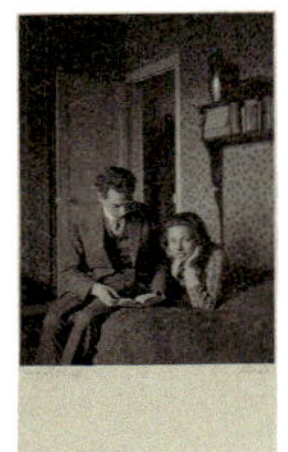

Cat. 163 *Nicolas and Ibi Salgo*,
1925–28
Collection of Jeanne
Salgo Aboudrar
Only known print

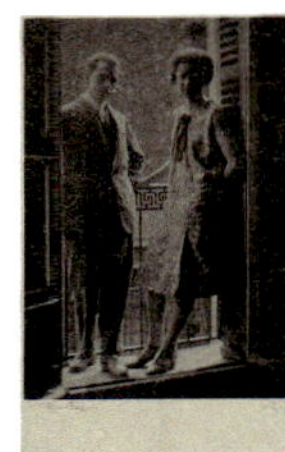

Cat. 164 *Nicolas and Ibi Salgo*,
1925–28
Collection of Jeanne
Salgo Aboudrar
Only known print

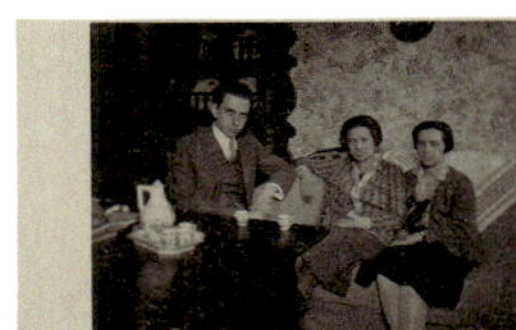

Cat. 165 *Nicolas Salgo,
Ibi Salgo, and Margarit Varga*,
1925–28
Collection of Jeanne
Salgo Aboudrar
Only known print

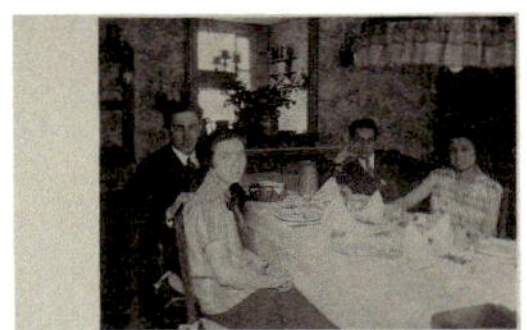

Cat. 166 *Nicolas and Ibi Salgo
with Ladislas and Margarit Varga*,
1925–28
Collection of Jeanne
Salgo Aboudrar
Only known print

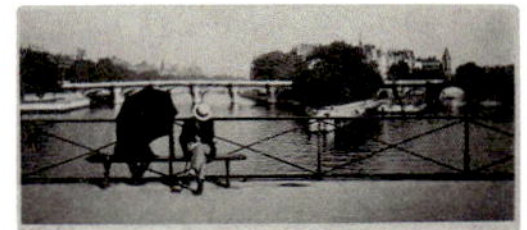

Cat. 167 *Michel Seuphor and
Friend on Pont des Arts*, 1926
New Orleans Museum of Art,
museum purchase,
Women's Volunteer
Committee Fund, 73.178
Only known print

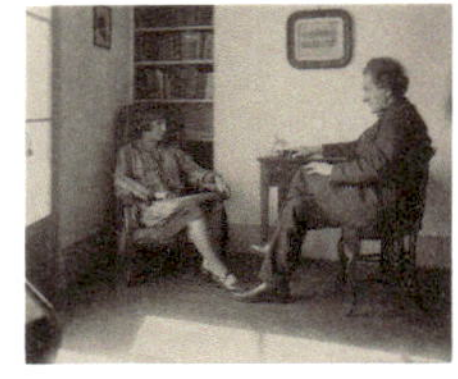

Cat. 168 *Jan Sliwinsky and
Girlfriend*, 1926–27
Keith de Lellis Gallery,
New York
Only known print

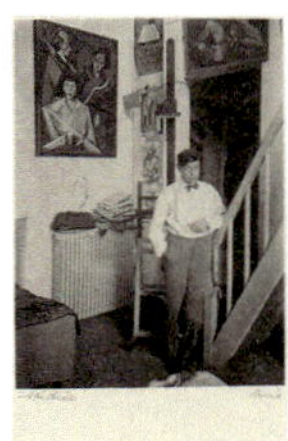

Cat. 169 *Lajos Tihanyi in
His Studio*, 1926–27
Petőfi Literary Museum,
Budapest, F.4439
Other known prints:
Hungarian Museum of
Photography, Kecskemét;
private collection

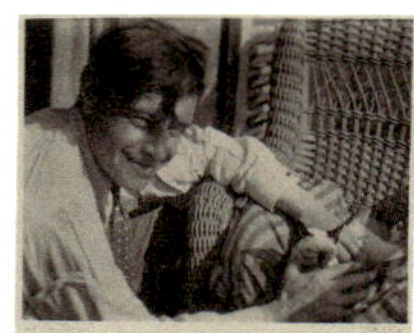

Cat. 170 *Lajos Tihanyi*, 1927
The Art Institute of Chicago,
gift of Nicholas and
Susan Pritzker, 2012.704
Only known print

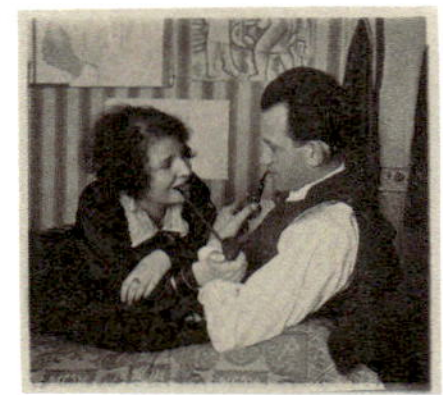

Cat. 176 *Gyula Zilzer and
Girlfriend*, 1925–26
Estate of André Kertész
Only known print

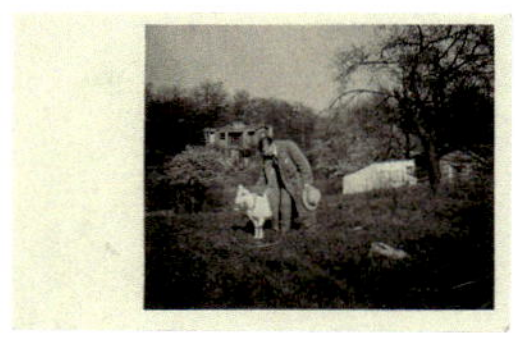

Cat. 171 *Lajos Tihanyi*, 1927
Petőfi Literary Museum,
Budapest, F.4451
Only known print

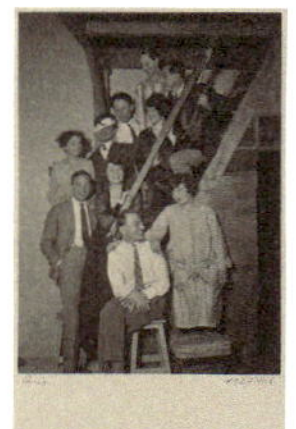

Cat. 177 *André Kertész and Friends
at Joseph Csáky's Studio*, 1927
The Museum of Fine Arts,
Houston, museum purchase
funded by the Caroline Wiess
Law Accessions Endowment
Fund, The Manfred Heiting
Collection, 2002.259
Other known prints: AEKF

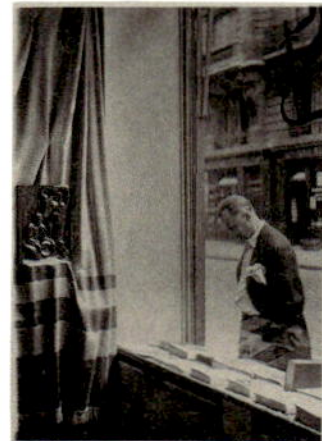

Cat. 172 *Edward Titus at
His Bookstore, Montparnasse*,
1928
New Orleans Museum of Art,
museum purchase,
Women's Volunteer
Committee Fund, 73.168
Only known print

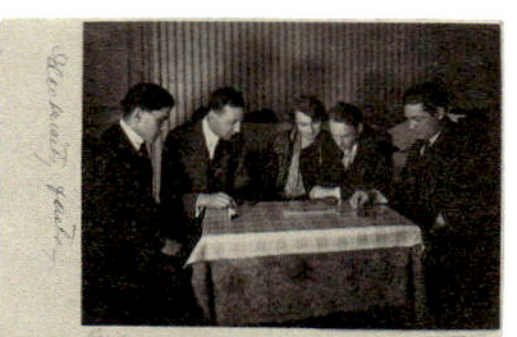

Cat. 178 *André Kertész and
Friends Playing Dominoes*, 1926
André and Elizabeth Kertész
Foundation
Only known print

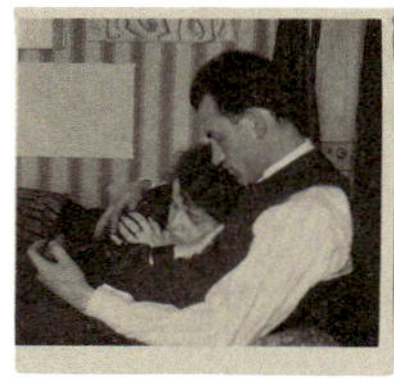

Cat. 173 *Gyula Zilzer and
Girlfriend*, 1925–26
The Art Institute of Chicago,
gift of Nicholas and
Susan Pritzker, 2012.696
Only known print

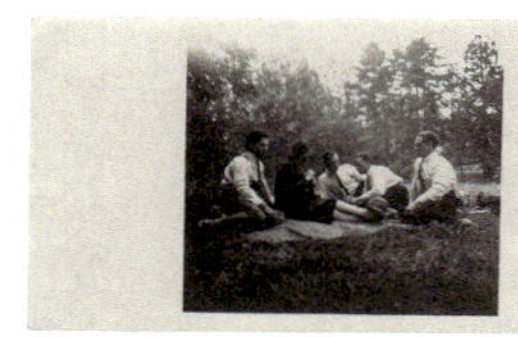

Cat. 179 *André Kertész and
Friends*, 1926
André and Elizabeth Kertész
Foundation
Other known prints: AEKF
(two additional prints)

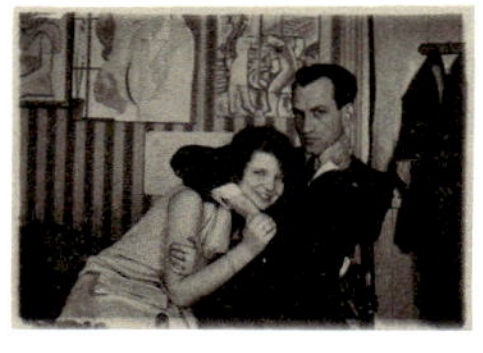

Cat. 174 *Gyula Zilzer and
Girlfriend*, 1925–26
André and Elizabeth Kertész
Foundation
Only known print

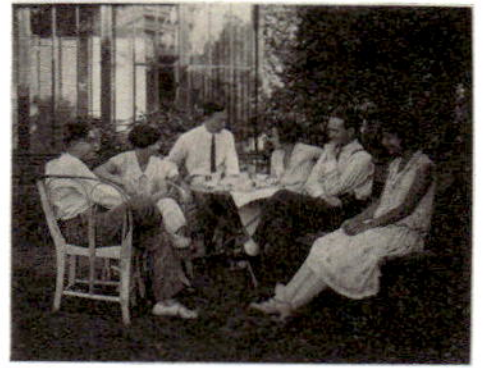

Cat. 180 *Frantisek Reichental,
"Dóra," André Kertész,
Vilma Mangold, Illés Kacér, and
"Ditta,"* c. 1927
Estate of André Kertész
Only known print

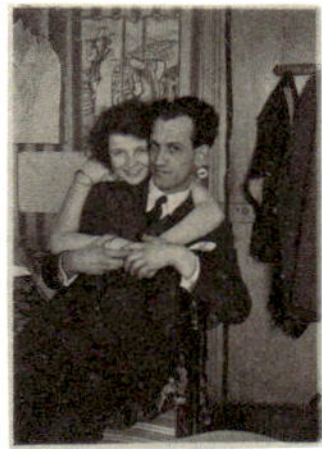

Cat. 175 *Gyula Zilzer and
Girlfriend*, 1925–26
Estate of André Kertész
Only known print

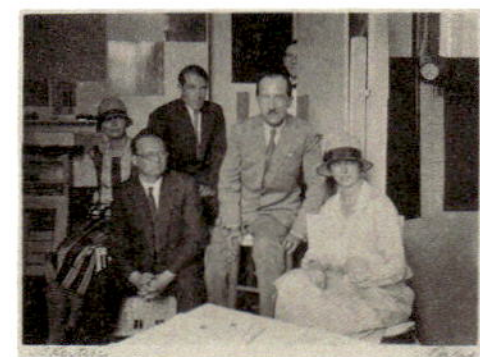

Cat. 181 *Willi Baumeister,
Piet Mondrian, Michel Seuphor,
and Friends in Mondrian's
Studio*, 1926
Family Holdings of
Nicholas and Susan Pritzker
Only known print

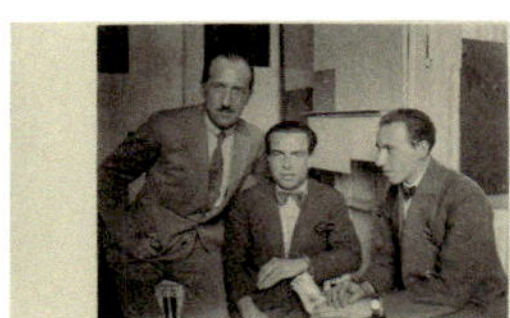

Cat. 182 *Piet Mondrian,*
Enrico Prampolini, and
Michel Seuphor, 1926
Stephen Daiter Gallery, Chicago
Other known prints:
KM; MFA Houston;
Collection of Ann and
Jürgen Wilde, Cologne

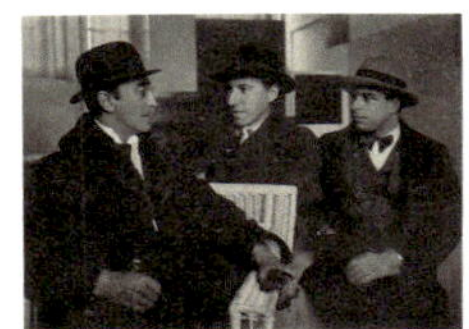

Cat. 183 *Paul Dermée,*
Michel Seuphor, and
Enrico Prampolini, 1927
Collection of Ann and
Jürgen Wilde, Cologne
Only known print

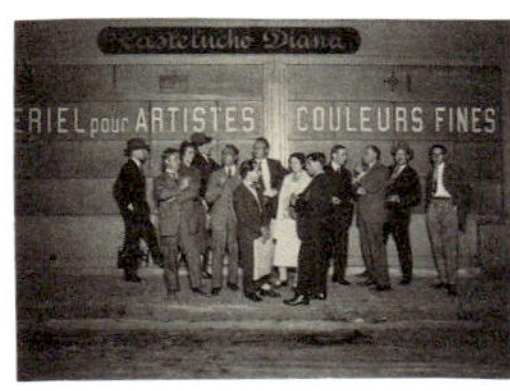

Cat. 184 *Ida Thal, Adolf Loos,*
Piet Mondrian, Michel Seuphor,
and Friends (*After the Soirée*),
1927
Private collection
Only known print

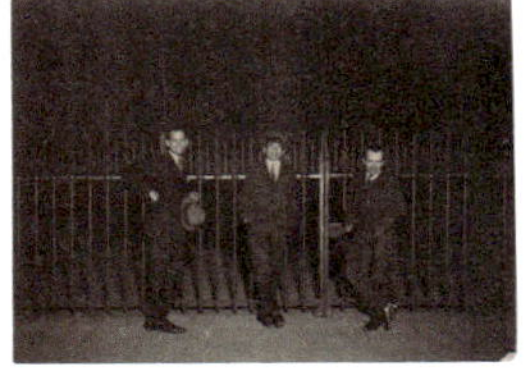

Cat. 185 *Gyula Zilzer,*
Rudolf Diener-Denes, and
Etienne Beöthy, 1926
André and Elizabeth Kertész
Foundation
Other known prints: AEKF
(additional print)

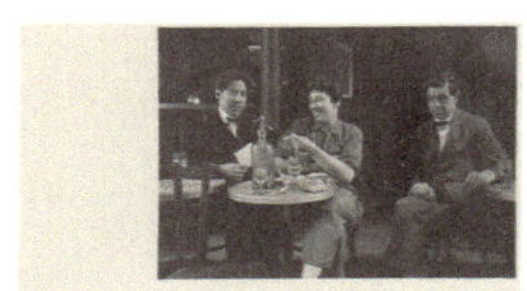

Cat. 186 *Josep Llorens Artigas,*
Vally Wieselthier, and
Lajos Tihanyi, 1927
The Art Institute of Chicago,
Wirt D. Walker Fund, 1984.548
Other known prints: AEKF
(three prints); Christian
Kietzmann

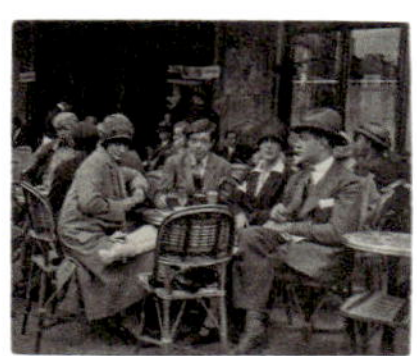

Cat. 187 *Lajos Tihanyi and*
Friends, Café du Dôme, 1925–26
André and Elizabeth Kertész
Foundation
Only known print

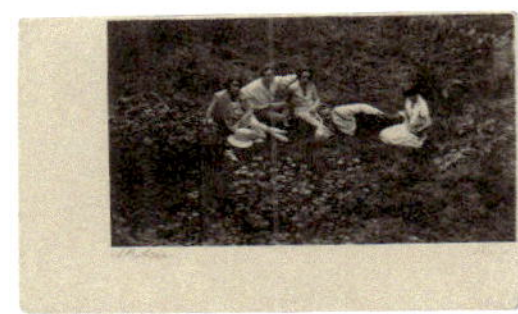

Cat. 188 *Frantisek Reichental*
(*Second from Left*) *and Friends,*
1925–28
Estate of André Kertész
Only known print

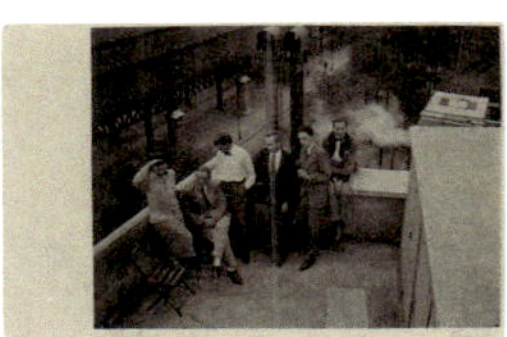

Cat. 189 *Elisabeth Hermann,*
Felix Albrecht Harta,
Lajos Tihanyi, Robbe Patson (?),
Friend, and Michel Seuphor,
Hôtel des Terraces, 1926–27
Petőfi Literary Museum,
Budapest, F.4463
Other known prints:
private collection

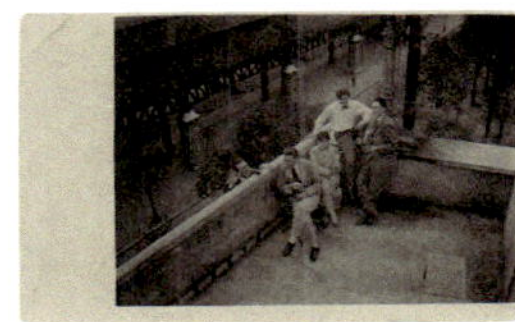

Cat. 190 *Michel Seuphor,*
Felix Albrecht Harta,
Elisabeth Hermann, Lajos Tihanyi,
and Friend, Hôtel des Terraces,
1926–27
Petőfi Literary Museum,
Budapest, F.4465
Only known print

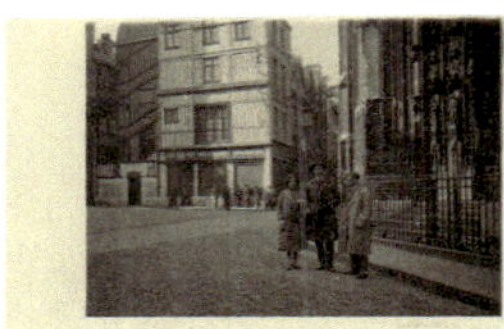

Cat. 191 *Lajos Tihanyi and*
Friends, Rouen, 1927
Petőfi Literary Museum,
Budapest, F.4468
Only known print

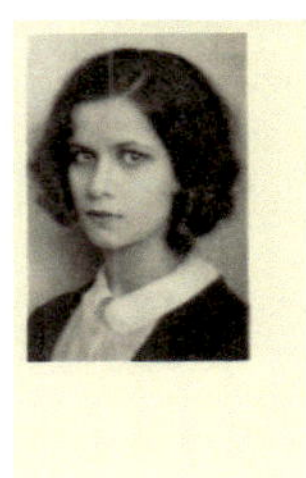

Cat. 192 *Unidentified Sitter*
(*Yugoslav Ballet Dancer*), 1926–27
Collection of John Erdman and
Gary Schneider
Only known print

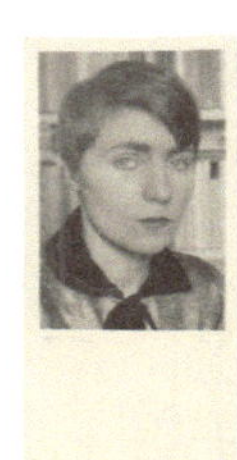

Cat. 193 *Unidentified Sitter*
(*Berenice Abbott?*), 1926–27
Jill Quasha, New York
Only known print

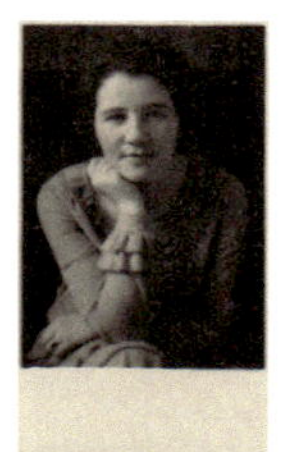

Cat. 194 *Unidentified Sitter,*
1925–28
Estate of André Kertész
Only known print

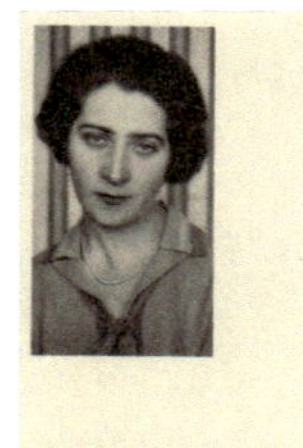

Cat. 200 *Unidentified Sitter,*
1925–28
Estate of André Kertész
Only known print

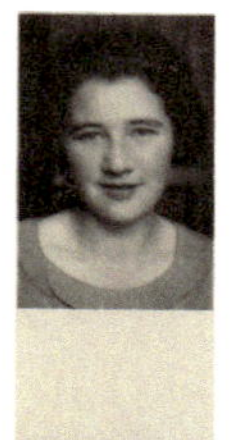

Cat. 195 *Unidentified Sitter,*
1925–28
Estate of André Kertész
Only known print

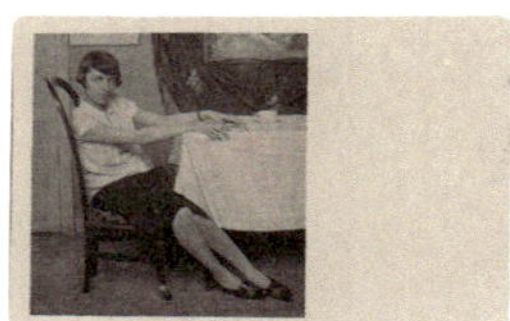

Cat. 201 *Unidentified Sitter*
(*German Journalist*), 1927
The Art Institute of Chicago,
gift of Nicholas and
Susan Pritzker, 2012.701
Only known print

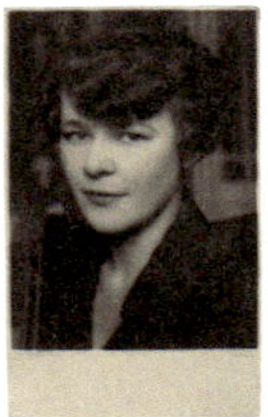

Cat. 196 *Unidentified Sitter,*
1925–28
Estate of André Kertész
Only known print

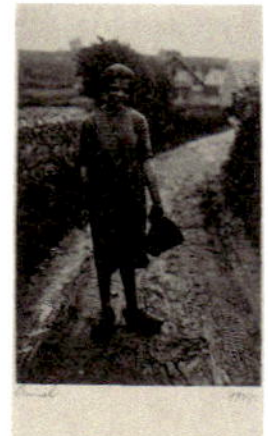

Cat. 202 *Unidentified Sitter,*
Primel, Brittany, 1927
Estate of André Kertész
Other known prints: AEKF
(additional print)

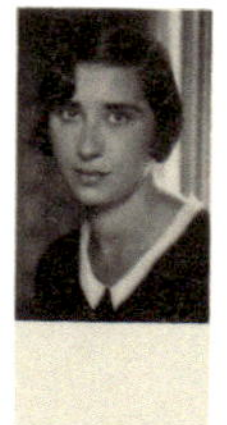

Cat. 197 *Unidentified Sitter,*
1925–28
Estate of André Kertész
Other known prints: AEKF
(additional print)

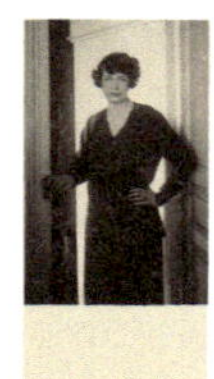

Cat. 203 *Unidentified Sitter,*
1927
The J. Paul Getty Museum,
Los Angeles, 86.XM.614.2
Only known print

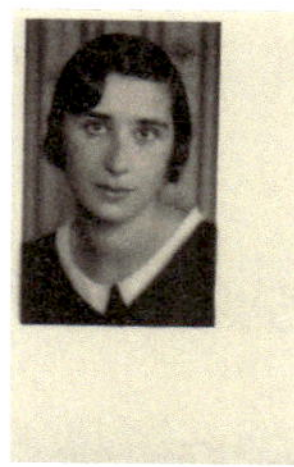

Cat. 198 *Unidentified Sitter,*
1925–28
Estate of André Kertész
Only known print

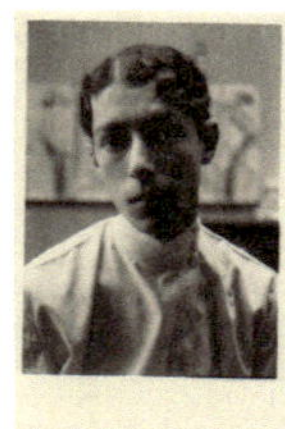

Cat. 204 *Unidentified Sitter*
(*Young Yugoslav Bibliophile*),
1925–28
Estate of André Kertész
Only known print

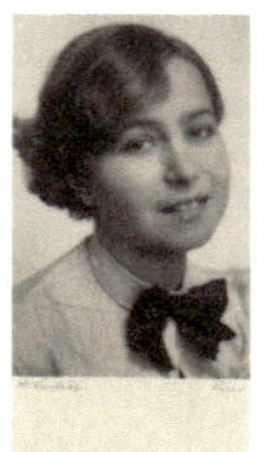

Cat. 199 *Unidentified Sitter,*
1927
Estate of André Kertész
Only known print

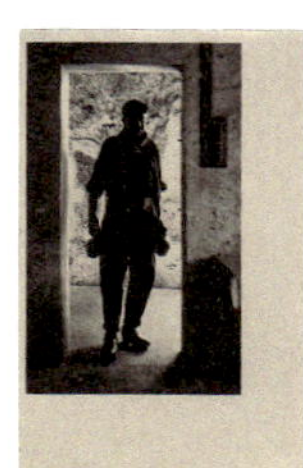

Cat. 205 *Unidentified Sitter,*
1925–28
Estate of André Kertész
Only known print

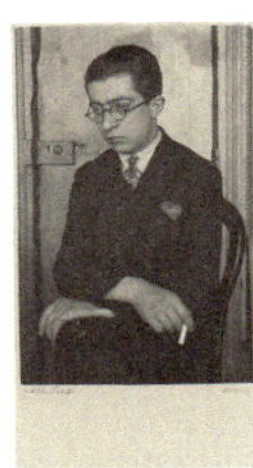

Cat. 206 *Unidentified Sitter (Young German Doctor)*, 1927
The Art Institute of Chicago, gift of Nicholas and Susan Pritzker, 2012.702
Only known print

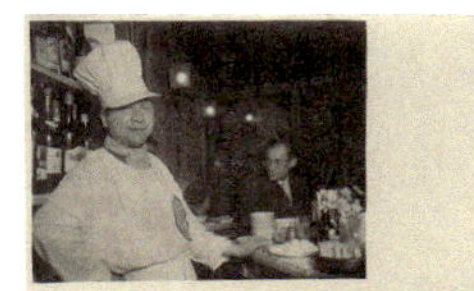

Cat. 212 *Unidentified Sitter (Chef)*, 1927
Estate of André Kertész
Only known print

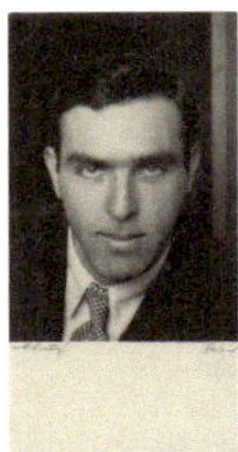

Cat. 207 *Unidentified Sitter (American Illustrator)*, 1925–28
André and Elizabeth Kertész Foundation
Only known print

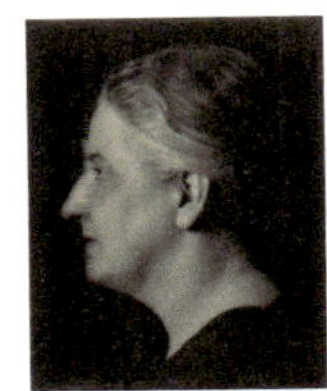

Cat. 213 *Unidentified Sitter*, 1925–28
Estate of André Kertész
Only known print

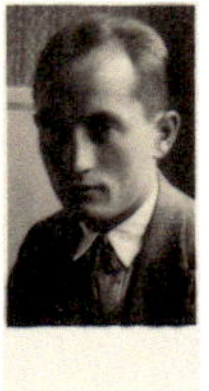

Cat. 208 *Unidentified Sitter*, 1925–28
San Francisco Museum of Modern Art, gift of Lisa and John Pritzker, 2016.155
Only known print

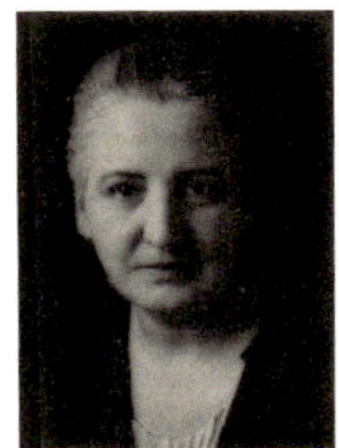

Cat. 214 *Unidentified Sitter*, 1925–28
Estate of André Kertész
Only known print

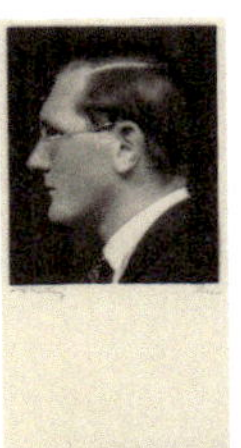

Cat. 209 *Unidentified Sitter*, 1925–28
Estate of André Kertész
Only known print

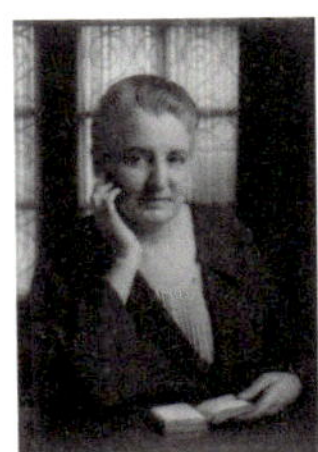

Cat. 215 *Unidentified Sitter*, 1925–28
Estate of André Kertész
Only known print

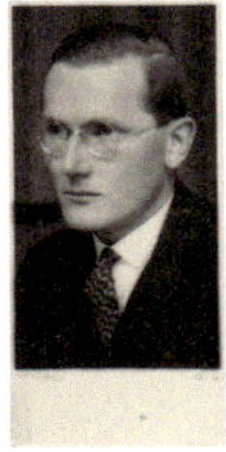

Cat. 210 *Unidentified Sitter*, 1925–28
San Francisco Museum of Modern Art, gift of Lisa and John Pritzker, 2016.156
Only known print

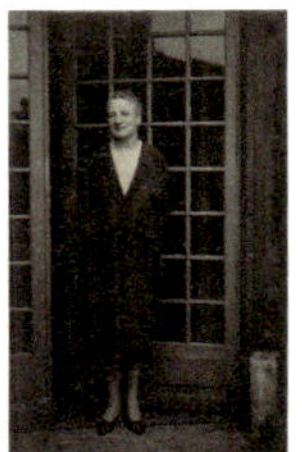

Cat. 216 *Unidentified Sitter*, 1925–28
Estate of André Kertész
Only known print

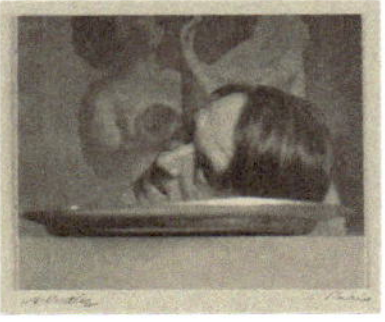

Cat. 211 *Unidentified Sitter (Head on Plate)*, c. 1928
The Metropolitan Museum of Art, New York, N.A. 2005.62
Only known print

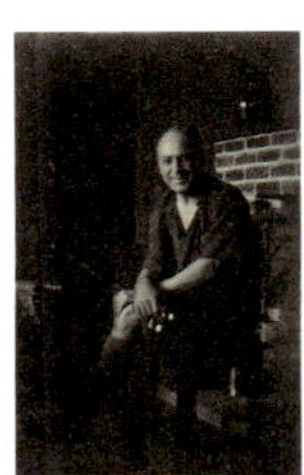

Cat. 217 *Unidentified Sitter*, 1925–28
Estate of André Kertész
Only known print

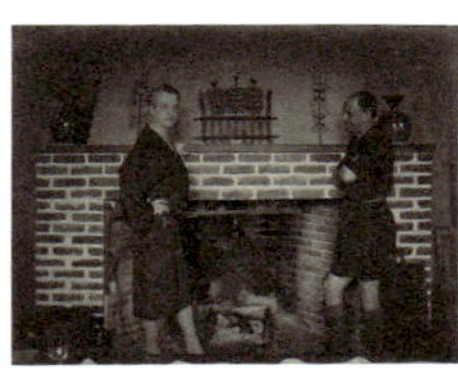

Cat. 218 *Unidentified Sitters,*
1925–28
Estate of André Kertész
Only known print

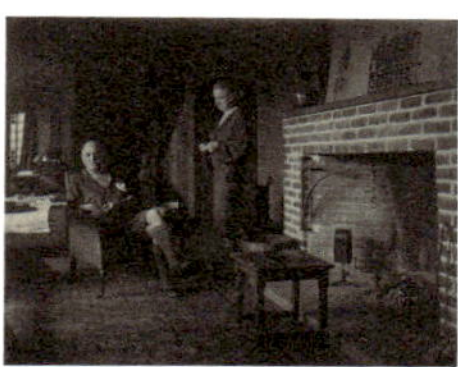

Cat. 219 *Unidentified Sitters,*
1925–28
Estate of André Kertész
Only known print

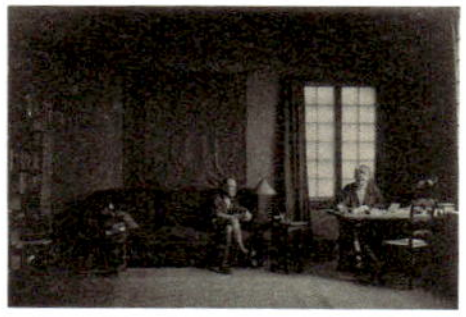

Cat. 220 *Unidentified Sitters,*
1925–28
Estate of André Kertész
Only known print

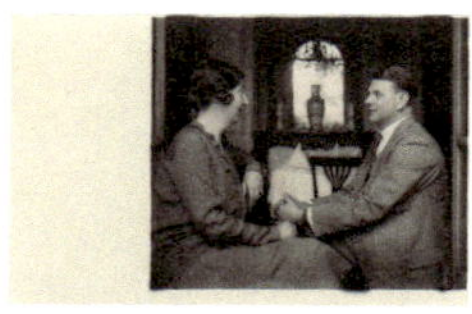

Cat. 221 *Unidentified Sitters,*
1926
The Art Institute of Chicago,
gift of Nicholas and
Susan Pritzker, 2012.715
Only known print

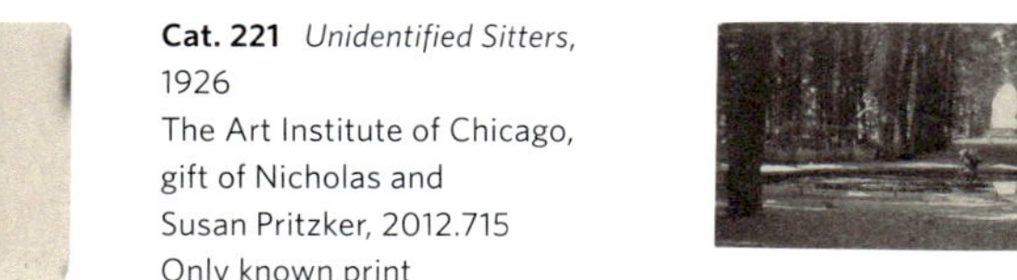

Cat. 222 *Unidentified Sitters,*
1925–28
Estate of André Kertész
Only known print

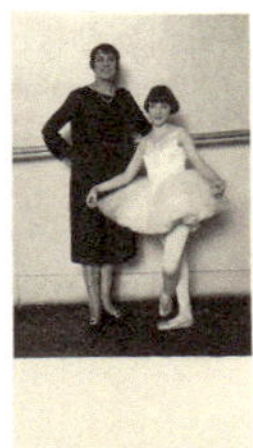

Cat. 223 *Unidentified Sitter,*
1927
Estate of André Kertész
Other known prints: AEKF
(additional print)

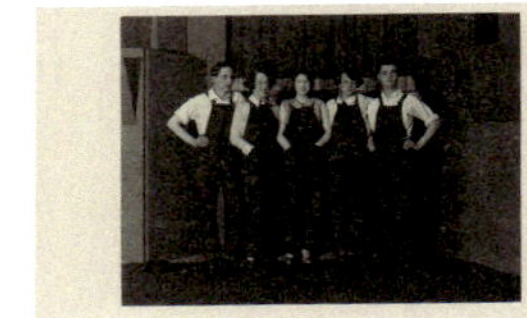

Cat. 224 *Arc-en-Ciel Puppet
Theatre,* c. 1928
Puppetry Collection of the
National Theatre Museum
and Institute, Budapest,
OSZMI-2006.14.1
Only known print

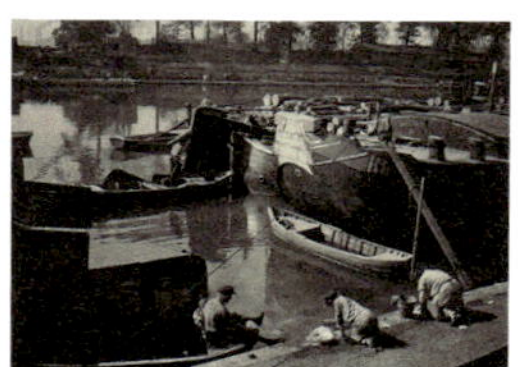

Cat. 225 *Banks of the Seine,*
1926
The Metropolitan Museum of
Art, New York, Gilman
Collection, purchase, Horace W.
Goldsmith Foundation Gift,
through Joyce and Robert
Menschel, 2005.100.915
Other known prints: George
Eastman Museum, Rochester,
NY; private collection,
New York

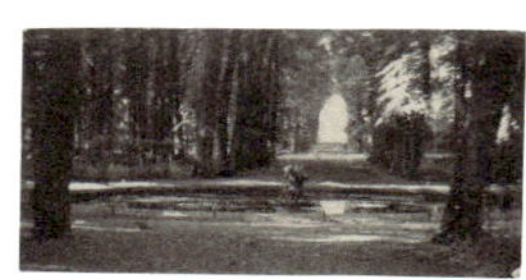

Cat. 226 *Park (Versailles?),*
1925–28
André and Elizabeth Kertész
Foundation
Only known print

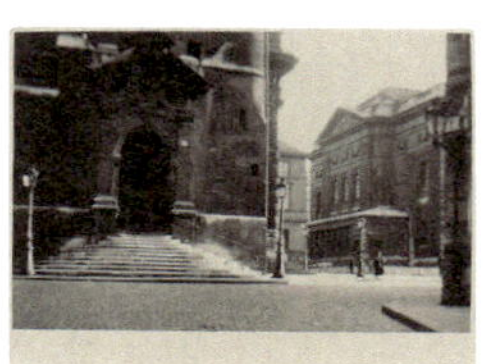

Cat. 227 *Latin Quarter,* 1926–28
New Orleans Museum of Art,
museum purchase,
Women's Volunteer
Committee Fund, 73.167
Other known prints: AIC

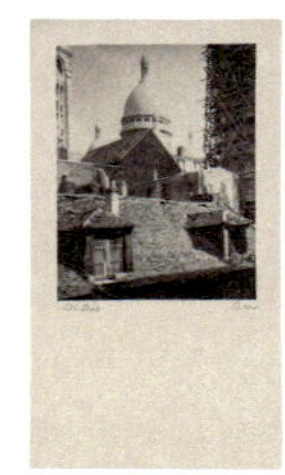

Cat. 228 *Sacre Coeur,* 1926
Städel Museum, Frankfurt,
Eigentum des Städelschen
Museums-Vereins e.V., St.F.106
Only known print

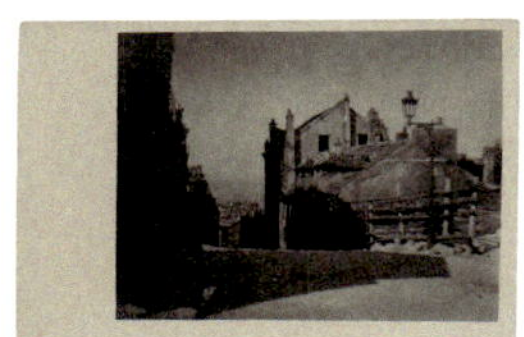

Cat. 229 *Montmartre*, 1925–28
James Hyman Gallery, London
Only known print

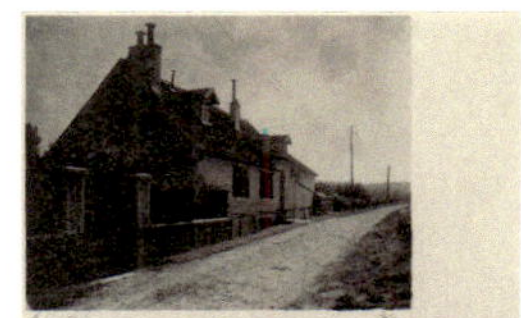

Cat. 235 *Pierre Mac Orlan's House*, 1925–28
Estate of André Kertész
Only known print

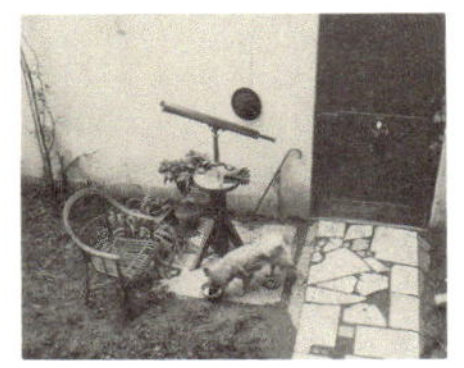

Cat. 230 *Jean Lurçat's Door*, 1927–28
The J. Paul Getty Museum, Los Angeles, 85.XM.259.16
Only known print

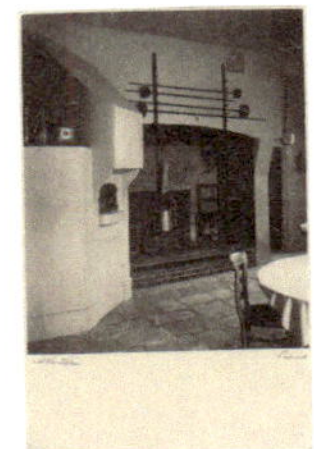

Cat. 236 *Inn, Sainte-Mesme*, 1927
André and Elizabeth Kertész Foundation
Only known print

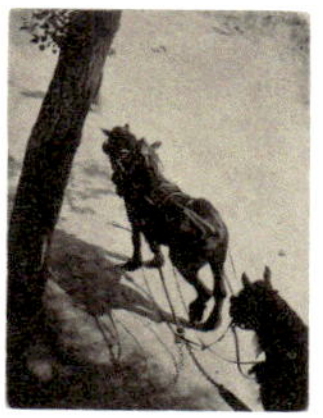

Cat. 231 *"Attelage,"* 1925
Estate of André Kertész
Only known print

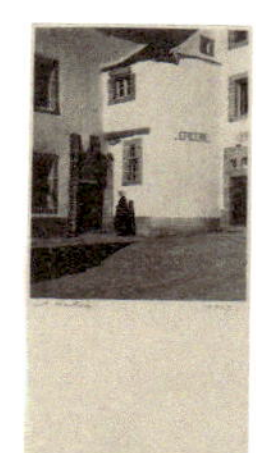

Cat. 237 *"Épicerie," Saint-Jean-du-Doigt, Brittany*, 1927
André and Elizabeth Kertész Foundation
Only known print

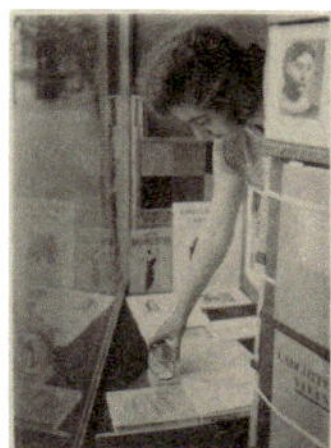

Cat. 232 *Window, L'Esthétique*, 1927
Kassák Múzeum, Budapest, KM-F-86.553
Only known print

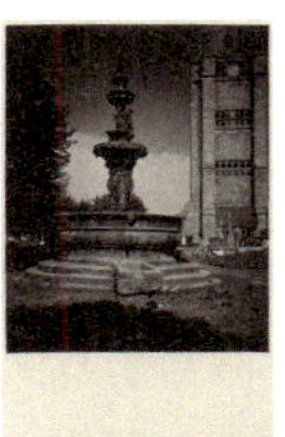

Cat. 238 *Fountain of Saint-Jean-du-Doigt, Brittany*, c. 1928
Estate of André Kertész
Only known print

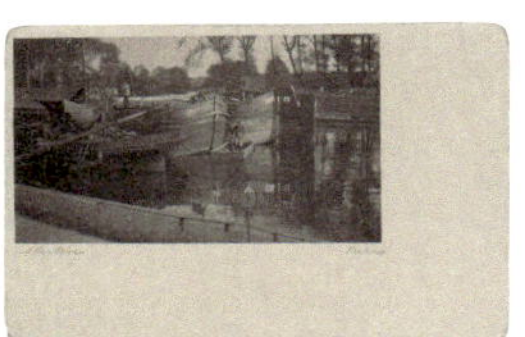

Cat. 233 *Banks of the Seine outside Paris*, 1926–27
The Art Institute of Chicago, Wirt D. Walker Fund, 1984.547
Only known print

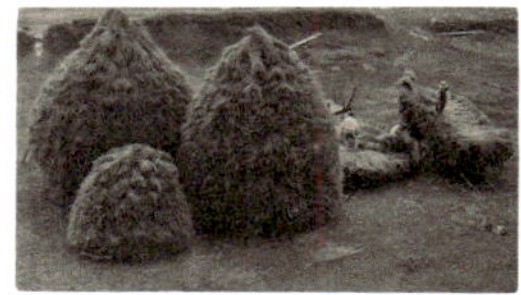

Cat. 239 *Primel, Brittany*, 1927
National Gallery of Art, Washington, DC, gift of the Andre and Elizabeth Kertesz Foundation, 2000.170.28
Other known prints: JPGM

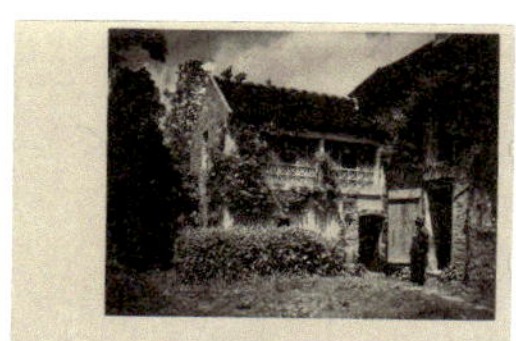

Cat. 234 *Unidentified House*, 1925–28
Estate of André Kertész
Only known print

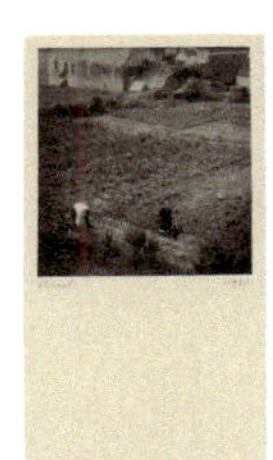

Cat. 240 *Primel, Brittany*, 1927
The J. Paul Getty Museum, Los Angeles, 86.XM.706.4
Only known print

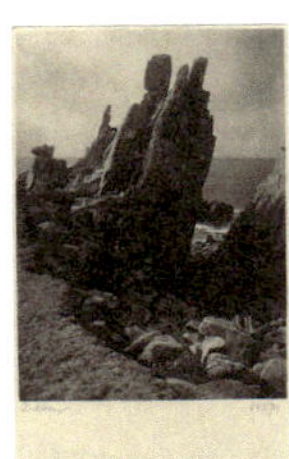

Cat. 241 *Diben, Brittany*, 1927
André and Elizabeth Kertész
Foundation
Other known prints: Collection of
Ann and Jürgen Wilde, Cologne

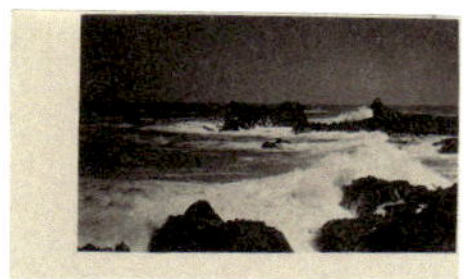

Cat. 242 *Brittany*, 1927
Estate of André Kertész
Only known print

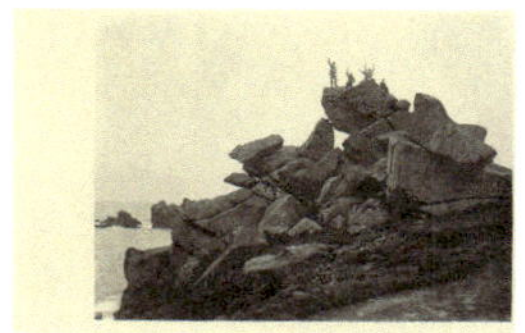

Cat. 243 *Brittany*, 1927
Vintage Works, Ltd.,
Chalfont, PA
Other known prints: Collection of
Ann and Jürgen Wilde, Cologne

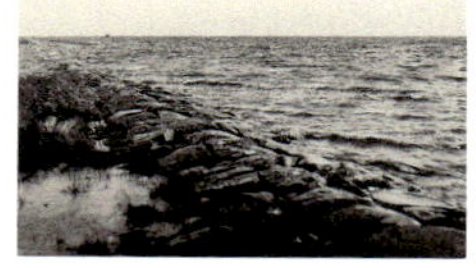

Cat. 244 *Brittany*, 1927
Collection of Ann and
Jürgen Wilde, Cologne
Only known print

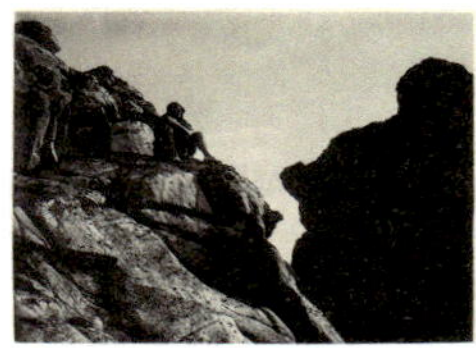

Cat. 245 *Brittany*, 1927
Collection of Ann and
Jürgen Wilde, Cologne
Only known print

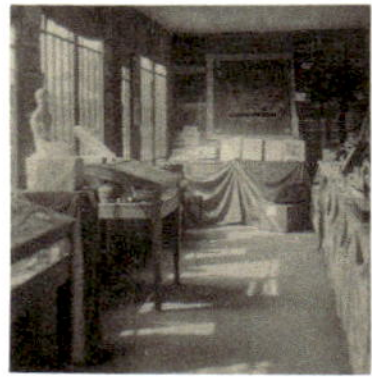

Cat. 246 *Library*, 1927
The J. Paul Getty Museum,
Los Angeles, 86.XM.706.6
Only known print

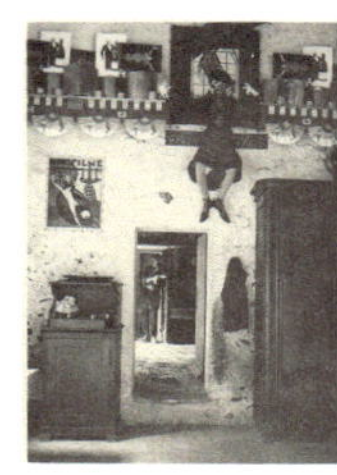

Cat. 247 *Pontoise*, 1927
Bluff Collection
Only known print

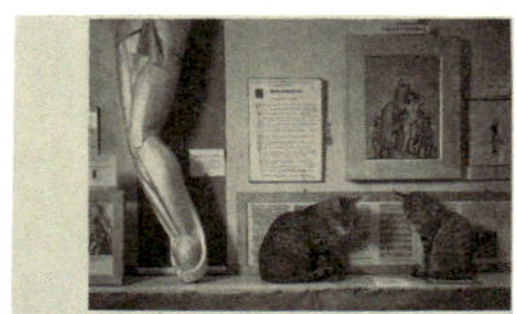

Cat. 248 *Cats with Sculpture by
Robert Lanz*, 1926
The Metropolitan Museum of
Art, New York, gift of
Joyce F. Menschel,
2013.1098.18
Only known print

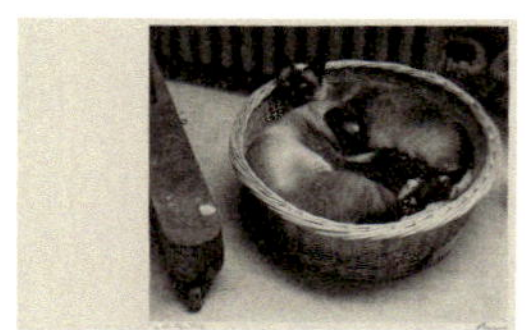

Cat. 249 *Cats in a Basket*, 1927
Jane Corkin, Toronto
Only known print

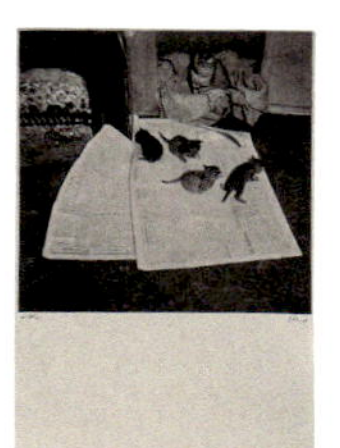

Cat. 250 *Cat and Kittens*, 1927
Smart Museum of Art,
University of Chicago, gift of
the Estate of Lester and
Betty Guttman, 2014.462
Only known print

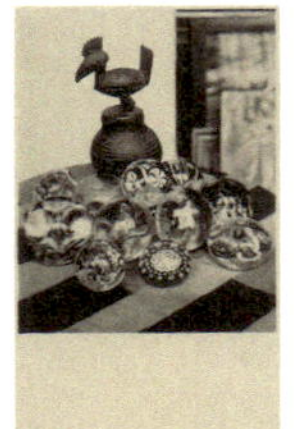

Cat. 251 *André Lhote's
Collection*, 1927–28
Private collection, Paris
Only known print

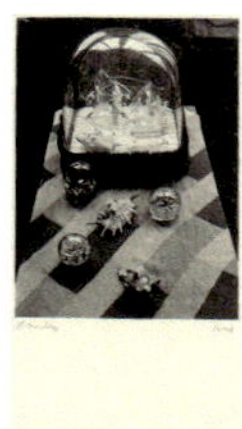

Cat. 252 *André Lhote's
Collection*, 1927–28
Amsab-Institute of Social
History, Ghent
Only known print

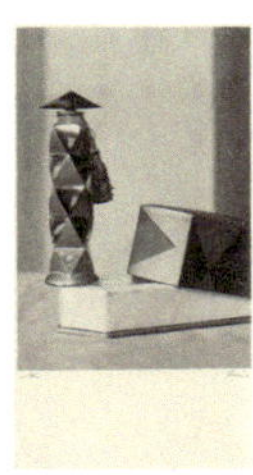

Cat. 253 *Arlequinade
Perfume Bottle,* 1926–27
Private collection, Frankfurt
Only known print

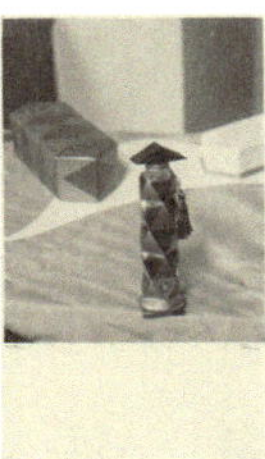

Cat. 254 *Arlequinade
Perfume Bottle,* 1926–27
Private collection, Frankfurt
Only known print

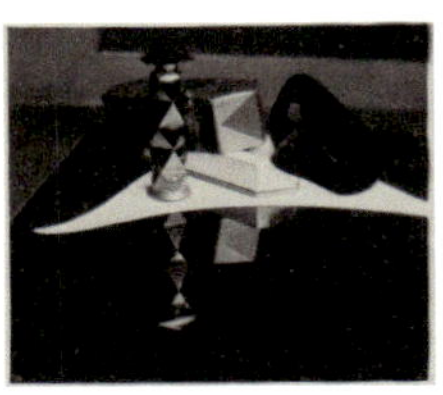

Cat. 255 *Arlequinade
Perfume Bottle,* 1926–27
Los Angeles County Museum of
Art, Ralph M. Parsons Fund,
AC1997.167.1
Only known print

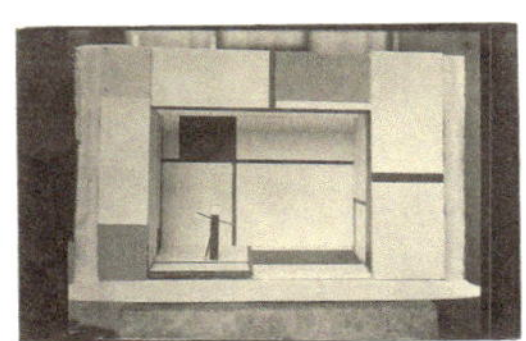

Cat. 256 *Theatrical Model by
Piet Mondrian for Act III of
Michel Seuphor's* The Ephemeral
Is Eternal, 1926
Private collection, Paris,
courtesy of Galerie Françoise
Paviot, Paris
Only known print

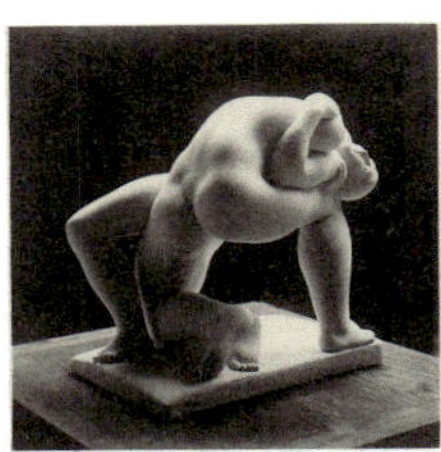

Cat. 257 *Etienne Beöthy's
Kissing Couple,* 1926–27
Collection of Ann and
Jürgen Wilde, Cologne
Only known print

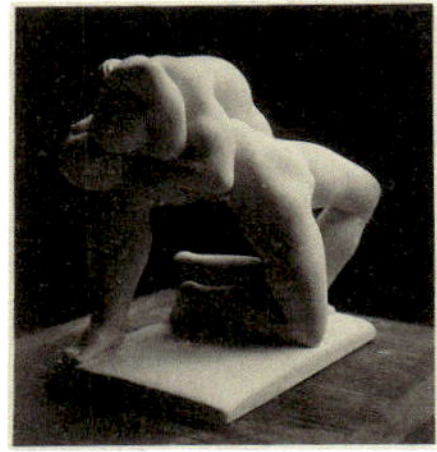

Cat. 258 *Etienne Beöthy's
Kissing Couple,* 1926–27
Collection of Ann and
Jürgen Wilde, Cologne
Only known print

CONTRIBUTORS

SARAH KENNEL is Curator of Photography at the High Museum of Art, Atlanta. Her recent exhibitions and publications include *Order of Imagination: The Photographs of Olivia Parker* (2019) and *Sally Mann: A Thousand Crossings* (2018). Much of her work examines dance and the visual arts in early twentieth-century Paris, and she has previously written an in-depth chronology on André Kertész for a catalogue by the National Gallery of Art in Washington, DC, where she was assistant curator.

SYLVIE PÉNICHON is Director of Photography and Media Conservation at the Art Institute of Chicago. She curated the exhibition *Conserving Photographs* (2018) and has contributed scholarship to exhibition catalogues *Moholy-Nagy: Future Present* (2016) and *Color: American Photography Transformed* (2013), among other publications. She is the author of *Twentieth-Century Color Photographs: Identification and Care* (2013), a comprehensive guide to understanding color photographs.

ELIZABETH SIEGEL is Curator of Photography and Media at the Art Institute of Chicago. She has overseen numerous exhibitions and publications, including *Playing with Pictures: The Art of Victorian Photocollage* (2009), *Abelardo Morell: The Universe Next Door* (2013), and *The Photographer's Curator: Hugh Edwards at the Art Institute of Chicago, 1959–1970* (2017), which received the Association of Art Museum Curators Award for Excellence for best digital publication in 2018.

PHOTOGRAPHY CREDITS

Unless otherwise noted, photographs of artworks in the collection of the Art Institute of Chicago are by Craig Stilwell with Aidan Fitzpatrick, with postproduction by Owen Conway with Jonathan Mathias, Imaging, the Art Institute of Chicago, and are copyrighted by the Art Institute of Chicago.

Every effort has been made to identify, contact, and acknowledge copyright holders for all reproductions; additional rights holders are encouraged to contact the Art Institute of Chicago. The following credits apply to all images in this book for which separate acknowledgment is due.

Siegel, figs. 3 (p. 16), **8** (p. 23), **10** (p. 26); **Pénichon, figs. 2** (p. 51), **5, right** (p. 54), **6** (p. 55): Donation André Kertész, ministère de la Culture (France), Médiathèque de l'architecture et du patrimoine, dist. RMN-GP. **Siegel, figs. 4** (p. 18), **11** (p. 27); **cats. 112, 114–18, 120** (p. 219); **123–25, 128, 130, 133** (p. 220); **139, 141–42, 145** (p. 221); **146, 149, 152, 154** (p. 222); **159** (p. 223); **174–76, 178–80** (p. 224); **185, 187–88** (p. 225); **194–200, 202, 204–5** (p. 226); **207, 209, 212–17** (p. 227); **218–20, 222–23, 226** (p. 228); **231, 234–38** (p. 229); **241–42** (p. 230): Robert Gurbo and Victor V. Gurbo. **Siegel, fig. 6** (p. 21); **Kennel, figs. 1–2** (pp. 37, 220); **cats. 1** (pp. 12, 61, 204), **2** (pp. 62, 204), **3** (pp. 63, 204), **5** (pp. 65, 204), **11** (pp. 75–76, 205), **12** (pp. 77, 205), **17** (pp. 82, 206), **18** (pp. 83, 206), **20** (pp. 86, 206), **25** (pp. 92, 207), **44** (pp. 113, 209), **62** (pp. 133, 212), **79** (pp. 153, 214), **249** (p. 230): Joseph Hartman. **Kennel, fig. 5** (p. 40): © Man Ray 2015 Trust / Artists Rights Society (ARS), NY / ADAGP, Paris 2021. Image Telimage, Paris. **Kennel, fig. 6** (p. 41): © 2021 Artists Rights Society (ARS), New York / ADAGP, Paris. **Kennel, fig. 7** (p. 42): © Estate Brassaï–RMN–Grand Palais. **Kennel, fig. 8** (p. 43); **cats. 10** (pp. 73, 205), **47–48** (pp. 116, 210), **49** (pp. 117–18, 210), **59** (pp. 130, 211), **105** (pp. 48, 189, 217), **239** (p. 229): Courtesy of the National Gallery of Art, Washington. **Kennel, fig. 10** (p. 45); **cats. 4** (pp. 64, 204), **55** (pp. 125, 211), **104** (pp. 187, 217), **211** (p. 227), **225** (p. 228), **248** (p. 230): Image copyright © The Metropolitan Museum of Art. Image source: Art Resource, NY. **Cats. 24** (pp. 91, 207), **107** (pp. 191–92, 217): Photograph © 2021 Museum of Fine Arts, Boston. **Cats. 26** (pp. 92, 207); **228** (p. 228): bpk Bildagentur / Städel Museum Frankfurt am Main, Germany / Art Resource, NY. **Cats. 30** (pp. 98, 208), **54** (pp. 123–24, 211), **57** (pp. 128, 211), **68** (pp. 141, 212), **158** (p. 223): Eileen Travell. **Cat. 35** (pp. 103, 208): San Francisco Museum of Modern Art. **Cats. 36** (pp. 104, 208),

90 (pp. 169–70, 215), **91** (pp. 171, 215), **100** (pp. 182, 217), **108** (pp. 193–95, 218), **147** (p. 222): Digital image © The Museum of Modern Art / Licensed by SCALA / Art Resource, NY. **Cats. 41** (pp. 110, 209); **45** (pp. 114, 210); **78** (pp. 152, 214); **140, 143** (p. 221); **208, 210** (p. 227): San Francisco Museum of Modern Art. Photograph: Don Ross. **Cat. 63** (pp. 135, 212): Ian Reeves. **Cat. 64** (pp. 136, 212): Reproduction by © Mustafa Önder at www.mustafaonder.com. **Cat. 73** (pp. 147–48): Margaret Fox. **Cat. 75** (pp. 150, 213): Princeton University Art Museum / Art Resource, NY. **Cat. 77** (pp. 151, 214): Courtesy of the Mattis-Hochberg Collection. **Cat. 103** (pp. 185–86, 217): Photo: Rob McKeever. **Cat. 136** (p. 221): © Stany Dederen. Courtesy of Gallery Fifty One, Antwerp. **Cat. 144** (p. 221): J. Arnold, Impart Photography. **Cats. 155–56** (p. 222); **cat. 243** (p. 230): Courtesy of Vintage Works, Ltd. **Cats. 160–66** (p. 223): Photo Raphaële Kriegel. **Cat. 184** (p. 225): Copyright 2013 Phillips Auctioneers LLC. All Rights Reserved. **Cat. 193** (p. 225): Photo by Adam Reich. **Cat. 229** (p. 229): Courtesy of James Hyman Gallery, London. **Cat. 247** (p. 230): Phocasso / JW White. **Cat. 250** (p. 230): Photograph © 2020 courtesy of The David and Alfred Smart Museum of Art, The University of Chicago. **Cat. 255** (p. 231): Digital image © 2021 Museum Associates / LACMA. Licensed by Art Resource, NY. **Cat. 256** (p. 231): Courtesy of Galerie Françoise Paviot, Paris.

André Kertész: Postcards from Paris was published in conjunction with an exhibition of the same title organized by the Art Institute of Chicago and the High Museum of Art, Atlanta.

Exhibition dates
The Art Institute of Chicago
October 2, 2021–January 17, 2022
High Museum of Art, Atlanta
February 18–May 29, 2022

Lead support for *André Kertész: Postcards from Paris* is generously provided by Nicholas and Susan Pritzker.

Major support is contributed by The André and Elizabeth Kertész Foundation.

Members of the Luminary Trust provide annual leadership support for the museum's operations, including exhibition development, conservation and collection care, and educational programming. The Luminary Trust includes an anonymous donor; Neil Bluhm and the Bluhm Family Charitable Foundation; Jay Franke and David Herro; Karen Gray-Krehbiel and John Krehbiel, Jr.; Kenneth C. Griffin; Caryn and King Harris, The Harris Family Foundation; Josef and Margot Lakonishok; Robert M. and Diane v.S. Levy; Ann and Samuel M. Mencoff; Sylvia Neil and Dan Fischel; Anne and Chris Reyes; Cari and Michael J. Sacks; and the Earl and Brenda Shapiro Foundation.

First edition
Printed in Italy

ISBN: 978-0-300-26003-8 (hardcover)
Library of Congress Control Number: 2021937148

Published by
The Art Institute of Chicago
111 South Michigan Avenue
Chicago, IL 60603-6404
artic.edu

Distributed by
Yale University Press
302 Temple Street
P.O. Box 209040
New Haven, CT 06520-9040
yalebooks.com/art

Publishing, the Art Institute of Chicago
Greg Nosan, Executive Director
Lisa Meyerowitz, Editorial Director
Joseph Mohan, Director of Production

Edited by Kit Shields
Production by Joseph Mohan and Ben Bertin
Photography research by Kylie Escudero and Pauline Lopez
Proofreading by Sarah Robinson
Indexing by Kate Mertes

Imaging, the Art Institute of Chicago
Bonnie Rosenberg, Director of Imaging
Aidan Fitzpatrick, Associate Director of Photography
Photography by Craig Stillwell with Aidan Fitzpatrick
Postproduction by Owen Conway with Jonathan Mathias
Preproduction and coordination by Elyse Allen
and Aidan Fitzpatrick

Design and typesetting by Jena Sher Graphic Design
Printing, separations, and binding by Trifolio, Verona, Italy

Cover (front and back): *Jean Jaffe*, 1926 (cat. 14)
Details: p. 4: *Quartet*, 1926 (cat. 95); p. 6: *Unidentified Sitter (Hungarian Woodcutter and Graphic Designer)*, 1927 (cat. 70); p. 12: *Self-Portrait*, 1927 (cat. 1); p. 34: *Magda Förstner*, 1927 (cat. 87); p. 48: *Fernand Léger's Studio*, 1926–27 (cat. 105); p. 59: *Eiffel Tower*, 1925 (cat. 6); p. 200: *Paul Arma's Hands*, 1928 (cat. 94)